Autodesk
3ds Max Design 2015:
A Tutorial Approach

CADCIM Technologies

525 St. Andrews Drive
Schererville, IN 46375, USA
(www.cadcim.com)

Contributing Authors

Sham Tickoo
Professor
Purdue University Calumet
Hammond, Indiana, USA

Rakesh Koul
CADCIM Technologies
USA

CADCIM Technologies

Autodesk 3ds Max Design 2015: A Tutorial Approach
Sham Tickoo

ISBN 978-1-936646-76-0

Copy Editors
Anju Jethwani
Rajendra Badola
Kusha Gupta

Technical Editor
Pradeep Mamgain

NOTICE TO THE READER

www.cadcim.com

DEDICATION

*To teachers, who make it possible to disseminate knowledge
to enlighten the young and curious minds
of our future generations*

*To students, who are dedicated to learning new technologies
and making the world a better place to live in*

THANKS

To employees of CADCIM Technologies for their valuable help

Online Training Program Offered by CADCIM Technologies

CADCIM Technologies provides effective and affordable virtual online training on various software packages including Computer Aided Design and Manufacturing (CAD/CAM), computer programming languages, animation, architecture, and GIS. The training is delivered 'live' via Internet at any time, any place, and at any pace to individuals as well as students of colleges, universities, and CAD/CAM training centers. The main features of this program are:

Training for Students and Companies in a Classroom Setting

Highly experienced instructors and qualified Engineers at CADCIM Technologies conduct the classes under the guidance of Prof. Sham Tickoo of Purdue University Calumet, USA. This team has authored several textbooks that are rated "one of the best" in their categories and are used in various colleges, universities, and training centers in North America, Europe, and in other parts of the world.

Training for Individuals

CADCIM Technologies with its cost effective and time saving initiative strives to deliver the training in the comfort of your home or workplace, thereby relieving you from the hassles of traveling to training centers.

Training Offered on Software Packages

CADCIM Technologies provides basic and advanced training on the following software packages:

CAD/CAM/CAE*: CATIA, Pro/ENGINEER Wildfire, SolidWorks, Autodesk Inventor, Solid Edge, NX, AutoCAD, AutoCAD LT, Customizing AutoCAD, EdgeCAM, ANSYS, Creo Direct, and AutoCAD MEP*

Computer Programming*: C++, VB.NET, Oracle, AJAX, and Java*

Animation and Styling*: Autodesk 3ds Max, Pixologic ZBrush, Character Animation, The Foundry NukeX, MAXON CINEMA 4D Studio, Autodesk Maya, eyeon Fusion, Adobe Flash Professional, and Autodesk Alias Design*

Architecture, Civil, and GIS*: Autodesk Revit Architecture, AutoCAD Civil 3D, Autodesk Revit Structure, AutoCAD Map 3D, Primavera, Staad Pro, and Navisworks*

*For more information, please visit the following link: **www.cadcim.com***

Note

If you are a faculty member, you can register by clicking on the following link to access the teaching resources: ***www.cadcim.com/Registration.aspx***. The student resources are available at ***www.cadcim.com***. We also provide **Live Virtual Online Training** on various software packages. For more information, write us at ***sales@cadcim.com***.

Table of Contents

Preface

Autodesk 3ds Max Design 2015

Welcome to the world of Autodesk 3ds Max Design, a 3D modeling, animation, and rendering software package developed by Autodesk Inc. It is widely used by architects, game developers, design visualization specialists, and visual effects artists. A wide range of modeling and texturing tools make it an ideal platform for 3D modelers and animators. The intuitive user interface and workflow tools of Autodesk 3ds Max Design have made the job of design visualization specialists easier.

Autodesk 3ds Max Design 2015: A Tutorial Approach is a tutorial-based textbook that introduces the readers to the basic features of 3ds Max Design 2015 created on real world model through tutorials. The textbook caters to the needs of both the novice and the advanced users of the software.

This textbook will help you unleash your creativity and help you create simple and complete 3D models and animations. The textbook will help the learners transform their imagination into reality with ease.

The main features of this textbook are as follows:

- **Tutorial Approach**

  The author has adopted the tutorial point-of-view and the learn-by-doing approach throughout the textbook. This approach helps the users Create 3D models and animations in the tutorials with ease.

- **Projects based on Real-World Models**

  The author has used 5 projects based on real-world models that allow the users to apply the skills learned in the text. In addition, there are 24 exercises that can be used by the readers to assess their knowledge.

- **Notes and Tips**

  Additional information related to various topics is provided to the users in the form of notes and tips.

- **Learning Objectives**

  The first page of every chapter summarizes the topics that are covered in that chapter. This helps the users to easily refer to a topic.

- **Self-Evaluation Test, Review Questions, and Exercises**

    Every chapter ends with Self-Evaluation Test so that the users can assess their knowledge of the chapter. The answers to Self-Evaluation Test are given at the end of the chapter. Also, the Review Questions and Exercises are given at the end of each chapter and they can be used by the Instructors as test questions and exercises.

Symbols Used in the Textbook

Note
The author has provided additional information to the users about the topic being discussed in the form of notes.

Tip
Special information and techniques are provided in the form of tips that helps in increasing the efficiency of the users.

Formatting Conventions Used in the Textbook

Refer to the following list for the formatting conventions used in this textbook.

- Names of tools, buttons, options, and menus are written in boldface.

    Example: The **Select and Move** tool, the **Geometry** button, the **Multiply** option, the **Create** menu, and so on.

- Names of dialog boxes, drop-down lists, windows, radio buttons, spinners, areas, and check boxes are written in boldface.

    Example: The **Save** dialog box, the **View** drop-down list, the **Frames** radio button, the **Material Editor** dialog box, the **Track View - Dope Sheet** window, the **Size** spinner, the **Mapping** area, the **Save File** check box, and so on.

- Values entered in spinners are written in boldface.

    Example: Set the value **0.5** in the **Amount** spinner.

- The path of choosing tool from the menu bar.

    Example: Choose **Tools > Align > Normal Align** from the menu bar.

- Names of the files are italicized

    Example: *c05_tut1_start.max*

Naming Conventions Used in the Textbook

The naming conventions used in this textbook are as follows:

Tool

If on selecting an item either from the **Command Panel** or from the **Main Toolbar**, a command is invoked to create/edit an object or perform some action, then that item is termed as **Tool**. For example: **Select and Rotate** tool, **Render Setup** tool, **Align** tool, **Mirror** tool, and so on.

Flyout

If on invoking a tool, a menu is displayed with options which perform similar type of function, then that menu is called a flyout.

Quad Menu

The quad menus provide quick access to the commonly used commands that are related to the current selection of an object. When you right-click on an object, a quad menu is displayed, as shown in Figure 1. Some of the options in the quad menus have an arrow on their right side. If you move the cursor on such options, a cascading menu will be displayed showing some more options related to the selected option, refer to Figure 1.

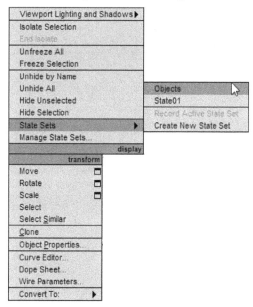

Figure 1 Quad menu displayed on right-clicking in the viewport

Dialog Box

In a dialog box, there are several options. Different terms are used to indicate various options of a dialog box. Refer to Figure 2 for different terminologies used in a dialog box.

Figure 2 Different terms used for the options in a dialog box

Button

The item in a dialog box that has a rectangular shape is termed as **Button**. For example, **OK** button, **Cancel** button, **Save** button, and so on, refer to Figure 3.

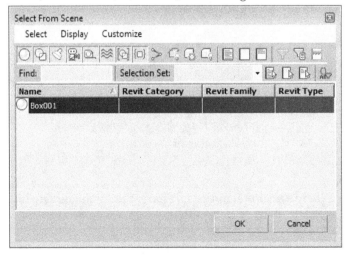

Figure 3 Buttons in the dialog box

Scene Explorer

The **Scene Explorer** is used to view, select, filter, and sort objects. It is also used to rename, delete, group, freeze, and hide the objects. The **Scene Explorer** is docked by default at the left of the interface in the default workspace, refer to Figure 4.

Figure 4 The Scene Explorer

Drop-down List

A drop-down list is the one in which a set of options are grouped together. You can set various parameters using these options. You can identify a drop-down list with a down arrow on it. For example, a drop-down list displayed in the **Output Size** area, refer to Figure 5.

Options

Options are the items that are available in shortcut menus, drop-down lists, dialog boxes, and so on, refer to Figure 6.

Figure 5 *Selecting an option from the drop-down list*

Figure 6 *Options displayed in the drop-down list*

Window

A window consists of various components such as tools, buttons, main menu, and so on. Different types of windows are available in Autodesk 3ds Max Design. Figure 7 shows the **Track View - Dope Sheet** window.

Figure 7 *The **Track View - Dope Sheet** window*

Free Companion Website

It has been our constant endeavor to provide you the best textbooks and services at affordable price. In this endeavor, we have come out with a Free Companion website that will facilitate the process of teaching and learning of Autodesk 3ds Max Design. If you purchase this textbook, you will get access to the files on the Companion website.

To access the files, you need to visit the resources section of the CADCIM website:

Faculty Resources

• **Technical Support**

   You can get online technical support by contacting *techsupport@cadcim.com*.

• **Instructor Guide**

   Solutions to all review questions and exercises in the textbook are provided in this guide to help the faculty members test the skills of the students.

• **PowerPoint Presentations**

   The contents of the book are arranged in PowerPoint slides that can be used by the faculty for their lectures.

• **3ds Max Design Files**

   The 3ds Max Design file used in tutorials and exercises are available for free download.

• **Rendered Images and Media Files**

   The media files used in the tutorials and rendered images of all tutorials are provided in the CADCIM website. You can use these images to compare them with your rendered images.

• **Additional Resources**

   You can access additional learning resources by visiting: *http://3dsmaxexperts.blogspot.com*

• **Colored Images**

   You can download the PDF file containing colored images of the screenshots used in this textbook from CADCIM website.

Student Resources

• **Technical Support**

   You can get online technical support by contacting *techsupport@cadcim.com*.

• **3ds Max Design Files**

   The 3ds Max Design files used in tutorials are available for free download.

• **Rendered Images and Media Files**

   The media files used in the tutorials and rendered images of all tutorials are provided in the CADCIM website. You can use these images to compare them with your rendered images.

- **Additional Resources**

   You can access additional learning resources by visiting: *http://3dsmaxexperts.blogspot.com*

- **Colored Images**

   You can download the PDF file containing colored images of the screenshots used in this textbook from CADCIM website.

- **Additional Project**

   Apart from tutorials, one student project has also been added in this textbook for the students to practice the tools learnt.

Stay Connected

You can now stay connected with us through Facebook and Twitter to get the latest information about our textbooks, videos, and teaching/learning resources. To stay informed of such updates, follow us on Facebook *(www.facebook.com/cadcim)* and Twitter (*@cadcimtech*). You can also subscribe to our YouTube channel *(www.youtube.com/cadcimtech)* to get the information about our latest video tutorials.

If you face any problem in accessing these files, please contact the publisher at *sales@cadcim.com* or the author at *stickoo@purduecal.edu* or *tickoo525@gmail.com*.

Chapter *1*

Introduction to Autodesk 3ds Max Design 2015

Learning Objectives

After completing this chapter, you will be able to:

• *Understand the Autodesk 3ds Max Design interface components*
• *Understand Scene Explorer/Layer Explorer*
• *Use controls for creating or modifying the objects*
• *Use hot keys in Autodesk 3ds Max Design*
• *Customize hot keys*
• *Customize the colors of the scene elements*

INTRODUCTION TO Autodesk 3ds Max Design 2015

Welcome to the world of Autodesk 3ds Max Design, an advanced application that is used to create still or animated 3D models and objects. With the help of this application, you can create realistic scenes by modifying objects, applying maps and materials to a scene, assigning environment to a scene, adding lights and cameras, effects in movies, and so on. Before working with Autodesk 3ds Max Design, you should have the basic knowledge of various tools and commands available in this software. In this chapter, you will learn the basic features of Autodesk 3ds Max Design.

GETTING STARTED WITH Autodesk 3ds Max Design

First, you need to install Autodesk 3ds Max Design 2015 on your computer. On installing the software, the **3ds Max Design 2015** shortcut icon will be created automatically on the desktop. Double-click on this icon to start Autodesk 3ds Max Design. Alternatively, you can start Autodesk 3ds Max Design from the taskbar. To do so, choose **Start > All Programs > Autodesk > Autodesk 3ds Max Design 2015 > 3ds Max Design 2015**, as shown in Figure 1-1.

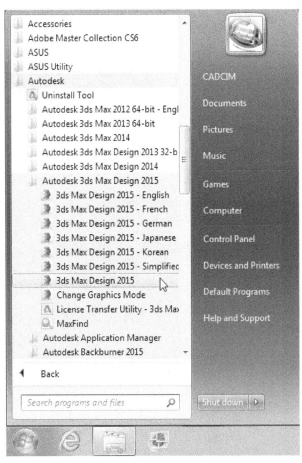

Figure 1-1 Starting Autodesk 3ds Max Design 2015 from the taskbar

The system will prepare to start 3ds Max Design 2015 by loading all the required files. If you are running 3ds Max Design 2015 for the first time, the **Autodesk Customer Involvement Program** dialog box will be displayed, as shown in Figure 1-2, and you will be prompted to enter the email address where the product team can contact you. This step is optional and you can skip it. Now, choose the **OK** button to close this dialog box. This entire information helps Autodesk to improve its product. You can also invoke the **Autodesk Customer Involvement Program** dialog box by choosing **Help > Speak Back > Customer Involvement Program** from the menu bar.

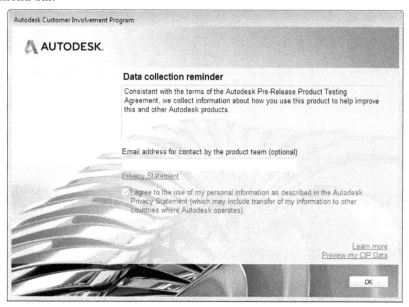

*Figure 1-2 The **Autodesk Customer Involvement Program** dialog box*

After all the required files are loaded, the 3ds Max Design interface will be displayed along with the **Welcome to 3ds Max** dialog box, refer to Figure 1-3. If you hover the mouse pointer at the top right corner of this dialog box, a layer will flip outside and a button **Start new or open a file**, will be displayed, as shown in Figure 1-3. Choose this button to create a new file or open an existing one. The **Welcome to 3ds Max** dialog box provides access to video tutorials that are helpful in learning the basics of 3ds Max Design. To start a tutorial, select one of the options in the **More 1-Minute Movies** drop-down list available on the left in this dialog box; the corresponding tutorial will be displayed in a separate window. Also, you can start a new scene, open an existing file, or any recently created files using this dialog box. Now, close the **Welcome to 3ds Max** dialog box.

Note

*In this textbook, the user interface has been customized so that you can view the objects clearly in the viewports. As a result, all screen shots have been taken in a customized user interface format. You can customize the user interface by using the **Customize User Interface** dialog box. To do so, choose **Customize > Customize User Interface** from the menu bar; the **Customize User Interface** dialog box will be displayed. Now, you can modify the geometry and background colors as per your requirements. On doing so, the color of user interface changes from dark grey to light grey.*

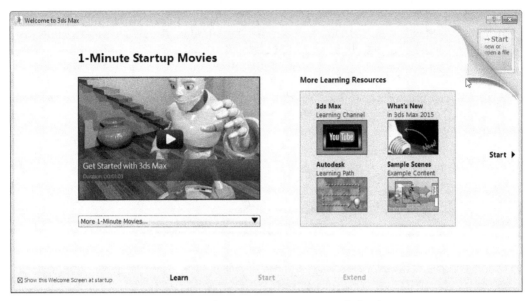

*Figure 1-3 The **Welcome to 3ds Max** dialog box*

STARTING A NEW FILE IN Autodesk 3ds Max DESIGN

To start a new file in Autodesk 3ds Max Design, choose the **Application** button located at the top left corner of the interface; the **Application** menu will be displayed. Next, choose **New > New All** from the **Application** menu; a new file will be displayed in the 3ds Max Design interface. Alternatively, press the CTRL+N keys; the **New Scene** dialog box will be displayed, as shown in Figure 1-4. By default, the **New All** radio button is selected in this dialog box. Choose the **OK** button; a new file will be displayed.

You can also reuse the objects from the current scene in the new scene. Select the **Keep Objects** radio button in the **New Scene** dialog box to keep only the objects from the current scene for the new file. However, on selecting this radio button, all the animation keys and links between the objects will be cleared. To keep the objects and the links between them, select the **Keep Objects and Hierarchy** radio button. However, in this case, the animation keys will be deleted.

Before starting a new scene in Autodesk 3ds Max Design, it is recommended to reset Autodesk 3ds Max Design and start afresh. By doing so, you will be able to reset all settings for the new scene. To reset Autodesk 3ds Max Design, choose **Reset** from the **Application** menu; the **3ds Max** message box will be displayed, as shown in Figure 1-5.

*Figure 1-4 The **New Scene** dialog box*

*Figure 1-5 The **3ds Max** message box*

Also, you will be prompted to specify if you really want to reset 3ds Max Design. Choose the **Yes** button; the 3ds Max Design will be reset.

Autodesk 3ds Max Design INTERFACE COMPONENTS

The 3ds Max Design interface screen consists of different components, as shown in Figure 1-6. These components are discussed next.

Figure 1-6 Different screen components of Autodesk 3ds Max Design interface

Menu Bar

The menu bar is located just below the title bar, refer to Figure 1-6 and contains various pull-down menus. Some of the pull-down menus are standard window menus such as **Edit**, **Help**, and so on while others are 3ds Max Design pull-down menus such as **Create**, **Modifiers**, **Animation**, **Graph Editors**, **Rendering**, **Customize**, and so on. The title of each pull-down menu indicates the purpose of commands in the menu. When you choose one of the menu titles, Autodesk 3ds Max Design displays the corresponding pull-down menu. Each menu consists of a collection of commands. In a pull-down menu, the dots after a command indicate that a dialog box will be displayed on choosing that command. An arrow next to a command indicates that a cascading menu will be displayed on placing the cursor on that command. For some of the commands in the pull-down menus, the keyboard shortcuts are displayed on their right side, as shown in Figure 1-7.

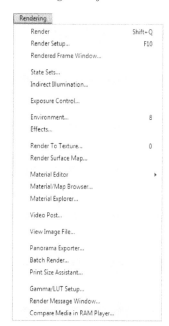

*Figure 1-7 The keyboard shortcuts in the **Rendering** pull-down menu*

Application Menu

The **Application** menu is used to manage the files created in 3ds Max Design. Choose the **Application** button on the top left of the 3ds Max Design screen; the **Application** menu will be displayed, as shown in Figure 1-8. This menu comprises the most commonly used file management options. The **Send to** option provides interoperability with other Autodesk applications such as Softimage, MotionBuilder, Maya, and Mudbox.

When you choose the **Send to** option from the **Application** menu, a cascading menu will be displayed. Choose the desired option from the cascading menu; a submenu will be displayed with the following options: **Send as New Scene**, **Update Current Scene**, **Add to Current Scene**, and **Select Previously Sent Objects**. You can choose the option from this menu as per your requirement.

On the right of the menu is the **Recent Documents** page that provides information about the files that were previously saved in 3ds Max Design, refer to Figure 1-8. You can change the size of the icons of the recent documents. To do so, choose the Icon or Image Display button from the **Application** menu, refer to Figure 1-8; a flyout will be displayed, as shown in Figure 1-9. Select the icon size from the flyout to change the size of the icons of the recent documents.

*Figure 1-8 The **Application** menu*

You can also use the keyboard shortcuts to work with the **Application** menu. To do so, press ALT+F; the **Application** menu will be displayed with all the shortcuts, as shown in Figure 1-10. Next, press the shortcut key as per your requirement; the corresponding command will be executed. Now, if you again choose the **Application** menu it will not display the shortcuts. You can repeat the process to view the shortcuts again.

Quick Access Toolbar

The **Quick Access Toolbar** comprises the most commonly used file management buttons, as shown in Figure 1-11. These buttons are also available in the **Application** menu. Apart from the commonly used buttons, the **Quick Access Toolbar** also contains the **Redo Scene Operation** and **Undo Scene Operation** buttons.

Figure 1-9 A flyout displayed on choosing the Icon or Image Display button

Workspaces

The workspace includes toolbars, menus, the ribbon, hotkeys, quad menus, and viewport layout presets. You can switch between different workspaces by choosing the required option from the **Workspaces** drop-down list located on the **Quick Access Toolbar**, refer to Figure 1-11. To create a new workspace, you need to change the interface setup as required and then choose the **Manage Workspaces** option from the **Workspaces** drop-down list; the **Manage Workspaces** dialog box will be displayed. In this dialog box, choose the **Save as New Workspace** button; the **Create New Workspace** dialog box will be displayed. Enter the name for the workspace in the **Name** text box in the **New Workspace** area and then choose the **OK** button to close the dialog box. Next, close the **Manage Workspaces** dialog box. The newly created workspace will be active now.

Figure 1-10 The **Application** menu with the shortcuts

Figure 1-11 The **Quick Access Toolbar**

In 3ds Max Design 2015, the new enhanced menu system comes with features such as improved layout, detailed tooltips that are linked to the relevant help topics in the documentation, drag and drop support for menu categories, and menu commands search using keyboard. To access enhanced menus, select the **Default with Enhanced Menus** option from the **Workspaces** drop-down list; the 3ds Max Design interface with the enhanced menus will be displayed. Figure 1-12 shows the enhanced **Lighting/Cameras** pull-down menu.

*Figure 1-12 The enhanced **Lighting/Cameras** pull-down menu displayed*

Toolbars

In Autodesk 3ds Max Design, the commands can be invoked by using the buttons or tools in the toolbars. By default, only the **Main Toolbar** will be displayed on Autodesk 3ds Max Design screen. However, you can display other toolbars such as **Snaps**, **Axis Constraints**, **Extras**, **MassFX Toolbar**, and so on in the 3ds Max Design screen. Also, you can move, resize, and undock them based on your requirements. To display these toolbars, right-click in the blank area on the **Main Toolbar**; a shortcut menu will be displayed with the names of all toolbars, as shown in Figure 1-13. Next, choose the required toolbar; the chosen toolbar will be displayed on the screen. Also, you can hide any of the displayed toolbars by choosing its label from the shortcut menu.

The **Main Toolbar** provides quick access to many tools and dialog boxes such as **Select and Link**, **Unlink Selection**, **Select Object**, **Material Editor**, and so on. This toolbar is docked just below the menu bar. You will learn more about the tools available in various toolbars in the later chapters.

Figure 1-13 The shortcut menu displayed to view the hidden toolbars

In 3ds Max Design 2015, the **Select and Place** tool is added in the **Main Toolbar** to position and orient an object with respect to another object. Using this tool, you can move an object along the surface of the another object as if it is magnetically attracted towards it. Also, the placed object changes its orientation according to the shape of the object on which it is placed. To place an object along the surface of other object, choose the **Select and Place** tool from the **Main Toolbar** and then click and drag the object to the other object.

*Figure 1-12 The enhanced **Lighting/Cameras** pull-down menu displayed*

Toolbars

In Autodesk 3ds Max Design, the commands can be invoked by using the buttons or tools in the toolbars. By default, only the **Main Toolbar** will be displayed on Autodesk 3ds Max Design screen. However, you can display other toolbars such as **Snaps**, **Axis Constraints**, **Extras**, **MassFX Toolbar**, and so on in the 3ds Max Design screen. Also, you can move, resize, and undock them based on your requirements. To display these toolbars, right-click in the blank area on the **Main Toolbar**; a shortcut menu will be displayed with the names of all toolbars, as shown in Figure 1-13. Next, choose the required toolbar; the chosen toolbar will be displayed on the screen. Also, you can hide any of the displayed toolbars by choosing its label from the shortcut menu.

The **Main Toolbar** provides quick access to many tools and dialog boxes such as **Select and Link**, **Unlink Selection**, **Select Object**, **Material Editor**, and so on. This toolbar is docked just below the menu bar. You will learn more about the tools available in various toolbars in the later chapters.

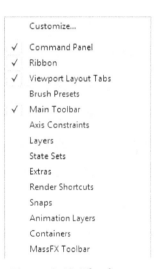

Figure 1-13 The shortcut menu displayed to view the hidden toolbars

In 3ds Max Design 2015, the **Select and Place** tool is added in the **Main Toolbar** to position and orient an object with respect to another object. Using this tool, you can move an object along the surface of the another object as if it is magnetically attracted towards it. Also, the placed object changes its orientation according to the shape of the object on which it is placed. To place an object along the surface of other object, choose the **Select and Place** tool from the **Main Toolbar** and then click and drag the object to the other object.

Figure 1-10 *The **Application** menu with the*
shortcuts

Figure 1-11 *The **Quick Access Toolbar***

In 3ds Max Design 2015, the new enhanced menu system comes with features such as improved layout, detailed tooltips that are linked to the relevant help topics in the documentation, drag and drop support for menu categories, and menu commands search using keyboard. To access enhanced menus, select the **Default with Enhanced Menus** option from the **Workspaces** drop-down list; the 3ds Max Design interface with the enhanced menus will be displayed. Figure 1-12 shows the enhanced **Lighting/Cameras** pull-down menu.

Command Panel

By default, the **Command Panel** is docked on the right of the 3ds Max Design screen. There are six tabs in the **Command Panel**: **Create**, **Modify**, **Hierarchy**, **Motion**, **Display**, and **Utilities**, as shown in Figure 1-14. Most of the 3ds Max Design modeling and animation tools are placed in these tabs. The tools in the **Command Panel** are used to create, modify, and animate the objects. Each tab has several rollouts that can be expanded or collapsed. The tabs in the **Command Panel** are discussed next.

 The **Create** tab is chosen by default. The tools in the **Create** tab are used to create objects, cameras, lights, and so on.

 The **Modify** tab is used to modify the selected objects by modifying their parameters, applying various modifiers, and editing the mesh as well as polygonal and patch objects.

 The **Hierarchy** tab is used to control the links in the hierarchy, joints, and inverse kinematics.

 The **Motion** tab is used to control the animation controllers and trajectories.

 The **Display** tab is used to hide and unhide the objects in the viewport.

*Figure 1-14 The **Command Panel***

 The **Utilities** tab is used to access various utility programs.

 Note
*You can undock the **Command Panel** and **Main Toolbar** and place them anywhere on the screen. To do so, move the cursor on the top of the **Main Toolbar**; the cursor will change into an arrow with two overlapping rectangles. Now, press and hold the left mouse button and drag the **Main Toolbar** to the desired location. Double-click on the **Main Toolbar** to dock it back to its default position.*

Scene Management

In 3ds Max Design 2015, the **Scene Explorer** is added to manage complex scenes in an efficient manner. You can also create and manage more than one **Scene Explorer** in a scene for better scene management. The **Scene Explorer** can also be switched to **Layer Explorer**. The **Scene Explorer**, **Layer Explorer**, and the process creating and managing more than one **Scene Explorer** is discussed next.

Scene Explorer

The **Scene Explorer** is used to view, select, filter, and sort objects. It is also used to rename, delete, group, freeze, and hide the objects. The **Scene Explorer** is docked by default at the left of the interface in the default workspace, refer to Figure 1-15.

Figure 1-15 The Scene Explorer

The options in the **Scene Explorer** menu bar are used to select objects, customize the **Scene Explorer** toolbar, change the display to specific type of objects in its list, and so on. The **Toggle Display** toolbar button is used to toggle the visibility of the **Scene Explorer** toolbar. The Search field is used to search an object from the list of objects and thereby adding a filter is added to the list of objects. The **Remove Filter** button is used to remove the applied filter. When you right-click in the area where the list of objects is displayed, a quad menu will be displayed. The options in this quad menu are used to rename the object, freeze the object, and so on. The name of the workspace used in the scene is displayed in the field located at the bottom of the **Scene Explorer**. The arrow at the left of this field is used to save the active **Scene Explorer** as the default **Scene Explorer**, default mass explorer, and so on. You can use the **Sort By Layer** button to switch the **Scene Explorer** to **Layer Explorer**. The **Layer Explorer** is discussed next.

Layer Explorer

The **Layer Explorer** is displayed in the interface on choosing the **Sort By Layer** button from the **Scene Explorer**, refer to Figure 1-15. By default, the **Layer Explorer** is displayed with **0 (default)** layer, as shown in Figure 1-16. You can create any number of layers in the **Layer Explorer** by using the **Create New Layer** button. To add an object to the newly created or existing layer, expand the **0 (default)** layer and then select the object from the list of objects in the **Layer Explorer** and right-click on it; a quad menu will be displayed, refer to Figure 1-17. Choose **Add Selection To > New Parent (pick)** from the quad menu and select the desired layer from the list of layers displayed; the selected object is transferred to the selected layer. You can also create a new layer and add the selected object to it by using the quad menu. To do so, select the object from the list of objects displayed. Next, right-click on it and then choose **Add Selected To > Create Layer** from the quad menu displayed; a new layer will be created and the selected object will be added to it. To rename a layer, right-click on it and choose **Rename** from the quad menu displayed.

*Figure 1-16 The **Layer Explorer***

Figure 1-17 The quad menu

Creating and Managing the Scene Explorer

In 3ds Max Design 2015, you can create new **Scene Explorer**(s) to manage complex scenes. You can also open a number of Scene Explorers simultaneously in a scene.

To create a new **Scene Explorer**, choose **Tools > New Scene Explorer** from the menu bar; the **Scene Explorer - Scene Explorer #** window will be opened, refer to Figure 1-18. You can also close the newly created **Scene Explorer**(s). To reopen the recently closed **Scene Explorer**, choose **Tools > Open Explorer: Scene Explorer #** from the menu bar. Alternatively, you can press ALT+CTRL+O to reopen it.

Figure 1-18 The Scene Explorer - Scene Explorer1 window

To manage various Scene Explorers, choose **Tools > Manage Scene Explorer** from the menu bar; the **Manage Scene Explorer** dialog box will be displayed, refer to Figure 1-19. Using this dialog box, you can select a **Scene Explorer** and set it as the default **Scene Explorer**, rename it, or delete it. You can also save a **Scene Explorer** for later use in other scenes.

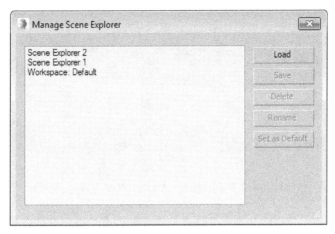

*Figure 1-19 The **Manage Scene Explorer** dialog box*

To save the **Scene Explorer**, choose the **Save** button; the **Save Scene Explorer** dialog box will be displayed. Next, enter the desired name in the **File name** text box and choose the **Save** button; the **Scene Explorer** is saved with the desired name. To use a saved **Scene Explorer** in other scenes, choose the **Load** button; the **Load Scene Explorer** dialog box will be displayed. Select the desired **Scene Explorer** from this dialog box and choose **Open**; the desired **Scene Explorer** will be opened in the current scene.

Viewports

When you start Autodesk 3ds Max Design, you are provided with a default interface. This interface consists of four equal sized viewports surrounded by tools and commands. These viewports are labeled as Top, Front, Left, and Perspective. The viewports in Autodesk 3ds Max Design are used to create 3D scenes. Also, they enable you to view a scene from different angles. When you create an object in the viewport, the Top, Front, and Left viewports will display the top, front, and left orthographic views of the object, respectively.

In 3ds Max Design, you can loop between viewports to make a particular viewport active by using the WINDOWS+SHIFT keys. The active viewport in 3ds Max Design is highlighted with a yellow border. Only one viewport can remain active at a time. All commands and actions in 3ds Max Design are performed in the active viewport. You can switch between the viewports by using the WINDOWS + SHIFT keys. However, if only one viewport is maximized, then on repeatedly pressing the WINDOWS + SHIFT keys, a window with available viewports will be displayed, refer to Figure 1-20. When the WINDOWS + SHIFT keys are released, the window will disappear and the viewport you have chosen will become active.

You can modify the size of the viewports by dragging the intersection of the viewports on the splitter bars. To restore the original layout, right-click on the intersection of the dividing lines; a shortcut menu will be displayed, as shown in Figure 1-21. Choose the **Reset Layout** option from the shortcut menu; the viewports will be restored to their default size.

Figure 1-20 *Selecting a viewport to make it active*

Figure 1-21 *Choosing the **Reset Layout** option from the shortcut menu*

On the bottom left corner of each viewport, there is a world-space tripod, as shown in Figure 1-22. The world-space tripod has three axes, X, Y, and Z, which are displayed in red, green, and blue colors, respectively. The tripod always refers to the world coordinate system, regardless of the local coordinate system. ViewCube is placed on the top right corner of the viewport, as shown in Figure 1-22. The ViewCube provides visual feedback of the current orientation of the viewport.

Note

The ViewCube will not be visible in the camera, light, and shape viewports.

It is important to note that the local coordinate system defines local position of an object in a scene, whereas the World coordinate system uses fixed axes to define the position of all objects in the world space. Each viewport has a grid placed in it, refer to Figure 1-22.

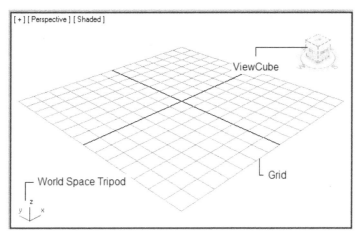

Figure 1-22 The world space tripod, grid, and ViewCube in the Perspective viewport

It is like a graph paper in which all the lines intersect each other at right angles. You can modify the spacing in the grids. The grids in all viewports act as an aid to visualize the spacing and distance while creating objects. Also, they are used as a construction plane to create and align the objects. You can also use the grids as a reference system while using the snap tools to align the objects. You can also hide the grid in the viewport. To do so, press the G key; the grid will disappear from the viewport. To make the grid visible, press the G key again.

On the top left corner of each viewport, there are three viewport labels: General viewport label, Point of view (POV) viewport label, and Shading viewport label, refer to Figure 1-23. When you click on any of the viewport labels, the corresponding flyout will be displayed, as shown in Figure 1-24. The options in these shortcut menus are used to modify various aspects of the active viewport.

You can configure the active viewport by using the options in the General viewport label menu. Choose the **Configure Viewports** option from this menu; the **Viewport Configuration** dialog box will be displayed. Various options in this dialog box can be used to configure the viewports. You already know that four equally sized viewports are displayed on the screen. However, you can change the viewport configuration based on your requirement. To change the basic configuration of the viewports, choose the **Layout** tab in the **Viewport Configuration** dialog box, refer to Figure 1-25. In the **Layout** tab, you can specify the division method of the viewports. There are 14 types of configurations displayed at the top in the tab. Select the required configuration and then choose the **OK** button; the viewports will be displayed according to the configuration that you have selected in the **Viewport Configuration** dialog box.

Note
The viewport configuration specifies how the viewports will be arranged on the screen.

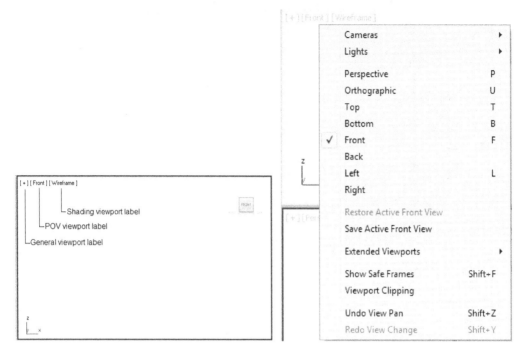

Figure 1-23 *The viewport labels in the Front viewport*

Figure 1-24 *The flyout displayed on clicking the POV viewport label*

Figure 1-25 *The **Layout** tab of the **Viewport Configuration** dialog box*

You can change the default viewport to any other viewport type available such as Bottom, Right, and so on, by using the options in the POV viewport label menu. To do so, click on the POV viewport label; a flyout will be displayed. Choose the viewport that you want to display.

You can also use the Shading viewport label menu for defining the type of shading displayed in the viewport. The different types of shading types are: **Realistic**, **Shaded**, **Consistent Colors**, **Wireframe**, **Edged Faces**, **Bounding Box**, **Hidden Line**, and so on. However, some other shading types are available in the cascading menu of the **Stylized** option, refer to Figure 1-26. These shading types are **Graphite**, **Color Pencil**, **Ink**, and so on. You can choose any one of the options to change the shading.

Figure 1-26 *Different shading types in the cascading menu of the* ***Stylized*** *option*

Viewport Navigation Controls

There are various tools available at the bottom right corner of the Autodesk 3ds Max Design screen, as shown in Figure 1-27. These tools are known as viewport navigation controls and they are used to control the display and navigation of the viewport. The tools displayed in the viewport navigation controls depend on the viewport selected. For example, if the Camera viewport is selected, its corresponding tools will be displayed in the viewport navigation control. These tools are discussed in detail in the later chapters.

Figure 1-27 *The viewport navigation controls*

Viewport Layout Tab Bar

The Viewport Layout tab bar enables you to store multiple viewport setups in a single scene. You can switch between different viewport setups with a click. This bar is active by default and is located on the extreme left of the interface screen, refer to Figure 1-6. By default, there is a single tab at the bottom of the bar that represents the startup layout. To add more layout tabs to the bar, click on the arrow button on the bar; the **Standard Viewport Layouts** flyout will be displayed. Next, choose the required option from the flyout; the chosen layout tab will be added to the bar. To remove a tab from the bar, right-click on the tab; a shortcut menu will be displayed. Next, choose **Delete Tab** from the shortcut menu.

Animation Playback Controls

The tools in the animation playback controls are displayed on the left side of the viewport navigation controls, refer to Figure 1-28. These tools are used to control the animation in the active viewport. Also, you can set the total number of frames, animation length, and other settings of the animation using these tools.

Figure 1-28   The animation playback controls

Animation Keying Controls

The tools in the animation keying controls are displayed on the left side of the animation playback controls, refer to Figure 1-29. These tools are used to enter or exit different animation modes.

Figure 1-29   The animation keying controls

Track Bar

The track bar lies between the time slider and the status bar, refer to Figure 1-30. It displays a timeline along with the frame numbers.

Figure 1-30 The track bar and the time slider

Time Slider

The time slider displays the current frame and the total number of frames in the current time segment, refer to Figure 1-31. You can view the animation at each frame by dragging the time slider. The time segment is the total range of frames that you can access using the time slider. By default, it ranges from 0 to 100. You can set the range using the **Time Configuration** dialog box, about which you will learn in the later chapters.

Status Bar

There are various tools in the status bar that provide information about the scene and the active command, as shown in Figure 1-31. The prompt line, which is located at the bottom of the screen, displays information about the active command or tool. On top of the status bar, a text box known as the status line is available. This status line displays the number of currently selected objects (current selection set). The **Selection Lock Toggle** tool on the right side of the status bar is used to lock the selection set. The Coordinate display/transform type-in area displays the X, Y, and Z coordinates of the cursor or the currently selected object. The Coordinate display/transform type-in area can also be used to enter transform values while moving, scaling, or rotating the selected object(s).

The Grid setting display area is placed on the right of the Coordinate display area. It displays the size of the grid. The time tag area located below the grid setting display area is used to assign the text labels at any point of time in your animation. Click on the time tag area; a flyout with the **Add Tag** and **Edit Tag** options will be displayed. Use these options to add or edit the text labels at any point of time in your animation.

Figure 1-31 The status bar

The **Progressive Display/Adaptive Degradation** button placed on the right of the prompt line is used to improve the viewport performance in a complex scene by decreasing the visual fidelity of some of the objects temporarily. This results in smoother viewport motions and object transformations in such scenes. It also improves viewport quality incrementally, depending on the availability of processing time. To activate this feature, right-click on the **Progressive Display** button; the **Viewport Configuration** dialog box will be displayed, as shown in Figure 1-32. The **Display Performance** tab is chosen by default in this dialog box. Now, change the settings in the **Display Performance** tab based on your requirement and choose the **OK** button.

*Figure 1-32 The **Viewport Configuration** dialog box*

SNAPS SETTINGS

Snaps restrict the movement of the cursor to a specific part of an object or grid. There are four tools available for snap settings in the **Main Toolbar**: **Snaps Toggle**, **Angle Snap Toggle**, **Percent Snap Toggle**, and **Spinner Snap Toggle**. If you right-click on the **Snaps Toggle**, **Angle Snap Toggle**, or **Percent Snap Toggle** tool, the **Grid and Snap Settings** dialog box will be displayed, as shown in Figure 1-33. In this dialog box, you can select different parts of the objects or grid where the cursor will snap to. You can turn the snap command on and off by pressing the S key or by invoking the **Snaps Toggle** tool. If you press and hold the mouse button on the **Snaps Toggle** tool, a flyout will be displayed. This flyout contains the **2D Snap**, **2.5 Snap**, and **3D Snap** tools, which can be invoked to snap the cursor.

*Figure 1-33 The **Grid and Snap Settings** dialog box*

Snaps Toggle

Main Toolbar:	Snaps Toggle
Menu bar:	Tools > Grids and Snaps > Snaps Toggle
Keyboard:	S

The **Snaps Toggle** tool is used to snap the objects on the grid. On invoking the **Snap Toggle** tool, a flyout will be displayed, as shown in Figure 1-34. This flyout has three tools and these tools are discussed next.

2D Snap

If you invoke the 2D Snap tool from the **Snaps Toggle** flyout, then the cursor snaps to the active grid in two dimensions, X and Y. The Z-axis is not taken into consideration.

*Figure 1-34 The **Snaps Toggle** flyout*

2.5D Snap

If you invoke the 2.5D Snap tool from the **Snaps Toggle** flyout, then the cursor snaps to the vertices and edges of the objects projected on the active grid.

3D Snap

If you invoke the 3D Snap tool from the **Snaps Toggle** flyout, then the cursor snaps to any object in 3D space using the **3D Snap** tool.

On moving the gizmo or snap handle, this axis center will act as the start snap point. This feature also helps in increasing the accuracy of snaps.

Angle Snap Toggle

Main Toolbar: Angle Snap Toggle
Menu bar: Tools > Grids and Snaps > Angle Snap Toggle
Keyboard: A

 The **Angle Snap Toggle** tool enables you to rotate an object in angular increments. The increment value is specified in the **Angle** spinner of the **Grid and Snap Settings** dialog box. By default, the value in the **Angle** spinner is set to 5.0.

Percent Snap Toggle

Main Toolbar: Percent Snap Toggle
Menu bar: Tools > Grids and Snaps > Percent Snap Toggle
Keyboard: CTRL+SHIFT+P

 The **Percent Snap Toggle** tool enables you to scale an object in percent increments. The increment value can be specified in the **Percent** spinner of the **Grid and Snap Settings** dialog box. By default, the value set in the **Percent** spinner is set to 10.0.

Spinner Snap Toggle

Main Toolbar: Spinner Snap Toggle

The **Spinner Snap Toggle** tool is used to set the single increment or decrement value for all spinners in Autodesk 3ds Max Design. By default, the increment or decrement value is set to 1. To specify the increment value, right-click on the **Spinner Snap Toggle** tool; the **Preference Settings** dialog box will be displayed. In this dialog box, choose the **General** tab, if it is not already chosen. Now, in the **Spinners** area, set a value in the **Snap** spinner, refer to Figure 1-35.

Figure 1-35 The Spinners area in the Preference Settings dialog box

Also, select the **Use Snap** check box and then choose the **OK** button; the **Spinner Snap Toggle** tool in the **Main Toolbar** is invoked. Now, when you use any spinner in 3ds Max Design, the value will increase or decrease according to the value that you have specified in the **Preference Settings** dialog box.

UNITS SETUP

The units setup in 3ds Max Design is used to specify the units that help in measuring the geometry in a scene. You can change the settings for units by using the **Customize** pull-down menu. To do so, choose **Customize > Units Setup** from the menu bar; the **Units Setup** dialog box will be displayed, as shown in Figure 1-36. By default, the **Generic Units** radio button is selected in the **Display Unit Scale** area in this dialog box. You can select any other radio button as per the requirement from the **Display Unit Scale** area of this dialog box and then choose the **OK** button; the limits in all spinners in 3ds Max Design will be modified accordingly.

Setting Grid Spacing

To set the spacing between the visible grids in the viewports, choose **Tools > Grids and Snaps > Grid and Snap Settings** from the menu bar; the **Grid and Snap Settings** dialog box will be displayed. Choose the **Home Grid** tab in this dialog box, as shown in Figure 1-37. In the **Grid Dimensions** area, set the value in the **Grid Spacing** spinner to specify the size of the smallest square of the grid. The value in the spinners will be measured in the units that you specify in the **Units Setup** dialog box. Set the value in the **Major Lines every Nth Grid Line** spinner to specify the number of squares between the major lines in the grid. Set the value in the **Perspective View Grid Extent** spinner to specify the size of the home grid in the Perspective viewport. Note that the default grid displayed in the viewports on starting 3ds Max Design is known as the Home Grid.

Figure 1-36   *The* **Units Setup** *dialog box*

Figure 1-37   *The* **Home Grid** *tab chosen in the* **Grid and Snap Settings** *dialog box*

In the **Dynamic Update** area, the **Active Viewport** radio button is selected by default. It is used to update the active viewport according to the new values of the **Grid and Snap Settings** dialog box. Select the **All Viewports** radio button to update all viewports simultaneously according to the new values that you set in the spinners of the **Grid and Snap Settings** dialog box.

UNDO AND REDO TOOLS

Quick Access Toolbar:	Undo Scene Operation or Redo Scene Operation
Menu bar:	Edit > Undo or Redo
Keyboard:	CTRL+Z (Undo) or CTRL+Y (Redo)

The **Undo** tool is used to revert the last actions performed while creating or modifying a model in Autodesk 3ds Max Design. To undo an action, invoke the **Undo Scene Operation** tool from the **Quick Access Toolbar** or press the CTRL+Z keys. You need to invoke the **Undo Scene Operation** tool repeatedly till all the previously performed actions are reversed. To reverse a number of actions at a time, click on the arrow of the **Undo Scene Operation** tool in the **Quick Access Toolbar**; a list of actions will be displayed, refer to Figure 1-38. Move the cursor over the number of actions that you want to reverse; the actions will be selected. Next, click on the list. By default, you can reverse your actions up to 20 times. If you want to change this number, choose **Customize > Preferences** from the menu bar; the **Preference Settings** dialog box will be displayed. By default, the **General** tab is chosen in this dialog box. In the **Scene Undo** area, set a new value in the **Levels** spinner, as shown in Figure 1-39.

Figure 1-38 *The list of actions displayed after choosing the **Undo Scene Operation** tool*

Figure 1-39 *The **Scene Undo** area in the **Preference Settings** dialog box*

The **Redo** tool is used to revert the last actions performed by the **Undo** tool. To redo an action, invoke the **Redo Scene Operation** tool from the **Quick Access Toolbar** or press the CTRL+Y keys. You need to invoke the **Redo Scene Operation** tool repeatedly till you want to reverse the actions performed earlier. To reverse a number of actions at a time, click on the arrow of the **Redo Scene Operation** tool in the **Quick Access Toolbar**; a list of last actions will be displayed. Move the cursor over the number of actions that you want to reverse; the actions will be selected. Next, click on the list; the selected action will be displayed.

HOLD AND FETCH TOOLS

Menu bar:	Edit > Hold or Fetch
Keyboard:	CTRL+H (Hold) or ALT+CTRL+F (Fetch)

Sometimes you may want to perform different experiments on a scene. In such as a case you need to hold the scene. The **Hold** tool is used to hold a scene and it saves the work in a temporary file with the name *maxhold.mx*.

The file is saved at the location *\Documents\3dsmaxDesign\autoback*. To perform an experiment using the new commands in a scene, invoke the **Hold** tool from the **Edit** menu or press the CTRL+H keys. Next, if you need to go back to the previous command, choose the **Fetch** tool from the **Edit** menu or press ALT+CTRL+F; the **About to Fetch. OK?** message box will be displayed, as shown in Figure 1-40. Choose the **Yes** button; the scene with the previous command will be displayed. In this way, you can go back to a series of commands using the **Hold** tool.

Figure 1-40 *The **About to Fetch. OK?** message box*

Note
*When you use the **Fetch** tool in a scene, the history of the actions performed so far will be deleted. As a result, you cannot undo or redo the actions performed before invoking this tool.*

HOT KEYS

In 3ds Max Design, you can use the hot keys to invoke some of the commonly used tools and commands. These keys are known as the hot keys. You can work faster and more efficiently using the hot keys. The major hot keys and their functions are listed next.

Main Toolbar

The hot keys that can be used to invoke the tools available in the **Main Toolbar** are given next:

H	Invokes the **Select From Scene** dialog box
S	Invokes the **Snaps Toggle** tool
A	Invokes the **Angle Snap Toggle** tool
CTRL+SHIFT+P	Invokes the **Percent Snap Toggle** tool
M	Invokes the **Material Editor** dialog box
SHIFT+Q	Invokes the **Render Production** tool

Viewport Navigation Controls

The hot keys that can be used to invoke the tools available in the viewport navigation controls are given next:

ALT+CTRL+Z	Performs the action of the **Zoom Extents** tool
ALT+W	Invokes the **Maximize Viewport Toggle** tool
ALT+Z	Invokes the **Zoom** tool
CTRL+W	Invokes the **Zoom Region** tool
CTRL+P	Invokes the **Pan View** tool
Scroll the middle mouse button	Zooms in or out the active viewport
CTRL+R	Invokes the **Orbit** tool
SHIFT+Z	Used to undo the **Zoom** or **Pan** command actions
ALT+ press and hold the middle mouse button and move the mouse	Performs the actions of the **Orbit** tool

The following hot keys are used to change the POV viewport labels:

V	Invokes the viewport quad menu
T	Invokes the Top viewport
F	Invokes the Front viewport
L	Invokes the Left viewport
P	Invokes the Perspective viewport
B	Invokes the Bottom viewport
U	Invokes the Orthographic viewport

Animation Playback Controls

The hot keys that can be used to invoke the tools available in the animation playback controls are given next:

N	Invokes the **Auto key** tool
Home	Go to start frame
End	Go to end frame
/ (backslash)	Plays animation
ESC	Stop the animation
, (comma)	Go to previous frame
. (period)	Go to next frame

Customizing the Hot Keys

In 3ds Max Design, you can create your own keyboard shortcuts. To do so, choose **Customize > Customize User Interface** from the menu bar; the **Customize User Interface** dialog box will be displayed, as shown in Figure 1-41. In this dialog box, the **Keyboard** tab is chosen by default. Next, select a command from the **Group** and **Category** drop-down lists; the list of corresponding actions will be displayed just below the **Category** drop-down list. Now, select one of the actions from the list and then enter the key that you want to assign to the selected action in the **Hotkey** text box. Next, choose the **Assign** button; the key is assigned to the selected action.

CUSTOMIZING THE COLORS OF THE USER INTERFACE

3ds Max Design allows you to modify the colors of the interface. You can modify the colors for almost every element in the interface. To modify the colors, choose **Customize > Customize User Interface** in the menu bar; the **Customize User Interface** dialog box will be displayed. Choose the **Colors** tab from this dialog box, refer to Figure 1-41. Next, select the category of the interface element from the **Elements** drop-down list; the list of the corresponding elements will be displayed just below the **Elements** drop-down list. Now, select one of the elements from the list and click on the Color swatch on the right of the **Elements** drop-down list; the **Color Selector** dialog box will be displayed. Select a new color and choose the **OK** button to close the **Color Selector** dialog box.

*Figure 1-41 The **Customize User Interface** dialog box*

To reset the new color to the default one, choose the **Colors** tab and then choose the **Reset** button at the bottom of the **Customize User Interface** dialog box; the **Revert Color File** message box will be displayed, as shown in Figure 1-42. Choose the **Yes** button; the default colors will be displayed in the color swatches.

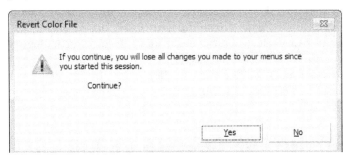

*Figure 1-42 The **Revert Color File** message box*

HELP PREFERENCES

When you choose **Help > Autodesk 3ds Max Help** from the menu bar, the 3ds Max help will be displayed. If you want to open help from a local drive, you need to download it from *http://www.autodesk.com/3dsmax-helpdownload-enu* and then install it on your system. Next, choose **Customize > Preferences** from the menu bar; the **Preference Settings** dialog box will be displayed. Choose the **Help** tab in this dialog box, refer to Figure 1-43. Select the **Local Computer/Network** radio button from the **Help Location** area and then choose the **Browse** button; the **Browse For Folder** dialog box will be displayed. Select the path where you have saved the file and then choose the **OK** button to exit the dialog box. Next, choose the **OK** button in the **Preference Settings** dialog box; the dialog box will be closed. Now, you can access the help from your local drive.

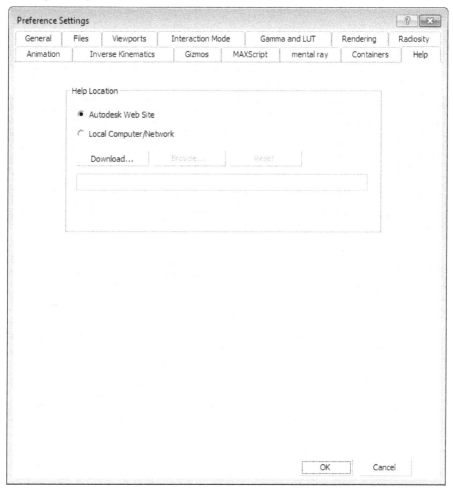

*Figure 1-43 The **Help** tab chosen in the **Preference Settings** dialog box*

In Autodesk 3ds Max Design, if you choose **Help > Search 3ds Max Commands** from the menu bar or press X, a search field will be displayed, refer to Figure 1-44. Next, enter the first few characters of a command; a list of command names that contain the specified text will be displayed, refer to Figure 1-45. Now, you can execute the desired command by choosing it from the list displayed.

Figure 1-44 *The search field*   **Figure 1-45** *List of commands displayed on entering first few characters*

Note

For the printing purpose, this textbook will follow the white background. However, for a better understanding and a clear visualization at various places, this textbook will follow other color schemes as well.

In addition, the **Shaded** *shading type is used throughout the textbook in all screen captures. Moreover, at some places in figures, grids will be hidden for better understanding and visualization. In some tutorials, you have been instructed to browse the images and 3ds Max Design files from the CADCIM website. Therefore, before starting the tutorials, download the images and 3ds Max Design files from www.cadcim.com. The path of the files is as follows: Textbooks > Animation and Visual Effects > 3ds Max Design > Autodesk 3ds Max Design 2015: A Tutorial Approach*

Self-Evaluation Test

Answer the following questions and then compare them to those given at the end of this chapter:

1. Which of the following tools is used to improve the performance of a viewport in a complex scene by temporarily decreasing the visual fidelity of some of the objects?

    (a) **Progressive Display**   (b) **Snaps Toggle** flyout
    (c) **Mirror**   (d) All of these

2. Which of the following tabs should be chosen to control the animation controllers?

    (a) **Motion**   (b) **Display**
    (c) **Hierarchy**   (d) None of these

3. Which of the following dialog boxes is used to set the spacing in the grids displayed in the viewports?

    (a) **Customize User Interface**   (b) **Grid and Snap Settings**
    (c) **Units Setup**   (d) All of these

4. Which of the following shortcut keys is used to invoke the **Pan** tool?

    (a) CTRL+P   (b) SHIFT+Z
    (c) CTRL+A   (d) CTRL+W

5. The _____ is located at the bottom of the screen and displays the information about the active command or tool.

6. The _____ dialog box, provides access to video tutorials that are helpful in learning the basics of 3ds Max Design.

7. Most of the 3ds Max Design modeling and animation tools can be invoked from the tabs located in the **Command Panel**. (T/F)

8. The default interface of 3ds Max Design consists of three equal sized viewports that are surrounded by tools and commands. (T/F)

9. In 3ds Max Design, you can modify the colors of almost every element in the interface. (T/F)

10. The tools in the animation playback controls are used to control the display of a viewport. (T/F)

Review Questions

Answer the following questions:

1. Which of the following tabs in the **Command Panel** is used to hide and unhide the objects in the viewport?

   (a) **Utilities**   (b) **Display**
   (c) **Motion**   (d) **Hierarchy**

2. Which of the following shortcut keys is used to loop between viewports to make a particular viewport active?

   (a) WINDOWS+SHIFT   (b) WINDOWS+ALT
   (c) WINDOWS+TAB   (d) WINDOWS+ENTER

3. Which of the following components displays the current frame and the total number of frames in the current time segment?

   (a) Status Bar   (b) Track Bar
   (c) Time slider   (d) None of these

4. The _____ provides visual feedback of the current orientation of the viewport.

5. The _____ is located between the time slider and the status bar.

6. The _____ tool located on the right of the status bar is used to lock a selection set.

7. The options in the _____ drop-down list are used to switch between the saved layout setups.

8. The **Viewport Layout Tab** bar enables you to store multiple viewport setups in a single scene. (T/F)

9. Snapping restricts the movement of the cursor to a specific part of an object or grid. (T/F)

10. The options in the General viewport label menu are used for defining the type of shadings displayed in the viewport. (T/F)

Answers to Self-Evaluation Test
1. a, **2.** a, **3.** b, **4.** a, **5.** prompt line, **6. Welcome to 3ds Max, 7.** T, **8.** F, **9.** T, **10.** F

Chapter 2

Primitive Objects-I

Learning Objectives

After completing this chapter, you will be able to:
- *Create primitive objects*
- *Modify primitive objects*
- *Use the Mirror and Align tools*

INTRODUCTION

In this chapter, you will learn to create primitive objects and modify them using modifiers such as **Edit Mesh** and **Edit Poly**. In addition, you will learn to use the **Mirror** and **Align** tools.

TUTORIALS

Tutorial 1

In this tutorial, you will create a model of a temple using various primitive objects, as shown in Figure 2-1.   **(Expected time: 20 min)**

Figure 2-1 *The model of a temple*

The following steps are required to complete this tutorial:

a.   Create the project folder.
b.   Create bottom part of the temple.
c.   Create pillars.
d.   Create the roof.
e.   Modify the roof objects.
f.   Add details to the dome.
g.   Change the background color of the scene.
h.   Save and render the scene.

Creating the Project Folder

Before starting a new scene, it is recommended that you create the project folder. Creating a project folder helps you keep all files of a project in an organized manner. Open Windows Explorer and browse to the *Documents* folder. In this folder, create a new folder with the name *3dsmaxdesign 2015*. The *3dsmaxdesign 2015* folder will be the main folder and it will contain all project folders that you will create while working on the tutorials of this textbook. Next, you will create first project folder for Tutorial 1 of this chapter. To do so, you need to follow the steps given next.

1. Start 3ds Max Design 2015.

2. If 3ds Max Design is already running, you need to reset it. To do so, choose the **Reset** option from the **Application** menu; the **3ds Max** message box is displayed. Choose the **Yes** button from the message box; a new screen is displayed with default settings.

Note
*The **Reset** option is used to restore 3ds Max Design settings to its startup defaults.*

3. Choose the **Application** button; the **Application** menu is displayed. Next, choose **Manage > Set Project Folder** from it; the **Browse For Folder** dialog box is displayed.

4. In the **Browse For Folder** dialog box, navigate to *\Documents\3dsmaxdesign*. Next, choose the **Make New Folder** button and create a new folder with the name *c02_tut1*. Next, choose the **OK** button to close the **Browse For Folder** dialog box.

5. Choose **Save** from the **Application** menu; the **Save File As** dialog box is displayed.

Note
*1. The scenes created in 3ds Max Design are saved with the .max extension. As the project folder is already created, the **scenes** folder is displayed in the **Save in** drop-down list of the **Save File As** dialog box.*

*2. You can also save a scene to a previous versions (2012, 2013, and 2014) of 3ds Max Design. To do so, select the desired option from the **Save as type** drop-down list in the **Save File As** dialog box.*

*3. After setting the project folder when you open or save a scene, the scenes folder of this project is selected by default in the **Save File As** and **Open File** dialog boxes.*

6. Enter **c02tut1** in the **File name** text box and then choose the **Save** button to close the dialog box.

When you start 3ds Max Design, the last project that you have worked with will be active and an empty scene will be displayed with the name **Untitled**. It is recommended that you frequently save the files while you are working on them by pressing the CTRL+S keys.

Autodesk 3ds Max Design creates a backup of the scene and saves changes periodically. In case of system failure, you can open the auto backup scene file and continue working on it. If you have not created the project folder, the default path for windows to save the auto backup file is as follows: *C:\users\<username>\My Documents\3dsmaxdesign\autoback*. However, if you have created the project folder, the backup file will be saved in the *autoback* subfolder of the project folder. When 3ds Max Design is auto saving a file, the information, **Autosave in progress... (Press ESC to cancel)** is displayed in the prompt line at the bottom of the interface. If the size of the file is too large and consuming long time to save, you can press the ESC key to interrupt the saving process. You can also set the number of autoback files, specify the names for these files, and set the backup time interval. To do so, choose **Customize > Preferences** from the menu bar; the **Preferences Settings** dialog box will be displayed. Next, choose the **Files** tab and then set the options as required in the **Auto Backup** area of the dialog box.

Creating Bottom Part of the Temple

In this section, you will create the bottom part of the temple using the **Box** tool.

1. Choose **Create > Geometry** in the **Command Panel**, if it is not already chosen; different tools and rollouts pertaining to the **Create** command are displayed in the **Command Panel**, refer to Figure 2-2.

*Figure 2-2 The tools and rollouts in the **Command Panel***

When you start 3ds Max Design, the **Geometry** button is chosen by default.

2. Invoke the **Box** tool from the **Object Type** rollout; the rollouts corresponding to the **Box** tool such as **Name and Color**, **Creation Method**, **Keyboard Entry**, and **Parameters** are displayed.

    The **+** sign on the left side of the rollout title bar indicates that the rollout is collapsed, while the **-** sign indicates that the rollout is expanded, refer to Figure 2-2.

3. Expand the **Keyboard Entry** rollout by clicking on its title bar and set the values as given next.

    Length: **360**   Width: **360**   Height: **20**

Choose the **Create** button; the box is created in all viewports with the name *Box001*. Enter **Bottom** in the **Name and Color** rollout; the box is renamed as *Bottom*.

4. Invoke the **Zoom Extents All** tool from the viewport navigation controls; *Bottom* is zoomed to its extents, refer to Figure 2-3.

[+][Perspective][Shaded]

Figure 2-3 *Bottom zoomed to its extents*

5. Make sure the **Box** tool is invoked.

6. In the **Keyboard Entry** rollout, set the values as given next.

Length: **60**   Width: **60**   Height: **30**

Choose the **Create** button; a box is created at the center of *Bottom*. Enter **Base01** in the **Name and Color** rollout; the box is renamed as *Base01*. Next, right-click to exit the **Box** tool.

7. Invoke the **Maximize Viewport Toggle** tool from the viewport navigation controls; all viewports are displayed with *Bottom* and *Base01*. Make sure the Top, Front, and Left viewports are in wireframe mode, refer to Figure 2-4.

   Tip: *You can also press ALT+W to toggle between the active viewport and four viewport display.*

8. Click in the Front viewport to activate it. Next, invoke the **Zoom** tool from the viewport navigation controls and zoom in the small box in the Front viewport.

Note

In 3ds Max Design 2015, you can switch between the viewports to make a particular viewport active by using the WINDOWS+SHIFT keys. The active viewport in 3ds Max Design is marked with a yellow highlighted border. Only one viewport can remain active at a time. If all viewports are visible, pressing the WINDOWS+SHIFT keys will make the subsequent viewports active one after the other. However, if only one viewport is maximized, then on pressing the WINDOWS+SHIFT keys repeatedly, a window with available viewports will be displayed. When the WINDOWS+SHIFT Keys are released, the window will disappear and the viewport you choose will becomes active. You can use this process to activate a viewport whenever you need to do so.

Figure 2-4 Bottom and Base01 displayed in viewports

9. Invoke the **Select and Move** tool by pressing the W key. In the Front viewport, select *Base01* and move it up along the Y-axis such that its bottom touches the top of the object *Bottom*. Now, release the left mouse button. Next, select the *Bottom* and invoke the **Zoom Extents** tool to zoom *Bottom*.

10. Activate the Top viewport and invoke the **Zoom Extents** tool from the viewport navigation controls area. Next, invoke the **Maximize Viewport Toggle** tool from the viewport navigation controls to maximize the viewport.

11. Move *Base01* to the lower-left corner of *Bottom*, as shown in Figure 2-5.

Note

*The **Axis Constraints** toolbar is not displayed by default. To display this toolbar, right-click on the empty area of the **Main Toolbar** and then choose the **Axis Constraints** option from the shortcut menu displayed.*

12. Choose the **Transform Gizmo Y Constraint** button from the **Axis Constraint** toolbar. Also, make sure the **Select and Move** tool is invoked from the **Main Toolbar**.

13. Press and hold the left mouse button along with the SHIFT key, drag *Base01* to the upper-left corner of *Bottom*. Next, release the left mouse button; the **Clone Options** dialog box is displayed. In this dialog box, make sure the **Copy** radio button is selected and then enter **Base02** in the **Name** text box, as shown in Figure 2-6. Next, choose the **OK** button to close the dialog box; *Base02* is created in the viewport.

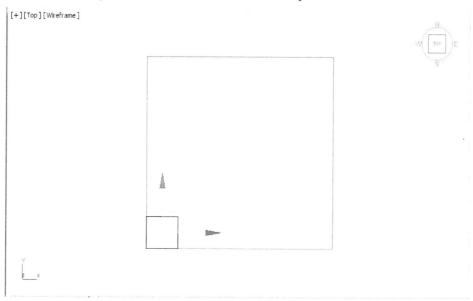

Figure 2-5 Alignment of Base01 to the lower-left corner of Bottom

*Figure 2-6 The **Clone Options** dialog box*

Note
When multiple objects are selected and moved with the SHIFT key pressed, a copy of each selected object is created.

14. Choose the **Transform Gizmo X Constraint** button from the **Axis Constraint** toolbar. Make sure the **Select and Move** tool is invoked and *Base02* is selected. Next, press and hold the CTRL key and select *Base01*. Now, release the CTRL key.

The CTRL key enables you to select multiple objects.

15. Press and hold the SHIFT key and drag both the objects to the right side of *Bottom*. Now, release the left mouse button; the **Clone Options** dialog box is displayed. In this dialog box, make sure the **Copy** radio button is selected and then enter **Base03** in the **Name** text box. Next, choose the **OK** button; a copy each of *Base01* and *Base02* is created. One of the copies is already renamed as *Base03*. Rename the other copy as **Base04**.

16. Invoke the **Maximize Viewport Toggle** tool from the viewport navigation controls to restore the previous viewport configuration. Next, invoke the **Zoom Extents All** tool. Adjust the Perspective viewport. Figure 2-7 shows the four bases of the temple.

Figure 2-7 Four bases of the temple

Creating Pillars

In this section, you will create the pillars for the temple by using the **Cylinder** tool.

1. Maximize the Top viewport using the **Maximize Viewport Toggle** tool from the viewport navigation controls. Next, choose **Create > Geometry** in the **Command Panel** and then invoke the **Cylinder** tool.

2. Expand the **Keyboard Entry** rollout and set the value **30** in the **Radius** spinner and **250** in the **Height** spinner. Next, choose the **Create** button from the **Keyboard Entry** rollout; the cylinder is created at the center of the object *Bottom*. Enter **Pillar01** in the **Name and Color** rollout.

This cylinder will act as a pillar in the model of the temple.

3. Press the ESC key to exit the **Cylinder** tool. Invoke the **Zoom Extents All** tool from the viewport navigation controls. If needed, invoke the **Zoom** tool and zoom in until the subgrid is displayed.

4. Make sure the **Select and Move** tool is invoked from the **Main Toolbar** and then drag *Pillar01* to the lower-left corner such that it is positioned on *Base01*, as shown in Figure 2-8.

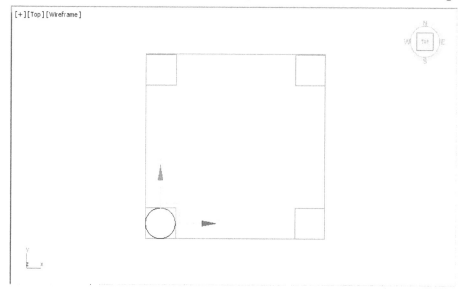

Figure 2-8 Aligning Pillar01 to Base01 in the Top viewport

5. Return to the four-viewport configuration by invoking the **Maximize Viewport Toggle** tool from the viewport navigation controls. Activate the Front viewport and maximize it. Choose the **Transform Gizmo Y Constraint** button. Next, click and drag *Pillar01* up such that its bottom touches the top of *Base01* in the viewport.

6. Return to the four-viewport configuration and activate the Top viewport. Next, maximize the Top viewport and then zoom in as needed to display the subgrid.

7. Make sure the **Select and Move** tool is invoked. Next, press and hold the SHIFT key and move *Pillar01* to the upper-left corner and position it on *Base02*. Next, release the left mouse button; the **Clone Options** dialog box is displayed. In this dialog box, make sure the **Copy** radio button is selected and enter **Pillar02** in the **Name** text box. Choose the **OK** button to close this dialog box; a copy with the name *Pillar02* is created.

8. Make sure that *Pillar02* is selected. Press and hold the CTRL key and select *Pillar01*. Next, choose the **Transform Gizmo X Constraint** button.

9. Press and hold the left mouse button along with the SHIFT key and move both objects to the right such that they are centered on the remaining two bases. Next, release the left mouse button; the **Clone Options** dialog box is displayed. In this dialog box, make sure the **Copy** radio button is selected and then enter **Pillar03** in the **Name** text box. Choose the **OK** button; two pillars are created. Name the other copy as **Pillar04**.

10. Return to the four-viewport configuration and invoke the **Zoom Extents All** tool from the viewport navigation controls, refer to Figure 2-9.

Figure 2-9   *The pillars created for the temple*

Creating the Roof

In this section, you will create the roof of the temple by using the **Sphere** tool.

1. Select *Bottom* and maximize the Front viewport. Make sure that the **Transform Gizmo Y Constraint** button is chosen. Press and hold the left mouse button along with the SHIFT key and drag *Bottom* upward. Next, release the left mouse button; the **Clone Options** dialog box is displayed. In this dialog box, make sure the **Copy** radio button is selected and then enter **Top** in the **Name** text box. Now, choose the **OK** button; a copy of *Bottom* with the name *Top* is created. Now, place it on top of the pillars using the **Select and Move** tool.

2. Return to the four-viewport configuration and invoke the **Zoom Extents All** tool to view the objects properly, refer to Figure 2-10.

3. Activate the Top viewport and choose **Create > Geometry** in the **Command Panel**. Next, invoke the **Sphere** tool.

4. In the **Keyboard Entry** rollout, set the value **170** in the **Radius** spinner. In the **Parameters** rollout, set the values as given next.

    Segments: **32**   Hemisphere: **0.5**

A hemisphere value of 0.5 creates one-half of a sphere.

Figure 2-10 *bottom copied to create top*

5. Choose the **Create** button in the **Keyboard Entry** rollout. Enter the name **Dome** in the **Name and Color** rollout; the sphere is renamed as *Dome*.

6. Maximize the Front viewport. Make sure the **Transform Gizmo Y Constraint** button is chosen. Next, invoke the **Select and Move** tool from the **Main Toolbar** and move *Dome* up such that its base is on the top surface of *Top*.

7. Invoke the **Zoom Extents All** tool. Make sure the **Geometry** button is chosen in the **Create** tab of the **Command Panel**. Next, invoke the **Sphere** tool.

8. In the **Keyboard Entry** rollout, set the value **110** in the **Radius** spinner. In the **Parameters** rollout, make sure the value **15** is set in the **Segments** spinner. Next, choose the **Create** button in the **Keyboard Entry** rollout; a sphere is created with the name *Sphere001*.

9. Make sure *Sphere001* is selected. Next, invoke the **Align** tool from the **Main Toolbar**; the cursor changes to reflect the active command.

   The **Align** tool can also be used to easily and quickly move the object.

10. Now, select *Dome*; the **Align Selection (Dome)** dialog box is displayed. In this dialog box, make sure the **Y Position** check box is selected in the **Align Position (Screen)** area. Next, clear the **X Position** and **Z Position** check boxes. Now, select the **Center** radio button from the **Current Object** area and the **Minimum** radio button from the **Target Object** area, as shown in Figure 2-11. Now, choose the **OK** button; *Sphere001* is now vertically aligned with the flat surface of *Dome*, as shown in Figure 2-12.

Figure 2-11 The **Align Selection(Dome)** dialog box

Figure 2-12 Alignment of Sphere001 with Dome

Modifying Roof Objects

In this section, you will modify roof objects using the **Boolean** tool and **Edit Mesh** modifier.

1. Maximize the Front viewport. Select *Top* from the **Scene Explorer**, as shown in Figure 2-13.

Figure 2-13 Selecting Top from Scene Explorer

The **Scene Explorer** provides the additional functionality to select, rename, delete, and hide the objects in the viewports.

2.   Select **Compound Objects** from the drop-down list below the **Geometry** button. Next, invoke the **Boolean** tool from the **Object Type** rollout; the rollouts corresponding to the **Boolean** tool are displayed. Make sure the **Subtraction (A-B)** radio button is selected in the **Operation** area of the **Parameters** rollout. Next, choose the **Pick Operand B** button in the **Pick Boolean** rollout. Finally, select *Sphere001* in the viewport; *Sphere001* is subtracted from *Top*, thus creating a hole.

     After performing the Boolean operation, invoke the **Select Object** tool from the **Main Toolbar** to prevent accidental selection of a different operand.

3.   Select *Dome* in the Front viewport.

4.   Choose the **Modify** tab in the **Command Panel**. From the **Modifier List** drop-down list, select the **Edit Mesh** option in the **OBJECT-SPACE MODIFIER** section. Next, choose the **Vertex** button in the **Selection** rollout; vertices of *Dome* are displayed, as shown in Figure 2-14.

     By choosing the **Vertex** button, you have entered the **Vertex** sub-object mode. The vertices which are not selected will be displayed in blue whereas the selected vertices will be displayed in red.

5.   Invoke the **Select and Move** tool and then choose the **Transform Gizmo Y Constraint** button.

6.   Select the top single vertex of the dome and drag the it down to about -3 units, using the coordinate display in the status bar. Release the left mouse button.

[+][Front][Wireframe]

Figure 2-14 *The* **Edit Mesh** *modifier assigned to Dome*

7. Choose the **Vertex** button from the **Selection** rollout to exit the sub-object mode. Next, return to the four-viewport configuration.

Adding Details to the Dome

In this section, you will use the **Sphere** and **Cone** tools to add more details to *Dome*.

1. Activate the Top viewport. Choose **Create > Geometry** in the **Command Panel**. Select **Standard Primitives** from the drop-down list. Then, invoke the **Sphere** tool from the **Object Type** rollout.

2. In the **Keyboard Entry** rollout, set the value **30** in the **Radius** spinner and choose the **Create** button; a sphere is created. Enter **Sphere** in the **Name and Color** rollout.

3. Invoke the **Select and Move** tool from the **Main Toolbar** and then move *Sphere* up in the Front viewport to place it on top of *Dome*.

4. Activate the Top viewport. Make sure the **Geometry** button is chosen in the **Create** tab of the **Command Panel**. Next, invoke the **Cone** tool from the **Object Type** rollout.

5. In the **Keyboard Entry** rollout, set the values as given next.

Radius 1: **30**   Radius 2: **0**   Height: **50**

Choose the **Create** button; a cone is created. Enter **Cone** in the **Name and Color** rollout.

6. Activate the Front viewport and move *Cone* on the top of *Sphere* by using the **Select and Move** tool from the viewport navigation controls. Next, invoke the **Zoom Extents All** tool from the viewport navigation controls, refer to Figure 2-15.

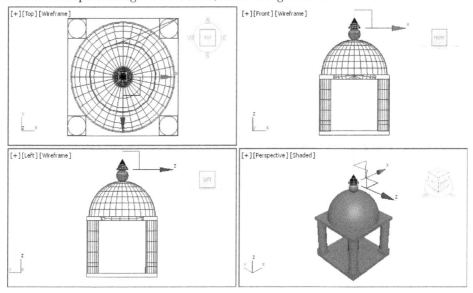

Figure 2-15 *The details added to the top of Dome*

7. Activate the Top viewport. Make sure the **Geometry** button is chosen in the **Create** tab of the **Command Panel**. Next, invoke the **Cone** tool in the **Object Type** rollout.

8. In the **Keyboard Entry** rollout, set the values as given next.

   Radius 1: **40**   Radius 2: **10**   Height: **70**

   Choose the **Create** button. Enter **Bell** in the **Name and Color** rollout.

9. Activate the Front viewport and invoke the **Select and Move** tool from the **Main Toolbar**. Move *Bell* such that half of it lies above *Top* and the other half of *Bell* lies below it, as shown in Figure 2-16.

Figure 2-16 *Adjustment of Bell at the center of Dome*

Changing the Background Color of the Scene

In this section, you will change the background color of the scene.

1.   Choose **Rendering > Environment** from the menu bar; the **Environment and Effects** dialog box is displayed with the **Environment** tab chosen.

2.   In the **Background** area of the **Common Parameters** rollout, choose the color swatch corresponding to the **Color** parameter; the **Color Selector: Background Color** dialog box is displayed. Select the white color and choose the **OK** button.

3.   Close the **Environment and Effects** dialog box.

Saving and Rendering the Scene

In this section, you will save the scene that you have created and then render it. You can also view the final rendered image of this model by downloading the *c02_3dsmaxdesign_2015_rndr.zip* file from *www.cadcim.com*. The path of the file is as follows: *Textbooks > Animation and Visual Effects > 3ds Max Design > Autodesk 3ds Max Design 2015: A Tutorial Approach*

1.   Choose **Save** from the **Application** menu.

2.   Activate the Perspective viewport. Next, invoke the **Render Production** tool from the **Main Toolbar**; the rendered image is displayed, refer to Figure 2-17.

   Tip: *You can press SHIFT+Q or F9 to render the active viewport.*

Figure 2-17 *The rendered image*

 Note
The process of texturing this model is discussed in Chapter 11.

Tutorial 2

In this tutorial, you will create the model of the table and the benches, as shown in Figure 2-18. **(Expected time: 30 min)**

Figure 2-18 *The table and benches*

The following steps are required to complete this tutorial:

a.   Create the project folder.
b.   Create the top of the table.
c.   Create the legs of the table.
d.   Create the base of the table.
e.   Create the rivets of the table.
f.   Create the benches.
g.   Save and render the scene.

Creating the Project Folder

Create the project folder with the name *c02_tut2* in the *3dsmaxdesign 2015* folder, as discussed in Tutorial 1.

Creating the Top of the Table

In this section, you will create the top of the table by using the **Box** tool.

1.   Invoke the **Maximize Viewport Toggle** tool and then activate the Top viewport.
     Choose **Create > Geometry** in the **Command Panel**; **Standard Primitives** is
     displayed in the drop-down list located below it. Next, invoke the **Box** tool from the
     Object Type rollout; various rollouts are displayed in the **Command Panel**.

2.   Expand the **Keyboard Entry** rollout and set the values as given next.

     Length: **100**   Width: **70**   Height: **1.5**

3.   Choose the **Create** button from the **Keyboard Entry** rollout; a box is created in all viewports,
     refer to Figure 2-19. In the **Name and Color** rollout, enter **Top** and press the ENTER key;
     the box is named as *Top*.

4.   Choose the **Modify** tab in the **Command Panel**. In the **Parameters** rollout, set the values
     as given next.

     Length Segs: **12**   Width Segs: **6**   Height Segs: **2**

     Next, you need to convert *Top* to editable poly to modify it at the sub-object level.

5.   Make sure the **Modify** tab is chosen and then select the **Edit Poly** option from the
     OBJECT-SPACE MODIFIERS section of the **Modifier List** drop-down list; the **Edit Poly**
     modifier is displayed in the modifier stack. In the modifier stack, click on the plus sign
     on the left of the **Editable Poly** to view all the sub-object levels.

6.   Make sure the Top viewport is activated and press the W key to invoke the **Select and Move**
     tool. Next, select the **Edge** sub-object level in the modifier stack. Select five vertical edges
     of *Top* using the CTRL key, as shown in Figure 2-20. In the **Selection** rollout, choose the
     Loop button; five edge loops are selected.

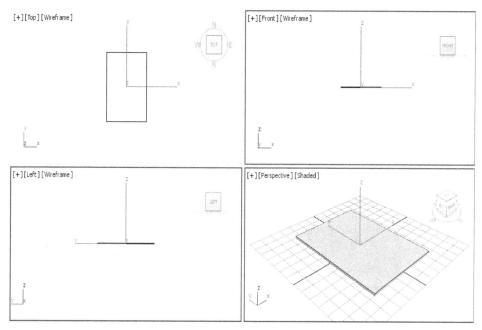

Figure 2-19 *The box created in all viewports*

7. In the **Edit Edges** rollout, choose the **Settings** button on the right of the **Chamfer** button; the **Chamfer** caddy control is displayed in the viewport. Set the value **0.2** in the **Chamfer-Amount** spinner, as shown in Figure 2-21 and choose the **OK** button; the selected edges are chamfered, as shown in Figure 2-22.

Figure 2-20 *Five vertical edges selected*

Figure 2-21 *Setting the value in the* ***Chamfer-Amount*** *spinner*

8. Maximize the Top viewport. Select the **Polygon** sub-object level in the modifier stack. In the **Selection** rollout, select the **Ignore Backfacing** check box and select the polygons, as shown in Figure 2-23. Next, press and hold the ALT key and draw a cross window around the polygons on the extreme left side of *Top*, as shown in Figure 2-24; the polygons in the cross window are deselected, as shown in Figure 2-25.

Figure 2-22 *The edges chamfered*

Figure 2-23 *The polygons selected*

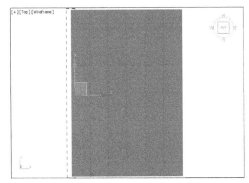

Figure 2-24 *Drawing a cross window around the polygons*

Figure 2-25 *The polygons deselected*

The **Ignore Backfacing** check box is selected to avoid selection of polygons from the opposite side of the object. You will notice that the polygons on the bottom of *Top* are not selected.

9.   Similarly, press the ALT key and deselect the polygons, refer to Figure 2-26. You will notice that only the polygons between the chamfered edges remain selected. Now, delete these polygons.

Figure 2-26 *The polygons to be deselected*

Creating the Legs of the Table

In this section, you will create the legs of the table by extruding the polygons of *Top*.

1. Activate the Bottom viewport and select the **Edge** sub-object level in the modifier stack. Select two horizontal edges from the viewport using the CTRL key, as shown in Figure 2-27. Next, in the **Selection** rollout, choose the **Loop** button; two edge loops are selected.

    Note
    *To activate the Bottom viewport, click on the POV viewport label in the Top viewport; a flyout is displayed. Choose the **Bottom** option; the Top viewport is switched into the Bottom viewport. Similarly, you can switch to any viewport by clicking on the POV viewport label.*

2. In the **Edit Edges** rollout, choose the **Settings** button on the right of the **Chamfer** button; the **Chamfer** caddy control is displayed in the viewport. Set the value **4** in the **Chamfer-Amount** spinner and **2** in the **Chamfer-Segments** spinner. Next, choose the **OK** button; the selected edges are chamfered.

3. Select the **Polygon** sub-object level from the modifier stack and select the polygons in the Bottom viewport by using the CTRL key, as shown in Figure 2-28. In the **Edit Polygons** rollout, choose the **Settings** button on the right of the **Extrude** button; the **Extrude Polygons** caddy control is displayed in the viewport. Set the value **7** in the **Extrude Polygons-Height** spinner, and choose the **OK** button; the selected polygons are extruded.

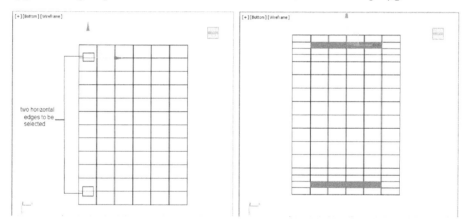

Figure 2-27 *Two horizontal edges selected in the Bottom viewport*   *Figure 2-28* *The polygons selected in the Bottom viewport*

4. Make sure the Bottom viewport is activated. Again, select the polygons by using the CTRL key, as shown in Figure 2-29. In the **Edit Polygons** rollout, choose the **Settings** button on the right of the **Extrude** button; the **Extrude Polygons** caddy control is displayed in the viewport. Set the value **50** in the **Extrude Polygons-Height** spinner, and choose the **OK** button; the selected polygons are extruded, refer to Figure 2-30.

    Next, you need to add edges to the extruded part of legs to add some details to it.

Figure 2-29 *The polygons selected*   **Figure 2-30** *The polygons extruded*

Creating the Base of the Table

In this section, you will create the base of the table using the **Box** tool and the **Edit Poly** modifier.

1. Activate the Front viewport. Choose **Create > Geometry** in the **Command Panel** and invoke the **Box** tool from the **Object Type** rollout. Expand the **Keyboard Entry** rollout and set the values as given next.

   Length: **12**   Width: **45**   Height: **5**

2. Choose the **Create** button from the **Keyboard Entry** rollout; a box is created in all viewports, In the **Name and Color** rollout, enter **base1** and press ENTER; the box is named as *base1*. Now, invoke the **Select and Move** tool from the **Main Toolbar** and move *base1* at the bottom of the leg.

3. Choose the **Modify** tab in the **Command Panel**. Next, in the **Parameters** rollout, set the values as given next.

   Length Segs: **4**   Width Segs: **12**   Height Segs: **2**

4. Make sure the **Modify** tab is chosen and then select the **Edit Poly** modifier from the **OBJECT-SPACE MODIFIERS** section of the **Modifier List** drop-down list; the **Edit Poly** modifier is displayed in the modifier stack. In the modifier stack, click on the plus sign on the left of the **Editable Poly** to view all sub-object levels.

5. Select the **Vertex** sub-object level. Make sure the Front viewport is activated. Next, select the vertices using the CTRL key, as shown in Figure 2-31 and move them slightly in the downward direction. Similarly, move other vertices of *base1* to get a shape, as shown in Figure 2-32. Next, select the **Vertex** sub-object level again in the modifier stack to deactivate it.

6. Activate the Bottom viewport and then switch to Top viewport as discussed earlier. Next, align *base1* in all viewports, as shown in Figure 2-33.

Figure 2-31 *The vertices to be selected*   **Figure 2-32** *The shape of base1*

Figure 2-33 *The base1 object aligned in all viewports*

Next, you need to create the copy of *base1* to act as a base for the other leg.

7.   Activate the Left viewport and make sure *base1* is selected. Press and hold the left mouse button along with the SHIFT key and then move the cursor toward the other leg. Next, release the left mouse button; the **Clone Options** dialog box is displayed. In this dialog box, make sure the **Copy** radio button is selected in the **Object** area and 1 is displayed in the **Number of Copies** spinner. Now, enter **base2** in the **Name** text box and choose the **OK** button; a copy of *base1* with the name *base2* is created.

8.   Align *base2* in all the viewports to position it at the bottom of the other leg, as shown in Figure 2-34.

Figure 2-34   *The base 2 object aligned in all viewports*

Next, you need to create the footrests for *table*.

9. Make sure the Left viewport is activated. Choose **Create > Geometry** in the **Command Panel** and invoke the **Box** tool from the **Object Type** rollout. Expand the **Keyboard Entry** rollout and set the values as given next.

Length: **5**   Width: **80**   Height: **2**

10. Choose the **Create** button from the **Keyboard Entry** rollout; a box is created in all viewports. Enter **footrest1** in the **Name and Color** rollout, and press the ENTER key; the box is named as *footrest1*. Invoke the **Select and Move** tool from the **Main Toolbar** and align *footrest1* in all viewports, as shown in Figure 2-35.

11. Create the copy of *footrest1* in the Front viewport as done in Step 7 and then align it in all viewports, as shown in Figure 2-36.

Figure 2-35 *The footrest1 object aligned in all viewports*

Figure 2-36 *The copy of footrest1 object aligned in all viewports*

Creating the Rivets of the Table

In this section, you will create a sphere and a cylinder to create the cap and the body of rivet, respectively.

1. Activate the Top viewport and choose **Create > Geometry** in the **Command Panel**; the **Standard Primitives** option is displayed in the drop-down list. Next, invoke the **Sphere** tool from the **Object Type** rollout; various rollouts are displayed in the **Command Panel**.

2. Expand the **Keyboard Entry** rollout and set the value **0.65** in the **Radius** spinner and choose the **Create** button; a sphere is created in all the viewports.

3. In the **Parameters** rollout, make sure that the **Smooth** check box and the **Chop** radio button are selected. Set the value **0.5** in the **Hemisphere** spinner.

4. Enter **cap** in the **Name and Color** rollout and use the color swatch in this rollout to change the color to black.

   Next, you need to create a cylinder for the body of the rivet.

5. Choose the **Cylinder** tool from **Create > Geometry > Standard Primitives > Object Type** rollout in the **Command Panel**.

6. In the **Keyboard Entry** rollout, set the values as given next.

   Radius: **0.241**   Height: **3.5**

7. Choose the **Create** button from the **Keyboard Entry** rollout; a cylinder is created.

8. Enter **body** in the **Name and Color** rollout and use the color swatch in this rollout to change the color to black. Next, right-click to exit the **Cylinder** tool.

9. Activate the Left viewport and invoke the **Select by Name** tool from the **Main Toolbar**; the **Select From Scene** dialog box is displayed. In this dialog box, select *cap* and *body* simultaneously by holding the CTRL key and then choose the **OK** button; the *cap* and the *body* are selected in the viewport.

    Note
   *You can also select cap and body from the **Scene Explorer** located at the left of the interface.*

10. Invoke the **Zoom Extents All Selected** tool from the **Main Toolbar** to magnify the selected objects in all viewports and click on an empty area of the screen to deselect the objects.

11. Align *cap* and *body* of the rivet in the Left viewport using the **Select and Move** tool, as shown in Figure 2-37.

    Note
   *You may need to use the **Zoom Region** and **Pan View** tools from the viewport navigation controls to align the cap and body of the rivet.*

Next, you need to group *body* and *cap* to create the rivet.

12. Select *cap* and *body* of the rivet in the **Scene Explorer**. Choose **Group > Group** from the menu bar; the **Group** dialog box is displayed. In this dialog box, enter **rivet001** in the **Group Name** text box and then choose the **OK** button; the **rivet001** group is created.

Next, you need to align *rivet001*.

13. In the Left viewport, make sure *rivet001* is selected. Next, right-click on the **Select andRotate** tool in the **Main Toolbar**; the **Rotate Transform Type-In** dialog box is displayed. Also, a circular gizmo along with the X, Y, and Z axes is displayed.

14. In the **Offset:Screen** area of the **Rotate Transform Type-In** dialog box, set **-90** in the **Z** spinner and press the ENTER key; *rivet001* gets rotated, as shown in Figure 2-38. Now, close the **Rotate Transform Type-In** dialog box.

Figure 2-37 The cap and body objects aligned in all viewports   *Figure 2-38* The rivet001 object rotated

15. Activate the Perspective viewport. Invoke the **Select and Place** tool from the **Main Toolbar**. Next, drag *rivet001* and place it on the *base2*. Now, align *rivet001* in all viewports, as shown in Figure 2-39.

The **Select and Place** tool is used to accurately position an object on the other object.

16. Activate the Front viewport. Create 3 more copies of *rivet001* as done earlier and align them in all viewports, as shown in Figure 2-40.

Next, you will use the **Mirror** tool to create the copy of these rivets.

17. Activate the Left viewport and select all rivets. Invoke the **Mirror** tool from the **Main Toolbar**; the **Mirror: Screen Coordinates** dialog box is displayed. In this dialog box, make sure the **X** radio button is selected in the **Mirror Axis** area and set the value **-81.9** in the **Offset** spinner. Next, select the **Copy** radio button in the **Clone Selection** area and choose the **OK** button; the copy of rivets is created, as shown in Figure 2-41.

 Note
*You may need to change the value in the **Offset** spinner as per requirement.*

Figure 2-39 *The rivet001 object aligned in all viewports*

Figure 2-40 *The copies of rivet001 aligned in all viewports*

Figure 2-41 *The copy of rivets created*

Creating the Benches
In this section, you will create the benches.

1. Create two copies similar to *table*, and then scale and align them, as shown in Figure 2-42.

Figure 2-42 *The table and benches objects aligned*

Saving and Rendering the Scene

In this section, you will save the scene that you have created and then render it. You can also view the final rendered image of this model by downloading the *c02_3dsmaxdesign_2015_rndr.zip* file from *www.cadcim.com*. The path of the file is as follows: *Textbooks > Animation and Visual Effects > 3ds Max Design > Autodesk 3ds Max Design 2015: A Tutorial Approach*

1. Change the background color of the scene to white by following the steps as given in Tutorial 1.

2. Choose **Save** from the **Application** menu.

3. Activate the Perspective viewport. Next, invoke the **Render Production** tool from the **Main Toolbar**; the rendered image is displayed, refer to Figure 2-43.

Figure 2-43   *The rendered image*

Self-Evaluation Test

Answer the following questions and then compare them to those given at the end of this chapter:

1. Which of the following shortcut keys is used to toggle between the active viewport and four viewport display?

    (a) ALT+W   (b) ALT+S
    (c) SHIFT+Q   (d) None of these

2. Which of the following tools is used to accurately position an object on the other object?

    (a) **Select and Scale**   (b) **Select and Place**
    (c) **Select and Rotate**   (d) **Select and Squash**

3. You need to press and hold the _____ key while moving the object using the **Select and Move** tool to create a copy of an object.

4. You need to set the value in the _____ spinner of the **Sphere Parameters** rollout to create a hemisphere.

5. You need to choose the **Geometry** button in the **Create** tab of the **Command Panel** and then select **Compound Objects** from the drop-down list to apply boolean operations on the objects. (T/F)

6. The **Ignore Backfacing** check box in the **Selection** rollout is used to avoid selection of polygons from the opposite side of the object. (T/F)

Review Questions

Answer the following questions:

1. Which of the following shortcut keys is used to render the active viewport?

   (a) ALT+Q   (b) SHIFT+Q
   (c) CTRL+S   (d) None of these

2. Which of the following provides the additional functionality to select, rename, delete, freeze, and hide the objects in the viewports?

   (a) **Select Object**   (b) **Select and Manipulate**
   (c) **Scene Explorer**   (d) **Schematic View**

3. The _____ tool available in the **Main Toolbar** is used to align the current object with the target object.

4. The _____ dialog box is used to create the copies of the selected object(s).

5. The _____ key is used to display grids in the viewport.

6. The **Edit Mesh** modifier is used to modify the object at sub-object level. (T/F)

EXERCISE

The rendered output of the model used in the following exercise can be accessed by downloading the *c02_maxdesign_2015_exr.zip* from *www.cadcim.com*. The path of the file is as follows: *Textbooks > Animation and Visual Effects > 3ds Max Design > Autodesk 3ds Max Design 2015: A Tutorial Approach*

Exercise 1

Create the models of chairs and center table, as shown in Figure 2-44.

Figure 2-44　*The models of chairs and center table*

Chapter 3

Primitive Objects-II

Learning Objectives

After completing this chapter, you will be able to:
- *Create primitive objects*
- *Modify primitive objects*
- *Use the Boolean and Array tools*

INTRODUCTION

In this chapter, you will create primitive and extended primitive objects. You will also modify them using the **Edit Poly** and **Edit Mesh** modifiers. In addition to this, you will learn to use the **Boolean** and **Array** tools.

TUTORIALS

Tutorial 1

In this tutorial, you will create the model of a hot air balloon consisting of a balloon, a basket, ropes, and a collar, refer to Figure 3-1. You will create these components using primitive objects.   **(Expected time: 25 min)**

Figure 3-1 *The model of hot air balloon*

The following steps are required to complete this tutorial:

a. Create the project folder.
b. Create a balloon.
c. Create the basket.
d. Create the ropes.
e. Create the collar.
f. Save and render the scene.

Creating the Project Folder

Create the project folder with the name *c03_tut1* in the *3dsmaxdesign 2015* folder as discussed in Tutorial 1 of Chapter 2.

Creating a Balloon

In this section, you will create a balloon using the **Sphere** tool.

1. Invoke the **Maximize Viewport Toggle** tool from the viewport navigation controls todisplay all four viewports. Next, activate the activate the Top viewport and choose **Create > Geometry** in the **Command Panel**. Now, invoke the **Sphere** tool from the **Object Type** rollout.

2. In the **Keyboard Entry** rollout, set **150** in the **Radius** spinner. In the **Parameters** rollout, set **16** in the **Segments** spinner. Next, choose the **Create** button in the **Keyboard Entry** rollout; a sphere is created. Enter **Balloon** in the **Name and Color** rollout. Right click in the viewport to exit the tool.

3. Activate the Perspective viewport. Next, invoke the **Zoom Extents All** tool from viewport navigation controls to zoom out the object in the Perspective viewport, refer to Figure 3-2.

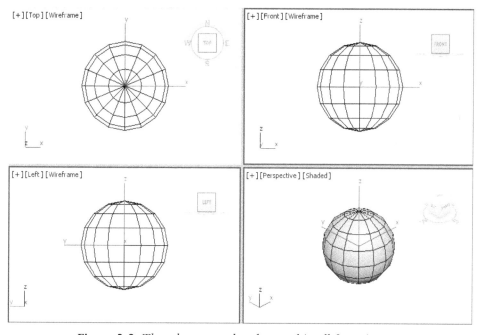

Figure 3-2 The sphere created and zoomed in all four viewports

4. Activate the Top viewport and click on the **Wireframe** Shading viewport label in the Top viewport to display a shortcut menu. Choose **Shaded** from the shortcut menu to display the mesh in the Top viewport.

5. Invoke the **Zoom All** tool from the viewport navigation controls and move the cursor down by pressing and holding the left mouse button in any viewport to display *Balloon* smaller than before. Right-click to exit the tool.

    The **Zoom All** tool simultaneously zooms in/out all viewports equally.

6. Activate the Front viewport and invoke the **2D Snap** tool from the **Snaps Toggle** flyout to turn on snaps. Right-click on this tool to open the **Grid and Snap Settings** dialog box. In the **Snaps** tab of this dialog box, make sure the **Grid Points** check box is selected and all other check boxes are cleared.

7. Close the **Grid and Snap Settings** dialog box.

8. Choose the **Transform Gizmo Y Constraint** button from the **Axis Constraints** toolbar.

Note

*The **Axis Constraints** tools do not normally work with snaps on. To overcome this problem, right-click on the **Snaps Toggle** tool to display the **Grid and Snap Settings** dialog box. Choose the **Options** tab and make sure the **Enable Axis Constraints** check box is selected in the **Translation** area.*

9. Maximize the Front viewport and zoom in, if needed, to display the subgrid. Invoke the **Select and Move** tool from the **Main Toolbar**. Select *Balloon*, if it is not already selected.

10. Choose the **Modify** tab in the **Command Panel**. In the **Modifier List** drop-down list, select **Edit Mesh** in the **OBJECT-SPACE MODIFIERS** section. Next, choose the **Vertex** button in the **Selection** rollout; the **Vertex** sub-object mode is selected.

Note

*In **Vertex** sub-object mode, selected vertices are displayed in red and unselected vertices in blue.*

11. Select the lowermost two layers of vertices by dragging a selection window around them in the Front viewport; the selected vertices turn red.

12. In the Front viewport, drag the vertices down 40 units in the -Y direction. This is shown as 0.0, –40.0, 0.0 in the coordinate display. The shape of the sphere changes into a balloon, refer to Figure 3-3.

Figure 3-3 *The shape of the sphere changed into a balloon*

Alternatively, right-click on the **Select and Move** tool from the **Main Toolbar**; the **Move Transform Type-In** dialog box is displayed. Next, set the value **–40** in the **Y** spinner of the **Offset: Screen** area.

13. Choose the **Vertex** button again in the **Selection** rollout to exit the sub-object mode. Return to four viewport configuration.

Creating the Basket

In this section, you will create a basket using the **Box** and **Boolean** tools.

1. Activate the Top viewport. Choose **Create > Geometry** in the **Command Panel**. Next, invoke the **Box** tool.

2. Expand the **Keyboard Entry** rollout and set the values as given next:

    Length: **160**   Width: **160**   Height: **80**

    Choose the **Create** button in the **Keyboard Entry** rollout. Enter **Basket01** in the **Name and Color** rollout; the box is named as *Basket01*.

3. Now, again in the **Keyboard Entry** rollout and set the values as given next:

    Length: **150**   Width: **150**   Height: **100**

    Next, choose the **Create** button and then enter **Basket02** in the **Name and Color** rollout; *Basket02* is created and it protrudes through the top of *Basket01*. Right-click to exit the **Box** tool.

4. Press and hold the CTRL key and select *Basket01* and *Basket02* in the **Scene Explorer**, as shown in Figure 3-4.

Figure 3-4 *Selecting Basket01 and Basket02 from the*
    Scene Explorer

5. Activate the Front viewport and then invoke the **Maximize Viewport Toggle** tool from the viewport navigation controls. Next, invoke the **Select and Move** tool from the **Main Toolbar**.

6. You need to move both baskets down vertically by 430 units. To do so, right-click on the **Select and Move** tool from the **Main Toolbar**; the **Move Transform Type-In** dialog box is displayed. Next, set **–430** in the **Y** spinner in the **Offset: Screen** area and press the ENTER key, refer to Figure 3-5.

Figure 3-5 The Move Transform Type-In dialog box

7. Close the **Move Transform Type-In** dialog box.

8. Select *Basket02* in the **Scene Explorer**; *Basket01* is deselected, while *Basket02* remains selected.

9. Right-click on the **Select and Move** tool; the **Move Transform Type-In** dialog box is displayed. Next, set **10** in the **Y** spinner in the **Offset:Screen** area and press the ENTER key; *Basket02* is moved up by 10 units in the Front viewport and then close this dialog box.

10. Select *Basket01* in the **Scene Explorer**. Make sure the **Geometry** button is chosen in the **Create** tab of the **Command Panel**. Next, select **Compound Objects** in the drop-down list below the **Geometry** button.

11. In the **Object Type** rollout, invoke the **Boolean** tool. Make sure that the **Subtraction (A-B)** radio button is selected in the **Operation** area of the **Parameters** rollout. Choose the **Pick Operand B** button in the **Pick Boolean** rollout. Select *Basket02* in the viewport; *Basket02* is subtracted from *Basket01* creating a hollow basket. Invoke the **Select Object** tool from the **Main Toolbar** to complete the operation.

12. Invoke the **Maximize Viewport Toggle** tool from the viewport navigation controls. Next, invoke the **Zoom Extents All** tool from the viewport navigation controls to view all objects properly, refer to Figure 3-6.

Creating the Ropes
In this section, you will create ropes using the **Cylinder** and **Array** tools.

1. Activate the Top viewport. Click on the **Shaded** viewport label on the top-left side of the viewport and then choose **Wireframe** from the flyout displayed.

2. Make sure the **Geometry** button is chosen in the **Create** tab of the **Command Panel**. Next, select **Standard Primitives** in the drop-down list below the **Geometry** button. Invoke the **Cylinder** tool from the **Object Type** rollout.

3. In the **Parameters** rollout, set **5** in the **Height Segs** spinner. In the **Keyboard Entry** rollout, set **4** in the **Radius** spinner, and **150** in the **Height** spinner. Next, choose the **Create** button. Enter **Rope01** in the **Name and Color** rollout; *Rope01* is created.

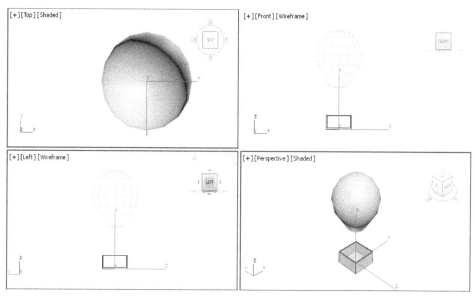

Figure 3-6 *Basket01 after performing the* **Boolean** *operation*

4. Invoke the **Select and Rotate** tool from the **Main Toolbar** and choose the **Transform Gizmo X Constraint** button from the **Axis Constraints** toolbar. Turn the snap off. Invoke the **Angle Snap Toggle** tool from the **Main Toolbar** to rotate *Rope01* in increments.

The **Angle Snap Toggle** tool in the **Main Toolbar** is used to rotate the object in the increments you set. By default, the rotations take place in 5-degree increments. Right-click on the **Angle Snap Toggle** tool; the **Grid and Snap Settings** dialog box is displayed. Set **30** in the **Angle** spinner in the **General** area of the **Options** tab, as shown in Figure 3-7. Close the **Grid and Snap Settings** dialog box.

Figure 3-7 *The* **Grid and Snap Settings** *dialog box*

5. In the Top viewport, move the cursor over the X-axis and rotate *Rope01* through an angle of 30 degrees; the rotation value is displayed in the coordinate display below the viewports.

Be careful that you do not override the axis constraint by accidentally selecting an unwanted portion of the transform gizmo.

6. Choose the **Transform Gizmo Y Constraint** button from the **Axis Constraints** toolbar. Right-click on the **Angle Snap Toggle** tool; the **Grid and Snap Settings** dialog box is displayed. Set **35** in the **Angle** spinner in the **General** area of the **Options** tab. Rotate *Rope01* through an angle of 35 degrees and then close this dialog box. Turn the **Angle Snap Toggle** off.

7. Activate the Front viewport. Invoke the **Select and Move** tool from the **Main Toolbar** and also choose the **Transform Gizmo XY Plane Constraint** button from the **Axis Constraints** toolbar. Next, move *Rope01* so that its lower end touches the upper-left corner or the basket. Activate the Left viewport and move *Rope01* such that its lower end touches the upper-left corner of the basket, as shown in Figure 3-8.

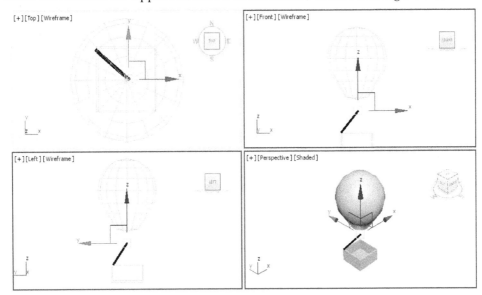

Figure 3-8 Rope01 in all viewports

8. Notice that the top of *Rope01* does not touch the bottom of *Balloon*. Invoke the **Zoom Region** tool. Next, zoom in on the bottom portion of *Balloon* and the upper portion of *Rope01* in the Front viewport.

9. Make sure *Rope01* is selected. Choose the **Modify** tab in the **Command Panel**. In the **Modifier List** drop-down list, select **Edit Mesh** in the **OBJECT-SPACE MODIFIERS** section. In the **Selection** rollout, choose the **Vertex** button to enter the sub-object mode and then select the upper vertices of *Rope01*; the vertices at the top turn red.

10. Choose the **Transform Gizmo Y Constraint** button from the **Axis Constraints** toolbar. Drag the selected vertices to touch the lower point of the balloon, as shown in Figure 3-9.

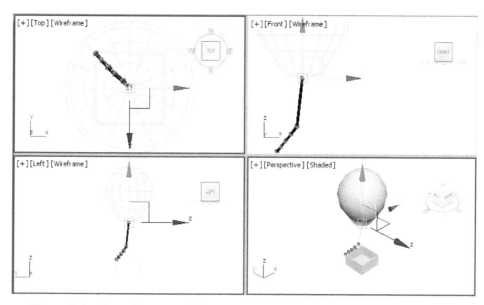

Figure 3-9 *The end vertices of the Rope01 moved to touch the bottom of the balloon*

11. Choose the **Vertex** button in the **Selection** rollout again to exit the sub-object mode. Invoke the **Zoom Extents** tool from the viewport navigation controls.

 Note
The ***View*** *option is selected in the* ***Reference Coordinate System*** *drop-down list by default. If you want to rotate objects about the world origin, you need to select the* ***World*** *option in this drop-down list provided the viewport is not centered at the origin. After rotating the objects, you may select the* ***View*** *option in the* ***Reference Coordinate System*** *drop-down list to avoid confusion.*

12. Activate the Top viewport. Next, invoke the **Use Transform Coordinate Center** tool from the **Use Pivot Point Center** flyout from the **Main Toolbar**. Select **World** in the **Reference Coordinate System** drop-down list. Next, choose **Tools > Array** from the menu bar; the **Array** dialog box is displayed, as shown in Figure 3-10.

13. Choose the **Reset All Parameters** button available at the bottom of the **Array** dialog box and set **90** in the **Incremental Z** spinner in the **Rotate** row. In the **Type of Object** area, select the **Copy** radio button. In the **Array Dimensions** area, select the **1D** radio button and set **4** in the **1D Count** spinner. Choose the **OK** button; ropes are placed at the four corners of the basket and extended to the bottom of *Balloon*, as shown in Figure 3-11.

14. Select **View** in the **Reference Coordinate System** drop-down list and change **Use Transform Coordinate Center** tool to **Use Pivot Point Center** tool in the flyout from the **Main Toolbar**. Rename the three newly created ropes as **Rope02, Rope03,** and **Rope04**.

Figure 3-10 The *Array* dialog box

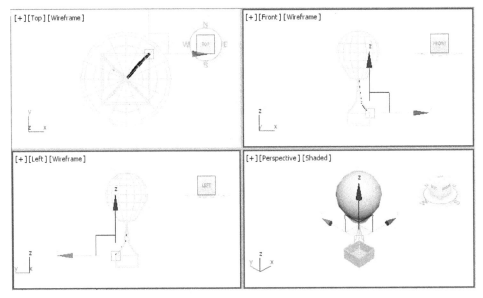

Figure 3-11 The four ropes placed at the four corners of basket

Creating the Collar

Next, you will create a collar and place it at the "kink" in the ropes.

1. Make sure the Top viewport is activated and then choose **Create > Geometry** in the **Command Panel**. Next, invoke the **Torus** tool from the **Object Type** rollout.

2. In the **Keyboard Entry** rollout, set the values **25** in the **Major Radius** spinner and **5** in the **Minor Radius** spinner. Choose the **Create** button and enter **Collar** in the **Name and Color** rollout.

3. Invoke the **Select and Move** tool from the **Main Toolbar**. In the Front viewport, move *Collar* down so that the "kinks" in the ropes are inside the collar, as shown in Figure 3-12 and then zoom the view properly as needed.

Figure 3-12 Alignment of collar with the ropes

4. Invoke the **Zoom Extents All** tool from the viewport navigation controls to view all objects properly.

 Note
The process of texturing this model has been discussed in Chapter 11.

Saving and Rendering the Scene

In this section, you will save the scene that you have created and then render it. You can also view the final rendered image of this model by downloading the *c03_3dsmaxdesign_2015_rndr.zip* file from *www.cadcim.com*. The path of the file is as follows: *Textbooks > Animation and Visual Effects > 3ds Max Design > Autodesk 3ds Max Design 2015: A Tutorial Approach*

1. Change the background color of the scene to white by following the steps as given in Tutorial 1 of Chapter 2.

2. Choose **Save** from the **Application** menu.

3. Activate the Perspective viewport. Next, invoke the **Render Production** tool from the **Main Toolbar**; the rendered image is displayed, as shown in Figure 3-13.

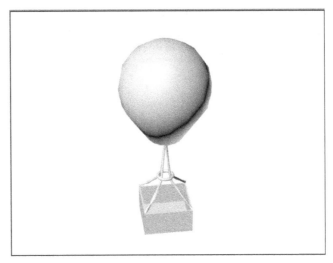

Figure 3-13 *The rendered image*

Tutorial 2

In this tutorial, you will create the model of a shed, as shown in Figure 3-14.

(Expected time: 40 min)

Figure 3-14 *The model of a shed*

The following steps are required to complete this tutorial:

a.   Create the project folder.
b.   Create the sides of the shed.
c.   Create the supports for the side.
d.   Create the top of the shed.
e.   Save and render the scene.

Creating the Project Folder

Create the project folder with the name *c03_tut2* in the *3dsmaxdesign 2015* folder as discussed in Tutorial 1 of Chapter 2.

Creating the Sides of the Shed

In this section, you will create one side of the shed and then copy it using the **Mirror** tool to create other sides.

1.   Invoke the **Maximize Viewport Toggle** tool from viewport navigation controls to display all four viewports and then activate the Top viewport and then maximize it. Choose **Create > Geometry** in the **Command Panel**; **Standard Primitives** is displayed in the drop-down list. Next, invoke the **Box** tool from the **Object Type** rollout; various rollouts are displayed in the **Command Panel**.

2.   Expand the **Keyboard Entry** rollout and set the values as given next:

Length: **3**   Width: **50**   Height: **19**

Note
*To view segments of objects in the Perspective viewport, you need to switch from **Shaded** view to **Shaded+Edge Faces** view. To do so, click on the **Shaded** viewport label in the Perspective viewport; a shortcut menu is displayed. Choose the **Edge Faces** option from it.*

3.   Choose the **Create** button from the **Keyboard Entry** rollout; a box is created. In the **Name and Color** rollout, enter **side1** and press ENTER; the box is named as *side1*.

4.   Choose the **Modify** tab in the **Command Panel**. Next, in the **Parameters** rollout, set the values as given next:

Length Segs: **1**   Width Segs: **18**   Height Segs: **1**

On setting these values, the modified *side1* is displayed in all viewports, as shown in Figure 3-15.

Next, you need to convert *side1* to editable poly to modify it at the sub-object level.

5.   Make sure the **Modify** tab is chosen and then select the **Edit Poly** modifier from the **OBJECT-SPACE MODIFIERS** section in the **Modifier List** drop-down list; the **Edit Poly** modifier is displayed in the modifier stack. In the modifier stack, click on the plus sign on the left of the **Editable Poly** to view all sub-object levels.

6. Activate the Front viewport. Select the **Polygon** sub-object level. Next, select the polygon of *side1*, as shown in Figure 3-16.

Figure 3-15 The side 1 displayed in all viewports

7. In the **Edit Polygons** rollout, choose the **Settings** button on the right of the **Extrude** button; the **Extrude Polygons** caddy control is displayed in the viewport, refer to Figure 3-17. Set the value **47** in the **Extrude Polygons-Height** spinner, and choose the **OK** button to close this caddy control; the selected polygon is extruded, as shown in Figure 3-18.

Figure 3-16 The polygon selected

*Figure 3-17 The **Extrude Polygons** caddy control*

8. Activate the Perspective viewport and select the **Edge** sub-object level. Next, select the edge as shown in Figure 3-19.

Figure 3-18 The selected polygon extruded

9. In the **Selection** rollout, choose the **Ring** button; the ring of edges is selected, as shown in Figure 3-20.

Figure 3-19 The edge selected   *Figure 3-20 The ring of edges selected*

10. In the **Edit Edges** rollout, choose the **Settings** button on the right of the **Connect** button; the **Connect Edges** caddy control is displayed in the viewport. Set the value **16** in the **Connect Edges Segments** spinner and choose the **OK** button to close this caddy control; edge loops are added, as shown in Figure 3-21.

11. Activate the Top viewport. Make sure the **Edge** sub-object level is selected. Next, select a vertical edge, refer to Figure 3-22. Next, choose the **Ring** button in the **Selection** rollout to select edges, as shown in Figure 3-22.

Figure 3-21 The edge loops added

Figure 3-22 The vertical edges selected

12. In the **Edit Edges** rollout, choose the **Settings** button on the right of the **Connect** button; the **Connect Edges** caddy control is displayed in the viewport. Set the value **2** in the **Connect Edges Segments** spinner and **15** in the **Connect Edges Pinch** spinner. Next, choose the **OK** button to close this caddy control; two edge loops are added, as shown in Figure 3-23.

13. Similarly, select horizontal edge, refer to Figure 3-24. Next, choose the **Ring** button in the **Selection** rollout to select edges, as shown in Figure 3-24. Now, repeat step 12 to add two edge loops, as shown in Figure 3-25.

Figure 3-23 Two edge loops added

Figure 3-24 The horizontal edges selected

Figure 3-25 Two edge loops added

14. Make sure the Top viewport is activated. Select the **Polygon** sub-object level in the **Selection** rollout. Next, select the **Ignore Backfacing** check box in the **Selection** rollout and then select the polygons, as shown in Figure 3-26.

15. In the **Edit Polygons** rollout, choose the **Settings** button on the right of the **Extrude** button; the **Extrude Polygons** caddy control is displayed in the viewport. Set the value **125** in the **Extrude Polygons-Height** spinner. Next, choose the **OK** button to close this caddy control; the polygons are extruded. Figure 3-27 shows the selected polygons extruded in the Perspective viewport.

Figure 3-26 The polygons selected   *Figure 3-27 The selected polygons extruded*

Next, you will create the horizontal strips of *side1*.

16. Make sure the Top viewport is activated. Choose **Create > Geometry** in the **Command Panel**; the **Standard Primitives** option is displayed in the drop-down list. Next, invoke the **Box** tool from the **Object Type** rollout; various rollouts are displayed in the **Command Panel**.

17. Expand the **Keyboard Entry** rollout and set the values as given next:

X: **0**   Y: **0**   Z: **27**
Length: **0.65**   Width: **47**   Height: **2.7**

18. Choose the **Create** button from the **Keyboard Entry** rollout; a box is created. In the **Name and Color** rollout, enter **hozt strip1** and press ENTER; the box is named as *hozt strip1*. Figure 3-28 shows *hozt strip1* in all viewports.

19. Activate the Front viewport and then invoke the **Select and Move** tool from the **Main Toolbar**. Make sure *hozt strip1* is selected. Next, press and hold the SHIFT key and drag the cursor in the Y direction till the value in the **Y** spinner of the coordinate display is changed to 12.7. Now, release the left mouse button; the **Clone Options** dialog box is displayed. In this dialog box, select the **Copy** radio button. Also, set the value in the **Number of Copies** spinner to **8** and then choose the **OK** button; the copies of *hozt strip1* are created. Figure 3-29 shows the copies of *hozt strip1* in the Perspective viewport.

Figure 3-28 *The hozt strip1 aligned*

Figure 3-29 *The copies of hozt strip1 created*

20. Similarly, create horizontal strips for the other portion of *side1*, as shown in Figure 3-30.

Next, you need to group all objects created in the scene.

Figure 3-30 *The copies of the horizontal strips created*

21. Select all objects in the scene and then choose **Group > Group** from the menu bar; the **Group** dialog box is displayed. In this dialog box, enter **side01** in the **Group name** text box and choose the **OK** button to close the dialog box; *side01* group is created.

Creating Supports for the Side
In this section, you will create supports for the side by using the **Box** tool.

1. Activate the Top viewport. Choose **Create > Geometry** in the **Command Panel**; the **Standard Primitives** option is displayed in the drop-down list. Next, invoke the **Box** tool from the **Object Type** rollout; various rollouts are displayed in the **Command Panel**.

2. Expand the **Keyboard Entry** rollout and set the values as given next:

   X: **0**   Y:**0**   Z: **0**
   Length: **49.8**   Width: **2.3**   Height: **17.5**

3. In the **Parameters** rollout, set the value in the **Height Segs** spinner to **6** and **Width Segs** spinner to **1**.

4. Choose the **Create** button from the **Keyboard Entry** rollout; a box is created. Enter **support1** in the **Name and Color** rollout; *support1* is created.

5. Switch the Left viewport to Right[Shaded+Edged Faces] viewport, as discussed earlier. Next, invoke the **Select and Move** tool and align *support1* in all viewports, as shown in Figure 3-31.

Figure 3-31 *The support1 aligned in all viewports*

Note

For alignment of objects in the scene, you may need to switch from one viewport to another. To do so, click on the POV viewport label in a viewport; a flyout is displayed. Choose the desired option to switch to that viewport.

6. Choose the **Modify** tab. Select the **Edit Poly** modifier from the **OBJECT-SPACE MODIFIERS** section in the **Modifier List** drop-down list; the **Edit Poly** modifier is displayed in the modifier stack. In the modifier stack, click on the plus sign on the left of the **Editable Poly** to view all sub-object levels.

7. Activate the Perspective viewport. Select the **Edge** sub-object level from the **Selection** rollout. Next, select two edges using the CTRL key, as shown in Figure 3-32 and then, choose the **Loop** button from the **Selection** rollout; two edge loops are selected.

8. In the **Edit Edges** rollout, choose the **Settings** button on the right of the **Chamfer** button; the **Chamfer** caddy control is displayed in the viewport. Set the value **0.1** in the **Chamfer-Amount** spinner and then choose the **OK** button to close this caddy control; two edge loops are added, as shown in Figure 3-33.

9. Select the **Polygon** sub-object level from the **Selection** rollout. Next, select the polygons in the Right, Front, and Back viewports using the CTRL key, as shown in Figure 3-34. Now, delete these polygons.

Figure 3-32 *Two edges selected*   **Figure 3-33** *Two edge loops added*

Figure 3-34 *The selected polygons*

Next, you need to create rivets to join the *support1* with *side01*.

10. Create rivets, as discussed in Tutorial 2 of Chapter 2. Next, align them, as shown in Figure 3-35.

11. Select *support1* as well as all rivets in the scene, and then choose **Group > Group** from the menu bar; the **Group** dialog box is displayed. In this dialog box, enter *support01* in the **Group name** text box and choose the **OK** button to close the dialog box; *support01* group is created.

Figure 3-35 The rivets aligned

12. Create a copy of *support 01* with the name *support02*. Now, align and rotate it, as shown in Figure 3-36.

Figure 3-36 The support02 aligned

Next, you need to create one more support similar to *support01*.

13. Activate the Top viewport and choose **Create > Geometry** in the **Command Panel**; the **Standard Primitives** option is displayed in the drop-down list. Next, invoke the **Box** tool from the **Object Type** rollout; various rollouts are displayed in the **Command Panel**.

14. Expand the **Keyboard Entry** rollout and set the values as given next:

    Length: **69**   Width: **2.3**   Height: **17.5**

15. In the **Parameters** rollout, set the value in the **Height Segs** spinner to **6** and **Width Segs** spinner to **1**.

16. Choose the **Create** button from the **Keyboard Entry** rollout; a box is created. Enter **support 03** in the **Name and Color** rollout; *support03* is created.

17. Repeat steps 6 to 9 to chamfer the edges and delete the polygons for *support03*. Next, align *support03* using the **Select and Move** and **Select and Rotate** tools from the **Main Toolbar**, as shown in Figure 3-37.

Figure 3-37 The support03 aligned

18. Select all objects in the scene and choose **Group > Group** from the menu bar; the **Group** dialog box is displayed. In this dialog box, enter **SIDE01** in the **Group name** text box and choose the **OK** button to close the dialog box; *SIDE01 group* is created.

    Now, you will create other sides of the shed using the **Mirror** tool.

19. Make sure the Top viewport is activated. Select *SIDE01* and invoke the **Mirror** tool from the **Main Toolbar**; the **Mirror: Screen Coordinates** dialog box is displayed. In this dialog box, select the **Y** radio button and set the value in the **Offset** spinner to **-165** in the **Mirror Axis** area. Next, make sure the **Copy** radio button is selected in the **Clone Selection** area and choose the **OK** button to close the dialog box; the copy of *SIDE01* is created with the name *SIDE002* and positioned, as shown in Figure 3-38.

Figure 3-38 The SIDE002 created and positioned

20. Make sure the Top viewport is activated. Next, select *side01* and *side002* and again invoke the **Mirror** tool from the **Main Toolbar**; the **Mirror: Screen Coordinates** dialog box is displayed. In this dialog box, select the **X** radio button and set the value in the **Offset** spinner to **-165** in the **Mirror Axis** area. Next, make sure the **Copy** radio button is selected in the **Clone Selection** area and then choose the **OK** button to close the dialog box; the copies of *SIDE01* and *SIDE002* are created with the name *SIDE003* and *SIDE004* and positioned, as shown in Figure 3-39.

Creating the Top of the Shed

In this section, you will create the top of the shed using the **Box** and **Hedra** tools.

1. Make sure the Top viewport is activated. Choose **Create > Geometry** in the **Command Panel**; **Standard Primitives** is displayed in the drop-down list. Next, invoke the **Box** tool from the **Object Type** rollout; various rollouts are displayed in the **Command Panel**.

2. Expand the **Keyboard Entry** rollout and set the values as given next:

   Length: **193.5**   Width: **193.5**   Height: **4.5**

3. In the **Parameters** rollout, set the values given next:

   Length Segs: **10**   Width Segs: **10**   Height Segs: **1**

Figure 3-39 The SIDE003 and SIDE004 positioned

Choose the **Create** button from the **Keyboard Entry** rollout; a box is created. In the **Name and Color** rollout, enter **Top1** and press ENTER; the box is named as *Top1*.

4. Invoke the **Select and Move** tool from the **Main Toolbar** and align *Top1* in all viewports, as shown in Figure 3-40.

5. Make sure *Top1* is selected and the Top viewport is activated. Next, choose the **Modify** tab in the **Command Panel**. Select the **Edit Poly** from the **Modifier List** drop-down list; the **Edit Poly** modifier is applied to *Top1* in the modifier stack.

6. Invoke the **Select Object** tool from the **Main Toolbar** and then select the **Polygon** sub-object level from the **Selection** rollout. Next, select middle polygons of *Top1* by dragging across window around the polygons, as shown in Figure 3-41. Next, delete them.

7. Choose **Create > Geometry** in the **Command Panel**. Select **Extended Primitives** from the drop-down list located below it. Next, invoke the **Hedra** tool from the **Object Type** rollout.

8. Click at a point in the Top viewport, drag the cursor, and then release the left mouse button; the hedra is created, as shown in Figure 3-42 and it is automatically named as *Hedra001*.

9. Choose the **Modify** tab in the **Command Panel**; various rollouts are displayed in the **Command Panel**. Make sure that the **Tetra** radio button is selected in the **Family** area of

the **Parameters** rollout. Next, scroll down in this rollout and set the value of **135** in the **Radius** spinner. Also, rename *Hedra001* as *Top2* in the **Name and Color** rollout.

Figure 3-40 Top 1 aligned in all viewports

10. Select the **Edit Poly** modifier from the **OBJECT-SPACE MODIFIER** section in **Modifier List** drop-down list; the **Edit Poly** modifier is displayed in the modifier stack. In the modifier stack, click on the plus sign on the left of the **Editable Poly** to view all sub-object levels.

11. Activate the Front viewport. Select the **Vertex** sub-object level from the modifier stack. Next, select the vertex of *Top2*, as shown in Figure 3-43. Invoke the **Select and Move** tool from the **Main Toolbar** and move the vertex, as shown in Figure 3-44.

Figure 3-41 The polygons selected

12. Select the **Edge** sub-object level from the **Selection** rollout and then select all edges of *Top2*. Next, choose the **Settings** button on the right of the **Chamfer** button; the **Chamfer** caddy control is displayed, as shown in Figure 3-45. Set the value **2.5** in the **Chamfer-Amount** spinner and make sure that the value in the **Segments** spinner is set to 1. Choose the **OK** button to close the caddy control; all edges of *Top2* are chamfered, refer to Figure 3-46. Select the **Edge** sub-object level in the modifier stack again to deactivate it.

Figure 3-42 Hedra001 created

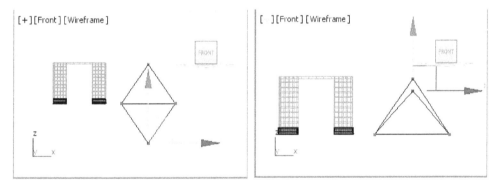

Figure 3-43 The selected vertex   *Figure 3-44 The vertex moved*

13. Make sure *Top2* is selected. Right-click on the **Select and Uniform Scale** tool; the **Scale Transform Type-In** dialog box is displayed. In the **Absolute:Local** area of this dialog box, set the value **50** in the **Z** spinner and press the ENTER key; *Top2* is scaled, as shown in Figure 3-47.

14. Close the **Scale Transform Type-In** dialog box.

15. Invoke the **Select and Move** tool from the **Main Toolbar** and align *Top2* in all viewports, as shown in Figure 3-48.

    Next, you will create a group of *Top1* and *Top2*.

Figure 3-45 The **Chamfer** caddy control

Figure 3-46 All edges chamfered

16. Select *Top1* and *Top2* in the viewport and choose **Group > Group** from the menu bar; the **Group** dialog box is displayed. In this dialog box, enter **Top** in the **Group name** dialog box and choose the **OK** button to close the dialog box.

Saving and Rendering the Scene

In this section, you will save the scene that you have created and then render it. You can also view the final rendered image of this model by downloading the *c03_3dsmaxdesign_2015_rndr.zip*

Figure 3-47 The Top 2 scaled

file from *www.cadcim.com*. The path of the file is as follows: *Textbooks > Animation and Visual Effects > 3ds Max Design > Autodesk 3ds Max Design 2015: A Tutorial Approach*

1. Change the background color of the scene to white by following the steps given in Tutorial 1 of Chapter 2.

2. Choose **Save** from the **Application** menu.

3. Activate the Perspective viewport. Next, invoke the **Render Production** tool from the **Main Toolbar**; the rendered image is displayed, refer to Figure 3-49.

Figure 3-48 *The Top 2 aligned*

Figure 3-49 *The rendered image*

Self-Evaluation Test

Answer the following questions and then compare them to those given at the end of this chapter:

1. Which of the following buttons is chosen by default in the **Create** tab of the **Command Panel**?

   (a) **Geometry**   (b) **Shapes**
   (c) **Lights**   (d) **Helpers**

2. Which of the following tools in the **Main Toolbar** is used to rotate the object in the increments?

   (a) **Spinner Snap Toggle**   (b) **Percent Snap Toggle**
   (c) **Angle Snap Toggle**   (d) None of these

3. Which of the following options is selected by default in the **Reference Coordinate System** drop-down list?

   (a) **World**   (b) **View**
   (c) **Screen**   (d) **Grid**

4. The _____ tool in the viewport navigation controls is used to view all objects properly in all viewports.

5. You can use the _____ tool from navigation viewport controls to zoom in on a small portion of an object by enclosing it in a selection window.

6. Choose **Array** from the _____ menu to display the **Array** dialog box.

7. Choose **Group** from the _____ menu to display the **Group** dialog box.

8. You can use the **Render Production** tool from the **Main Toolbar** to render the active viewport. (T/F)

Review Questions

Answer the following questions:

1. Which of the following dialog boxes is invoked by right-clicking on the **Select and Move** tool?

   (a) **Scale Transform Type-In**   (b) **Rotate Transform Type-In**
   (c) **Move Transform Type-In**   (d) None of these

2. Which of the following dialog boxes is displayed by right-clicking on the **Snaps Toggle** tool?

    (a) **Select from Scene**   (b) **Grid and Snap Settings**
    (c) **Preference Settings**   (d) **Environment and Effects**

3. The _____ tool is used to zoom an object equally in all viewports.

4. The _____ tool is used to create the duplicate copies of the other sides of objects.

5. The _____ is used to select the objects in the scene.

6. The **Axis Constraints** tools in the **Axis Constraints** toolbar do not normally work with snaps on. (T/F)

7. The **Snaps Toggle** tool is used to rotate the object in the increments you set. (T/F)

EXERCISE

The rendered output of the model used in the following exercise can be accessed by downloading the *c03_maxdesign_2015_exr.zip* from *www.cadcim.com*. The path of the file is as follows: *Textbooks > Animation and Visual Effects > 3ds Max Design > Autodesk 3ds Max Design 2015: A Tutorial Approach*

Exercise 1

Create the scene of a bench umbrella and table on the ground, as shown in Figure 3-50.

Figure 3-50 *The scene of a bench umbrella and a table*

Chapter 4

Working with Splines-I

Learning Objectives

After completing this chapter, you will be able to:

- *Create 2D shapes*
- *Modify splines*
- *Change bezier splines*
- *Work with transform centers*

INTRODUCTION

In 3ds Max Design, splines are used to create various shapes. The advantage of using splines in place of primitive objects is that they require less number of segments to create an object. In this chapter, you will learn to create different types of splines and to modify them using the **Edit Spline** modifier.

TUTORIAL

Tutorial 1

In this tutorial, you will create different 2D splines such as a line, circle, rectangle, arc, and text. You will modify the vertices and segments, and also adjust the splines using bezier handles. In addition, you will transform the shapes using different transform centers.

(Expected time: 25 min)

The following steps are required to complete this tutorial:

a. Create the project folder.
b. Create 2D Shapes.
c. Modify vertices, segments, and splines.
d. Change bezier splines.
e. Lock handles.
f. Create and modify splines.
g. Copy an object.

Creating the Project Folder

Create a project folder with the name *c04_tut1* in the *3dsmaxdesign 2015* folder as discussed in Tutorial 1 of Chapter 2.

Creating 2D Shapes

In this section, you will first create 2D shapes in the form of spline polygons.

1. Invoke the **Maximize Viewport Toggle** tool. Make sure the grid is displayed in the Top, Left, and Front viewports. If the grid is not already displayed, press the G key it.

2. Activate the Top viewport and then invoke the **Maximize Viewport Toggle** tool from the viewport navigation controls to maximize the Top viewport.

3. Invoke the **2D Snap** tool from the **Snaps Toggle** flyout in the **Main Toolbar** to turn on snaps. Right-click on the **2D Snap** tool; the **Grid and Snap Settings** dialog box is displayed. In the **Snaps** tab, make sure that only the **Grid Points** check box is selected and then close the dialog box.

4. Choose **Create > Shapes** in the **Command Panel**. Next, invoke the **Line** tool from the **Object Type** rollout.

5. Click at a point in the viewport to create the first vertex. Next, move the mouse and click at points where you need to create the rest of the vertices; a line is created in the Top viewport, refer to Figure 4-1 (top-left). Next, right-click to exit the tool.

6. Invoke the **Zoom** tool from the viewport navigation controls. Click near the center of the viewport and drag the cursor vertically downward. Release the mouse button after increasing the drawing display area.

7. Invoke the **Rectangle** tool from the **Object Type** rollout.

8. Press and hold the mouse button at a point and then drag the cursor to select the diagonally opposite corner; a rectangle is created, refer to Figure 4-1. You can press and hold the CTRL key to make a square. Right-click to exit the tool.

9. Invoke the **Circle** tool from the **Object Type** rollout. Next, press and hold the mouse button at a point as the center of the circle and then drag the cursor to set the radius, refer to Figure 4-1.

10. Invoke the **Arc** tool from the **Object Type** rollout. Press and hold the mouse button at a point to create the first endpoint of the arc. Next, drag to create the second point and then release the left mouse button. Now, drag and click again in the viewport to specify third and fourth point to set the radius of the arc, refer to Figure 4-1.

Figure 4-1 *Different spline shapes created in the Top viewport*

11. Invoke the **Text** tool from the **Object Type** rollout. In the **Parameters** rollout, select **Arial** from the drop-down list, if it is not already selected. Next, enter **G** in the **Text** edit box.

12. Click at a point in the viewport to position the text, refer to Figure 4-1. Invoke the **Select and Move** tool from the **Main Toolbar**. Next, press and hold the left mouse button and drag the cursor to move the text and place it on the screen at a proper position. You can also scale the text as required by using the **Select and Uniform Scale** tool.

13. Click on the empty area of the viewport to deselect any selected shape.

14. Invoke the **Zoom Extents** tool from the viewport navigation controls to view the text clearly in the viewport. Next, choose **Edit > Hold** from the menu bar to copy the current state to a buffer. This can be retrieved later using the **Fetch** option.

Modifying Vertices, Segments, and Splines

In this section, you will convert the alignment of vertices from linear to curved and vice versa.

1. Select the text object and then select the circle using the SHIFT key.

2. Choose the **Modify** tab in the **Command Panel**. Select **Edit Spline** from the **Modifier List** drop-down list. Next, choose the **Vertex** button in the **Selection** rollout; the **Edit Spline** modifier is applied to the shapes and the **Vertex** sub-object mode is activated. The vertices of both the shapes are displayed in the viewport.

3. Right-click on the vertex on the right side of the circle; a quad menu is displayed. Choose **Corner** from the upper-left quadrant of the quad menu, as shown in Figure 4-2.

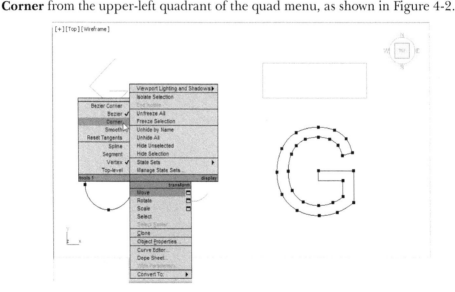

*Figure 4-2 Choosing **Corner** from the upper-left quadrant of the quad menu*

4. Right-click on the vertex on the left side of the text and choose **Corner** from the upper-left quadrant of the quad menu displayed; the curved vertices are changed to corner, as shown in Figure 4-3.

5. Right-click on the vertex on the right side of the circle; the quad menu is displayed. Choose **Smooth** from the upper-left quadrant of the quad menu to make the circle smooth. Choose the **Vertex** button to exit the sub-object mode. Now, select the rectangle.

Figure 4-3 The curved vertices changed to corner

 Note
You cannot select a new shape when you are in the sub-object mode.

6. Select **Edit Spline** from the **OBJECT-SPACE MODIFIERS** section in the **Modifier List** drop-down list. Next, choose the **Vertex** button in the **Selection** rollout; the **Edit Spline** modifier is applied to the rectangle and the **Vertex** sub-object mode is activated. Also, the vertices are displayed in the viewport.

7. Right-click on the lower-left vertex of the rectangle; the quad menu is displayed. Choose **Smooth** in the upper-left quadrant of the quad menu. Now, right-click on the upper-right vertex of the rectangle and then choose **Smooth** from the quad menu displayed; the two linear vertices become curved, resulting in a curved shape, as shown in Figure 4-4. Similarly, you can convert the linear segments into curved segments and vice versa.

8. Choose the **Segment** button in the **Selection** rollout; the **Segment** sub-object mode of the **Edit Spline** modifier of the rectangle is activated.

9. Drag a selection window around the rectangle to select all segments. The segments turn red. Right-click anywhere on the rectangle to display the quad menu. Choose **Line** from the upper-left quadrant; the curved segments become linear and the rectangle is restored, as shown in Figure 4-5. You can also convert the linear spline into a curved spline and vice versa.

10. Choose the **Segment** button in the **Selection** rollout to exit the sub-object mode.

11. Select the object created using the **Line** tool. Next, make sure the **Modify** tab is chosen in the **Command Panel**. In the **Selection** rollout, choose the **Spline** button to enter the **Spline** sub-object mode.

Figure 4-4 *Two corners of the rectangle changed to smooth curves*

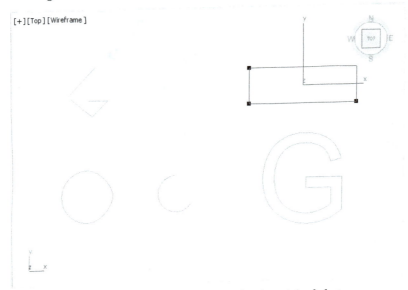

Figure 4-5 *The rectangle restored to its original shape*

Note
*The **Edit Spline** modifier need not to be applied to the shapes created using the **Line** tool.*

12. Right-click on the spline; the quad menu is displayed. Choose **Curve** from the upper-left quadrant of the quad menu; the whole spline becomes curved, as shown in Figure 4-6.

[+][Top][Wireframe]

Figure 4-3 *The curved vertices changed to corner*

Note
You cannot select a new shape when you are in the sub-object mode.

6. Select **Edit Spline** from the **OBJECT-SPACE MODIFIERS** section in the **Modifier List** drop-down list. Next, choose the **Vertex** button in the **Selection** rollout; the **Edit Spline** modifier is applied to the rectangle and the **Vertex** sub-object mode is activated. Also, the vertices are displayed in the viewport.

7. Right-click on the lower-left vertex of the rectangle; the quad menu is displayed. Choose **Smooth** in the upper-left quadrant of the quad menu. Now, right-click on the upper-right vertex of the rectangle and then choose **Smooth** from the quad menu displayed; the two linear vertices become curved, resulting in a curved shape, as shown in Figure 4-4. Similarly, you can convert the linear segments into curved segments and vice versa.

8. Choose the **Segment** button in the **Selection** rollout; the **Segment** sub-object mode of the **Edit Spline** modifier of the rectangle is activated.

9. Drag a selection window around the rectangle to select all segments. The segments turn red. Right-click anywhere on the rectangle to display the quad menu. Choose **Line** from the upper-left quadrant; the curved segments become linear and the rectangle is restored, as shown in Figure 4-5. You can also convert the linear spline into a curved spline and vice versa.

10. Choose the **Segment** button in the **Selection** rollout to exit the sub-object mode.

11. Select the object created using the **Line** tool. Next, make sure the **Modify** tab is chosen in the **Command Panel**. In the **Selection** rollout, choose the **Spline** button to enter the **Spline** sub-object mode.

Figure 4-4 *Two corners of the rectangle changed to smooth curves*

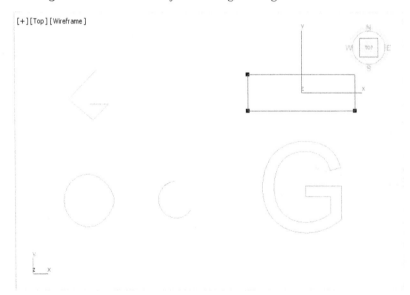

Figure 4-5 *The rectangle restored to its original shape*

 Note
*The **Edit Spline** modifier need not to be applied to the shapes created using the **Line** tool.*

12. Right-click on the spline; the quad menu is displayed. Choose **Curve** from the upper-left quadrant of the quad menu; the whole spline becomes curved, as shown in Figure 4-6.

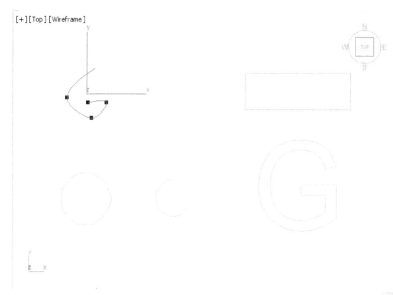

Figure 4-6 *The curved line spline*

Changing Bezier Splines

There are two types of bezier vertices: the **Bezier** vertex and the **Bezier Corner** vertex. In this section, you will adjust spline curvature with the help of bezier handles.

1. To restore the shapes from the buffer, choose **Edit > Fetch** from the menu bar; the **About to Fetch. OK?** message box is displayed, as shown in Figure 4-7. Choose the **Yes** button from the message box to restore the buffer.

Figure 4-7 The **About to Fetch. OK?** *message box*

2. Select the rectangle in the viewport and then make sure the **Modify** tab is chosen in the **Command Panel**. Select **Edit Spline** from **OBJECT-SPACE MODIFIERS** section in the **Modifier-List** drop-down list; the **Edit Spline** modifier is applied. Next, choose the **Vertex** button in the **Selection** rollout to enter into the **Vertex** sub-object mode.

3. Right-click on the top-left vertex of the rectangle; the quad menu is displayed. Choose **Bezier** from the upper-left quadrant of the quad menu; the two vector handles are displayed. They are in a straight line, forcing the left segment into a curve.

    The bezier vertex is a tangent vector.

4. Invoke the **Select and Move** tool from the **Main Toolbar**. Next, invoke the **2D Snap** tool again from the **Snaps Toggle** flyout in the **Main Toolbar** to turn it off. Drag one of the handles to form the shape shown in Figure 4-8; both handles move such that the vertex remains tangent to the segments.

Figure 4-8 Shape of the rectangle after dragging one of the handles

Note
As choosing the transform gizmo button sets an axis constraint, it is often difficult to move the handles as desired while the transform gizmo is active. Therefore, you may need to turn off the transform gizmo while working with bezier handles. To turn off the transform gizmo, choose **Views > Show Transform Gizmo** *from the menu bar. Choosing* **Show Transform Gizmo** *for a second time will restore the transform gizmo in the viewport.*

5. Press and hold the SHIFT key and move the left handle up toward the left direction; the SHIFT key breaks the tangent by allowing you to move only the selected handle, converting the bezier vertex into a bezier corner vertex; only the segment associated with this handle is affected, whereas the other handle remains unchanged, as shown in Figure 4-9.

6. Right-click on the same vertex again to display the quad menu and choose **Bezier** from it; the changed segment automatically assumes its previous shape, forcing the moved handle to be in a straight line with the unchanged handle.

Locking Handles

For any vertex, there are two bezier handles that are used to set the tangency. By selecting the **Lock Handles** check box in the **Selection** rollout and selecting the **Alike** radio button, you can simultaneously transform all similar bezier handles (all lead-in handles or all lead-out handles) for the selected vertices. When the **All** radio button is active, you can simultaneously move both handles for all the selected vertices. In this section, you will explore the use of the **Lock Handles** check box and the radio buttons discussed above.

Figure 4-9 Curved line segments of the spline

1. Choose **Edit > Fetch** from the menu bar; the **About to Fetch. OK?** message box is displayed.

2. Choose the **Yes** button in this message box; the original shape of the rectangle is restored.

3. Select the rectangle and apply an **Edit Spline** modifier, as discussed earlier.

4. Choose the **Vertex** button in the **Selection** rollout and select all the vertices in the shape by dragging a selection window around the rectangle; the bezier handles are displayed on all the vertices.

5. In the **Selection** rollout, clear the **Lock Handles** check box, if it is selected.

6. Invoke the **Select and Move** tool. Next, select the lower handle of the top-left vertex. Now, drag it to left; only the selected handle is affected, and only the segment connected to it changes, as shown in Figure 4-10.

7. Choose the **Undo** button to reverse the changes. In the **Selection** rollout, select the **Lock Handles** check box. Also, make sure the **Alike** radio button is selected. Moreover, all vertices in the rectangle are selected in the viewport.

8. Select the lower handle of the top-left corner vertex and drag it to left; the selected handle and all other lead-in handles for the selected vertices are affected, and all segments connected to them are changed, as shown in Figure 4-11.

9. Press CTRL + Z to reverse the changes. In the **Selection** rollout, select the **All** radio button.

Figure 4-10 *Adjusting the bezier handles*

Figure 4-11 *All similar bezier handles affected by the **Lock Handles** check box and the **Alike** radio button*

10. Select the lower handle of the top-left corner vertex and drag it to left. Release the left mouse button; all the handles are affected and all the segments are changed, refer to Figure 4-12.

Figure 4-12 All bezier handles affected on selecting the **All** radio button

Creating and Modifying Splines

In this section, you will create some more splines and modify them using options in the rollouts.

1. Choose **New > New All** from the **Application** menu; the **Autodesk 3ds Max Design 2015** message box is displayed, as shown in Figure 4-13. Choose the **Don't Save** button in this message box; all shapes are removed and a blank screen is displayed. The viewport layout, which is a maximized Top viewport, is retained.

Figure 4-13 The **Autodesk 3ds Max Design 2015** message box

2. Choose **Create > Shapes** in the **Command Panel**. Next, invoke the **Ellipse** tool from the **Object Type** rollout. Create an ellipse in the Top viewport.

    Before creating the ellipse, you may need to turn on the **Snap Toggle** tool, if it is off.

3. Invoke the **Rectangle** tool from the **Object Type** rollout. Press and hold the CTRL key and draw a square, as shown in Figure 4-14.

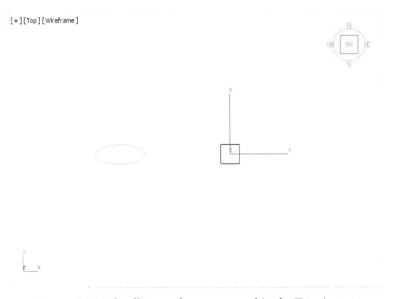

[+][Top][Wireframe]

Figure 4-14 The ellipse and square created in the Top viewport

4. Invoke the **Select Object** tool, press and hold the CTRL key, and select the ellipse so that both the ellipse and the rectangle are selected.

5. Choose the **Modify** tab in the **Command Panel**. Select **Edit Spline** from the **OBJECT-SPACE MODIFIERS** section in the **Modifier List** drop-down list; the **Edit Spline** modifier is applied to both shapes.

6. Choose the **Segment** button in the **Selection** rollout.

7. Select the lower-right segment of the ellipse. Press and hold the CTRL key and select the left and lower sides of the square as well; all three segments turn red indicating that they are selected.

8. Choose the **Delete** button in the **Geometry** rollout or press the DELETE key; the selected segments are deleted from the shapes and the ellipse and the square become two open splines, as shown in Figure 4-15.

9. Choose the **Spline** button in the **Selection** rollout.

10. Click anywhere on the remaining portion of the square; the spline turns red, indicating selection. Notice that the ellipse is not selected.

11. Choose the **Close** button in the **Geometry** rollout; the end vertices of the two remaining segments are joined by a curved segment and the spline is closed, as shown in Figure 4-16.

12. Choose the **Undo** button to reverse the changes. Next, choose the **Vertex** button in the **Selection** rollout.

Figure 4-15 *Selected segments deleted from the shapes*

Figure 4-16 *The closed spline*

13. Choose the **Connect** button in the **Geometry** rollout. Next, select an end vertex of the square segment and then drag the cursor toward the other end vertex. When you move the cursor over the other end vertex, the cursor icon gets changed. Also, a dashed line is attached to the cursor while dragging, as shown in Figure 4-17.

Figure 4-17 *A dashed line attached to the end vertices*

14. Release the mouse button; the two vertices are joined by a straight segment, as shown in Figure 4-18.

Figure 4-18 *The two vertices joined by a straight segment*

15. Choose the **Undo** button to reverse the changes. Next, choose the **Insert** button in the **Geometry** rollout.

16. Move the cursor and place it near the middle of the top segment of the remaining square; the cursor icon changes.

17. Click anywhere in the top segment to insert the vertex and then move the cursor down. Click again to position the vertex.

18. Move the cursor to the left and click to place another vertex, refer to Figure 4-19. Right-click to complete the command.

Figure 4-19 New vertices added to the segment

19. Choose the **Undo** button to reverse the changes. Next, invoke the **Select Object** tool and select the white colored end vertex. The direction of the spline runs from the first vertex to the last vertex. The first vertex is yellow in color.

20. Choose the **Make First** button in the **Geometry** rollout; the selected vertex becomes yellow in color, indicating that now it is the first vertex. Since the vertex is selected, it is red in color.

21. Choose the **Insert** button in the **Geometry** rollout. Next, move the cursor and place it near the middle of the top segment of the remaining portion of the square; the cursor icon changes.

22. Click to place the vertex and then move it down. Click again to position the vertex.

23. Move the cursor to the right and click again to place another vertex. Right-click to complete the command.

   As the direction of the spline has changed, the resulting shape is different from the one created previously by adding vertices, refer to Figure 4-20.

   Next, you will work with transform centers. There are three types of transform centers: pivot point, selection, and transform coordinate. The effect on objects due to rotation and scale transforms differs depending on the type of transform center selected.

[+][Top][Wireframe]

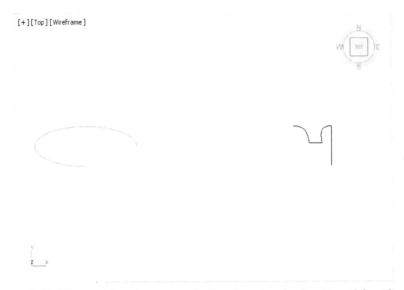

Figure 4-20 *The resulting shape created after changing the direction of the spline*

24. Choose **New > New All** from the **Application** menu; the **Autodesk 3ds Max Design 2015** message box is displayed. Choose the **Don't Save** button in the message box; all shapes are removed.

25. Invoke the **Zoom Extents** tool. Next, choose **Create > Shapes** in the **Command** **Panel**. Next, invoke the **Rectangle** tool. Draw a small rectangle near the upper-left corner of the Top viewport.

26. Invoke the **Ellipse** tool and draw a small ellipse close to the rectangle, as shown in Figure 4-21.

27. Choose **Edit > Hold** from the menu bar to copy the current state to a buffer. This can be retrieved later using the **Fetch** option.

28. Make sure the **Snaps Toggle** tool is turned off. Next, invoke the **Select and** **Rotate** tool and make sure the **Transform Gizmo Z Constraint** button is chosen. Make sure the ellipse is selected, and then invoke the **Angle Snap Toggle** tool to turn the angle snap on.

The **Use Pivot Point Center** tool in the **Main Toolbar** is selected by default.

29. Rotate the ellipse until 0.00, 0.00, 90.0 is shown in the coordinate display; the ellipse is rotated about its pivot point, which is in the center of the ellipse, as shown in Figure 4-22.

30. Invoke the **Select and Uniform Scale** tool from the **Main Toolbar** and make sure the **Transform Gizmo XY Plane Constraint** button is chosen in the **Axis Constraints** toolbar. Select the rectangle and scale it until 50, 50, 50 is shown in the coordinate display; the rectangle is scaled about its pivot point which is in the center of the rectangle, as shown in Figure 4-23.

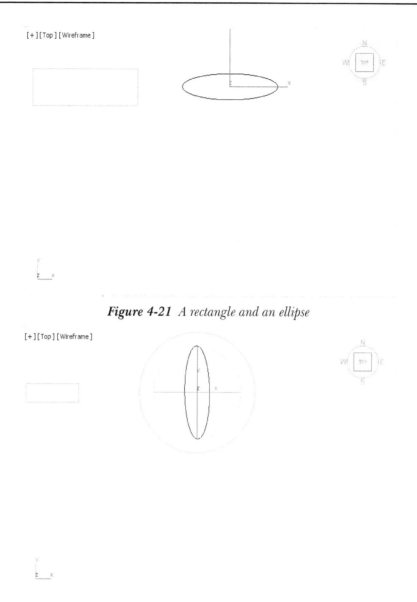

Figure 4-21 *A rectangle and an ellipse*

Figure 4-22 *The ellipse rotated*

31. Choose **Edit > Fetch** from the menu bar to retrieve the original drawing; the **About to Fetch. OK** dialog box is displayed. Choose the **Yes** button in this dialog box; the original shape of the rectangle and the ellipse is restored.

32. Invoke the **Select and Rotate** tool and make sure the **Transform Gizmo Z Constraint** button is chosen. Make sure the **Snaps Toggle** tool is deactivated and the **Angle Snap Toggle** tool is invoked.

Figure 4-23 *The rectangle scaled to its pivot point*

33. Use the CTRL key to select both the ellipse and the rectangle. Make sure the **Use selection Center** tool is invoked from the **Use Pivot Point Center** flyout in the **Main Toolbar**, which shows the transform gizmo at the center point of the combined selection.

34. Rotate both objects until 0.00, 0.00, 40.00 is shown in the coordinate display; the objects are rotated about their combined center point, as shown in Figure 4-24.

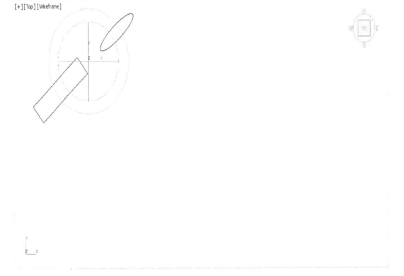

Figure 4-24 *Both objects rotated around the center of their combined center point*

35. Restore the original drawing by choosing the **Undo** button. Make sure the **Select and Rotate** tool is invoked in the **Main Toolbar**.

36. Select only the ellipse. Next, invoke the **Use Transform Coordinate Center** tool from the **Use Selection Center** flyout. Also, select **World** from the **Reference Coordinate System** drop-down list located next to the **Select and Scale** flyout. Note that the axis tripod moves to the world origin, which is probably near the center of the viewport.

37. Make sure that the **Angle Snap Toggle** tool is invoked from the **Main Toolbar** and rotate the ellipse until 0.00, 0.00, -90.00 is shown in the coordinate display; the ellipse is rotated with respect to the origin of the world space, as shown in Figure 4-25.

*Figure 4-25   The ellipse rotated after selecting **World** in the **Reference Coordinate System** drop-down list*

Copying an Object

In this section, you will use the SHIFT key with the transform commands to make a copy of the original object.

1. Choose **New > New All** from the **Application** menu; the **Autodesk 3ds Max Design 2015** message box is displayed. Choose the **Don't Save** button; all the shapes are removed and a blank Top viewport is displayed.

2. Choose **Create > Shapes** in the **Command Panel**. Next, invoke the **Rectangle** tool from the **Object Type** rollout. Expand the **Keyboard Entry** rollout and set the values as given next:

Length: **100**   Width: **100**

Choose the **Create** button; a square is created in the center of the Top viewport.

3. Invoke the **Select and Rotate** tool and make sure the **Transform Gizmo Z Constraint** button is chosen. Select **View** from the **Reference Coordinate System** drop down list, if it is not already selected. Make sure the **Use Pivot Point Center** tool is also invoked. Also, ensure that the snap is turned off and the **Angle Snap Toggle** tool is invoked.

4. Press and hold the SHIFT key and make sure the square is selected and then rotate it. Next, release the mouse button and the SHIFT key when the square is rotated about 45 degrees; the **Clone Options** dialog box is displayed. Notice that the original square remains at its position, while its copy is rotated about its pivot point.

5. Make sure that the **Copy** radio button is selected in the **Object** area of the **Clone Options** dialog box. Choose the **OK** button in the dialog box; a copy of the square rotated at an angle of 45 degrees is created, as shown in Figure 4-26.

6. Invoke the **Select and Uniform Scale** tool from the **Main Toolbar**. Next, press and hold the SHIFT key and select the original square and scale it up to 50 percent of its original size; the **Clone Options** dialog box is displayed.

7. Choose the **OK** button in the **Clone Options** dialog box; a copy of the square scaled down to half of its original size is created inside the two overlapping squares.

8. Select the first square that you cloned, press and hold the SHIFT key, and scale the square to 50 percent of its original size. Choose **OK** in the **Clone Options** dialog box; a copy of the rotated square, scaled down to half its size, is created, as shown in Figure 4-27.

Figure 4-26 A copy of the square created by rotating it at 45 degrees

Figure 4-27 Both squares copied and scaled down to 50 percent of their original size

Self-Evaluation Test

Answer the following questions and then compare them to those given at the end of this chapter:

1. Which of the following options is used to convert a curved spline into a linear spline?

   (a) **Bezier**   (b) **Bezier Corner**
   (c) **Corner**   (d) **Smooth**

2. Which of the following buttons is used to enter the spline sub-object mode?

   (a) **Spline**   (b) **Line**
   (c) **Vertex**   (d) None

3. You need to choose _____ from the **Edit** menu to copy the existing state on the screen to a buffer.

4. When you choose the **Vertex** button in the **Selection** rollout to turn it on, the _____ of the selected shape are displayed.

5. You can change the curvature through a vertex by manipulating the _____ of the vertex.

6. There are two types of bezier vertices, **Bezier** and _____.

7. The two bezier handles at any vertex are used to move the lead in and out of the vertex. (T/F)

8. When the **Connect** button in the **Geometry** rollout (in the **Vertex** sub-object mode) is used, the two vertices of a spline are joined by a curved segment. (T/F)

9. The first vertex in a spline has white color. (T/F)

10. The **Edit Spline** modifier need not to be applied to the shapes created using the **Line** tool. (T/F)

Review Questions

Answer the following questions:

1. Which of the following tools is used to bring the transform gizmo to the center point of the selected object?

   (a) **Use Transform Coordinate Center**   (b) **Use Pivot Point Center**
   (c) **Use Selection Center**   (c) **Select and Uniform Scale**

2. Which modifier is used to modify the shape of the splines?

    (a) **Edit Poly**   (b) **Edit Spline**
    (c) **Edit Mesh**   (d) None of these

3. The _____ option is used to convert a linear spline into a curved spline.

4. The _____ option is used to restore the previously saved state from the buffer.

5. To turn the transform gizmo on and off, choose _____ from the **Views** menu.

6. The _____ button is used to bring the transform gizmo to the center point of the selected object.

7. The **Edit Spline** modifier helps you to modify the shape of splines. (T/F)

8. When the **Use Selection Center** tool becomes active on using the **Rotate** command, the selected objects are rotated along their individual pivot points. (T/F)

9. The first vertex of the spline is always yellow colored. (T/F)

10. You cannot select a new shape when you are in the sub-object mode. (T/F)

EXERCISE

Exercise 1

Draw the following shapes by using the dimensions of your choice, refer to Figure 4-28. Make copies and transform them as required.   **(Expected time: 20 min)**

Figure 4-28 Drawing different shapes

Answers to Self-Evaluation Test
1. c, **2.** a, **3. Hold**, **4.** vertices, **5.** bezier handles, **6. Bezier Corner**, **7.** T, **8.** F, **9.** F, **10.** T

Chapter 5

Working with Splines-II

INTRODUCTION

In the previous chapter, you learned to create and modify different shapes using splines. In this chapter, you will learn to create 3D objects using splines. You will also learn the use of the **Lathe** modifier.

TUTORIALS

Tutorial 1

In this tutorial, you will create a model of a table consisting of a top, frame, and legs by extruding simple shapes. You will also create a jug with a handle and place it on the table, refer to Figure 5-1.   (**Expected time: 30 min**)

Figure 5-1 *The model of a table and jug*

The following steps are required to complete this tutorial:

a. Create the project folder.
b. Create the top.
c. Extrude the top.
d. Create the frame.
e. Create the leg.
f. Copy the legs.
g. Rotate the table.
h. Create the jug.
i. Create the handle.
j. Loft the handle.
k. Join the handle to the jug.
l. Save and render the scene.

Creating the Project Folder

Create the project folder with the name *c05_tut1* in the *3dsmaxdesign 2015* folder, as discussed in Tutorial 1 of Chapter 2.

Creating the Top

In this section, you will create a top of the table using the **Rectangle** tool.

1. Choose **Create > Shapes** in the **Command Panel**; the **Splines** option is displayed in the drop-down list located below the **Shapes** button.

2. Invoke the **Rectangle** tool from the **Object Type** rollout.

3. Invoke the **Maximize Viewport Toggle** tool from viewport navigation controls to display all viewports. Activate the Top viewport.

4. Expand the **Keyboard Entry** rollout and set the value **200** in both the **Length** and **Width** spinners. Next, choose the **Create** button; a rectangle is created.

5. Invoke the **Zoom Extents All** tool from viewport navigation controls to zoom the rectangle to its extents in all viewports, as shown in Figure 5-2.

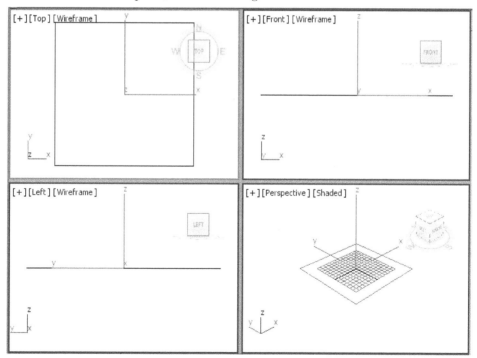

Figure 5-2 *The rectangle created for the table top*

6. In the **Name and Color** rollout, enter **Top** as the name of the object.

Extruding the Top

In this section, you will extrude *Top* to give it a thickness.

1. Make sure *Top* is selected. Next, choose the **Modify** tab in the **Command Panel.**

2. Select **Extrude** from the **OBJECT-SPACE-MODIFIERS** section in the **Modifier List** drop-down list; the **Extrude** modifier is applied to the rectangle.

3. In the **Parameters** rollout, set the value **10** in the **Amount** spinner and press the ENTER key; *Top* is extruded by 10 units, as shown in Figure 5-3.

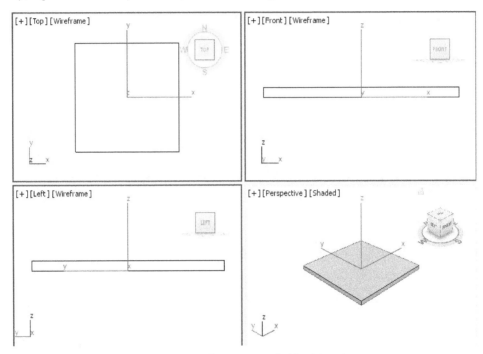

Figure 5-3 The Top extruded by 10 units

Creating the Frame

In this section, you will create a frame to support the legs of the table using the **WRectangle** tool.

1. Make sure the Top viewport is activated.

2. Choose **Create > Shapes** in the **Command Panel**; the **Splines** option is displayed in the drop-down list below the **Shapes** button. Select **Extended Splines** from this drop-down list; the extended spline tools are displayed in the **Object Type** rollout. Next, invoke the **WRectangle** tool.

3. Expand the **Keyboard Entry** rollout and set the values in the spinners as given next:

Length: **160**   Width: **160**   Thickness: **12**

Choose the **Create** button; *WRectangle001* spline is created.

4. In the **Name and Color** rollout, enter **Frame** as the name of the object.

    Next, you need to extrude *Frame*.

5. Make sure *Frame* is selected. Next, choose the **Modify** tab in the **Command Panel**.

6. Select **Extrude** from the **OBJECT-SPACE-MODIFIERS** section in the **Modifier List** drop-down list; the **Extrude** modifier is applied to *Frame*.

7. In the **Parameters** rollout, set the value **15** in the **Amount** spinner; *Frame* is extruded by 15 units, as shown in Figure 5-4.

Figure 5-4 The Frame extruded by 15 units

8. Invoke the **Select and Move** tool from the **Main Toolbar** and then choose the **Transform Gizmo Y Constraint** button from the **Axis Constraints** toolbar.

9. In the Front viewport, move *Frame* so that its bottom touches the upper part of *Top*, as shown in Figure 5-5.

Creating the Leg

In this section, you will create a leg at one of the corners of *Frame* using the **Rectangle** tool.

1. Activate the Top viewport and then choose **Create > Shapes** in the **Command Panel**.

Figure 5-5 *The Frame aligned*

2. Select **Splines** from the drop-down list located below the **Shapes** button and then invoke the **Rectangle** tool from the **Object Type** rollout.

3. Expand the **Keyboard Entry** rollout and set the values **20** in the **Length** and **Width** spinners. Next, choose the **Create** button; the rectangle is created at the center of the table.

4. In the **Name and Color** rollout, enter **Leg01** as the name of the object.

5. Make sure *Leg01* is selected. Next, choose the **Modify** tab in the **Command Panel**.

6. Select **Extrude** from the **OBJECT-SPACE-MODIFIERS** section in the **Modifier List** drop-down list; the **Extrude** modifier is applied to the rectangle.

7. In the **Parameters** rollout, set the value **100** in the **Amount** spinner; *Leg01* is extruded by 100 units.

8. Invoke the **Select and Move** tool from the **Main Toolbar** and then choose the **Transform Gizmo XY Plane Constraint** button from the **Axis Constraints** toolbar.

9. Move *Leg01* to the lower-left inner corner of *Frame*.

10. Activate the Front viewport. Choose the **Transform Gizmo Y Constraint** button from the **Axis Constraints** toolbar and move *Leg01* up so that its bottom touches the upper part of *Top* (not *Frame*).

11. Invoke the **Zoom Extents All** tool from viewport navigation controls to view all objects properly.

Copying the Legs

In this section, you will copy *Leg01* to the other three corners of *Frame*.

1. Activate the Top viewport. Make sure the **Select and Move** tool is invoked and then choose the **Transform Gizmo Y Constraint** button from the **Axis Constraints** toolbar, if it is not already invoked.

2. Select *Leg01* and then choose **Edit > Clone** from the menu bar; the **Clone Options** dialog box is displayed.

3. In this dialog box, enter **Leg02** in the **Name** text box and make sure the **Copy** radio button is selected, as shown in Figure 5-6. Next, choose the **OK** button; *Leg02* is created over *Leg01*.

*Figure 5-6 The **Clone Options** dialog box*

4. Move *Leg02* to the upper-left corner of the frame.

5. Select *Leg02* and then choose **Edit > Clone** from the menu bar; the **Clone Options** dialog box is displayed. In this dialog box, enter **Leg03** in the **Name** text box and then choose the **OK** button. Next, choose the **Transform Gizmo X Constraint** button. Next, move *Leg03* to the upper-right corner of the frame.

6. Similarly, create a copy of *Leg03*. Next, name it as **Leg04** and place it at the lower-right corner of *Frame*; the four legs of table are created and aligned, as shown in Figure 5-7.

7. Select all objects in the viewport. Choose **Group > Group** from the menu bar; the **Group** dialog box is displayed. In this dialog box, enter **Table** in the **Group name** text box and then choose the **OK** button to close the dialog box; *Table* group is created.

Figure 5-7 *The four legs of the table created and aligned to their correct places*

Rotating the Table

In this section, you will rotate the table so that it stands up on its legs.

1. Activate the Front viewport. Invoke the **Select and Rotate** tool from the **Main Toolbar** and then choose the **Transform Gizmo Y Constraint** button from the **Axis Constraints** toolbar.

2. Invoke the **Use Selection Center** tool from the Pivot Point flyout in the **Main Toolbar**.

    The **Use Selection Center** tool enables you to rotate the selected objects around their collective geometric center.

3. Right-click on the **Select and Rotate** tool in the **Main Toolbar**; the **Rotate Transform Type-In** dialog box is displayed. Set the value **180** in the **Z** spinner in the **Offset:Screen** area of this dialog box and then press the ENTER key; *Table* is rotated in upright position, as shown in Figure 5-8. Next, close this dialog box.

4. Invoke the **Zoom Extents All** tool from viewport navigation controls; *Table* is zoomed to its extents in all four viewports after rotated upright to stand on its legs, refer to Figure 5-8.

5. Use the **Maximize Viewport Toggle** tool from the viewport navigation controls to maximize the Front viewport.

Figure 5-8 *Table rotated upright to stand on its legs*

Creating the Jug

In this section, you will create a jug on the table by using the **Line** tool and the **Lathe** modifier.

1. Maximize the Front viewport and invoke the **Use Pivot Point Center** tool from the Pivot Point flyout in the **Main Toolbar**.

2. Invoke the **Zoom Region** tool from viewport navigation controls and zoom in on a small area surrounding the center of *Top*, as shown in Figure 5-9.

3. Choose **Create > Shapes** in the **Command Panel**. Make sure **Splines** is selected in the drop-down list below the **Shapes** button.

4. Invoke the **Line** tool from the **Object Type** rollout.

5. In the Front viewport, place the cursor over the center of the top surface of *Top*. Now, click at this point to specify it as the first vertex of the line.

6. Similarly, click at different points to create the profile of the jug, as shown in Figure 5-10. Note that the profile consists of nearly parallel segments. This will give the jug the required thickness when the **Lathe** modifier is applied to the shape.

Figure 5-9 The center of Table zoomed in the front viewport

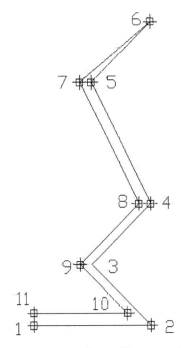

Figure 5-10 The profile curve of the Jug

7. Right-click to exit the **Line** tool; a double-line profile of the jug is created. Use the **Zoom** and **Pan** tools, if needed, to display the entire profile of the jug, refer to Figure 5-11.

[+][Front][Wireframe]

Figure 5-11 *The profile of the Jug*

8. Enter **Jug** in the **Name and Color** rollout.

Next, you will smoothen *Jug* by modifying its vertices.

9. With *Jug* selected, choose the **Modify** tab in the **Command Panel**. In the **Selection** rollout, choose the **Vertex** button; the **Vertex** sub-object mode is selected and the vertices appear on the profile.

10. Right-click on the inner vertex, refer to Figure 5-12; the quad menu is displayed. Choose **Bezier** from the upper-left quadrant of the quad menu; the spline is curved and the bezier handles are displayed, as shown in Figure 5-12.

11. Invoke the **Select and Move** tool from the **Main Toolbar** and choose the **Transform Gizmo XY Plane Constraint** button from the **Axis Constraints** toolbar.

12. Next, hold the upper green handle and drag it to left so that the curve looks similar to the one shown in Figure 5-13. If you make a change by mistake, choose the **Undo Scene Operation** button to undo the previous change.

13. Similarly, change the curvature of the other vertices and move some of them to get the shape of *Jug* similar to the one shown in Figure 5-14. You can move a vertex by directly clicking on it.

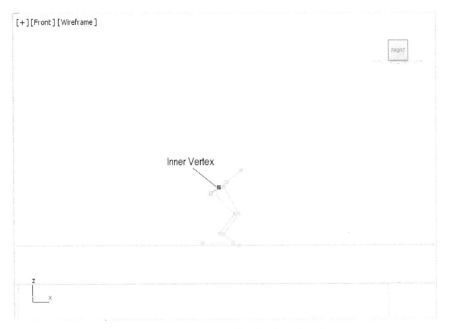

Figure 5-12 *The bezier handles displayed at the vertex*

Figure 5-13 *The curve reshaped by dragging the bezier handle*

 Note
You will find snaps useful for selecting vertices, but you may need to disable snaps while moving or changing the curvature of vertices.

[+][Front][Wireframe]

Figure 5-14 *The curve edited by moving the bezier handles of the vertices*

14. In the **Selection** rollout, choose the **Vertex** button again to exit the sub-object mode.

   Next, you will spin the profile of *Jug* around its axis to form a complete jug.

15. Invoke the **Maximize Viewport Toggle** tool from the viewport navigation controls
   to restore all four viewports. Make sure the profile is selected and invoke the **Zoom
   Extents All Selected** tool from the viewport navigation controls; the profile is zoomed
   to its extent in all viewports.

16. Choose the **Modify** tab in the **Command Panel**. Select **Lathe** from the **OBJECT-SPACE-
   MODIFIERS** section in the **Modifier List** drop-down list; the profile spins around its axis
   at the middle.

17. To properly align the shape, select the **Min** radio button in the **Align** area of the **Parameters**
   rollout; the profile form the shape of a jug, refer to Figure 5-15. Invoke the **Zoom Extents
   All Selected** tool from the viewport navigation controls to zoom the object to its extent.

18. Invoke the **Zoom Extents All** tool from the viewport navigation controls; all objects are
   zoomed to their extents in all viewports.

Creating the Handle
In this section, you will create a handle for *Jug* by using the **Circle** and **Loft** tools.

1.   Maximize the Front viewport. Invoke the **Zoom Region** tool from the viewport navigation
   controls and zoom in the right-hand side of *Jug* such that you can create more space to
   accommodate the handle.

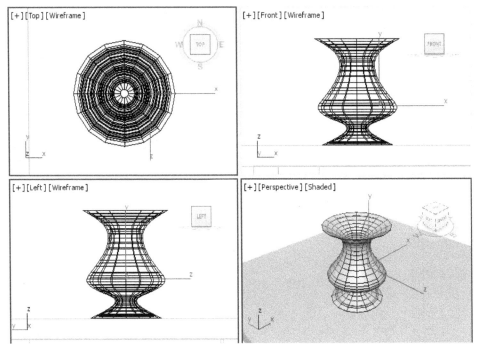

Figure 5-15   *The profile rotated to form the Jug*

2.   Choose **Create > Shapes** in the **Command Panel**. Next, make sure the **Line** tool is invoked from the **Object Type** rollout.

3.   Click at a point slightly below the neck. Make sure to place it inside the outer line of *Jug*, as shown in Figure 5-16.

Figure 5-16   *The first vertex placed within the profile*

4. Similarly, click at other points to form a curve, refer to Figure 5-17. Right-click to exit the **Line** tool; the shape of the handle is created, as shown in Figure 5-17.

[+][Front][Wireframe]

Figure 5-17 *The curve for the handle of the Jug*

You may need to adjust the coordinates given, depending on the profile of your *Jug*.

5. In the **Name and Color** rollout, enter **Handle** as the name of the object.

6. With *Handle* selected, choose the **Modify** tab in the **Command Panel**. In the **Selection** rollout, choose the **Vertex** button; the **Vertex** sub-object mode is selected and the vertices appear on the profile.

7. Invoke the **Select and Move** tool from the **Main Toolbar** and right-click on the second vertex. Choose **Bezier** from the quad menu and then move *Handle* to get the desired curve. Similarly, modify the rest of the vertices of *Handle* as needed to form a curved shape, as shown in Figure 5-18.

8. Choose the **Vertex** button again to exit the vertex selection mode.

Lofting the Handle

In this section, you will add thickness to the handle. This can be done by creating a circle and then lofting it along a path.

1. Choose **Create > Shapes** in the **Command Panel**. Next, invoke the **Circle** tool. Create a circle anywhere in the viewport, as shown in Figure 5-19. Set the value **0.5** in the **Radius** spinner of the **Parameters** rollout.

[+] [Front] [Wireframe]

Figure 5-18 The Handle modified by moving the bezier handles

[+] [Front] [Wireframe]

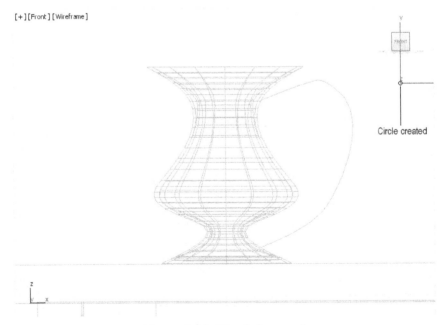

Figure 5-19 The circle created

2. Select *Handle* from the **Scene Explorer** located left of the interface.

3. Choose **Create > Geometry** in the **Command Panel**. Select **Compound Objects** from the drop-down list located below it. Next, invoke the **Loft** tool from the **Object Type** rollout; different rollouts for the loft object are displayed.

4. In the **Creation Method** rollout, make sure the **Instance** radio button is selected and then choose the **Get Shape** button; the shape of the cursor changes.

5. Select the circle. Next, right-click in the viewport to exit the tool.

   The circle is placed on the vertices of the path (*Handle*) and is automatically named as **Loft001**.

6. Enter **Handle** in the **Name and Color** rollout. Invoke the **Select Object** tool to complete the operation.

7. Delete the circle. Next, invoke the **Maximize Viewport Toggle** tool to restore the four-viewport configuration. Now, invoke the **Zoom Extents All** tool to view all objects properly.

Joining the Handle and the Jug

In this section, you will join *Handle* with *Jug* using the **Boolean** tool.

1. Invoke the **Zoom Region** tool from the viewport navigation controls to zoom in the Top viewport and make sure that *Handle* is centered on *Jug*. If not, move *Handle* as required.

2. Make sure *Handle* is selected and also make sure the **Compound Objects** is selected in the drop-down list below the **Geometry** button. Next, invoke the **Boolean** tool from the **Object Type** rollout; different rollouts for a boolean object are displayed.

3. In the **Operation** area of the **Parameters** rollout, select the **Union** radio button.

4. In the **Pick Boolean** rollout, choose the **Pick Operand B** button. Next, select *Jug* in any viewport. Invoke the **Select Object** tool from the **Main Toolbar** to complete the operation; *Jug* and *Handle* are joined to make a single object, as shown in Figure 5-20.

5. In the **Name and Color** rollout, enter the name of the object as **jug**. Invoke the **Zoom Extents All** tool from viewport navigation controls.

Saving and Rendering the Scene

In this section, you will save the scene that you have created and then render it. You can also view the final rendered image of this scene by downloading the *c05_3dsmaxdesign_2015_rndr.zip* file from *www.cadcim.com*. The path of the file is as follows: *Textbooks > Animation and Visual Effects > 3ds Max Design > Autodesk 3ds Max Design 2015: A Tutorial Approach*

1. Choose **Save** from the **Application** menu.

2. Change the background color to white, as discussed in earlier chapters.

Figure 5-20 *Using the boolean operation to join Handle and Jug*

3. Activate the Perspective viewport. Next, invoke the **Render Production** tool from the **Main Toolbar**; the rendered image is displayed, refer to Figure 5-21.

Figure 5-21 *The rendered image*

Tutorial 2

In this tutorial, you will create the model of a lamp post, as shown in Figure 5-22 using various spline tools. **(Expected time: 25 min)**

Figure 5-22 The model of a lamp post

The following steps are required to complete this tutorial:

a. Create the project folder.
b. Create the base.
c. Create the pillar.
d. Create the joint.
e. Create the lamp holder.
f. Add details.
g. Save and render the scene.

Creating the Project Folder

Create a project folder with the name *c05_tut2* in the *3dsmaxdesign 2015* folder as discussed in Tutorial 1 of Chapter 2.

Creating the Base

In this section, you will create the base of the lamp post by using the **Box** tool.

1. Invoke the **Maximize Viewport Toggle** tool from viewport navigation controls to switch to the four viewport configuration. Next, activate the Top viewport and then choose **Create > Shapes** in the **Command Panel**; the **Splines** option is displayed in the drop-down list located below it. Next, invoke the **Rectangle** tool from the **Object Type** rollout.

2. Expand the **Keyboard Entry** rollout and set the values in the spinners as given next:

   Length: **3**   Width: **3**

   Choose the **Create** button; a square is created in all viewports.

3. Enter **base** in the **Name and Color** rollout. Invoke the **Zoom Extents All** tool; *base* is zoomed in all viewports, as shown in Figure 5-23.

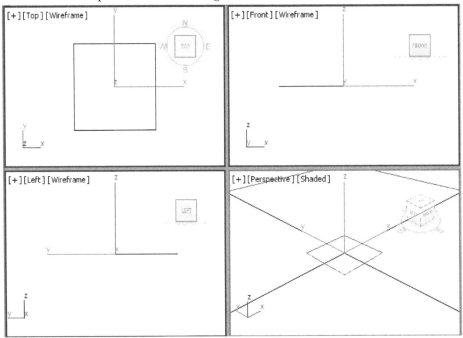

Figure 5-23 The base zoomed in all viewports

4. Choose the **Modify** tab in the **Command Panel**. Next, select the **Extrude** option from the **OBJECT-SPACE-MODIFIERS** section in the **Modifier List** drop-down list; the **Extrude** modifier is applied to *base* and displayed in the modifier stack. Also, various rollouts of this modifier are displayed in the **Command Panel**.

5. In the **Parameters** rollout, set the value **0.4** in the **Amount** spinner and press the ENTER key; *base* is extruded, as shown in Figure 5-24.

Creating the Pillar

In this section, you will create the pillar of the lamp post using the **Line** tool.

1. Activate the Front viewport. Next, invoke the **Maximize Viewport Toggle** tool from viewport navigation controls to maximize the Front viewport.

2. Invoke the **Zoom** tool and zoom out to create more space at the top of *base*. Choose **Create > Shapes** in the **Command Panel**; the **Splines** option is displayed in the drop-down list. Next, invoke the **Line** tool from the **Object Type** rollout.

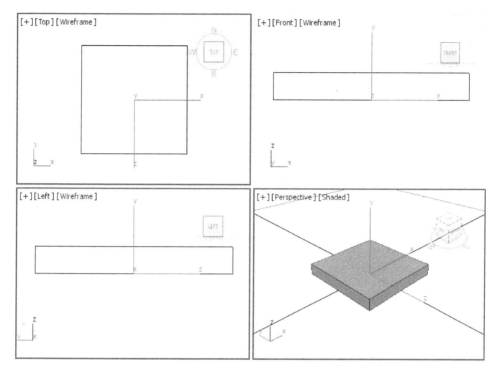

Figure 5-24 *The base extruded in all viewports*

3. Click at the center of the top edge of *base* and create a curved shape, as shown in Figure 5-25. Enter **pillar** in the **Name and Color** rollout. Next, right-click to exit the **Line** tool.

To get the perfect shape shown in Figure 5-25, you need to follow the steps given next.

 Note
To achieve the smoothness in the curve, the number of vertices should be more.

4. Choose the **Modify** tab and then in the modifier stack, click on the plus sign on the left of the **Line** to view all sub-object levels. Next, select the **Vertex** sub-object level. Now, select the vertices one by one and move them by using the **Select and Move** tool from the **Main Toolbar** to get the desired shape.

5. Select the upper vertices of *pillar*, as shown in Figure 5-26 and then right-click; a quad menu is displayed. Choose **Smooth** from the quad menu; the upper portion of *pillar* is smoothened. Select the **Vertex** sub-object level again to exit the sub-object mode.

Next, you will add thickness to *pillar*.

6. Expand the **Rendering** rollout and select the **Enable In Renderer** and **Enable In Viewport** check boxes.

7. Make sure the **Radial** radio button is selected and set the value **0.15** in the **Thickness** spinner; the thickness is added to *pillar*, as shown in Figure 5-27.

Figure 5-25 *The line created*   **Figure 5-26** *The selected vertices*

Creating the Joint

In this section, you will create a joint between the pillar and the lamp holder using the **Ellipse** tool.

1. Activate the Left viewport. Next, invoke the **Maximize Viewport Toggle** tool from viewport navigation controls to maximize the Left viewport.

2. Choose **Create > Shapes** in the **Command Panel**; the **Splines** option is displayed in the drop-down list below the **Shapes** button. Next, invoke the **Ellipse** tool from the **Object Type** rollout.

3. Expand the **Keyboard Entry** rollout and set the values of the parameters as given next:

    Length: **0.3**   Width: **0.2**

    Choose the **Create** button; an ellipse is created in the viewport. Enter **joint** in the **Name and Color** rollout.

4. In the **Rendering** rollout, make sure that the **Enable In Renderer** and **Enable In Viewport** check boxes are selected. Also, make sure that the **Radial** radio button is selected. Next, set the value **0.05** in the **Thickness** spinner and press the ENTER key; *joint* is displayed at the bottom of the viewport, as shown in Figure 5-28.

Figure 5-27 *The thickness added to pillar*   **Figure 5-28** *The joint displayed*

5. Invoke the **Maximize Viewport Toggle** tool to display all viewports. Make sure the **Select and Move** tool is invoked in the **Main Toolbar** and align *joint* in all viewports, as shown in Figure 5-29.

Figure 5-29 *The joint aligned in all viewports*

Creating the Lamp Holder

In this section, you will create the lamp holder using the **NGon** tool and the **Edit Poly** modifier.

1. Activate the Top viewport. Choose **Create > Shapes** in the **Command Panel**; the **Splines** option is displayed in the drop-down list below the **Shapes** button. Next, invoke the **NGon** tool from the **Object Type** rollout.

2. Expand the **Keyboard Entry** rollout and set the value **0.4** in the **Radius** spinner. Choose the **Create** button; *NGon001* is created in the viewport. Enter **lamp holder** in the **Name and Color** rollout. In the **Parameters** rollout, set the value **8** in the **Sides** spinner.

3. Choose the **Modify** tab in the **Command Panel**. Next, select **Extrude** from the **Modifier List** drop-down list; the **Extrude** modifier is applied to *lamp holder*.

4. Set the value **1.2** in the **Amount** spinner of the **Parameters** rollout and press the ENTER key; *lamp holder* is extruded. Next, align it in all viewports, as shown in Figure 5-30.

   The *lamp holder* is aligned slightly below *joint* because you will modify its shape in the following steps by applying the **Edit Poly** modifier.

5. Select **Edit Poly** from the **OBJECT-SPACE-MODIFIERS** section in the **Modifier List** drop-down list; the **Edit Poly** modifier is applied to *lamp holder*.

Figure 5-30 The lamp holder aligned in all viewports

6. Click on the plus sign in the modifier stack; all sub-object levels are displayed. Select the **Edge** sub-object level. Now, activate the Front viewport and select the edge, as shown in Figure 5-31.

7. In the **Selection** rollout, choose the **Ring** button; the ring of edges are selected. Next, in the **Edit Edges** rollout, choose the **Settings** button on the right of the **Chamfer** button; the **Chamfer** caddy control is displayed in the viewport. Set the value **0.03** in the **Chamfer-Amount** spinner and **1** in the **Segments** spinner and then choose the **OK** button to close the caddy control; the selected edges are chamfered, as shown in Figure 5-32.

Figure 5-31 The edge selected

Figure 5-32 Selected edges chamfered

8. Select the **Polygon** sub-object level from the **Selection** rollout and then select all polygons between the chamfered edges, as shown in Figure 5-33.

Figure 5-33 *The selected polygons between chamfered edges*

9. In the **Edit Polygons** rollout, choose the **Settings** button on the right of the **Bevel** button; the **Bevel** caddy control is displayed in the viewport. Set the value -**0.01** in the **Bevel-Height** spinner and **-0.02** in the **Bevel-Outline** spinner and then choose the **OK** button to close the caddy control; the selected polygons are beveled, as shown in Figure 5-34.

10. Select the uppermost and lowermost polygons, as shown in Figure 5-35.

11. In the **Edit Polygons** rollout, choose the **Settings** button on the right of the **Bevel** button; the **Bevel** caddy control is displayed in the viewport. Set the value **0.13** in the **Bevel-Height** spinner and **-0.08** in the **Bevel-Outline** spinner and then choose the **OK** button to close the caddy control; the selected polygons are beveled, as shown in Figure 5-36.

Figure 5-34 *The selected polygons beveled*

Figure 5-35 *The selected polygons*

Figure 5-36 *The selected polygons beveled*

12. Select the **Polygon** sub-object level again in the **Selection** rollout to deactivate it.

13. Invoke the **Select and Move** tool from the **Main Toolbar** and align *lamp holder*, refer to Figure 5-36.

Adding Details

In this section, you will use the **Line** tool to add details to the lamp post.

1. Activate the Front viewport. Choose **Create > Shapes** in the **Command Panel**; the **Splines** option is displayed in the drop-down list. Next, invoke the **Line** tool from the **Object Type** rollout.

2. In the **Rendering** rollout, make sure that the **Enable In Renderer** and **Enable In Viewport** check boxes are selected. Also, set the value of **0.06** in the **Thickness** spinner.

3. In the **Creation Method** rollout, make sure the **Smooth** radio buttons are selected in the **Initial Type** and **Drag Type** areas. Next, create a curve, as shown in Figure 5-37. Right-click to exit the **Line** tool.

4. Repeat steps 1, 2, and 3 and create second curve, as shown in Figure 5-38.

   Next, you will create two joints between the curves and *pillar*.

5. Make sure the **Line** tool is activated. In the **Rendering** rollout, make sure the **Enable in Renderer** and **Enable In Viewport** check boxes are selected. Also, set the value **0.03** in the **Thickness** spinner. Next, create two joints, as shown in Figure 5-39.

Figure 5-37 The curve created

Figure 5-38 The second curve created

Figure 5-39 Two joints created

Saving and Rendering the Scene

In this section, you will save the scene that you have created and then render it. You can also view the final rendered image of this model by downloading the *c05_3dsmaxdesign_2015_rndr.zip* file from *www.cadcim.com*. The path of the file is as follows: *Textbooks > Animation and Visual Effects > 3ds Max Design > Autodesk 3ds Max Design 2015: A Tutorial Approach*

1. Change the background color of the scene to white, as discussed in Tutorial 1 of Chapter 2.

2. Choose **Save** from the **Application** menu.

3. Activate the Perspective viewport. Next, invoke the **Render Production** tool from the **Main Toolbar**; the rendered image is displayed, refer to Figure 5-40.

Figure 5-40 The rendered image

Self-Evaluation Test

Answer the following questions and then compare them to those given at the end of this chapter:

1. Which of the following tools is used to render a scene?

    (a) **Rendered Frame Window**   (b) **Render Production**
    (c) **Render Setup**   (d) None of these

2. You need to choose _____ from the **Edit** menu to invoke the **Clone Options** dialog box.

3. You can use the _____ tool to switch between the single and four-viewports configuration.

4. The _____ button is used to reverse the latest changes made.

5. When you choose **Bezier** from the quad menu, the spline becomes a straight line at the selected vertex along with the display of a single Bezier handle. (T/F)

6. You need to increase the number of vertices in a curve to achieve smoothness in it. (T/F)

Review Questions

Answer the following questions:

1. Which of the following tools is used to arrange the objects, lights, and cameras in a viewport?

    (a) **Select and Uniform Scale**   (b) **Select and Move**
    (c) **Select and Rotate**   (d) All of these

2. The _____ button in the **Align** area of the **Parameters** rollout is used to properly align a shape created using the **Lathe** modifier.

3. The _____ tool enables you to rotate the selected objects around their collective geometric center.

4. The _____ modifier is used to spin a spline around its axis to form an object.

5. You can draw a square by invoking the **Rectangle** tool and then dragging the cursor while holding down the CTRL key. (T/F)

EXERCISE

The rendered output of the model used in the following exercise can be accessed by downloading *c05_maxdesign_2015_exr.zip* from *www.cadcim.com*. The path of the file is as follows: *Textbooks > Animation and Visual Effects > 3ds Max Design > Autodesk 3ds Max Design 2015: A Tutorial Approach*

Exercise 1

Create a cup and a saucer, as shown in Figure 5-41 by using the profile curves shown in Figure 5-42.   **(Expected time: 25 min)**

Figure 5-41 The cup and saucer

Figure 5-42 Profile curves of the cup and saucer

Chapter 6

Lofting, Twisting, and Deforming Objects

Learning Objectives

After completing this chapter, you will be able to:

• *Loft spline objects along a path*
• *Change the skin display*
• *Change the path levels*
• *Add different shapes to the loft object*
• *Remove twists from twisted loft objects*
• *Use various deformation tools on a loft object*

INTRODUCTION

Lofting is a technique to create a 3D object by repeating a shape along a path. In this chapter, you will learn to loft splines, twist the lofted objects, and use various deformation tools to modify them.

TUTORIALS

Tutorial 1

In this tutorial, you will create an ellipse and then loft it along a path to create a 3D object. You will also change various skin parameters to get desired shapes.   **(Expected time: 20 min)**

The following steps are required to complete this tutorial:

a.   Create the project folder.
b.   Loft spline objects.
c.   Change the shape of the lofted object.
d.   Cap loft objects.

Creating the Project Folder

Create the project folder with the name *c06_tut1* in the *3dsmaxdesign 2015* folder, as discussed in Tutorial 1of Chapter 2.

Lofting Spline Objects

In this section, you will create a line and an ellipse and then loft the line using the **Loft** tool.

1.   Invoke the **Maximize Viewport Toggle** tool from the viewport navigation controls to display all viewports. If the grid is not displayed in the viewports, click on the viewport label; a flyout is displayed. Choose **Show Grids** from the flyout to display grids in the viewport.

2.   Invoke the **Zoom** tool from the viewport navigation controls. Zoom in on the Top, Front, and Left viewports to display the subgrid, if it is not already displayed.

3.   Invoke the **2D Snap** tool from the **Snaps Toggle** flyout in the **Main Toolbar** to turn on snapping. Right-click on the **2D Snap** tool; the **Grid and Snap Settings** dialog box is displayed. In the **Snaps** tab, ensure that only the **Grid Points** check box is selected. Next, close the dialog box.

4.   Choose **Create > Shapes** in the **Command Panel**. Next, invoke the **Line** tool from the **Object Type** rollout.

5. Activate the Front viewport. Expand the **Keyboard Entry** rollout and enter the following values in the **X**, **Y**, and **Z** spinners. You need to choose the **Add Point** button after every XYZ coordinate entry:

X: **0**   Y:**100**   Z: **0**
X: **0**   Y:**0**   Z: **0**

Choose the **Finish** button. Next, right-click to exit the tool.

This line is the path for the loft object.

6. Invoke the **Ellipse** tool from the **Object Type** rollout.

7. Activate the Top viewport. In the **Keyboard Entry** rollout, set **50** in the **Length** spinner and **100** in the **Width** spinner. Next, choose the **Create** button; an ellipse is created in all viewports. Right-click to exit the tool. Now, align the shapes, as shown in Figure 6-1 and invoke the **Zoom Extents All** tool from the viewport navigation controls to view the created shapes properly, refer to Figure 6-1.

Figure 6-1 *A straight line and an ellipse*

The ellipse is the shape for the loft object.

8. Invoke the **2D Snap** tool again from the **Snaps Toggle** flyout in the **Main Toolbar** to turn the snaps off. Next, select the line in any viewport.

9. Choose **Create > Geometry** in the **Command Panel**. Next, select **Compound Objects** from the drop-down list below the **Geometry** button. Next, invoke the **Loft** tool from the **Object Type** rollout.

10. In the **Creation Method** rollout, make sure the **Instance** radio button is selected. Then, choose the **Get Shape** button.

11. Select the ellipse in any viewport. Next, right-click to exit the creation of the loft.

    The ellipse (shape) is placed along the line (path) at its first vertex. The first vertex of the path is indicated by a small yellow cross mark.

12. With the lofted object selected, invoke the **Zoom Extents All Selected** tool from the viewport navigation controls; the lofted object is zoomed to its extents in all viewports, as shown in Figure 6-2.

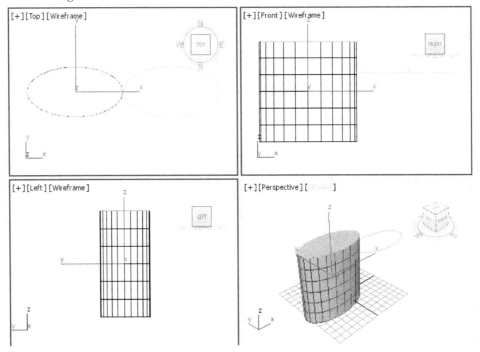

Figure 6-2 The lofted object zoomed to its extents in all viewports

 Note

*1. You can change the number of steps using the **Shape Steps** spinner in the **Options** area of the **Skin Parameters** rollout to increase or decrease the smoothness of the loft object around (not along) the path.*

2. You can add different shapes at different levels of the path to create a complex loft object. Use of multiple shapes on a path for creating a loft object is explained in detail in Tutorial 3.

Changing the Shape of the Lofted Object

In this section, you will change the shape of the lofted object by using different shapes along its path.

1. Choose **Edit >Hold** from the menu bar. Next, select the lofted object, if it is not already selected.

2. Invoke the **2D Snap** tool from the **Snaps Toggle** flyout in the **Main Toolbar** to turn on snapping.

3. Choose **Create > Shapes** in the **Command Panel**. Next, invoke the **Rectangle** tool from the **Object Type** rollout.

4. In the Top viewport, draw a rectangle that fits inside the original ellipse and then right-click to exit the tool.

5. Select the lofted object in any viewport and choose the **Modify** tab in the **Command Panel**.

6. In the **Path Parameters** rollout, select the **On** check box to activate the **Snap** spinner. Make sure the **Percentage** radio button is selected.

7. Set the value **50** in the **Path** spinner; the small yellow cross mark, which indicates the current level moves to the middle, or 50% of the entire path.

   Note
   *If the yellow cross mark is not at the center of the path when the **Path** spinner is set to **50**, the path may have been created with one or more bezier vertices. To rectify this, click on the plus sign next to **Loft** in the modifier stack and select the **Path** level from the sub-object hierarchy. Expand the **Line** level and select the **Vertex** sub-object mode. Right-click on the vertices of each of the paths and make sure that the **Corner** option is chosen in the quad menu displayed. When you are done, click on the **Loft** twice in the modifier stack to exit sub-object mode and then repeat step 7.*

8. Choose the **Get Shape** button in the **Creation Method** rollout. Then, select the rectangle in any viewport. Choose the **Get Shape** button again to deactivate it; the rectangle is added as a shape at the 50% mark and the lofted object is updated, as shown in Figure 6-3.

9. Now, set the value **100** in the **Path** spinner. In the **Creation Method** rollout, make sure the **Get Shape** button is chosen. Then, select the original ellipse in any viewport; the ellipse is added as a shape at the end of the path, as shown in Figure 6-4.

   The lofted object now starts as an ellipse, tapers to a rectangle, and then tapers back to an ellipse.

   Note
   *You can change the number of path steps in the **Skin Parameters** rollout to increase or decrease the smoothness along the length of a lofted object.*

Figure 6-3 *A rectangular section created in the middle of the loft*

Figure 6-4 *The ellipse added as a shape at the end of the path*

Capping Loft Objects

In this section, you will use the capping options to open and then close the ends of a lofted object.

1. Expand the **Skin Parameters** rollout and then clear the **Cap Start** check box in the **Capping** area; the top end of the lofted object (beginning of the path) opens, as shown in Figure 6-5.

Figure 6-5 The top end of the loft object opened

2. To get a better view of the model, use the **Orbit SubObject** tool from the viewport navigation controls to adjust the Perspective viewport.

   As you rotate the view, notice that the other side of the lofted object is not displayed in the shaded viewports. This is because the skin is one-sided. A two-sided material can be applied to see the other side of the lofted object.

3. Clear the **Cap End** check box from the **Capping** area in the **Skin Parameters** rollout; the bottom end of the loft object opens and a hollow cylinder is created because the skin is generated on an open path.

4. Choose **Save** from the **Application** menu to save the scene.

Tutorial 2

In this tutorial, you will create a lofted object using the **Loft** tool and position the shapes at different levels in a path. You will also align the shape vertices to remove the twist from the loft. In addition, you will move the shapes to different levels on the path and then make the path curved.   **(Expected time: 25 min)**

The following steps are required to complete this tutorial:

a.   Create the project folder.
b.   Loft multiple objects.
c.   Remove the twist.
d.   Move and modify shapes.
e.   Change the shape of the path.
f.   Move shapes with respect to the path.

Creating the Project Folder

Create the project folder with the name *c06_tut2* in the *3dsmaxdesign 2015* folder, as discussed in Tutorial 1 of Chapter 2.

Lofting Multiple Objects

In this section, you will loft multiple shapes along a path.

1.   Invoke the **Maximize Viewport Toggle** tool from the viewport navigation controls to display the four-viewport configuration.

2.   Right-click on the **Snaps Toggle** tool; the **Grid and Snap Settings** dialog box is displayed. Make sure that only the **Grid Points** check box is selected. Next, close the dialog box.

3.   Invoke the **Zoom** tool from the viewport navigation controls. Zoom in the Top, Front, and Left viewports until the subgrid is displayed.

4.   Choose **Create > Shapes** in the **Command Panel**. Next, invoke the **Line** tool from the **Object Type** rollout.

5.   Activate the Front viewport. Expand the **Keyboard Entry** rollout and enter the following values in the **X**, **Y**, and **Z** spinners. You need to choose the **Add Point** button after every XYZ coordinate entry:

X: **0**   Y: **130**   Z: **0**
X: **0**   Y: **0**   Z: **0**

Choose the **Finish** button. Next, right-click to exit the tool. This line is the path for creating the lofted object.

6. Activate the Top viewport. Invoke the **Ellipse** tool from the **Object Type** rollout. In the **Keyboard Entry** rollout, set **60** in the **Length** spinner and **100** in the **Width** spinner. Next, choose the **Create** button; an ellipse is created in all viewports. Right-click to exit the tool.

7. Invoke the **Rectangle** tool from the **Object Type** rollout. In the **Keyboard Entry** rollout, set **130** in the **Length** and **Width** spinners. Next, choose the **Create** button; a rectangle is created in all viewports. Right-click to exit the tool. Now, align the shapes, as shown in Figure 6-6 and invoke the **Zoom Extents All** tool. The rectangle is the second shape to be lofted. The line, ellipse, and rectangle are created, refer to Figure 6-6.

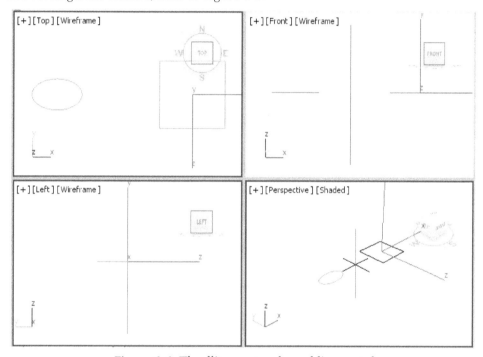

Figure 6-6 *The ellipse, rectangle, and line created*

8. Select the line in any viewport.

9. Choose **Create > Geometry** in the **Command Panel**. Select **Compound Objects** from the drop-down list below the **Geometry** button. Next, invoke the **Loft** tool from the **Object Type** rollout.

10. In the **Creation Method** rollout, make sure that the **Instance** radio button is selected. Next, choose the **Get Shape** button.

11. Select the ellipse in any viewport and select it; an instance of the ellipse (shape) is placed at the first vertex of the line (path). The current level, indicated by a small yellow cross, is positioned at the first vertex of the path. Since the line was drawn from the top to the bottom, the first vertex is at the top of the viewport. Next, right-click to exit the tool. The lofted object is shown in Figure 6-7.

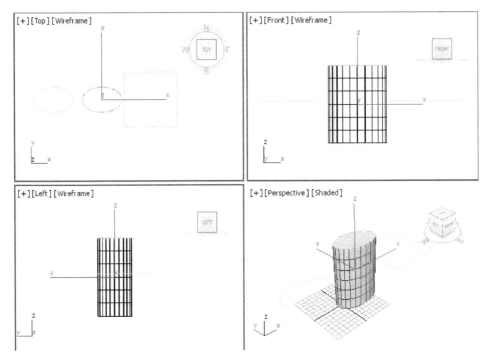

Figure 6-7 The lofted object and the shapes zoomed to their extents in all viewports

12. Select the lofted object, if it is not already selected.

13. Choose the **Modify** tab in the **Command Panel**. In the **Path Parameters** rollout, select the **On** check box; the **Snap** spinner is enabled.

14. Set the value **100** in the **Path** spinner; the yellow cross moves to the last vertex of the path.

15. In the **Creation Method** rollout, choose the **Get Shape** button. Select the rectangle in any viewport and select it. Choose the **Get Shape** button again to complete the operation; an instance of the rectangle is placed along the line at its last vertex. Now, the ellipse is on one end of the path and the rectangle is on the other end.

    When an object is created by lofting multiple shapes, the first vertex of one shape is joined with the first vertex of the next shape. The other vertices are joined with their corresponding vertices. If the vertices are not aligned, the object is twisted.

16. Select the lofted object, if it is not already selected. Invoke the **Zoom Extents All Selected** tool; the lofted object is zoomed to its extents in all viewports, refer to Figure 6-8. You will notice the twist in the lofted object.

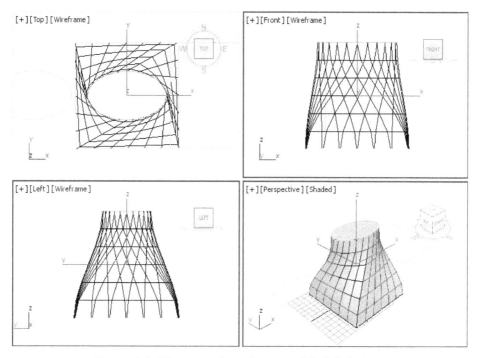

Figure 6-8 *The rectangle used as one of the lofted objects*

Removing the Twist

In this section, you will remove the twist in the lofted object. To avoid twisting of lofted object, the vertices of the shapes should be aligned. This can be done by using the **Compare** button in the **Shape Commands** rollout. This rollout is available when the **Shape** sub-object mode is active for the lofted object.

1. Make sure the lofted object is selected. Next, choose **Loft** in the modifier stack from the **Modify** tab in the **Command Panel**. The modifier stack appears in the window below the **Modifier List** drop-down list.

2. Click on the + sign next to **Loft** to display the sub-object hierarchy. Make sure the **Shape** sub-object level is selected, as shown in Figure 6-9; the **Shape** level is displayed in yellow indicating that it is the current sub-object mode. Also, the **Shape Commands** rollout is displayed.

3. Choose the **Compare** button in the **Shape Commands** rollout; the **Compare** window is displayed, as shown in Figure 6-10.

4. Choose the **Pick Shape** button in the **Compare** window. Next, move the cursor over the ellipse in the lofted object; the shape of the cursor changes. Now, click to select the ellipse in any viewport.

    The ellipse is displayed in the **Compare** window. The first vertex of the ellipse is displayed as a small square.

Figure 6-9 *The **Shape** sub-object level*
selected in the modifier stack

5. With the **Pick Shape** button chosen, move the cursor over the rectangle in the lofted
    object and select it; the rectangle with its first vertex is displayed in the **Compare**
    window. You can use the **Zoom Extents** tool located at the bottom of the **Compare**
    window to display both shapes in the window, if needed, as shown in Figure 6-11.

Figure 6-10 *The **Compare** window*   *Figure 6-11* *The ellipse and rectangle displayed*
                                             *in the **Compare** window*

6. Choose the **Pick Shape** button to deactivate it. Activate the Front viewport and select
    the rectangle in the lofted object. Next, right-click on the **Select and Rotate** tool from
    the **Main Toolbar**; the **Rotate Transform Type-In** dialog box is displayed. In this dialog
    box, set the value **-45** in the **Z** spinner of the **Offset: Local** area and then close the dialog
    box; the vertices of both the shapes are aligned in the **Compare** window, as shown in
    Figure 6-12.

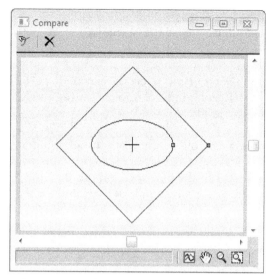

Figure 6-12 *The rectangle rotated to align first vertices of both shapes*

7. Close the **Compare** window; the lofted object with aligned sides is displayed in all viewports and the twist is removed from the lofted object, as shown in Figure 6-13.

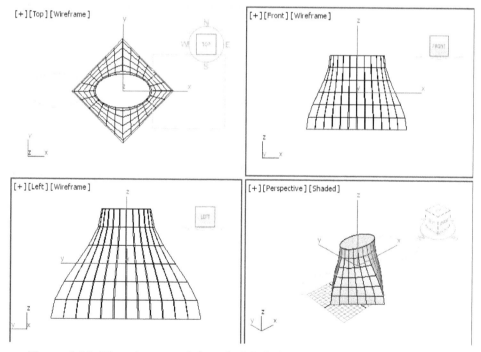

Figure 6-13 *The twist removed from the lofted object by rotating the rectangle shape*

Moving and Modifying Shapes

In this section, you will modify the shape of the lofted object by moving and modifying the shapes along the path.

1. Invoke the **Select Object** tool and select the rectangle in the lofted object, if it is not already selected; the **Rectangle** level appears in the modifier stack below the **Loft** level and its sub-object levels.

2. In the **Shape Commands** rollout, the **Path Level** spinner displays 100, indicating the level on which the rectangle is placed. Set **60** in this spinner and press the ENTER key; the rectangle moves to the 60% location on the path. The lofted object starts as an ellipse, gradually changes to a rectangle at 60%, and finishes as a rectangle, as shown in Figure 6-14.

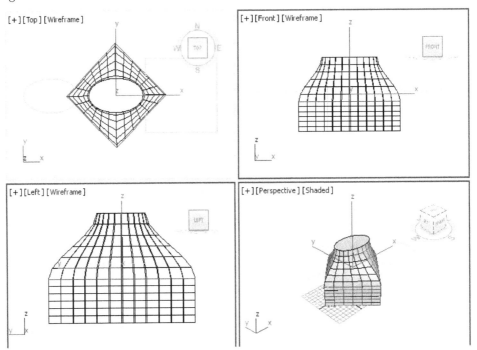

Figure 6-14 The rectangle shape moved to the 60% position on the path

3. Select the ellipse on the loft (at 0%). In the modifier stack, select the **Ellipse** level; the rollouts for the ellipse are displayed.

4. In the **Parameters** rollout, set the value **150** in the **Width** spinner and press the ENTER key; the width of the ellipse is increased, as shown in Figure 6-15.

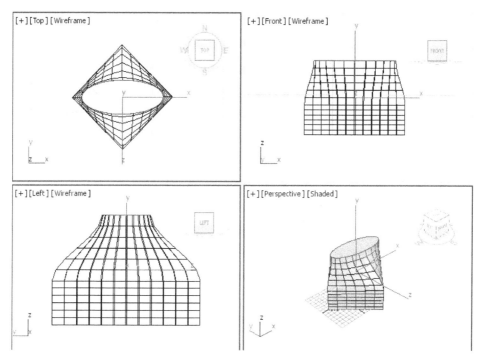

Figure 6-15 *Width of the ellipse increased*

Changing the Shape of the Path

In this section, you will modify the lofted object by changing the shape of the path along which it is lofted.

1. In the modifier stack, select the **Path** level to exit the **Shape** sub-object mode and enter into the **Path** sub-object mode; the **Line** level appears in the modifier stack below the **Path** level of the **Loft** sub-object hierarchy.

2. Select the **Line** level in the modifier stack; the rollouts for a line are displayed. In the selection rollout, choose the **Vertex** button; the **Vertex** sub-object mode is selected for the line.

3. Invoke the **Select and Move** tool from the **Main Toolbar** and make sure the **Transform Gizmo XY Plane Constraint** button is chosen from the **Axis Constraints** toolbar.

4. In the Front viewport, select the first vertex (upper vertex) and move it about 30 units to the left and 20 units down, as shown in Figure 6-16; the lofted object tilts at an angle.

5. Invoke the **Zoom Extents All Selected** tool. Now, in the Front viewport, right-click on the same vertex; the quad menu is displayed. Choose **Bezier** from the upper-left quadrant; the bezier handle is displayed. Since this is an end vertex, there is only one handle.

6. Using the **Select and Move** tool from the **Main Toolbar**, move the bezier handle to the right so that the path is slightly curved; the lofted object curves with the path, as shown in Figure 6-17.

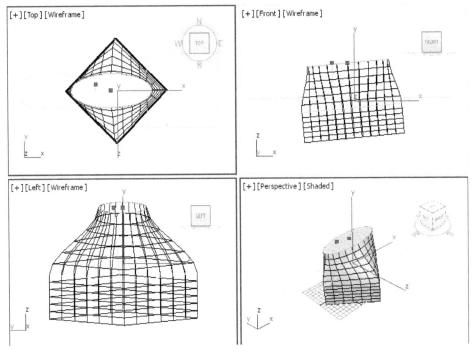

Figure 6-16 The top vertex of the path moved

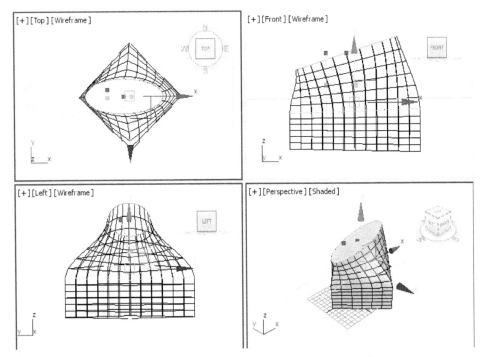

Figure 6-17 The lofted object curves with the path

Moving Shapes with Respect to the Path

The shapes are always perpendicular to the path along which you loft them. In this section, you will move the shape with respect to the path using the sub-object mode.

1. In the modifier stack, select the **Shape** level. Next, make sure the **Select and Move** tool is invoked from the **Main Toolbar** and choose the **Transform Gizmo Z Plane Constraint** button from the **Axis Constraints** toolbar.

2. In the Front viewport, make sure the ellipse in the lofted object is selected. Next, move it downward. Notice that the shape moves perpendicular to the path. Also, the object is slightly skewed as the ellipse moves away from the path, as shown in Figure 6-18.

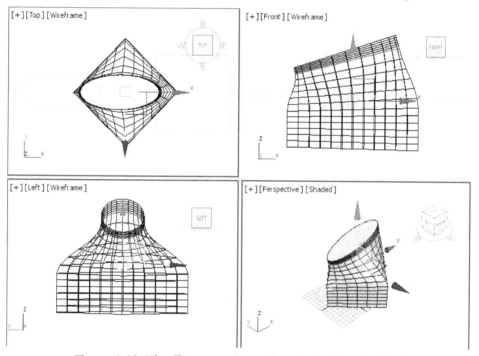

Figure 6-18 *The ellipse moved away from the path (to the right)*

3. In the **Align** area of the **Shape Commands** rollout, choose the **Right** button; the ellipse is shifted to the left such that its right edge lies on the path, as shown in Figure 6-19.

4. In the **Align** area of the **Shape Commands** rollout, choose the **Center** button; the ellipse is centered on the path.

5. Choose **Save** from the **Application** menu to save the scene.

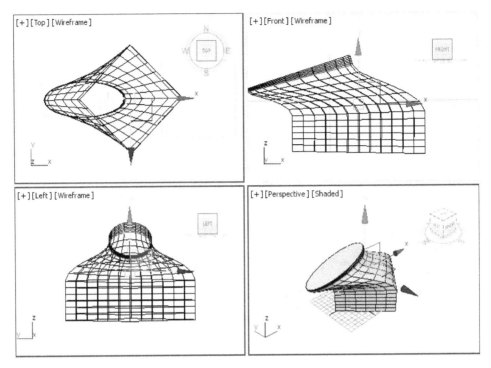

*Figure 6-19 The ellipse aligned on the right by using the **Right** button*

Tutorial 3

In this tutorial, you will draw a circle and loft it along a line. Next, you will use the deformation tools such as **Scale**, **Twist**, **Teeter**, **Bevel**, and **Fit** to modify the loft object to obtain different shapes.   **(Expected time: 25 min)**

The following steps are required to complete this tutorial:

a. Create the project folder.
b. Create and loft shapes.
c. Use the scale deformation.
d. Use the twist deformation.
e. Use the teeter deformation.
f. Use the bevel deformation.
g. Use the fit deformation.

Creating the Project Folder

Create the project folder with the name *c06_tut3* in the *3dsmaxdesign 2015* folder, as discussed in Tutorial 1 of Chapter 2.

Creating and Lofting Shapes

1. Invoke the **Maximize Viewport Toggle** tool from the viewport navigation controls to display all four viewports.

2. Activate the **Snap Toggle** tool by right-clicking on the **3D Snap** tool from the **Snaps Toggle** flyout in the **Main Toolbar**; the **Grid and Snap Settings** dialog box is displayed. In the **Snaps** tab, select the **Grid Points** check box, if it is not already selected, and then close the dialog box.

3. Choose **Create > Shapes** in the Command Panel. Next, use the **Line** and **Circle** tools from the **Object Type** rollout to create a line (from bottom to top) and a circle in the Top viewport; a line and a circle are created, refer to Figure 6-20. Exit the **Line** and **Circle** tools by pressing the ESC key. Next, invoke the **Zoom Extents All** tool from the viewport navigation controls.

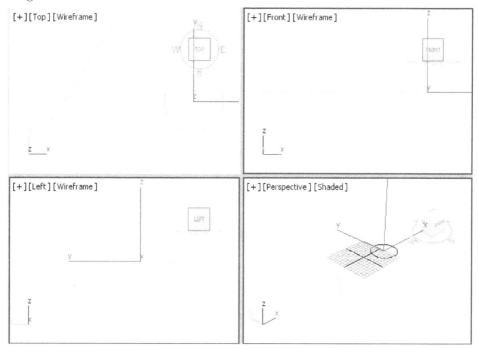

Figure 6-20 *A line and a circle created*

4. Select the line, if it is not already selected. Next, choose the **Geometry** button in the **Create** tab of the **Command Panel** and then select **Compound Objects** from the drop-down list. Invoke the **Loft** tool from the **Object Type** rollout.

5. In the **Creation Method** rollout, choose the **Get Shape** button and then select the circle; the circle is lofted along the line.

6. Expand the **Skin Parameters** rollout and set **3** in the **Shape Steps** spinner and **10** in the **Path Steps** spinner.

7. Invoke the **Zoom Extents All Selected** tool from the viewport navigation controls to zoom the lofted object to its extents, as shown in Figure 6-21.

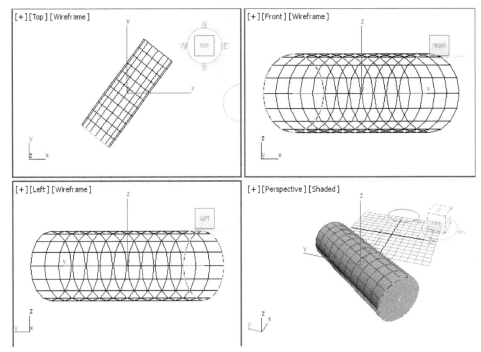

Figure 6-21 The lofted object zoomed

Using the Scale Deformation

In this section, you will deform the lofted object using the **Scale Deformation(X)** dialog box.

1. Make sure the lofted object is selected and then choose the **Modify** tab in the **Command Panel**.

2. Expand the **Deformations** rollout to display all five deformation buttons are listed in this rollout.

3. Choose the **Scale** button in the **Deformations** rollout; the **Scale Deformation(X)** dialog box is displayed, as shown in Figure 6-22.

    In this dialog box, the horizontal red line represents the path steps along the X axis of the lofted object. The left point of the line represents the first vertex of the path. The number in the ruler at the top represents the length of the path in percentage. The vertical location of the line in the dialog box represents the scale in percentage, as noted on the vertical ruler. The left and right vertices at the same vertical point (100) show that the lofted object is not scaled.

4. Invoke the **3D Snap** tool from the **Snaps Toggle** flyout in the **Main Toolbar** to turn snapping on.

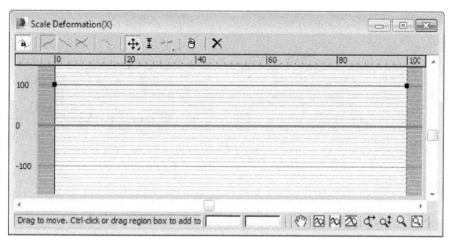

Figure 6-22 *The **Scale Deformation(X)** dialog box*

When you select any of the snap tools, the cursor snaps to the vertical gridlines in the **Scale Deformation(X)** dialog box.

5. Choose the **Move Control Point** button in the **Scale Deformation(X)** dialog box, if it is not already chosen.

6. Move the right vertex down by six lines until 40 is displayed in the right text box at the bottom of the dialog box, as shown in Figure 6-23; the lofted object tapers to 40% of its original size at the last vertex, refer to Figure 6-24.

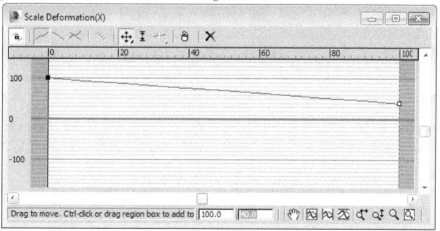

Figure 6-23 *The vertex moved in the **Scale Deformation(X)** dialog box*

7. Choose the **Insert Corner Point** button in the **Scale Deformation(X)** dialog box and then click on the red line near 40 (refer to the ruler at the top); a vertex is added at this point. To move the vertex to the precise position, enter **40** in the left-hand text box at the bottom of the dialog box and then press the ENTER key. In this way, the corner vertex is placed at the precise position.

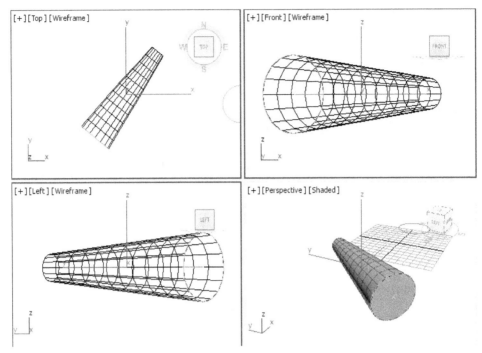

*Figure 6-24 The lofted object tapered after moving the vertex in the **Scale Deformation(X)** dialog box*

8. Choose the **Move Control Point** button and move this new vertex straight up above the top (100%) line by two lines, until 120 is displayed in the right text box at the bottom of the dialog box.

9. Choose the **Insert Corner Point** button and then click on the red line near 60 (refer to the ruler at the top). Next, enter **60** in the left text box and then press the ENTER key to place the vertex at the precise position.

10. Choose the **Move Control Point** button and move this new vertex below the top (100%) line by nine lines, until 10 is displayed in the right text box at the bottom of the dialog box, refer to Figure 6-25; a complex shape is created for the lofted object and is displayed in the viewports, as shown in Figure 6-26.

   Note
   *You can right-click on the control point to display the shortcut menu from which you can select **Bezier-Smooth** or **Bezier-Corner** to display the handles. By adjusting these handles, you can make curved deformations.*

11. Close the **Scale Deformation(X)** dialog box.

    Notice that the **Lightbulb** button next to the **Scale** button in the **Deformations** rollout is now activated, indicating that the deformation operation is on.

12. Choose the **Lightbulb** button next to the **Scale** button to turn the deformation off.

Figure 6-25 *Two vertices added and moved in the **Scale Deformation(X)** dialog box*

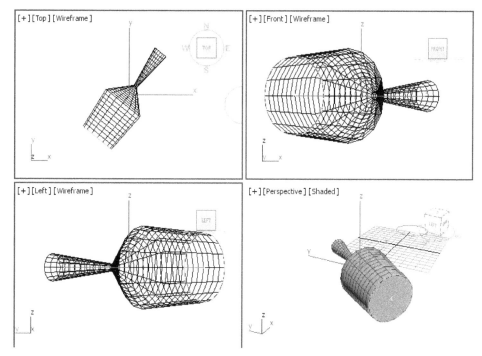

Figure 6-26 *The modified lofted object after adding and moving the vertices*

Using the Twist Deformation

In this section, you will deform the lofted object using the **Twist Deformation** dialog box.

1. In the **Deformations** rollout, choose the **Twist** button; the **Twist Deformation** dialog box is displayed, which is similar to the **Scale Deformation** dialog box, but with the red horizontal line at the 0 position. The horizontal line represents the degree of twist along the path axis.

2. Choose the **Insert Corner Point** button in this dialog box and then click on the red line near 40 (refer to the ruler at the top). Next, enter **40** in the left text box and then press the ENTER key to insert the point at the precise position.

3. Choose the **Move Control Point** button and move the left vertex up to 200 degrees (200 is displayed in the right text box). If 200 is not visible in the graph, use the scroll bar to view the point, refer to Figure 6-27; the lofted object twists 200 degrees between the starting point of the path and a point at 40% of the path's overall length, refer to Figure 6-28.

Figure 6-27 *Moving the vertex up to 200 degrees*

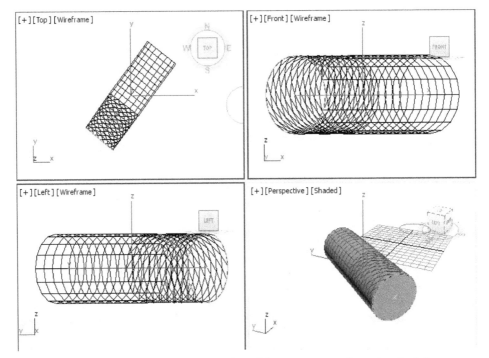

Figure 6-28 *The modified loft object after adding a vertex and moving the left vertex*

4. Close the **Twist Deformation** dialog box.

 Note
*If the twist is not readily visible in the shaded viewport, click on the **Realistic** label to display the shortcut menu and then choose **Edged Faces** from the shortcut menu to get a better display.*

5. In the **Deformations** rollout, choose the **Lightbulb** button next to the **Twist** button to turn the deformation off.

Using the Teeter Deformation

In this section, you will deform the lofted object using the **Teeter Deformation(Y)** dialog box.

1. In the **Deformations** rollout, choose the **Teeter** button; the **Teeter Deformation(X)** dialog box is displayed. The red horizontal line at the 0 position represents the teeter along X axis.

2. The **Make Symmetrical** button is activated by default. Choose this button to turn it off. Then, choose the **Display Y Axis** button; the red line turns green. This allows the lofted object to be teetered along the Y axis. The title bar of the dialog box indicates the presently displayed axis.

3. Choose the **Insert Corner Point** button in the dialog box and then click on the green line (Y axis) near 60. Enter **60** in the left-hand text box and press the ENTER key to place the vertex at the precise position.

4. Choose the **Move Control Point** button in the dialog box and move the right vertex up by five lines so that 50 is displayed in the right text box in the dialog box, as shown in Figure 6-29; the end of the lofted object is tilted 50 degrees along the Y axis, as shown in Figure 6-30.

Figure 6-29 Moving the right-hand vertex up by five lines

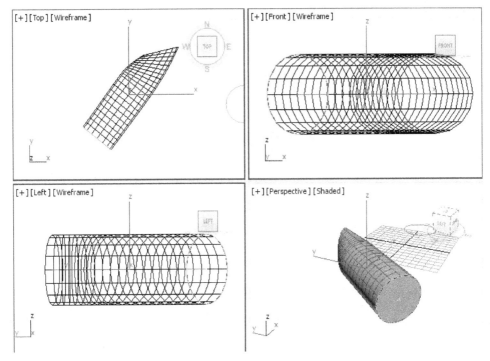

Figure 6-30 *The lofted object tilted along the Y axis*

5. Close the **Teeter Deformation(Y)** dialog box. In the **Deformations** rollout, choose the **Lightbulb** button next to the **Teeter** button to turn the deformation off.

Using the Bevel Deformation

In this section, you will bevel the lofted object using the **Bevel Deformation** dialog box.

1. In the **Deformations** rollout, choose the **Bevel** button; the **Bevel Deformation** dialog box is displayed. The **Bevel Deformation** dialog box works similar to the **Scale Deformation** dialog box. This dialog box is used to bevel the object equally on both X and Y axes.

2. Choose the **Insert Corner Point** button and then click on the red line near 40. Next, enter **40** in the left text box and press the ENTER key to place the vertex precisely. Similarly, place another corner point at 50.

3. Insert another corner point near 60. Next, enter **60** in the left-hand text box and press the ENTER key to place the vertex precisely.

4. Choose the **Move Control Point** button and move the vertex at point 50 down by 4 lines so that – 40 is displayed in the right text box, as shown in Figure 6-31; a lofted object is beveled at this point, as shown in Figure 6-32.

5. Close the **Bevel Deformation** dialog box. In the **Deformations** rollout, choose the **Lightbulb** button next to the **Bevel** deformation to turn the deformation off.

*Figure 6-31 The three vertices added in the **Bevel Deformation** dialog box and the middle vertex moved down*

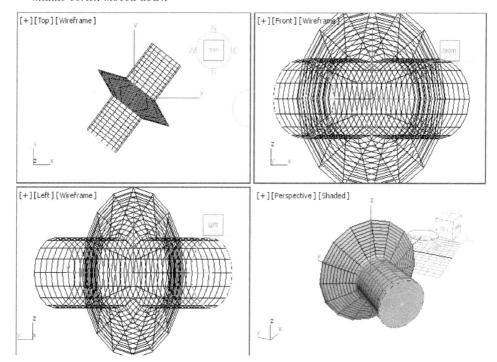

Figure 6-32 The lofted object beveled after inserting three vertices and moving the middle one

Using the Fit Deformation

In this section, you will deform the lofted object using the **Fit Deformation(X)** dialog box.

1. Choose **Create> Shapes** in the **Command Panel**. Next, invoke the **Line** tool from the **Object Type** rollout.

2. In the Top viewport, use the **Line** tool to draw a closed shape that represents the way you want the side view of the loft object to appear. Make the shape approximately of the same length as the loft object. Next, enter **Fit Shape (Side)** in the **Name and Color** rollout to rename the objects, refer to Figure 6-33.

Figure 6-33 *Two closed shapes created in the Top viewport*

To draw the fit shape, maximize, zoom, and pan the viewport as needed. Edit the lines at the **Vertex** sub-object level to add smoothness and to get the desired shapes. In order to easily visualize the results of the fit deformation, both the shapes drawn should be of full size, and should have the same length.

3. Draw another closed shape that represents the way you want the loft object to appear when viewed from the top. Next, enter **Fit Shape (Top)** in the **Name and Color** rollout. Invoke the **Zoom Extents All** tool to zoom the objects to their extents, as shown in Figure 6-33.

4. Make sure the object level is activated. Select the lofted object and make sure the **Modify** tab is chosen in the **Command Panel**. In the **Deformations** rollout, choose the **Fit** button; the **Fit Deformation(X)** dialog box is displayed. Unlike the other deformation tools, the **Fit Deformation(X)** dialog box enables you to deform the lofted object by loading the shapes, rather than by editing a baseline.

    The top and side profiles of the lofted object are adjusted so that they can be fitted inside the shapes you select as the fit shapes.

5. In the **Fit Deformation(X)** dialog box, make sure the **Make Symmetrical** button is chosen to turn off the forced symmetry. Also, make sure the **Display X Axis** button is chosen. Next, choose the **Get Shape** button at the top of the dialog box and select *Fit Shape (Top)* in any of the viewports; *Fit Shape (Top)* is displayed in the **Fit Deformation(X)** dialog box.

   You must select the shape using the cursor.

6. Invoke the **Zoom** tool and zoom in the graph to view the entire *Fit Shape (Top)*, refer to Figure 6-34.

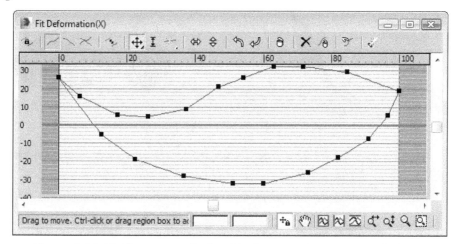

Figure 6-34 *Fit Shape (Top) displayed in the **Fit Deformation(X)** dialog box*

7. Choose the **Display Y Axis** button. Choose the **Get Shape** button at the top of the dialog box and select *Fit Shape (Side)* in any of the viewports; *Fit Shape (Side)* is displayed in the **Fit Deformation(Y)** dialog box, as shown in Figure 6-35.

Figure 6-35 *Fit Shape (Side) displayed in the **Fit Deformation(Y)** dialog box*

Note
*When you adjust the fit shapes at the **Vertex** sub-object level in the **Fit Deformation** dialog box, the lofted object will be automatically updated in the viewports to reflect the change.*

8. Close the **Fit Deformation(Y)** dialog box. Make sure the **Zoom Extents All Selected** tool is invoked from the viewport navigation controls; the lofted object is displayed in the viewports. The shape of the lofted object is clearly determined by the fit shapes, as shown in Figure 6-36.

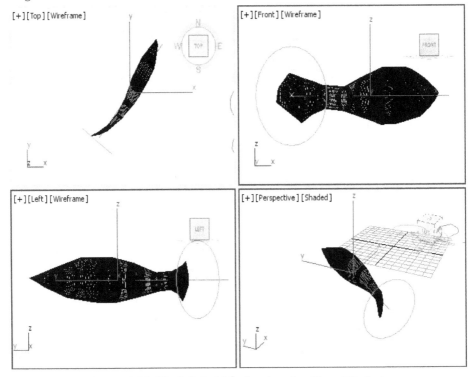

Figure 6-36 The lofted object showing the effect of fit shapes

In the **Deformations** rollout, you may turn on different deformations individually and in combinations by choosing the **Lightbulb** buttons next to the deformation names.

 Note
*While applying the **Scale**, **Teeter**, or **Fit** deformation to a lofted object, you can make changes to the X and Y axes separately by using the **Make Symmetrical** button.*

9. Choose **Save** from the **Application** menu to save the scene.

Self-Evaluation Test

Answer the following questions and then compare them to those given at the end of this chapter:

1. Which of the following shortcut keys is used to invoke the **Angle Snap Toggle** tool?

    (a) A   (b) Z
    (c) C   (d) None of these

2. Which of the following buttons in the **Creation Method** rollout is used to select the shape of the loft feature?

    (a) **Get Path**   (b) **Get Shape**
    (c) both of the above   (d) None of the above

3. Which of the following rollouts in the **Command Panel** is available when the **Shape** sub-object mode is active for the lofted object?

    (a) **Surface Properties**   (b) **Shape Commands**
    (c) **Soft Selection**   (d) **Geometry**

4. To avoid twisting of multiple shapes while lofting them, _____ of the shapes should be aligned.

5. In the **Teeter Deformation** dialog box, the currently displayed axis is indicated in the _____ of the dialog box.

6. The _____ button in the **Compare** window is used to load shapes into the window.

7. The _____ option in the **Align** area of the **Shape Commands** rollout centers the shape on the path.

8. You can loft a number of different _____ along a single path.

9. Select the _____ check box in the **Skin Parameters** rollout to display the skin of the lofted object.

10. You can add shapes along different _____ of a path.

11. Select the _____ check box in the **Path Parameters** rollout to enable the **Snap** spinner.

12. The **Bevel Deformation** dialog box is used to bevel an object equally on both X and Y axes. (T/F)

13. The lightbulb buttons next to the deformation names are used to turn on or off the effects of deformations. (T/F)

14. When you apply a fit deformation to a lofted object, the shapes used to create the loft are replaced with the fit shapes. (T/F)

15. You can apply a maximum of three deformations to a lofted object. (T/F)

16. When applying the **Scale**, **Teeter**, or **Fit** deformation to a lofted object, you can make the changes to the X and Y axes separately by making the **Make Symmetrical** button inactive. (T/F)

17. The shapes in the lofted object can be moved to different levels of the path. (T/F)

18. Once the lofted object is created, the shape of the path cannot be changed. (T/F)

19. The shapes can be moved with respect to the path using the sub-object mode. (T/F)

20. You can use the capping options to open or close the ends of a lofted object. (T/F)

Review Questions

Answer the following questions:

1. Which of the following buttons in the **Fit Deformation** dialog box is used to move control vertices?

    (a) **Insert corner Point**   (b) **Move Control Point**
    (c) **Scale Control Point**   (d) **Delete Control Point**

2. The _____ button is used to insert new values in the **Scale Deformation** dialog box.

3. The _____ button is used to create 3D objects by lofting 2D objects along a spline path.

4. If the vertices of the lofted object are not aligned, the object gets _____ .

5. The shapes are always _____ to the path along which you loft them.

6. In the **Creation Method** rollout, you need to make sure that the _____ radio button is selected before lofting the object.

7. In the **Skin Parameters** rollout, clear the _____ check box to open the top end of the lofted object.

8. To get a better view of the model, use the _____ button to adjust the view in the Perspective viewport.

9. In the **Fit Deformation** dialog box, the green horizontal line represents the X axis. (T/F)

10. The **Bevel Deformation** dialog box works similar to the **Scale Deformation** dialog box. (T/F)

11. The shapes in the lofted object can be moved and copied to different levels of the path. (T/F)

12. If you modify the path along which you loft the objects, the lofted object also gets modified. (T/F)

13. You cannot increase or decrease the smoothness of the lofted object around the created path. (T/F)

EXERCISES

The rendered output of the model used in the following exercises can be accessed by downloading the *c06_3dsmaxdesign_2015_exr.zip* from *www.cadcim.com*. The path of the file is as follows: *Textbooks > Animation and Visual Effects > 3ds Max Design > Autodesk 3ds Max Design 2015: A Tutorial Approach*

Exercise 1

In this exercise, you will create a propeller using a circle and an ellipse, refer to Figure 6-37. Both these shapes will be lofted along straight lines, as shown in Figure 6-38. Add material, lights, and camera, and then render the model, refer to Figure 6-39.

(Expected time: 30 min)

Figure 6-37 *The circular and ellipse shapes*   **Figure 6-38** *Shapes to be lofted*

Figure 6-39 *The propeller model*

Exercise 2

In this exercise, you will draw shapes and loft them to create the travel mug, as shown in Figures 6-40 and 6-41. The lofted objects must be modified to create the final model. Next, add lights and materials to the objects.   **(Expected time: 30 min)**

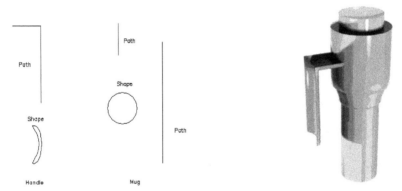

Figure 6-40 *Lofted shapes*   *Figure 6-41* *The travel mug*

Answers to Self-Evaluation Test

1. a, **2.** b, **3.** b, **4.** vertices, **5.** title bar, **6. Pick Shape**, **7. Center**, **8.** shapes, **9. Skin**, **10.** levels, **11. On**, **12.** T, **13.** T, **14.** T, **15.** F, **16.** T, **17.** T, **18.** F, **19.** T, **20.** T

Chapter 7

Material Editor:
Creating Materials

Learning Objectives

After completing this chapter, you will be able to:

- *Create materials in the material library*
- *Apply ambient and diffuse properties of the materials*
- *Assign materials to the objects*
- *Render the scene for the final output*

INTRODUCTION

In this chapter, you will create and apply materials to 3D objects. You will use the **Material Editor** dialog box to create materials and then apply them to 3D objects. The materials you create will be stored in a material library. Later, these materials can be assigned to other 3D objects.

TUTORIAL

Before starting the tutorial, you need to download the *c07_3dsmaxdesign_2015_tut.zip* file from *www.cadcim.com*. The path of the file is as follows: *Textbooks > Animation and Visual Effects > 3ds Max Design > Autodesk 3ds Max Design 2015: A Tutorial Approach*

Extract the contents of the zip file and save them in the *Documents* folder.

Tutorial 1

In this tutorial, you will create the materials to be applied to a traffic signal. You will create shiny red, green, and yellow materials for lights using the **Material Editor** dialog box, as shown in Figure 7-1.   **(Expected time: 25min)**

Figure 7-1 *The traffic signal model with materials applied*

The following steps are required to complete this tutorial:

a.   Create the project folder.
b.   Open the file.
c.   Create a new material library.
d.   Create the red light material.
e.   Create the yellow light material.
f.   Create the green light material.
g.   Save the material library.
h.   Assign materials to objects.
i.   Save and render the scene.

Creating the Project Folder

Create the project folder with the name *c07_tut1* in the *3dsmaxdesign 2015* folder, as discussed in Tutorial 1 of Chapter 2.

Opening the File

1. Choose **Open** from the **Application** menu; the **Open File** dialog box is displayed. In this dialog box, browse to the location *\Documents\c07_3dsmaxdesign_2015_tut.zip* and select the **c07_tut1_start.max** file from it. Choose the **Open** button to open this file; a modeled traffic signal is displayed in the Perspective viewport, as shown in Figure 7-2. Two materials have been defined and assigned in the scene: one material is assigned to the case and the other to three hoods.

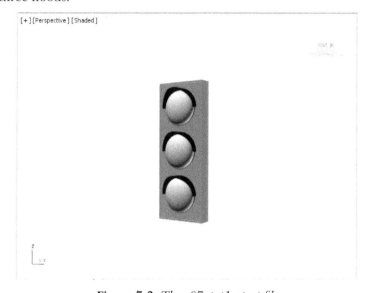

Figure 7-2 The c07_tut1_start file

Note
*While opening a Max file, if the **Missing External Files** message box is displayed, choose the **Continue** button. Next, press SHIFT + T; the **Asset Tracking** window will be displayed. In this window, right-click on the file name whose status is displayed as **File Missing**; a quad menu will be displayed. Choose **Browse** from it; the **Browse Image File** dialog box will be displayed. Navigate to the folder where you have saved the images and then choose the **Open** button; you will notice that the status of the selected file is changed to **Found** in the **Asset Tracking** window. Repeat this process for other such files as well and then close this window.*

2. Choose **Save As** from the **Application** menu; the **Save File As** dialog box is displayed. Browse to the location *\Documents\3dsmaxdesign 2015\c07_tut1\scenes*. Save the file with the name *c07tut1.max* at this location.

Creating a New Material Library

In this section, you will create a new material library in which you can store new materials.

1. Choose **Rendering > Material Editor > Compact Material Editor** from the menu bar; the **Material Editor** dialog box is displayed, as shown in Figure 7-3. You will notice that the **Case** and **Hood** materials are already defined.

*Figure 7-3 The **Material Editor** dialog box*

2. Choose the **Get Material** button in the **Material Editor** dialog box; the **Material/Map Browser** dialog box is displayed.

3. Choose the **Material/Map Browser Options** button in the **Material/Map Browser** dialog box; the Material/Map Browser Options flyout is displayed, as shown in Figure 7-4. Select **New Material Library** from the Material/Map Browser Options flyout; the **Create New Material Library** dialog box is displayed, as shown in Figure 7-5.

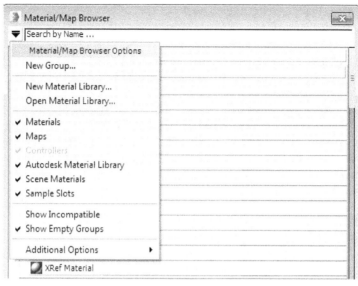

Figure 7-4 The **Material/Map Browser Options** *drop-down list*

Figure 7-5 The **Create New Material Library** *dialog box*

4. Enter **signal** as the new name for the material library and choose the **Save** button; the new **signal** material library is displayed in the **Material/Map Browser** dialog box.

5. Close the **Material/Map Browser** dialog box to return to the **Material Editor** dialog box.

Creating the Red Light Material

In this section, you will create material for the red light of the signal.

1. Select the first material sample slot in the **Material Editor** dialog box to make it the current sample; the properties for the material are displayed below the material samples.

2. Choose the **Arch & Design** button available in the **Material Editor** dialog box to change the material type; the **Material/Map Browser** dialog box is displayed. In this dialog box, select **Standard** from the **Materials > Standard** rollout and then choose the **OK** button; the **Arch & Design** material is replaced by the **Standard** material in the **Material Editor** dialog box. Also, various rollouts are displayed in the **Material Editor** dialog box to modify the **Standard** material.

3. In the **Shader Basic Parameters** rollout, make sure **Blinn** is selected in the drop-down list. This sets the rendering characteristics of the color being created.

    Note
    *If the material is transparent or semi transparent, or if the object on which the material is to be assigned is an open-ended object, like an uncapped loft, you need to select the **2-Sided** check box in the **Shader Basic Parameters** rollout.*

4. In the **Blinn Basic Parameters** rollout, choose the **Ambient** color swatch; the **Color Selector: Ambient Color** dialog box is displayed.

    If the lock button between the **Ambient** and **Diffuse** color swatches (to the left of the labels) is active, choose it to make it inactive. Otherwise, the same color will be used for ambient and diffuse settings.

5. In this dialog box, set the values as given next:

    Hue: **255**   Sat: **255**   Value: **89**

    Choose the **OK** button to exit the **Color Selector**: **Ambient Color** dialog box; the ambient portion of the material color is set to maroon.

    Note
    *The **Value** spinner controls the brightness of a color. Lower the value in this spinner, darker will be the ambient portion of the color.*

6. Choose **Rendering > Environment** from the menu bar; the **Environment and Effects** dialog box is displayed. In this dialog box, the **Environment** tab is chosen by default. Next, choose the **Ambient** color swatch in the **Global Lighting** area of the **Common Parameters** rollout; the **Color Selector: Ambient Light** dialog box is displayed. Using this dialog box, you can adjust the color and intensity of ambient light in the scene.

Note

Autodesk 3ds Max Design uses the ambient and diffuse properties of a material to shade an object as if it is three-dimensional. The ambient portion of a color describes the part of an object that is not under direct light, but in shadow. The diffuse portion of a color describes the part that is in normal lighting conditions. By adjusting only these two values, a matte or a non-glossy material is created.

7. In the **Color Selector: Ambient Light** dialog box, set the value **29** in the **Value** spinner. Note the change in the material sample in the **Material Editor** dialog box. Choose the **OK** button to exit the **Color Selector: Ambient Light** dialog box. Also, close the **Environment and Effects** dialog box.

Changing the value of the ambient light setting from 0 to 29 adds a small amount of white ambient light to the scene. If the ambient light value is set to 0 (black), the **Ambient** color settings for the material have no effect. As ambient light is increased in the scene, the ambient color portion of the material has more effect on the material's overall appearance.

8. Choose the **Diffuse** color swatch in the **Blinn Basic Parameters** area of the **Material Editor** dialog box; the **Color Selector: Diffuse Color** dialog box is displayed. In this dialog box, set the values as given next:

Red: **168**   Green: **0**   Blue: **0**

This sets the diffuse portion of the color to medium red.

9. Choose the **OK** button to close the **Color Selector: Diffuse Color** dialog box; the new material is displayed in the **Material Editor** dialog box.

You need to set the specular value for shiny materials. Shiny materials are represented by highlights when rendered. The specular portion of the color describes hue, saturation, and intensity of the highlights visible when a shiny object is rendered. The strength and shape of the highlight is controlled by the specular highlight settings.

Now, you will make the material shiny.

10. With the first material sample slot selected, choose the **Specular** color swatch in the **Blinn Basic Parameters** rollout; the **Color Selector: Specular Color** dialog box is displayed.

11. In the **Color Selector: Specular Color** dialog box, set the values as given next:

Red: **255**   Green: **200**   Blue: **200**

This will lighten the specular color.

12. Choose the **OK** button to close the **Color Selector: Specular Color** dialog box.

13. In the **Specular Highlights** area of the **Blinn Basic Parameters** rollout, set the value **60** in the **Specular Level** spinner and **20** in the **Glossiness** spinner.

The **Specular Level** spinner determines the intensity or brightness of the specular highlight. The **Glossiness** spinner determines the size of the specular highlight.

Now, you need to name the material and put it in the material library. After the material is saved in the library, it can be accessed and assigned to objects in other scenes.

14. Change the name of the material to **Red light** by entering it in the drop-down list located on the left of the **Standard** button in the **Material Editor** dialog box.

The name of the material is changed and it appears in the **Material Editor** dialog box as well.

15. Choose the **Put To Library** button in the **Material Editor** dialog box; a flyout is displayed.

16. Choose **signal.mat** (the newly created material library) from the flyout, as shown in Figure 7-6; the **Put To Library** dialog box is displayed, as shown in Figure 7-7.

*Figure 7-6 Choosing **signal.mat** from the flyout*

17. The name *Red light* appears in the **Name** text box. You can either put this material into the library by using the default name or give it a new name. To use the current name, choose the **OK** button; the current material is added under the *signal* material library.

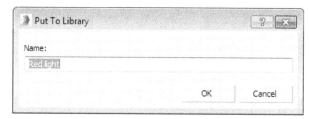

*Figure 7-7 The **Put To Library** dialog box*

18. Choose the **Get Material** button in the **Material Editor** dialog box; the **Material/Map Browser** dialog box is displayed. In this dialog box, click on **signal.mat** to expand it, if not already expanded. You will notice that the *Red light* material is added to it, as shown in Figure 7-8.

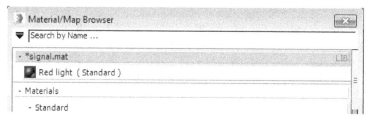

*Figure 7-8 The **Red light** material added to the material library*

19. Close the **Material/Map Browser** dialog box to return to the **Material Editor** dialog box.

Note
You can copy material by dragging it from one sample slot to another.

Creating the Yellow Light Material

In this section, you will create material for the yellow light of the signal.

1. Select the second available material sample slot in the **Material Editor** dialog box.

2. Choose the **Arch & Design** button to change the material type; the **Material/Map Browser** dialog box is displayed. In this dialog box, select **Standard** from the **Materials > Standard** rollout and then choose the **OK** button; the **Arch & Design** material is replaced by the **Standard** material in the **Material Editor** dialog box. Also, various rollouts are displayed in the **Material Editor** dialog box to modify the **Standard** material.

3. In the **Shader Basic Parameters** rollout, make sure **Blinn** is selected in the drop-down list.

4. In the **Blinn Basic Parameters** rollout, unlock the **Ambient** and **Diffuse** color swatches, if locked. Next, choose the **Ambient** color swatch; the **Color Selector: Ambient Color** dialog box is displayed.

5. In this dialog box, set the values as given next:

Red: **245**   Green: **183**   Blue: **15**

6. Choose the **OK** button to close the **Color Selector: Ambient Color** dialog box.

    Since the value of the ambient light setting has already been increased for the scene, you do not need to adjust the value.

7. Choose the **Diffuse** color swatch in the **Material Editor** dialog box; the **Color Selector: Diffuse Color** dialog box is displayed.

8. In the **Color Selector: Diffuse Color** dialog box, set the values as given next:

    Red: **245**   Green: **183**   Blue: **15**

    Note
    *The **Red**, **Green**, **Blue** spinners control the amount of color being mixed together. Greater the value, lighter will be the color. Setting all three colors to **0** creates a black material, whereas setting all three colors to **255** creates a white material.*

9. Choose the **OK** button to close the **Color Selector: Diffuse Color** dialog box.

    Now, you will make the material shiny.

10. Choose the **Specular** color swatch in the **Blinn Basic Parameters** rollout; the **Color Selector: Specular Color** dialog box is displayed.

11. In this dialog box, set the values as given next:

    Red: **255**   Green: **255**   Blue: **62**

12. Choose the **OK** button to close the **Color Selector: Specular Color** dialog box.

13. In the **Material Editor** dialog box, set the values in the **Specular Highlights** area as given next:

    Specular Level: **60**   Glossiness: **20**

    Now, you need to name the material and put it in the material library.

14. Change the name of the material to **Yellow light** by entering it in the drop-down list located on the left of the **Standard** button in the **Material Editor** dialog box.

15. Choose the **Put to Library** button in the **Material Editor** dialog box; a flyout is displayed.

16. Choose **signal.mat** (newly created material library) from the flyout; the **Put To Library** dialog box is displayed.

17. The name **Yellow light** is displayed in the **Name** text box. To use the same name, choose the **OK** button; the current material is added under the *signal* material library.

Creating the Green Light Material
In this section, you will create material for the green light of the signal.

1. Select the third material sample slot in the **Material Editor** dialog box.

2. Choose the **Arch & Design** button to change the material type; the **Material/Map Browser** dialog box is displayed again. In this dialog box, select **Standard** from the **Materials > Standard** rollout and then choose the **OK** button; the **Arch & Design** material is replaced by the **Standard** material in the **Material Editor** dialog box. Also, various rollouts are displayed in the **Material Editor** dialog box to modify the **Standard** material.

3. In the **Shader Basic Parameters** rollout, make sure **Blinn** is selected in the drop-down list.

4. In the **Blinn Basic Parameters** rollout, unlock the **Diffuse** and **Ambient** colors. Choose the **Ambient** color swatch; the **Color Selector: Ambient Color** dialog box is displayed. In this dialog box, set the values as given next:

    Red: **0**   Green: **50**   Blue: **0**

    The ambience level of the material color is set to dark green.

5. Choose the **OK** button to close the **Color Selector: Ambient Color** dialog box.

6. Choose the **Diffuse** color swatch in the **Material Editor** dialog box; the **Color Selector: Diffuse Color** dialog box is displayed. In this dialog box, set the values as given next:

    Red: **0**   Green: **225**   Blue: **0**

    The diffuse portion of the material color is set to bright green.

7. Choose the **OK** button to close the **Color Selector: Diffuse Color** dialog box.

    Now, you will make the material shiny.

8. Choose the **Specular** color swatch in the **Blinn Basic Parameters** rollout; the **Color Selector: Specular Color** dialog box is displayed.

9. In this dialog box, set the values as given next:

    Red: **0**   Green: **47**   Blue: **0**

10. Choose the **OK** button to close the **Color Selector: Specular Color** dialog box.

11. In the **Specular Highlights** area of the **Blinn Basic Parameters** rollout, set the values as given next:

    Specular Level: **60**   Glossiness: **20**

Now, you need to make the material self-illuminating to make the object appear glowing. It is achieved by replacing a percentage of the ambient color with the diffuse color in the shadowed areas of the object.

12. In the **Self-Illumination** area of the **Blinn Basic Parameters** rollout, set the value in the **Color** spinner to **85**. If you set the value in the **Color** spinner closer to 100, the material appears brighter.

    Now, you need to name the material and put it in the material library.

13. Change the name of the material to **Green light** by entering it in the drop-down list located on the left of the **Standard** button in the **Material Editor** dialog box.

14. Choose the **Put to Library** button in the **Material Editor** dialog box; a flyout is displayed. Choose **signal** from the flyout; the **Put To Library** dialog box is displayed.

15. The name *Green light* is displayed in the **Name** text box. To use the same name, choose the **OK** button; the current material is added under the *signal* material library.

Saving the Material Library

The changes made to the material library must be saved. Else, they will be lost when you exit the current file in 3ds Max Design. In this section, you will save the material library.

1. Choose the **Get Material** button in the **Material Editor** dialog box; the **Material/Map Browser** dialog box is displayed. Next, right-click on the **signal.mat** rollout; a shortcut menu is displayed. Choose **Save** from the shortcut menu, as shown in Figure 7-9; the **Export Material Library** dialog box is displayed.

2. Close the **Material/Map Browser** dialog box.

Assigning Materials to Objects

The materials have been created and the material library is saved. In this section, you will assign materials to the objects in the scene.

1. Select **Red** from the **Scene Explorer** located left on the interface; *Red* is selected in the viewport.

2. In the **Material Editor** dialog box, select the material sample slot which is named as *Red light*; the *Red light* material is set as the current material.

3. Choose the **Assign Material to Selection** button; the currently selected material is assigned to *Red*. Similarly, assign the material *Yellow light* to *Yellow* and *Green light* to *Green*. Next, close the **Material Editor** dialog box.

Figure 7-9 *Saving the material library*

Note
A material can also be assigned to an object by dragging the material sample slot into the scene and dropping it on the object.

Saving and Rendering the Scene

In this section, you will save the scene that you have created and then render it. You can also view the final rendered image of this model by downloading the *c07_3dsmaxdesign_2015_rndr.zip* file from *www.cadcim.com*. The path of the file is as follows: *Textbooks > Animation and Visual Effects > 3ds Max Design > Autodesk 3ds Max Design 2015: A Tutorial Approach*

1. Choose **Save** from the **Application** menu.

2. Activate the Perspective viewport. Next, invoke the **Render Production** tool from the **Main Toolbar**; the rendered image is displayed, refer to Figure 7-10.

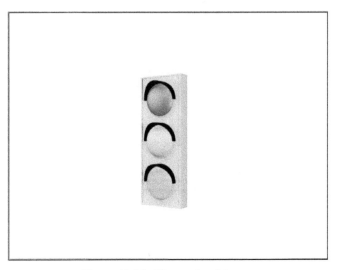

Figure 7-10 *The rendered image*

Self-Evaluation Test

Answer the following questions and then compare them to those given at the end of this chapter:

1. Which of the following buttons is used to invoke the **Material/Map Browser** dialog box?

    (a) **Put to Library**   (b) **Get Material**
    (c) **Go to Parent**   (d) None of these

2. The _____ dialog box displays all materials available in the currently open material library.

3. The _____ portion of a color describes the part of an object that is not under direct light but in shadow.

4. By adjusting the _____ and _____ portions of a material, you can create a matte, or a non-glossy material.

5. While defining a material, if you set the value of the red, green, and blue colors to _____, it will create a black material.

6. The _____ portion of the color describes the highlights of a shiny material.

7. The appearance of the highlights in a material is controlled by the _____ and _____ spinners.

8. Once the material is saved in the library, it can be assigned to objects. (T/F)

Review Questions

Answer the following questions:

1. Which of the following color swatches in the **Blinn Basic Parameters** rollout specifies the part of an object under normal light conditions?

    (a) **Ambient**   (b) **Diffuse**
    (c) **Specular**   (d) None of these

2. The 3ds Max Design uses the _____ and _____ properties of a material to shade an object.

3. If an object is transparent, semitransparent, or open ended, you need to select the _____ check box in the **Shader Basic Parameters** rollout.

4. If the lock button is turned on between the **Ambient** and **Diffuse** color swatches, then different colors will be applied for ambient and diffuse settings. (T/F)

5. Lower the value of the ambient color, darker will be the colored portion. (T/F)

EXERCISE

The rendered output of the model used in the exercise given next can be accessed by downloading the *c07_maxdesign_2015_exr.zip* from *www.cadcim.com*. The path of the file is as follows: *Textbooks > Animation and Visual Effects > 3ds Max Design > Autodesk 3ds Max Design 2015: A Tutorial Approach*

Exercise 1

Create the materials needed to texture a scene containing five crayons, as shown in Figure 7-11. You will need five colors of your choice for the wrappers of crayons and five shiny colors for the crayons.   **(Expected time: 25min)**

Figure 7-11 *The crayons*

Chapter 8

Material Editor:
Texture Maps-I

Learning Objectives

After completing this chapter, you will be able to:
• *Apply texture maps*
• *Apply bump maps*

INTRODUCTION

In this chapter, you will learn to create materials using texture maps. Multiple texture maps can be used to create complex materials. In addition, you will also learn to use the bump maps.

TUTORIAL

Before starting the tutorial, you need to download the *c08_3dsmaxdesign_2015_tut.zip* file from *www.cadcim.com*. The path of the file is as follows: *Textbooks > Animation and Visual Effects > 3ds Max Design > Autodesk 3ds Max Design 2015: A Tutorial Approach*

Extract the contents of the zip file and save them in the *Documents* folder.

Tutorial 1

In this tutorial, you will create materials and then apply them to a checkerboard, as shown in Figure 8-1.   **(Expected time: 20 min)**

Figure 8-1 *The checkerboard after applying materials*

The following steps are required to complete this tutorial:

a. Create the project folder.
b. Open the file.
c. Create a new material library.
d. Create checkerboard border material.
e. Create the board material.
f. Create the red checker material.
g. Create the black checker material.
h. Save the material library.
i. Assign materials.
j. Save and render the scene.

Creating the Project Folder

Create the project folder with the name *c08_tut1* in the *3dsmaxdesign 2015* folder, as discussed in earlier chapters.

Opening the File

1. Open Windows Explorer and then browse to *\Documents\c08_3dsmaxdesign_2015_tut*. Next, copy the *checkerb.jpg, checkerr.jpg, checker1.jpg*, and *marble.gif* files to *\Documents\3dsmaxdesign 2015\c08_tut1\sceneassets\images*.

2. Choose **Open** from the **Application** menu; the **Open File** dialog box is displayed. In this dialog box, browse to the location *\Documents\c08_3dsmaxdesign_2015_tut.zip* and select the **c08_tut1_start.max** file from it. Choose the **Open** button to open the file, refer to Figure 8-2.

Figure 8-2 The c08_tut1_start file

3. Choose **Save As** from the **Application** menu; the **Save File As** dialog box is displayed. Browse to the location *\Documents\3dsmaxdesign 2015\c08_tut1\scenes*. Save the file with the name *c08tut1.max* at this location.

Creating a New Material Library

In this section, you will create a new material library by using the **Material Editor** dialog box.

1. Choose **Rendering > Material Editor > Compact Material Editor** from the menu bar; the **Material Editor** dialog box is displayed, as shown in Figure 8-3.

2. In this dialog box, choose the **Get Material** button; the **Material/Map Browser** dialog box is displayed.

3. Choose the **Material/Map Browser Options** button from the **Material/Map Browser**
    dialog box; a flyout is displayed. Choose **New Material Library** from the flyout, as
    shown in Figure 8-4; the **Create New Material Library** dialog box is displayed, as
    shown in Figure 8-5.

Figure 8-3 The Material Editor dialog box

As the project folder is already set, the *materiallibraries* folder of this project is displayed
in the **Save in** drop-down list.

4. In this dialog box, enter **Checker Board** in the **File name** text box and then choose the
    Save button; the new material library named **Checker Board** is created in the **Material/
    Map Browser** dialog box.

5. Close the **Material/Map Browser** dialog box to return to the **Material Editor** dialog box.

Creating Checker Board Border Material
In this section, you will create a checker board material.

1. Select the first material sample slot in the **Material Editor** dialog box to make it the current
    sample slot.

*Figure 8-4 Choosing **New Material Library** from the flyout*

*Figure 8-5 The **Create New Material Library** dialog box*

2. Choose the **Arch & Design** button to change the material type; the **Material/Map Browser** dialog box is displayed. In this dialog box, select **Standard** from the **Materials > Standard** rollout and then choose the **OK** button; the **Arch & Design** material is replaced by the **Standard** material in the **Material Editor** dialog box. Also, various rollouts are displayed in the **Material Editor** dialog box to modify the **Standard** material.

3. In the **Shader Basic Parameters** rollout, make sure **Blinn** is selected in the drop-down list. Next, expand the **Maps** rollout, refer to Figure 8-6.

4. Choose the **Diffuse Color** map button, which is currently labeled as **None**; the **Material/ Map Browser** dialog box is displayed showing the types of maps that can be added.

Tip: *You can also double-click on* **Standard** *to select it and then close the* **Material/Map Browser** *dialog box.*

5. Select the **Bitmap** map from the **Maps > Standard** rollout and then choose the **OK** button; the **Select Bitmap Image File** dialog box is displayed, as shown in Figure 8-7.

Figure 8-6 The **Maps** *rollout expanded*

6. In this dialog box, make sure **All Formats** is displayed in the **Files of type** drop-down list. As the project folder is already set, the *images* folder of this project is displayed in the **Look in** drop-down list. Select the file **marble.gif** and then choose the **Open** button; the image file is loaded and the parameters are displayed for the map in the **Material Editor** dialog box.

7. Click and hold on the **Sample Type** button located on the right side of the **Material Editor** dialog box; a flyout is displayed. Choose the **Square** button to switch the sample from sphere to square, refer to Figure 8-8.

8. Choose the **Show Shaded Material in Viewport** button in the **Material Editor** dialog box. This will make the bitmap image visible in the shaded viewport when you assign material to the object.

9. In the **Coordinates** rollout, clear the **Use Real-WorldScale** check box. Next, set the value **0.1** in the **U:Tiling** and **V:Tiling** spinners, as shown in Figure 8-9.

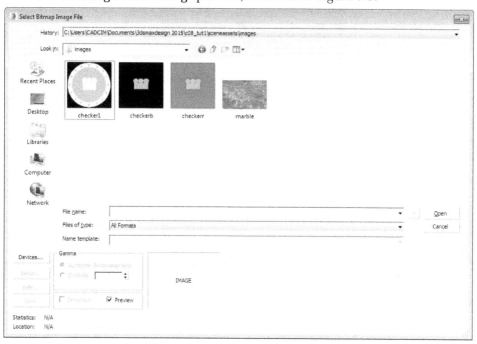

Figure 8-7 The *Select Bitmap Image File* dialog box

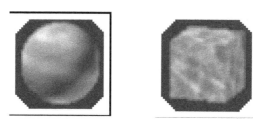

Figure 8-8 The sample switched from sphere to square in the *Material Editor* dialog box

10. Choose the **Go To Parent** button to return to the root level.

    Next, you will name the material created.

11. Choose the **Put to Library** button in the **Material Editor** dialog box; a flyout is displayed.

12. Choose the **Checker Board.mat** option from the flyout; the **Put To Library** dialog box is displayed.

*Figure 8-9 The **Coordinates** rollout after modifying the parameters*

13. Enter **Checker Board border** as the name of the new material in the **Put To Library** dialog box and choose the **OK** button; the material is assigned the name *Checker Board border* and is added to the **Checker Board** material library.

Creating the Board Material

In this section, you will create the board material.

1. In the **Material Editor** dialog box, select the second material sample slot. Next, choose the **Arch & Design** button to change the material type; the **Material/Map Browser** dialog box is displayed.

2. In this dialog box, select the **Standard** material from **Materials > Standard** rollout and then choose the **OK** button; the **Arch & Design** material is replaced by the **Standard** material. Also, various rollouts are displayed in the **Material Editor** dialog box to modify the **Standard** material.

3. Expand the **Maps** rollout and then choose the **Diffuse Color** map button that is currently labeled as **None**; the **Material/Map Browser** dialog box is displayed showing the types of maps that can be added.

4. Select the **Checker** map from the **Maps > Standard** rollout and choose the **OK** button; various rollouts for the **Checker** map are displayed in the **Material Editor** dialog box.

5. Make sure the **Use Real-World Scale** check box is cleared in the **Coordinates** rollout. Next, set the value **1** in the **Width:Tilling** and **Height:Tilling** spinners.

    The material currently resembles a portion of a black and white checkerboard.

6. Choose the **Show Shaded Material in Viewport** button in the **Material Editor** dialog box. Next, choose the **Go To Parent** button to return to the root level.

    Next, you will name the material created.

7. Choose the **Put to Library** button in the **Material Editor** dialog box; a flyout is displayed.

8. Choose the **Checker Board.mat** option from the flyout; the **Put To Library** dialog box is displayed.

9. Enter **Board** as the name of the new material in the **Put To Library** dialog box. Choose the **OK** button; the material is assigned the name *Board* and is added to the **Checker Board** material library.

Creating the Red Checker Material

In this section, you will create a red checker material with diffuse color and bump map. Also, you will assign the image to the bump map to make the surface of a material appear raised and lowered. Bump maps use a selected image file to make the surface of a material appear raised and lowered. Lighter pixels in the map will make the corresponding areas on the object appear to be raised while darker pixels on the map will make the corresponding areas on the object appear lowered. The value in the **Bump** spinner controls the intensity of the bumps.

1. Select the third material sample slot. Next, choose the **Arch & Design** button to change the material type; the **Material/Map Browser** dialog box is displayed.

2. In this dialog box, select the **Standard** material from **Materials > Standard** rollout and then choose the **OK** button; the **Arch & Design** material is replaced by the **Standard** material. Also, various rollouts are displayed in the **Material Editor** dialog box to modify the **Standard** material.

3. Expand the **Maps** rollout. Next, choose the **Diffuse Color** map button that is currently labeled as **None**; the **Material/Map Browser** dialog box is displayed showing the types of maps that can be added.

4. Select the **Bitmap** map from the **Maps > Standard** rollout and choose the **OK** button; the **Select Bitmap Image File** dialog box is displayed.

5. In this dialog box, make sure **All Formats** is selected in the **Files of type** drop-down list. As the project folder is already set, the *images* folder of this project is displayed in the **Look in** text box of this dialog box. Select the **checkerr.jpg** file and choose the **Open** button to open the image file.

6. In the **Coordinates** rollout of the **Material Editor** dialog box, clear the **Use Real-World Scale** check box. Set the value **1.0** in the **U: Tiling** and **V: Tiling** spinners.

7. Click and hold the **Sample Type** button on the right side of the **Material Editor** dialog box and choose the **Square** button to switch the sample from a sphere to a square, as done earlier.

   The material currently resembles a red checker with a gold crown at the center. To make the checker appear three-dimensional, you need to apply a bump map.

8. Choose the **Go To Parent** button in the **Material Editor** dialog box; the root level in the material definition is displayed.

9. In the **Maps** rollout, set the value in the **Bump** spinner to **90**.

   Now, a bump map needs to be assigned.

10. Choose the **Bump** map button, currently labeled as **None**; the **Material/Map Browser** dialog box is displayed again.

11. Select the **Bitmap** map from the **Maps > Standard** rollout and choose the **OK** button; the **Select Bitmap Image File** dialog box is displayed.

12. In this dialog box, make sure **All Formats** is selected in the **Files of type** drop-down list. As the project folder is already set, the *images* folder of this project is displayed in the **Look in** text box of this dialog box. Select the file **checker1.jpg** and choose the **Open** button; the selected image is displayed in the selected sample slot.

    You will notice that the preview displayed in the **Select Bitmap Image File** dialog box is a grayscale bitmap. The white area will be raised the most while the black area will not be raised at all.

13. In the **Coordinates** rollout of the **Material Editor** dialog box, clear the **Use Real-World Scale** check box. Set the value **1.0** in the **U: Tiling** and **V: Tiling** spinners.

14. Choose the **Show Shaded Material in Viewport** button in the **Material Editor** dialog box.

    Next, you will make the material shiny.

15. Choose the **Go To Parent** button in the **Material Editor** dialog box to return to the root level in the material definition and then collapse the **Maps** rollout.

16. Choose the **Specular** color swatch in the **Blinn Basic Parameters** rollout; the **Color Selector: Specular Color** dialog box is displayed.

17. In this dialog box, set the value **255** in the **Red**, **Green**, and **Blue** spinners; the specular color is set to white.

18. Choose the **OK** button to close the **Color Selector: Specular Color** dialog box.

19. In the **Specular Highlights** area of the **Blinn Basic Parameters** rollout, set the value **60** in the **Specular Level** spinner.

20. Set the value **20** in the **Glossiness** spinner.

    Next, you will name the material created.

21. Choose the **Put to Library** button in the **Material Editor** dialog box; a flyout is displayed.

22. Choose the **Checker Board.mat** from the flyout; the **Put To Library** dialog box is displayed.

23. Enter **Checker Red** as the name of the new material in the dialog box and choose the **OK** button; the material is added to the **Checker Board** material library.

Creating the Black Checker Material

In this section, you will create the black checker material.

1. Select the material sample slot next to the **Checker Red** material and choose the **Arch & Design** button to change the material type to **Standard** as discussed earlier.

2. Expand the **Maps** rollout and then choose the **Diffuse Color** map button, currently labeled **None**; the **Material/Map Browser** dialog box is displayed, showing the types of maps that may be added.

3. Select the **Bitmap** map from the **Maps > Standard** rollout and choose the **OK** button; the **Select Bitmap Image File** dialog box is displayed.

4. In this dialog box, make sure **All Formats** is selected in the **Files of type** drop-down list. As the project folder is already set, the *images* folder of this project is displayed in the **Look in** text box of this dialog box. Select the file **checkerb.jpg** and choose the **Open** button to open the image file; the selected image is displayed in the selected sample slot.

5. In the **Coordinates** rollout of the **Material Editor** dialog box, clear the **Use Real-World Scale** check box. Set the value **1.0** in the **U: Tiling** and **V: Tiling** spinners.

6. Click and hold the **Sample Type** button in the **Material Editor** dialog box and choose the **Square** button to switch the sample from a sphere to a square; the material currently resembles a black checker with a gold crown in the center.

7. Choose the **Go To Parent** button in the **Material Editor** dialog box; you will return to the root level in the material definition.

8. In the **Maps** rollout, set the value **90** in the **Bump** spinner; the intensity of the bump map is set.

   Now, a bump map needs to be assigned.

9. Choose the **Bump** map button, currently labeled **None**.

10. Select the **Bitmap** map from the **Maps > Standard** rollout and choose the **OK** button; the **Select Bitmap Image File** dialog box is displayed.

11. In this dialog box, select **All Formats** in the **Files of type** drop-down list. As the project folder is already set, the *images* folder of this project is displayed in the **Look in** text box of this dialog box. Select the file **checker1.jpg** and choose the **Open** button; a bump map is assigned to the material.

12. In the **Coordinates** rollout of the **Material Editor** dialog box, clear the **Use Real-World Scale** check box. Set the value **1.0** in the **U: Tiling** and **V: Tiling** spinners.

13. Choose the **Show Shaded Material in Viewport** button in the **Material Editor** dialog box.

   Next, you will make the material shiny.

14. Choose the **Go To Parent** button in the **Material Editor** dialog box to return to the root level in the material definition. Next, collapse the **Maps** rollout.

15. Choose the **Specular** color swatch in the **Blinn Basic Parameters** rollout; the **Color Selector: Specular Color** is displayed.

16. In this dialog box, set the value **255** in the **Red**, **Green**, and **Blue** spinners; the specular color is set to white. Now, choose the **OK** button to close the **Color Selector: Specular Color** dialog box.

17. In the **Specular Highlights** area of the **Blinn Basic Parameters** rollout, set the value **60** in the **Specular Level** spinner.

18. Set the value **15** in the **Glossiness** spinner.

   Next, you will name the material created.

19. Choose the **Put to Library** button in the **Material Editor** dialog box; a flyout is displayed.

20. Choose **Checker Board.mat** option (new material library that you have created); the **Put To Library** dialog box is displayed.

21. Enter **Checker Black** as the name of the new material in the **Put To Library** dialog box and choose the **OK** button; the material is assigned the name **Checker Black** and is added to the current material library.

Note
*While creating dark-colored material, you may choose the **Background** button in the **Material Editor** dialog box to change the sample material window background color from black to a multicolored pattern.*

Saving the Material Library
In this section, you will save the material library.

1. Choose the **Get Material** button in the **Material Editor** dialog box; the **Material/Map Browser** dialog box is displayed.

2. Right-click on **CheckerBoard.mat** in the **Material/Map Browser** dialog box; a flyout is displayed. Choose **Save** from the flyout, as shown in Figure 8-10.

Figure 8-10 Saving the Material Library

3. Close the **Material/Map Browser** dialog box.

Assigning Materials

In this section, you will assign materials to all objects in the scene.

1. Make sure the Camera viewport is activated.

2. Select **border** from the **Scene Explorer** located left of the interface.

3. In the **Material Editor** dialog box, select the **Checker Board border** material. Next,
    choose the **Assign Material to Selection** button; the currently selected object is
    assigned the **Checker Board border** material.

    Next, you will assign material to *Board*.

4. Select *Board* in any viewport; *Board* is highlighted and the object name *Board* is displayed
    in the **Name and Color** rollout.

5. In the **Material Editor** dialog box, select the **Board** material.

6. Choose the **Assign Material to Selection** button; the **Board** material is assigned to the
    board part of the checkerboard.

    Next, you will assign the **Checker Red** material to the **Checker-r** group.

7. Select **Checker-r** from the **Scene Explorer** located left of the interface.

8. In the **Material Editor** dialog box, select the **Checker Red** material.

9. Choose the **Assign Material to Selection** button; the **Checker Red** material is assigned
    to one group of checkers.

    Next, you will assign the **black** checker material to the **checker-b** group.

10. Select **Checker-b** from the **Scene Explorer** located left of the interface.

11. In the **Material Editor** dialog box, select the **Checker Black** material.

12. Choose the **Assign Material to Selection** button; the **Checker Black** material is assigned
    to the other group of checkers. Next, close the **Material Editor** dialog box.

Saving and Rendering the Scene

In this section, you will save the scene that you have created and then render it. You can also
view the final rendered image of this model by downloading the *c08_3dsmaxdesign_2015_rndr.zip*
file from *www.cadcim.com*. The path of the file is as follows: *Textbooks > Animation and Visual
Effects > 3ds Max Design > Autodesk 3ds Max Design 2015: A Tutorial Approach*

1. Choose **Save** from the **Application** menu.

2. Make sure the Camera viewport is activated. Next, invoke the **Render Production** tool from the **Main Toolbar**; the rendered image is displayed, as shown in Figure 8-11.

Figure 8-11 *The rendered scene after assigning materials*

Self-Evaluation Test

Answer the following questions and then compare them to those given at the end of this chapter:

1. Which of the following buttons in the **Material Editor** dialog box is used to display the material in the viewport?

    (a) **Show Shaded Material in Viewport** (b) **Assign Material to Selection**
    (c) **Show End Result** (d) **Put Material to Scene**

2. Which of the following buttons in the **Material Editor** dialog box is used to save the current material in a material library ?

    (a) **Get Material** (b) **Assign Material to Selection**
    (c) **Put To Library** (d) **Go To Parent**

3. Which of the following buttons in the **Material Editor** dialog box is used to change the sample material window background color from black to a multicolored pattern?

    (a) **Background** (b) **Sample Type**
    (c) **Get Material** (d) **Assign Material to Selection**

4. Which of the following tools is used to invoke the **Material Editor** dialog box from the **Main Toolbar**?

    (a) **Render Setup**   (b) **Render Production**
    (c) **Material Editor**   (d) **Manage Layers**

5. The _____ maps can be assigned to create complex materials.

6. A texture map will not be displayed in the viewports unless the _____ button is active.

7. Lighter pixels in an image used as a bump map will appear to be _____, while the darker pixels will appear to be _____.

8. In 3ds Max Design, you can assign more than one texture map to each material. (T/F)

9. The **Standard** material type is selected by default in the **Material Editor** dialog box. (T/F)

10. The **Scene Explorer** is used to select and highlight the objects in the viewports. (T/F)

Review Questions

Answer the following questions:

1. Which of the following areas of the **Blinn Basic Parameters** rollout is used to control the intensity and shape of highlights on a glossy material?

    (a) **Self-Illumination**   (b) **Specular Highlights**
    (c) Both of these   (d) None of these

2. The _____ button is used to create a new material library.

3. The value in the _____ spinner controls the intensity of the bumps.

4. The _____ button is used to put a material in the library.

5. The **Get Material** button helps you display the material in the viewport. (T/F)

EXERCISES

The rendered image of the scene used in the following exercises can be accessed by downloading the *c08_3dsmaxdesign_2015_exr.zip* from *www.cadcim.com*. The path of the file is as follows: *Textbooks > Animation and Visual Effects > 3ds Max Design > Autodesk 3ds Max Design 2015: A Tutorial Approach*

Exercise 1

Extract the contents of the *c08_3dsmaxdesign_2015_exr.zip* and then open the *c08_exr1_start* file from it. Next, create materials and then apply them to a company logo. Figure 8-12 shows the final rendered image of the company logo.   **(Expected time: 20 min)**

Figure 8-12 Company Logo

Exercise 2

Open the *c08_exr2_start* file. Next, create and apply materials needed for the model of a vise, refer to Figure 8-13.   **(Expected time: 25 min)**

Figure 8-13 The model of a Vise

Answers to Self-Evaluation Test
1. a, **2.** c, **3.** a, **4.** c. **5.** Texture, **6. Show Shaded Material in Viewport**, **7.** raised, lowered **8.** T, **9.** F, **10.** T

Chapter 9

Material Editor: Texture Maps-II

Learning Objectives

After completing this chapter, you will be able to:
- *Create transparent materials*
- *Apply transparency maps to objects*
- *Create procedural maps*

INTRODUCTION

In this chapter, you will create materials using opacity and procedural maps. An opacity map is used to control the transparency of a material. It can be applied to a simple 3D object to give it an appearance of a complex shape. Unlike a bitmap which contains a fixed number of pixels, a procedural map is generated in two or in three dimensions by using a mathematical algorithm.

TUTORIAL

Before starting the tutorial, you need to download the *c09_3dsmaxdesign_2015_tut.zip* file from www.cadcim.com. The path of the file is as follows: *Textbooks > Animation and Visual Effects > 3ds Max Design > Autodesk 3ds Max Design 2015: A Tutorial Approach*

Extract the contents of the zip file and save them in the *Documents* folder.

Tutorial 1

In this tutorial, you will create materials that use special texture maps. You will use the opacity and diffuse color maps to make a square block look like a flower, refer to Figure 9-1.

(Expected time: 20 min)

Figure 9-1 *The vase and flower models*

The following steps are required to complete this tutorial:

a. Create the project folder.
b. Open the file.
c. Create a new material library.
d. Create the vase material.
e. Create the flower material.
f. Create the wood block material.
g. Assign the material to the objects.
h. Save and render the scene.

Creating the Project Folder
Create the project folder with the name *c09_tut1* in the *3dsmaxdesign 2015* folder as discussed in earlier chapters.

Opening the File
1. Open Windows Explorer and then browse to *\Documents\c09_3dsmaxdesign_2015_tut*. Next, copy all the image files to *\Documents\3dsmaxdesign 2015\c09_tut1\sceneassets\images*.

2. Choose **Open** from the **Application** menu; the **Open File** dialog box is displayed. In this dialog box, browse to the location *\Documents\c09_3dsmaxdesign_2015_tut* and select the **c09_tut1_start.max** file from it. Choose the **Open** button to open the file, refer to Figure 9-2.

[+][Camera-Flower][Shaded]

Figure 9-2 *The c09_tut1_start file*

3. Choose **Save As** from the **Application** menu; the **Save File As** dialog box is displayed. Browse to the location *\Documents\3dsmaxdesign 2015\c09_tut1\scenes*. Save the file with the name *c09tut1.max* at this location.

Creating New Material Library

In this section, you will create new material library which will contain materials created in the scene.

1. Choose **Rendering > Material Editor > Compact Material Editor** from the menu bar; the **Material Editor** dialog box is displayed. You will notice that in the first slot there is a material named *Stem* which is applied to the flower stems.

2. Choose the **Get Material** button in the **Material Editor** dialog box; the **Material/Map Browser** dialog box is displayed.

3. Choose the **Material/Map Browser Options** button from the **Material/Map Browser** dialog box; the Material/Map Browser Options flyout is displayed. Select **New Material Library** from the Material/Map Browser Options flyout; the **Create New Material Library** dialog box is displayed.

   As the project folder is already set, the *materiallibraries* folder of this project is displayed in the **Save in** drop-down list of this dialog box.

4. Enter **Still-Life** in the **File name** text box as the new name for the material library and choose the **Save** button; the new **Still-Life** material library is created in the **Material/Map Browser** dialog box.

5. Close the **Material/Map Browser** dialog box to return to the **Material Editor** dialog box.

Creating the Vase Material

In this section, you will create the transparent vase material by setting different parameters in the **Material Editor** dialog box.

1. Select the second material sample slot in the **Material Editor** dialog box to make it the current sample.

2. Choose the **Arch & Design** button to change the material type; the **Material/Map Browser** dialog box is displayed. In this dialog box, select the **Standard** material from the **Maps > Standard** rollout and then choose the **OK** button; the **Arch & Design** material is replaced by the **Standard** material. Also, various rollouts are displayed in the **Material Editor** dialog box to modify the **Standard** material.

3. In the **Shader Basic Parameters** rollout, select **Blinn** from the drop-down list, if it is not already selected.

4. In the **Blinn Basic Parameters** rollout, unlock the **Ambient** and **Diffuse** color swatches. Next, choose the **Ambient** color swatch; the **Color Selector: Ambient Color** dialog box is displayed.

5. In the **Color Selector: Ambient Color** dialog box, set the values as given next:

   Red: **133** Green: **166** Blue: **47**

   The ambient color is set to green. Choose the **OK** button to close the **Color Selector: Ambient Color** dialog box.

6. Choose **Rendering > Environment** from the menu bar; the **Environment and Effects** dialog box is displayed. In the **Global Lighting** area of the **Common Parameters** rollout, choose the **Ambient** color swatch; the **Color Selector: Ambient Light** dialog box is displayed. In this dialog box, set the value **75** in the **Value** spinner and then choose the **OK** button to close the dialog box. Next, close the **Environment and Effects** dialog box.

   This ambient light will bring out the ambient portion of the material color, which was added in the previous steps. If the ambient light value remained at 0, the ambient color settings would have no effect on the appearance of the material.

7. In the **Material Editor** dialog box, choose the **Diffuse** color swatch; the **Color Selector: Diffuse Color** dialog box is displayed.

8. In this dialog box, set the values as given next and then choose the **OK** button to close this dialog box:

   Red: **153** Green: **175** Blue: **255**

9. In the **Material Editor** dialog box, choose the **Specular** color swatch; the **Color Selector: Specular Color** dialog box is displayed.

10. In this dialog box, set the values as given next:

    Red: **255** Green: **255** Blue: **255**

11. Close the **Color Selector: Specular Color** dialog box.

12. In the **Specular Highlights** area of the **Blinn Basic Parameters** rollout, set the value **60** in the **Specular Level** spinner.

13. Set the value **40** in the **Glossiness** spinner and **30** in the **Opacity** spinner.

    Note that smaller the opacity value, more transparent the material will be.

14. Choose the **Background** button located in the right side of the **Material Editor** dialog box; the background is displayed in the selected sample slot. This helps to view the effect of transparency settings in a better way; refer to Figure 9-3.

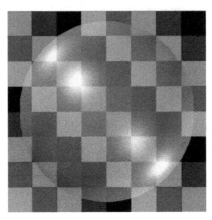

Figure 9-3 *The background displayed in the material*
*sample slot in the **Material Editor** dialog box*

Next, you will name the material and save it in the material library.

15. Choose the **Put to Library** button in the **Material Editor** dialog box; a flyout is displayed. Choose **Still-Life.mat** from the flyout; the **Put To Library** dialog box is displayed.

If the **Material Editor** message box is displayed prompting to put the entire material/ map tree to the library, choose the **Yes** button. If you are at the root level of the material definition, the **Material Editor** message box does not appear because the entire tree is added by default.

16. Enter **Vase** as the name of the new material in the **Put To Library** dialog box and choose the **OK** button; the material is assigned the name *Vase* and is added to the **Still-Life** material library.

Creating the Flower Material
In this section, you will create the flower material using the opacity maps.

1. In the **Material Editor** dialog box, select the third material sample slot and choose the **Arch & Design** button to change the material type; the **Material/Map Browser** dialog box is displayed. Select **Standard** from the **Materials > Standard** rollout and choose the **OK** button; the **Arch & Design** material is replaced by the **Standard** material. Also, various rollouts are displayed in the **Material Editor** dialog box to modify the **Standard** material.

2. Expand the **Maps** rollout. Next, choose the **Diffuse Color** map button, currently labeled **None**; the **Material/Map Browser** dialog box is displayed showing the types of maps that may be added.

3. Select the **Bitmap** map from the **Maps > Standard** rollout and choose the **OK** button; the **Select Bitmap Image File** dialog box is displayed.

4. In this dialog box, make sure **All Formats** is selected in the **Files of type** drop-down list. As the project folder is already set, the *images* folder of this project is displayed in the **Look in** drop down list of this dialog box. Select the **daisy.tif** file and choose the **Open** button; the image file is loaded and the parameters are displayed for the map in the **Material Editor** dialog box.

5. In the **Material Editor** dialog box, click and hold the **Sample Type** button located on the right side of the material slots. Now, choose the **Square** button from the flyout displayed; the sample slot in the **Material Editor** dialog box changes into square shape.

6. In the **Coordinates** rollout, clear the **Use Real-World Scale** check box and set the value **1** in the **U: Tiling** and **V: Tiling** spinners.

   The material currently is an image of a daisy. When the material is applied to an object, you want the background portion of the image to be transparent. This can be done with an opacity map. The map consists of another image of the daisy with the daisy portion completely white (opaque) and the background portion completely black (transparent).

7. Choose the **Go to Parent** button in the **Material Editor** dialog box to move one level up; the root level of the material is displayed.

8. In the **Maps** rollout, choose the **Opacity** map button that is currently labeled as **None**; the **Material/Map Browser** dialog box is displayed showing the types of maps that can be added.

9. Select the **Bitmap** map from the **Maps > Standard** rollout and choose the **OK** button; the **Select Bitmap Image File** dialog box is displayed.

10. In this dialog box, make sure **All Formats** is selected in the **Files of type** drop-down list. As the project folder is already set, the *images* folder of this project is displayed in the **Look in** drop down list of this dialog box. Select the **daisy-o.tga** file and choose the **Open** button; the image file is loaded and the parameters are displayed for the map in the **Material Editor** dialog box.

    You will notice that the preview of image displayed in the **Select Bitmap Image File** dialog box has black and white areas. The white area will be opaque while the black area will be transparent when the material is rendered.

11. In the **Coordinates** rollout, clear the **Use Real-World Scale** check box and set the value **1.0** in the **U: Tiling** and **V: Tiling** spinners.

12. Choose the **Background** button in the **Material Editor** dialog box; the material sample slot reflects the effect of opacity map, as shown in Figure 9-4.

*Figure 9-4 The material sample slot displayed in
the **Material Editor** dialog box*

 Note
*The transparent area of the material will still accept specular highlights. In other words, it will
look like a clear glass. If you want the transparent areas of the material to be completely invisible,
you can set **0** in the **Specular Level** spinner of the **Blinn Basic Parameters** rollout or add a
specular level map that matches the opacity map.*

Next, you will name the material and save it in the material library.

13. Choose the **Put to Library** button in the **Material Editor** dialog box; a flyout is
    displayed. Choose **Still-Life.mat** from the flyout; the **Put To Library** dialog box is
    displayed.

    If the **Material Editor** message box is displayed prompting to put the entire material/
    map tree to the library, choose the **Yes** button. If you are at the root level of the material
    definition, the **Material Editor** message box does not appear because the entire tree is
    added by default.

14. Enter **Daisy** as the name of the new material in the **Put To Library** dialog box and then
    choose the **OK** button; the material is assigned the name *Daisy* and is added to the **Still-Life**
    material library.

Creating the Wood Block Material

In this section, you will create a wood procedural map.

1. Select the fourth material sample slot in the **Material Editor** dialog box and choose the
    Arch & Design button to change the material type; the **Material/Map Browser** dialog box
    is displayed. In this dialog box, select **Standard** from the **Materials > Standard** rollout
    and then choose the **OK** button; the **Arch & Design** material is replaced by the **Standard**
    material in the **Material Editor** dialog box.

2. Expand the **Maps** rollout. Next, choose the **Diffuse Color** map button that is currently
    labeled as **None**; the **Material/Map Browser** dialog box is displayed, showing the types
    of maps that can be added.

3. Select **Wood** from the **Maps > Standard** rollout and choose the **OK** button; the **Material/ Map Browser** dialog box is closed and the parameters for the wood map are displayed in the **Material Editor** dialog box.

    Various settings in the **Wood Parameters** rollout in the **Material Editor** dialog box allow you to control the appearance of the wood material.

4. Adjust the color settings and other parameters as per your requirement.

    As you change parameters, the material sample is dynamically updated.

    Next, you will name the material and save it in the material library.

5. Choose the **Go to Parent** button in the **Material Editor** dialog box to move one level up; the root level of the material is displayed. Next, choose the **Put to Library** button in the **Material Editor** dialog box; a flyout is displayed.

6. Choose **Still-Life.mat** from the flyout; the **Put To Library** dialog box is displayed.

7. Enter **Wood** as the name of the new material in the **Put To Library** dialog box and choose the **OK** button; the material is assigned the name *Wood* and is added to the **Still-Life** material library.

    Next, you will save the **Still-Life** material library.

8. Choose the **Get Material** button in the **Material Editor**; the **Material/Map Browser** dialog box is displayed.

9. Right-click on the **Still-Life.mat** in the **Material/Map Browser** dialog box; a flyout is displayed. Choose **Save** from the flyout, as shown in Figure 9-5.

10. Close the **Material/Map Browser** dialog box.

Assigning Materials to the Objects

In this section, you will assign materials to the objects in the scene.

1. Close the **Material/Map Browser** dialog box to make more room on the screen.

2. Activate the Camera-Flower [Shaded] viewport.

3. Invoke the **Render Production** tool from the **Main Toolbar**; the **Rendered Frame** window is displayed, refer to Figure 9-6.

    You will notice that all the objects except the stems are currently assigned a default material. Notice that the flowers are created as simple 3D boxes. The opacity map on *Daisy* material will give the flowers their shape. The stems already have an appropriate material assigned. Also, the required mapping coordinates have already been applied to the objects.

Figure 9-5 Saving the material library

4. Close the rendered image. Next, invoke the **Select Object** tool from the **Main Toolbar**. Next, select *Vase* in the Camera-Flower [Shaded] viewport; the object is highlighted and *Vase* is displayed in the **Name and Color** rollout.

5. In the **Material Editor** dialog box, select the material sample slot which is named as *Vase* and then choose the **Assign Material to Selection** button; the *Vase* material is assigned to *Vase*. Next, choose the **Show Shaded Material in Viewport** button to display the material on *Vase* in the viewport.

6. Similarly, assign *Daisy* material to the two boxes representing the daisies. Also, assign *Wood* material to *Base*. Next, choose the **Show Shaded Material in Viewport** button to display the material on *Base* in the viewport.

Figure 9-6 *The **Rendered Frame** window*

The two boxes for the daisies are a single object.

7. Close the **Material Editor** dialog box.

Saving and Rendering the Scene

In this section, you will save the scene that you have created and then render it. You can also view the final rendered image of this model by downloading the *c09_3dsmaxdesign_2015_rndr.zip* file from *www.cadcim.com*. The path of the file is as follows: *Textbooks > Animation and Visual Effects > 3ds Max Design > Autodesk 3ds Max Design 2015: A Tutorial Approach*

1. Change the background color of the scene to light grey.

2. Choose **Save** from the **Application** menu.

3. Make sure the Camera-Flower [Shaded] viewport is activated. Next, invoke the **Render Production** tool from the **Main Toolbar**; the rendered image is displayed, refer to Figure 9-7.

Figure 9-7 *The rendered image with materials assigned to the objects*

Self-Evaluation Test

Answer the following questions and then compare them to those given at the end of this chapter:

1. Which of the following maps is used to control transparency of the material?

    (a) **Opacity**   (b) **Procedural**
    (c) **Mix**   (d) None of these

2. Which of the following maps will be created to represent a solid piece of wood?

    (a) **Opacity**   (b) **Procedural**
    (c) **Mix**   (d) None of these

3. Which of the following buttons is used to move one root level up in the **Material Editor** dialog box?

    (a) **Go to Parent**   (b) **Get Material**
    (c) **Material/Map Navigator**   (d) **Put Material to Scene**

4. In an opacity map, _____ pixels will be completely transparent and _____ pixels will be opaque.

5. The lower the value in the **Opacity** spinner, the higher will be the transparency of the material. (T/F)

6. As we change the parameters of the material types in the **Material Editor** dialog box, the material sample is dynamically updated. (T/F)

Review Questions

Answer the following questions:

1. Which of the following buttons in the **Material Editor** is used to display the opacity effect in the selected material slot color swatch?

    (a) **Background**   (b) **Make Preview**
    (c) **Backlight**   (d) None of these

2. The opacity maps help control the _____ of a material.

3. The _____ button in the **Main Toolbar** is used to render the current frame.

4. If you apply a procedural map to an object with a whole cut in it, the texture will still appear correct. (T/F)

EXERCISES

The rendered output of the models used in the following exercises can be accessed by downloading the *c09_maxdesign_2015_exr.zip* from *www.cadcim.com*. The path of the file is as follows: *Textbooks > Animation and Visual Effects > 3ds Max Design > Autodesk 3ds Max Design 2015: A Tutorial Approach*

Exercise 1

Extract the contents of the *c09_3dsmaxdesign_2015_exr.zip* and then open *c09_exr01_start.max*. Next, create materials to assign to three glasses placed on a tray, as shown in Figure 9-8. You will require three transparent materials with different opacity settings.

(Expected time: 20 min)

Figure 9-8 Three glasses with assigned materials

Exercise 2

Open *c09_exr02_start.max*. Create materials needed to assign to a scene displaying a broken piece of marble and a wooden board with a notch cut in it, as shown in Figure 9-9. In this exercise, you need to create two procedural map materials.   **(Expected time: 15 min)**

Figure 9-9 *Broken piece of marble and a wooden board*

Chapter *10*

Material Editor: Controlling Texture Maps

Learning Objectives

After completing this chapter, you will be able to:

- *Modify mapping parameters*
- *Apply decal texture maps*
- *Apply reflection maps*
- *Set up background bitmaps*

INTRODUCTION

In this chapter, you will learn to control texture maps by modifying the mapping parameters in the **Material Editor** dialog box. You will also learn to use reflection maps to provide a photo-realistic appearance to a scene.

TUTORIAL

Before starting the tutorial, you need to download the *c10_3dsmaxdesign_2015_tut.zip* file from *www.cadcim.com*. The path of the file is as follows: *Textbooks > Animation and Visual Effects > 3ds Max Design > Autodesk 3ds Max Design 2015: A Tutorial Approach*

Extract the content of the zip file and save it in the *Documents* folder.

Tutorial 1

In this tutorial, you will apply textures to the objects in the scene, as shown in Figure 10-1.

(Expected time: 20 min)

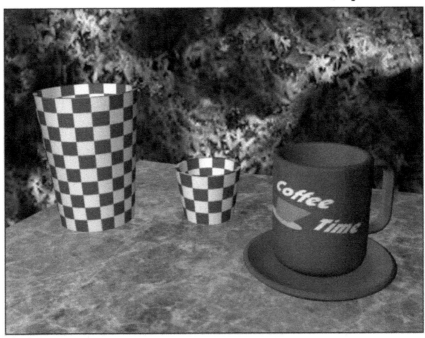

Figure 10-1 *The textured scene*

The following steps are required to complete this tutorial:

a.   Create the project folder.
b.   Open the file.
c.   Create a new material library.
d.   Create material for mug.
e.   Create material for mug handle and saucer.
f.   Create material for tabletop.

g. Set the environment background.
h. Create material for paper cups.
i. Save the material library.
j. Save and render the scene.

Creating the Project Folder

Create a project folder with the name *c10_tut1* in the *3dsmaxdesign 2015* folder, as discussed in earlier chapters.

Opening the File

1. Open Windows Explorer and then browse to *\Documents\c10_3dsmaxdesign_2015_tut*. Next, copy the *Logo.tga, Marbtea.gif*, and *Foliage.jpg* files to *\Documents\3dsmaxdesign 2015\c10_tut1\ sceneassets\images*.

2. Choose **Open** from the **Application** menu; the **Open File** dialog box is displayed. In this dialog box, browse to the location *\Documents\c10_3dsmaxdesign_2015_tut* and select the *c10_tut1_start.max* file from it. Choose the **Open** button to open the file, refer to Figure 10-2.

Figure 10-2 The c10_tut1_start file

3. Choose **Save As** from the **Application** menu; the **Save File As** dialog box is displayed. Browse to the location *\Documents\3dsmaxdesign 2015\c10_tut1\scenes*. Save the file with the name *c10tut1.max* at this location.

Creating a New Material Library

In this section, you will create a new material library in which new materials can be stored.

1. Choose **Rendering > Material Editor > Compact Material Editor** from the menu bar; the **Material Editor** dialog box is displayed.

2. Choose the **Get Material** button in the **Material Editor** dialog box; the **Material/Map Browser** dialog box is displayed.

3. Choose the **Material/Map Browser Options** button from the **Material/Map**
    Browser dialog box; a flyout is displayed. Select **New Material Library** from this
    flyout; the **Create New Material Library** dialog box is displayed.

    As the project folder is already set, the *materiallibraries* folder of this project is displayed
    in the **Save in** drop-down list.

4. Enter **MugLogo** in the **File name** text box and choose the **Save** button; the new material
    library **MugLogo.mat** is created at the specified location and displayed in the **Material/
    Map Browser** dialog box.

5. Close the **Material/Map Browser** dialog box to return to the **Material Editor** dialog
    box.

Creating Material for Mug

In this section, you will create a new material for *Mug*.

1. Select the first material sample slot in the **Material Editor** dialog box to make it the current
    sample slot.

2. Choose the **Arch & Design** button to change the material type; the **Material/Map**
    Browser dialog box is displayed. Select **Standard** from the **Materials > Standard**
    rollout and then choose the **OK** button; the **Arch & Design** material is replaced by the
    Standard material. Also, various rollouts are displayed in the **Material Editor** dialog box
    to modify the **Standard** material.

3. In the **Shader Basic Parameters** rollout, select **Blinn** from the drop-down list, if it is not
    already selected.

4. Expand the **Maps** rollout. Next, choose the **Diffuse Color** map button currently labeled
    as **None**; the **Material/Map Browser** dialog box is displayed showing the types of maps
    that can be added.

5. Select the **Bitmap** map from the **Maps > Standard** rollout and then choose the **OK** button;
    the **Material/Map Browser** dialog box is closed and the **Select Bitmap Image File** dialog
    box is displayed.

6. In this dialog box, make sure **All Formats** is selected in the **Files of type** drop-down list.
    Select the **logo.tga** file and then choose the **Open** button; the image file is loaded and
    the parameters for modifying the map are displayed in the **Material Editor** dialog box.

7. In the **Material Editor** dialog box, click and hold the **Sample Type** button located
    on the right side of the material slots. Now, choose the Square button from the
    flyout displayed; the sample slot in the **Material Editor** dialog box changes into a
    square shape.

8. In the **Coordinates** rollout, clear the **Use Real-World Scale** check box and set the value
    1.0 in the **U: Tiling** and **V: Tiling** spinners.

Note

*The **Use Real-World Scale** option is useful if the objects in the scene are drawn to scale, or if the material is to be assigned to multiple objects of different sizes. This feature will be explained later in this chapter.*

9. Choose the **Go to Parent** button in the **Material Editor** dialog box to move one level up.

Next, you will assign material to *Mug*.

10. Select **Mug** from the **Scene Explorer**; *Mug* is highlighted.

11. In the **Material Editor** dialog box, make sure the first material sample slot is selected.

12. Choose the **Assign Material to Selection** button; the material is assigned to *Mug*.

13. Choose the **Show Shaded Material in Viewport** button below the material sample slot; the texture map now appears on the object in the shaded viewports.

Next, you will modify the mapping parameters such as the scale, placement, and rotation angle of the bitmap image. These parameters can be controlled using the options in the **Coordinates** rollout. You will start by modifying the logo's scale.

14. In the **Maps** rollout, choose the **Diffuse Color** map button which is currently labeled **Map #x (logo.tga)**; you return to the map level of the material definition where the **Coordinates** rollout displays options for the texture map, as shown in Figure 10-3.

15. Set the value **2.0** in the **U: Tiling** spinner; the logo is set horizontally, to half of its original size.

Setting 2.0 in the **U: Tiling** spinner scales down the image so that it can fit twice in its original space.

16. Set the value **2.0** in the **V: Tiling** spinner; the logo is set vertically to half of its original size.

The logo is half of its original size and fits better on *Mug*. However, the image is repeating on both the horizontal and vertical axes. To create a decal texture map on *Mug*, the tiling must be turned off.

17. In the **Coordinates** rollout, clear the **U: Tile** check box; the logo no longer repeats on the horizontal axis.

18. Clear the **V: Tile** check box; the logo no longer repeats on the vertical axis.

To apply the same color on the mug, you need to define the basic color of the mug to dark green.

*Figure 10-3 The **Coordinates** rollout in the **Material Editor** dialog box*

19. Choose the **Go to Parent** button in the **Material Editor** dialog box to return to the root level of the material definition.

20. In the **Blinn Basic Parameters** rollout, choose the **Ambient** color swatch; the **Color Selector: Ambient Color** dialog box is displayed.

21. In the **Color Selector: Ambient color** dialog box, set the values as given next and then choose the **OK** button to close this dialog box:

Red: **15**   Green: **80**   Blue: **0**

The ambient and diffuse colors are currently locked. Therefore, when the ambient color is set to dark green, the diffuse color changes as well.

You also need to set the specular color to dark green. For this, you need to either choose the **Specular** color swatch and change the color values or you can lock the specular and diffuse (and therefore ambient) colors.

22. Choose the **Lock** button (between the **Diffuse** and **Specular** color swatches). The **Lock Diffuse and Specular?** message box is displayed, as shown in Figure 10-4. Choose the **Yes** button in the message box. Next, invoke the **Render Production** tool from the **Main Toolbar**; the render image is displayed and you will notice that a single logo is displayed on the all-green mug.

*Figure 10-4 The **Lock Diffuse and Specular?** message box*

Next, you will position the logo. To position the logo on *Mug*, you need to return to the map level of the rollout.

23. Choose the **M** button next to the **Diffuse** color swatch in the **Blinn Basic Parameters** rollout. Alternatively, you can choose the **Diffuse Color** map button in the **Maps** rollout.

24. Set the value **–0.12** in the **U: Offset** spinner; the logo is moved to the left of its original position.

   The distance the logo moves is based on the size of the bitmap image and the tiling setting. When the tiling is set to 1, a value of 0.5 will move any image to the right up to a distance equal to half of the image's width. Since the tiling is set to 2.0, a value of –0.12 in the offset spinner moves the logo to a distance equal to approximately a quarter of its width (–0.12 × 2 = –0.24).

25. Set the value **0.2** in the **V: Offset** spinner; the logo moves up from its original position.

   Next, you will render the scene to view the changes made so far.

26. Make sure the Camera01 viewport is activated, if it is not already activated.

27. Invoke the **Render Production** tool from the **Main Toolbar**; the rendered image is displayed on the screen. Close the render window.

   Next, you will rotate the logo.

28. In the **Coordinates** rollout for the map, set the value **20** in the **W: Angle** spinner; the logo is rotated clockwise.

29. Set the value **–0.1** in the **U: Offset** spinner; the logo moves left.

30. Set the value **0.1** in the **V: Offset** spinner; the logo rotates and reposition itself on *Mug*.

    Next, you will add a reflection map. A reflection map makes a 3D scene appear more realistic by causing objects to reflect a background image or surrounding elements in the scene.

31. Choose the **Go to Parent** button in the **Material Editor** dialog box; you will return to the root level of the material definition.

32. In the **Maps** rollout, set the value **20** in the **Reflection** spinner.

    This value in the **Reflection** spinner controls the amount of reflection in the material.

33. Choose the **Reflection** map button, which is currently labeled as **None**; the **Material/Map Browser** dialog box is displayed showing the types of maps that can be added.

34. Select **Reflect/Refract** from the **Maps > Standard** rollout and then choose the **OK** button; various rollouts for the **Reflect/Refract** map are displayed in the **Material Editor** dialog box.

    The **Reflect/Refract** map type automatically generates a reflection from the other elements in the scene and places it on the material during rendering.

35. Choose the **Go to Parent** button to return to the root level of the material definition.

    Next, you will name and save the material.

36. Choose the **Put to Library** button in the **Material Editor** dialog box; a flyout is displayed.

37. Choose **MugLogo.mat** from the flyout; the **Put to Library** dialog box is displayed.

38. Enter **Logo** in the **Name** text box and then choose the **OK** button; the material is assigned the name *Logo* and is added to the **MugLogo** material library.

Creating Material for Mug Handle and Saucer

In this section, you will create a material for mug handle and saucer in the scene. This new material should be identical to the material on the mug, but without the logo. For this, you need to copy *Logo* material and modify the copy by removing the bitmap. In this way, all the color and reflection settings for *Logo* material are automatically copied to the new material.

1. Select and hold *Logo* material sample slot. Drag the sample slot to the next unused material sample slot and release the mouse button; a duplicate copy of the material is created.

2. Make sure the copied material and not the original, is active, . Also make sure the **Maps** rollout is expanded. Drag and drop the **Specular Color** map button or any other map button labeled **None** to the **Diffuse Color** map button; the map is removed from the **Diffuse Color** map button. It means that the logo is removed from the material.

   Next, you will name and save the material.

3. Choose the **Put to Library** button in the **Material Editor** dialog box; a flyout is displayed.

4. Choose **MugLogo.mat** from the flyout; the **Put to Library** dialog box is displayed.

5. Enter **No-Logo** in the **Name** text box and choose the **OK** button; the material is assigned the name *No-Logo* and is added to the **MugLogo** material library.

   Next, you will assign the **No-Logo** material to the handle of the mug.

6. Select the mug handle from the **Scene Explorer** or in the viewport; *Handle* is highlighted and is displayed in the **Name and Color** rollout.

7. Choose the **Assign Material to Selection** button in the **Material Editor** dialog box; the *No-Logo* material is assigned to *Handle*.

8. Select *Saucer* in any viewport. Next, choose the **Assign Material to Selection** button in the **Material Editor** dialog box; the *No-Logo* material is assigned to *Saucer*.

9. Make sure the Camera01[Shaded] viewport is activated. Next, invoke the **Render Production** tool from the **Main Toolbar** to view the new changes at rendering; the rendered image is displayed. Now, close the render window.

 Note
Reflection maps are not displayed in the viewport. The scene must be rendered to see the effects of a reflection map.

Creating Material for Tabletop

In this section, you will create material for *Tabletop* which should reflect the background and any of the objects on the tabletop.

1. Activate the next unused material sample slot in the **Material Editor** dialog box.

2. Choose the **Arch & Design** button to change the material type; the **Material/Map Browser** dialog box is displayed. Select **Standard** from the **Materials > Standard** rollout and then choose the **OK** button; the **Arch & Design** material is replaced by the **Standard** material. Also, various rollouts are displayed in the **Material Editor** dialog box to modify the **Standard** material.

3. In the **Shader Basic Parameters** rollout, select **Blinn** in the drop-down list, if it is not already selected.

4. Expand the **Maps** rollout. Next, choose the **Diffuse Color** map button which is currently labeled as **None**; the **Material/Map Browser** dialog box is displayed showing the types of maps that can be added.

5. Select **Mix** from the **Maps > Standard** rollout and then choose the **OK** button; the map type is set as combination of two colors or images. The **Material/Map Browser** dialog box is closed and the **Mix Parameters** rollout is displayed in the **Material Editor** dialog box.

6. Choose the **Color #1** map button currently labeled **None**; the **Material/Map Browser** dialog box is displayed showing the types of maps that can be added.

7. Select the **Bitmap** map from the **Maps > Standard** rollout and choose the **OK** button; the **Material/Map Browser** dialog box is closed and the **Select Bitmap Image File** dialog box is displayed. As the project folder is already set, the *images* folder of this project is displayed in the **Look in** text box of this dialog box.

8. Select the file **Marbtea.gif** and choose the **Open** button; you are moved to the next level of the material definition and various rollouts for the **Bitmap** map are displayed in the **Material Editor** dialog box.

Note

*If a file type other than the currently selected file, is opened earlier, you need to select **All Formats** in the **File of type** drop down list to display the currently selected file .*

9. In the **Coordinates** rollout, make sure the **Use Real-World Scale** check box is selected. Set the value **250** in the **Width: Size** and **Height: Size** spinners; The material currently resembles a piece of granite. However, there is no reflection. To add the reflection, you need to set the second color of the mix as a reflection map.

10. Choose the **Go to Parent** button; you are moved one level up in the material definition to the mix map level.

    Notice how the **Color #1** button is now labeled **Map #x (Marbtea.gif)**.

11. Choose the **Color #2** map button, currently labeled **None**; the **Material/Map Browser** dialog box is displayed showing the types of maps that can be added.

12. Select the **Reflect/Refract** type from the **Maps > Standard** rollout and then choose the **OK** button; you are moved to the next level of the material definition and various rollouts for the **Reflect/Refract** map are displayed in the **Material Editor** dialog box.

    You will notice that the first color (the granite bitmap) currently overlays the second color (the reflection map) completely. To avoid this, you need to set the amount of mixing for the two maps in the **Mix Amount** spinner.

13. Choose the **Go to Parent** button; you are returned to the **Mix** map level.

14. In the **Mix Parameters** rollout, set the value **10** in the **Mix Amount** spinner; 90% of the first color (the granite bitmap) and 10% of the second color (the reflection map) create a combined texture map.
    Next, you will name and save the material.

15. Choose the **Go to Parent** button; you are returned to the root level of the material definition. Now, choose the **Put to Library** button in the **Material Editor** dialog box; a flyout is displayed.

16. Choose **MugLogo.mat** from the flyout; the **Put to Library** dialog box is displayed.

17. Enter **Table** in the **Put To Library** dialog box and choose the **OK** button; the material is assigned the name *Table* and is added to the **MugLogo** material library.

    Next, you will assign *Table* material to *Tabletop*.

18. Select *Tabletop* from the **Scene Explorer** or in the viewport; *Tabletop* is highlighted.

19. Choose the **Assign Material to Selection** button in the **Material Editor** dialog box. Next, choose the **Show Shaded Material in Viewport** button; the material *Table* is assigned to *Tabletop*. Render the scene to view the material.

Setting the Environment Background

In this section, you will use a bitmap image as a background for a rendered scene. With reflection maps active, it will appear that the background is actually being reflected on the objects in the scene.

1. Activate the next unused material sample slot in the **Material Editor** dialog box.

2. Choose the **Arch & Design** button to change the material type; the **Material/Map Browser** dialog box is displayed. Select **Standard** from the **Materials > Standard** rollout and then choose the **OK** button; the **Arch & Design** material is replaced by the **Standard** material. Also, various rollouts are displayed in the **Material Editor** dialog box to modify the **Standard** material.

3. Select **Blinn** from the drop-down list in the **Shader Basic Parameters** rollout, if it is not already selected.

4. Expand the **Maps** rollout. Next, choose the **Diffuse Color** map button which is currently labeled as **None**; the **Material/Map Browser** dialog box is displayed showing the types of maps that can be added.

5. Select the **Bitmap** map from the **Maps > Standard** rollout and choose the **OK** button; the **Material/Map Browser** dialog box is closed and the **Select Bitmap Image File** dialog box is displayed. As the project folder is already set, the *images* folder of this project is displayed in the **Look in** drop-down list.

6. Select the **Foliage.jpg** file and choose the **Open** button; the image file is loaded and the parameters for the map are displayed in the **Material Editor** dialog box.

7. Click on the drop-down list located below the material sample slots. By default, the name, **Map #x**, is displayed. Rename it to **Foliage** and press the ENTER key.

8. In the **Coordinates** rollout, select the **Environ** radio button. Select **Screen** from the **Mapping** drop-down list, if it is not already selected. Set the value **1.0** in the **U: Tiling** and **V: Tiling** spinners, as shown in Figure 10-5; the bitmap image will be scaled to fit the screen when it is rendered.

9. Choose the **Go to Parent** button to return to the root level of the material.

Next, you will name and save the material.

10. Choose the **Put to Library** button in the **Material Editor** dialog box; a flyout is displayed.

11. Choose **MugLogo.mat** from the flyout; the **Put to Library** dialog box is displayed.

12. Enter the name **Background Material** in the **Put To Library** dialog box and choose the **OK** button; the material is assigned the name *Background Material* and is added to the **MugLogo** material library.

13. Choose **Rendering > Environment** from the menu bar; the **Environment and Effects** dialog box is displayed, as shown in Figure 10-6.

14. Choose the **Environment Map** button in the **Background** area, currently labeled as **None**; the **Material/Map Browser** dialog box is displayed.

15. Expand the **Sample Slots** rollout, if it is not already expanded and then select **Diffuse Color: Foliage Map (Foliage.jpg),** as shown in Figure 10-7. Choose the **OK** button; the **Instance or Copy?** dialog box is displayed, as shown in Figure 10-8.

16. Make sure the **Instance** radio button is selected in the **Method** area of the **Instance or Copy?** dialog box and then choose the **OK** button.

By selecting the **Instance** radio button, any changes made to the map in the **Material Editor** dialog box are automatically transferred to the environment background.

17. Close the **Environment and Effects** dialog box; a bitmap image of bushes will fill the background when the scene is rendered.

Figure 10-5 *The settings displayed in the* **Coordinates** *rollout*

Figure 10-6 *The* **Environment and Effects** *dialog box*

Figure 10-7 *Selecting* **Diffuse Color: Foliage Map (Foliage.jpg)** *from the* **Sample Slots** *rollout*

*Figure 10-8   The **Instance or Copy?** dialog box*

Creating Material for Paper cups

In this section, you will create material for the paper cups using the **Checker** map.

1. Choose the **Display** tab of the **Command Panel**; various rollouts are displayed. In the **Hide** rollout, choose the **Unhide by Name** button; the **Unhide Objects** dialog box is displayed.

2. In this dialog box, select **PaperCup_Lrg** and **PaperCup_Sm**, as shown in Figure 10-9 and then choose the **Unhide** button.

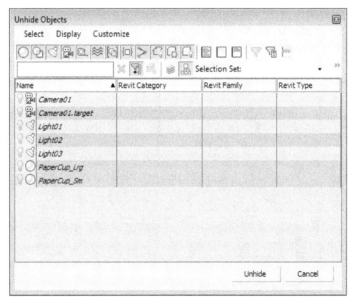

*Figure 10-9   Selecting **PaperCup_Lrg** and **PaperCup_Sm** in the **Unhide Objects** dialog box*

3. Select the next unused sample slot in the **Material Editor** dialog box. Choose the **Arch & Design** button to change the material type; the **Material/Map Browser** dialog box is displayed.

4. Select **Standard** from the **Materials > Standard** rollout and then choose the **OK** button; the **Arch & Design** material is replaced by the **Standard** material. Also, various rollouts are displayed in the **Material Editor** dialog box to modify the **Standard** material.

5. Expand the **Maps** rollout and choose the **Diffuse Color** map button, currently labeled as **None**; the **Material/Map Browser** dialog box is displayed.

6. Select the **Checker** map from **Maps > Standard** rollout in the **Material/Map Browser** dialog box and then choose the **OK** button; the **Material/Map Browser** dialog box is closed and various rollouts for the **Checker** map are displayed in the **Material Editor** dialog box.

7. In the **Material Editor** dialog box, expand the **Checker Parameters** rollout, if it is not already expanded. Next, choose the first **Color** swatch; the **Color Selector: Color 1** dialog box is displayed.

8. In the **Color Selector**: **Color 1** dialog box, set the values as given next:

    Red: **15**   Green: **80**   Blue: **0**

    The green color matching the diffuse color of the saucer and the cup, is set.

9. In the **Checker Parameters** rollout, choose the second **Color** swatch; the **Color Selector: Color 2** dialog box is displayed, refer to Figure 10-10. In this dialog box, set the values as given next:

    Red: **244**   Green: **244**   Blue: **0**

    Close the **Color Selector: Color 2** dialog box. Yellow color approximately matching the yellow color in the logo, is set.

10. In the **Coordinates** rollout, clear the **Use Real-World Scale** check box. Set the value **8** in the **U: Tiling** and **V: Tiling** spinners and then choose the **Go to Parent** button.

    These settings specify that the map will be repeated 8 times across an object's U dimension, and 8 times across the object's V dimension. The actual size of the map in rendering will depend on the size of the object to which it is assigned.

11. Select *PaperCup_Lrg* and *PaperCup_Sm* in any viewport. Choose the **Assign Material to Selection** button in the **Material Editor** dialog box to assign material to cups. Next, choose the **Show Shaded Material in Viewport** button to display the textured material on cups in the viewport. Enter the name **Paper Cup** in the drop-down list below the material sample slots; the material created is named as *Paper Cup*.

12. Make sure the Camera01 viewport is activated. Invoke the **Render Production** tool from the **Main Toolbar**.

    Note the difference in the appearance of the material on *PaperCup_Lrg* and *PaperCup_Sm*. *PaperCup_Lrg* is wider and much taller than *PaperCup_Sm*, so the checkerboard pattern in the material is larger. Also, *PaperCup_Lrg* is taller than it is wide, so the material pattern appears stretched out vertically.

*Figure 10-10 The **Color Selector: Color 2** dialog box displayed*

13. In the **Material Editor** dialog box, make sure the *Paper Cup* material is selected. Choose the map button (currently labeled as **M**) to the right of the **Diffuse** color swatch; you are navigated to the diffuse color map level of the material definition.

14. In the **Coordinates** rollout of the **Material Editor** dialog box, select the **Use Real-World Scale** check box. Set the value **50** in the **Width: Size** and **Height: Size** spinners. Close the **Material Editor** dialog box; you will notice that the map is appearing distorted.

The **Use Real-World Scale** check box is selected to maintain a consistent appearance when a material is applied to objects of different sizes. If you clear this check box, the appearance of the material map during rendering depends on the size of the object on which the map is applied, and the number of times the map is tiled on the object.

15. Select *PaperCup_Sm* in any viewport. Choose the **Modify** tab in the **Command Panel**. Select **Tube** in the modifier stack. In the **Parameters** rollout for the tube, select the **Real-World Map Size** check box.

16. Select *PaperCup_Lrg* in any viewport. Choose the **Modify** tab in the **Command Panel**. Select **Tube** in the modifier stack. In the **Parameters** rollout for the tube, select the **Real-World Map Size** check box.

17. Invoke the **Render Production** tool from the **Main Toolbar**.

   As the material map size is now based on drawing units instead of object size, the material appears same on both the cups. Next, you will name and save the material.

18. In the **Material Editor** dialog box, select *Paper Cup* material sample slot.

19. Choose the **Go to Parent** button. Next, choose the **Put to Library** button in the **Material Editor** dialog box; a flyout is displayed.

20. Choose **MugLogo.mat** from the flyout; the **Put to Library** dialog box is displayed.

21. Accept the name *Paper Cup* by choosing the **OK** button in the **Put To Library** dialog box; the *Paper Cup* material is added to the **MugLogo** material library.

Saving the Material Library

In this section, you will save the material library. You need to save the changes to the material library before you exit 3ds Max Design.

1. Choose the **Get Material** button in the **Material Editor** dialog box; the **Material/Map Browser** dialog box is displayed.

2. Right-click on the **MugLogo.mat** rollout; a shortcut menu is displayed. Choose **Save** from the shortcut menu, as shown in Figure 10-11.

3. Close the **Material/Map Browser** dialog box and the **Material Editor** dialog box.

Figure 10-11 *Saving the material library*

Saving and Rendering the Scene

In this section, you will save the scene that you have created and then render it. You can also view the final rendered image of this model by downloading the *c10_3dsmaxdesign_2015_rndr.zip* file from *www.cadcim.com*. The path of the file is as follows: *Textbooks > Animation and Visual Effects > 3ds Max Design > Autodesk 3ds Max Design 2015: A Tutorial Approach*

1. Choose **Save** from the **Application** menu.

2. Activate the Camera01 viewport. Next, invoke the **Render Production** tool from the **Main Toolbar**; the rendered image is displayed, refer to Figure 10-12.

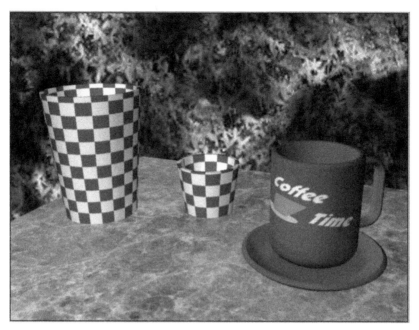

Figure 10-12 *The rendered image*

Self-Evaluation Test

Answer the following questions and then compare them to those given at the end of this chapter:

1. Which of the following buttons in the **Material Editor** dialog box is used to assign a material to an object?

    (a) **Show Shaded Material in Viewport**   (b) **Assign Material to Selection**
    (c) **Show End Result**   (d) **Put Material to Scene**

2. Which of the following rollouts is used to adjust scaling, placement, and rotation angle of a bitmap image?

    (a) **Maps**   (b) **Blinn Basic Parameters**
    (c) **Coordinates**   (d) None of these

3. You need to turn off the _____ option in the **Coordinates** rollout to stop repetition of a bitmap texture of the object.

4. You need to _____ the scene to see the effects of a reflection map if the material is not visible on objects.

5. The **Environment and Effects** dialog box is used to set the background of a rendered scene. (T/F)

Review Questions

Answer the following questions:

1. Which of the following maps is used to generate a reflection from other elements in a scene and then places it on the material during rendering?

    (a) **Reflect/Refract**   (b) **Mix**
    (c) **Bitmap**   (d) None of these

2. Which of the following buttons in the **Material Editor** dialog box is used to return to the root level of the material?

    (a) **Get Material**   (b) **Go to Parent**
    (c) **Put Material to Scene**   (d) **Make Material Copy**

3. The _____ map makes a 3D scene appear more realistic by causing objects to reflect a background image or other surrounding elements in a scene.

4. The _____ check box is selected to maintain a consistent appearance when a material is applied to objects of different sizes.

5. The actual size of a map in rendering depends on the size of the _____ to which it is assigned.

6. Bitmap images can be created in a paint program. (T/F)

EXERCISE

The rendered output of the model used in the following exercise can be accessed by downloading the *c10_maxdesign_2015_exr.zip* from *www.cadcim.com*. The path of the file is as follows: *Textbooks > Animation and Visual Effects > 3ds Max Design > Autodesk 3ds Max Design 2015: A Tutorial Approach*

Exercise 1

Extract the contents of the *c10_3dsmaxdesign_2015_exr.zip* and then open *c10_exr01_start.max*. Next, create a decal material to apply on the vise, as shown in Figure 10-13.

(Expected time: 20 min)

Figure 10-13 Vise with decal material

Answers to Self-Evaluation Test
1. b, **2.** c, **3. Tile**, **4.** render, **5.** T

Chapter 11

Material Editor: Miscellaneous Materials

Learning Objectives

After completing this chapter, you will be able to:

- *Use standard Autodesk materials*
- *Apply the UVW Map modifier*
- *Apply materials to different faces of an object*
- *Create background for the scene*
- *Add background to the scene*

INTRODUCTION

In this chapter, you will assign materials to the objects created in Chapters 2 and 3 using the standard material library *3dsmax.mat*.

TUTORIALS

Before starting the tutorials, you need to download the *c11_3dsmaxdesign_2015_tut.zip* file from *www.cadcim.com*. The path of the file is as follows: *Textbooks > Animation and Visual Effects > 3ds Max Design > Autodesk 3ds Max Design 2015: A Tutorial Approach*

Extract the contents of the zip file and save them in the *Documents* folder.

Tutorial 1

In this tutorial, you will assign different materials to the temple created in Tutorial 1 of Chapter 2, refer to Figure 11-1. **(Expected time: 20 min)**

Figure 11-1 *The textured model of the temple*

The following steps are required to complete this tutorial:

a. Create the project folder.
b. Open the file.
c. Assign material to cone, sphere, and dome.
d. Assign material to top and Bell.
e. Apply material to pillars.
f. Save and render the scene.

Creating the Project Folder

Create the project folder with the name *c11_tut1* in the *3dsmaxdesign 2015* folder, as discussed in earlier chapters.

Opening the File

1. Open Windows Explorer and then browse to *\Documents\c11_3dsmaxdesign_2015_tut*. Next, copy *3dsmax.mat* to *\Documents\3dsmaxdesign 2015\c11_tut1\materiallibraries*. Also, copy *cedfence.jpg*, *lakerem2.jpg*, *balmoral.jpg*, and *whtgran.jpg* to *\Documents\3dsmaxdesign 2015\ c11_tut1\sceneassets\images* and to *\Documents\3dsmaxdesign 2015\c11_tut1*.

2. Choose **Open** from the **Application** menu; the **Open File** dialog box is displayed. In this dialog box, browse to the location *\Documents\c11_3dsmaxdesign_2015_tut* and select the **c11_tut1_start.max** file from it. Choose the **Open** button to open the file, refer to Figure 11-2.

[+] [Perspective] [Shaded]

Figure 11-2 The c11_tut1_start.max file

Note

Instead of following step 2, you can directly open the file that you created in Tutorial 1 of Chapter 2 and then follow step 3 given below to save it.

3. Choose **Save As** from the **Application** menu; the **Save File As** dialog box is displayed. Save the file with the name *c11tut1.max*.

You will notice that the saving location of this file is *\Documents\3dsmaxdesign 2015\c11_tut1\ scenes*.

Applying Material to Cone, Sphere, and Dome

In this section, you will choose materials from the library of materials and then apply the selected materials to cone, sphere, and dome.

1. Select *Cone* and *Sphere*. Next, choose **Rendering > Material Editor > Compact Material Editor** from the menu bar; the **Material Editor** dialog box is displayed, as shown in Figure 11-3.

*Figure 11-3 The **Material Editor** dialog box*

2. Make sure the first sample slot is selected, and then choose the **Get Material** button; the **Material/Map Browser** dialog box is displayed, as shown in Figure 11-4.

3. In this dialog box, choose the **Material/Map Browser Options** button; the Material/Map Browser flyout is displayed.

4. Select **Open Material Library** from this flyout; the **Import Material Library** dialog box is displayed.

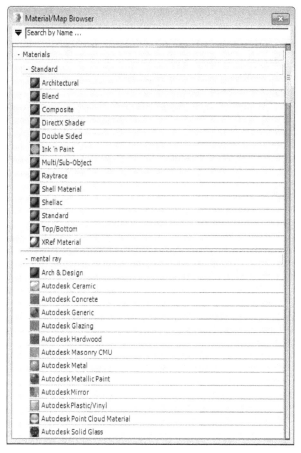

Figure 11-4 The **Material/Map Browser** *dialog box*

As the project folder is already set, the *materiallibraries* folder of this project is displayed in the **Look in** text box.

5. Now, select **3dsmax** and then choose the **Open** button; different materials present in *3dsmax* library are displayed in the **Material/Map Browser** dialog box.

6. Double-click on the material **Metal_Black_Plain (Standard)** from the *3dsmax.mat* material library of the **Material/Map Browser** dialog box to load it into the **Material Editor** dialog box. Make sure *cone* and *sphere* are selected in the viewport and then choose the **Assign Material to Selection** button in the **Material Editor** dialog box; the material *Metal_Black_Plain* is assigned to *cone* and *sphere*. Close the **Material/Map Browser** dialog box.

7. Select *Dome* from the **Scene Explorer** or in the viewport. In the **Material Editor** dialog box, select the second sample slot and choose the **Get Material** button; the **Material/Map Browser** dialog box is displayed.

8. In this dialog box, double-click on the material **Metal_Dark_Gold (Standard)** from the *3dsmax.mat* material library. Next, choose the **Assign Material to Selection** button in the **Material Editor** dialog box; the material *Metal_Dark_Gold* is assigned to *Dome*. Close the **Material/Map Browser** dialog box.

Applying Material to Top and Bell

In this section, you will choose materials from the library of materials and then apply the selected materials to *Top* and *Bell*.

1. Select *Top* from the **Scene Explorer** or in the viewport. In the **Material Editor** dialog box, select the third sample slot and choose the **Get Material** button; the **Material/Map Browser** dialog box is displayed.

2. In this dialog box, double-click on the material **Stones_Balmoral (Standard)** from the *3dsmax.mat* material library. Next, choose the **Assign Material to Selection** button in the **Material Editor** dialog box. Minimize the **Material Editor** dialog box and close the **Material/Map Browser** dialog box; the material *Stones_Balmoral* is assigned to *Top*.

3. Make sure *Top* is selected. Next, choose the **Modify** tab in the **Command Panel**. Select **UVW Map** from the **Modifier List** drop-down list; the **UVW Map** modifier is applied to *Top*.

4. In the **Mapping** area of the **Parameters** rollout, clear the **Real-World Map Size** check box. Select the **Box** radio button.

5. Set the values in the spinners as given next:

   Height: **360.36**   U Tile: **4**   V Tile: **4**   W Tile: **4**

   The mapping coordinates are applied to *Top*. Note that although *Top* is rectangular, the **UVW Map** modifier gizmo is made cubic. This is done so that the map has the same scale on each side.

   If the **UVW Map** modifier gizmo were rectangular, the material would appear squashed on the short sides of the object.

6. Select *Bell* from the **Scene Explorer**. In the **Material Editor** dialog box, select the fourth sample slot and choose the **Get Material** button; the **Material/Map Browser** dialog box is displayed.

7. In this dialog box, double-click on the material **Stones_White_Granite (Standard)** from the *3dsmax.mat* material library. Next, choose the **Assign Material to Selection** button in the **Material Editor** dialog box; the material *Stones_White_Granite* is assigned to *Bell*. Close the **Material/Map Browser** dialog box.

8. In the **Shader Basic Parameters** rollout of the **Material Editor** dialog box, select the **2-Sided** check box and set the value **35** in the **Opacity** spinner; a transparent material is created.

9. Make sure *Bell* is selected and then choose the **Modify** tab in the **Command Panel**. Select **UVW Map** from the **Modifier List** drop-down list; the **UVW Map** modifier is applied to *Bell*.

10. In the **Mapping** area of the **Parameters** rollout, clear the **Real-World Map Size** check box, and select the **Cylindrical** radio button; the cylindrical mapping coordinates are applied to *Bell*.

Applying Material to Pillars

In this section, you will choose materials from the library of materials and then apply the selected materials to pillars.

1. Select *Pillar01, Pillar02, Pillar03,* and *Pillar04*. In the **Material Editor** dialog box, select the second sample slot.

2. Choose the **Assign Material to Selection** button in the **Material Editor** dialog box; the material *Metal_Dark_Gold* is assigned to *Pillar01, Pillar02, Pillar03,* and *Pillar04*. Click anywhere in the viewport to deselect the pillars.

3. Select *Pillar01* and make sure the **Generate Mapping Coords** check box is selected in the **Parameters** rollout of the Modify panel. Next, clear the **Real-World Map Size** check box.

4. Repeat step 3 for *Pillar02, Pillar03,* and *Pillar04*.

5. Select *Base01, Base02, Base03,* and *Base04*.

6. In the **Material Editor** dialog box, select the sample slot containing the material *Stones_Balmoral*. Next, choose the **Assign Material to Selection** button; the material *Stones_Balmoral* is assigned to *Base01, Base02, Base03,* and *Base04*.

7. Apply a **UVW Map** modifier to all base objects, as done earlier. In the **Mapping** area in the **Parameters** rollout of the Modify panel, clear the **Real-World Map Size** check box. Select the **Box** radio button.

8. Set the values in the respective spinners as given next:

   Length: **360.36**   Width: **360.36**   Height: **360.36**
   U Tile: **4**   V Tile: **4**   W Tile: **4**

9. Select *Bottom* from the **Scene Explorer** or in the viewport. In the **Material Editor** dialog box, select the fifth sample slot. Next, choose the **Get Material** button; the **Material/Map Browser** dialog box is displayed.

10. Double-click on the material **Wood_Cedfence (Standard)** in the **Material/Map Browser** dialog box. Next, choose the **Assign Material to Selection** button in the **Material Editor** dialog box; the material *Wood_Cedfence* is assigned to *Bottom*.

11. Apply the **UVW Map** modifier to *Bottom*, as done earlier. In the **Mapping** area in the **Parameters** rollout of the Modify panel, clear the **Real-World Map Size** check box and make sure the **Box** radio button is selected.

12. In the **Mapping** area of the **Parameters** rollout, set the values in the respective spinners as given next:

U Tile: **2**   V Tile: **2**   W Tile: **2**

The box mapping coordinates are applied to *Bottom*.

13. Close the **Material Editor** and **Material/Map Browser** dialog boxes.

Saving and Rendering the Scene

In this section, you will save the scene that you have created and then render it. You can also view the final rendered image of this model by downloading the *c11_3dsmaxdesign_2015_rndr.zip* file from *www.cadcim.com*. The path of the file is as follows: *Textbooks > Animation and Visual Effects > 3ds Max Design > Autodesk 3ds Max Design 2015: A Tutorial Approach*

1. Choose **Save** from the **Application** menu.

2. Make sure the Perspective viewport is activated. Next, invoke the **Render Production** tool from the **Main Toolbar**; the rendered image is displayed, as shown in Figure 11-5.

Figure 11-5 *The rendered image*

Tutorial 2

In this tutorial, you will texture a scene created in Tutorial 1 of Chapter 3, refer to Figure 11-6.

(Expected time: 25 min)

Figure 11-6 The textured scene

The following steps are required to complete this tutorial:

a. Create the project folder.
b. Open the file.
c. Assign material to balloon.
d. Assign material to ropes.
e. Assign material to collar.
f. Assign material to basket.
g. Add lights and camera.
h. Set the background.
i. Save and render the scene.

Creating the Project Folder

Create the project folder with the name *c11_tut2* in the *3dsmaxdesign 2015* folder, as discussed in earlier chapters.

Opening the File

1. Open Windows Explorer and then browse to *\Documents\c11_3dsmaxdesign_2015_tut*. Next, copy *3dsmax.mat* to *\Documents\3dsmaxdesign 2015\c11_tut2\materiallibraries*. Also, copy *carpttan.jpg, cedfence.jpg, carptblu.jpg, and Background_Falls.jpg* to *\Documents\3dsmaxdesign 2015\c11_tut2\\sceneassets\images* and to *\Documents\3dsmaxdesign 2015\c11_tut2*.

2. Choose **Open** from the **Application** menu; the **Open File** dialog box is displayed. In this dialog box, browse to the location *Documents\c11_3dsmaxdesign_2015_tut* and select the **c11_tut2_start.max** file from it. Choose the **Open** button to open the file, refer to Figure 11-7.

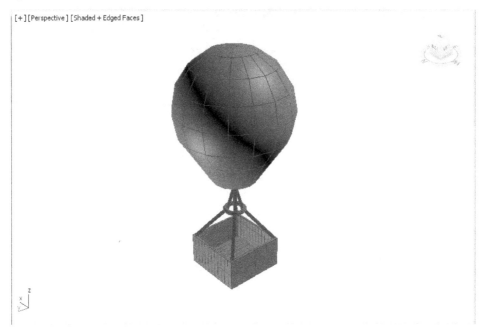

Figure 11-7 The c11_tut2_start.max file

3. Choose **Save As** from the **Application** menu; the **Save File As** dialog box is displayed. Browse to the location *Documents\3dsmaxdesign 2015\c11_tut2\scenes*. Save the file with the name *c11tut2.max* at this location.

Note
Instead of following step 1, you can directly open the file that you created in Tutorial 1 of Chapter 3 and then follow step 2 given next to save it.

Assigning Multi/Sub-Object Material to Balloon

In this section, you will assign different materials to different portions of the balloon. This can be accomplished by using the multi/sub-object type of material.

1. Choose **Rendering > Material Editor > Compact Material Editor** from the menu bar; the **Material Editor** dialog box is displayed.

2. Make sure the first material sample slot is selected in this dialog box. Next, choose the **Arch & Design** button; the **Material/Map Browser** dialog box is displayed, as shown in Figure 11-8.

*Figure 11-8 The **Material/Map Browser** dialog box*

3. In this dialog box, select **Multi/Sub-Object** from **Materials > Standard** rollout and then choose the **OK** button; the **Replace Material** dialog box is displayed, as shown in Figure 11-9.

*Figure 11-9 The **Replace Material** dialog box*

4. Select the **Discard old material?** radio button and then choose the **OK** button; the **Arch & Design** button is labeled as **Multi/Sub-Object** in the **Material Editor** dialog box with ten materials listed.

5. Rename the material as **Balloon Material** in the material name drop-down list located below the material sample slots and then press the ENTER key; the material created is renamed as *Balloon Material*.

6. In the **Multi/Sub-Object Basic Parameters** rollout, choose the **Set Number** button; the **Set Number of Materials** dialog box is displayed, as shown in Figure 11-10.

Figure 11-10 The Set Number of Materials dialog box

7. Set the value **3** in the **Number of Materials** spinner and then choose the **OK** button.

    The material now has three slots instead of ten for submaterials.

8. Choose the button labeled as **None** placed on the right of the first material; the **Material/Map Browser** dialog box is displayed.

9. Select **Standard** from the **Materials > Standard** rollout and then choose the **OK** button.

10. Choose the **Go to Parent** button in the **Material Editor** dialog box. Next, choose the color swatch on the right of the first material to display the **Color Selector** dialog box. Select the blue color and drag the arrow to set the intensity of your choice, refer to Figure 11-11.

Figure 11-11 Setting the color of the material to blue using the Color Selector dialog box

11. Choose the **OK** button in the **Color Selector** dialog box; the first material changes to blue color.

12. Similarly, make the second material red and the third material yellow.

13. Select *Balloon* in the Front viewport. Make sure the sample slot containing *Balloon Material* is activated in the **Material Editor** dialog box. Next, choose the **Assign Material to Selection** button in the **Material Editor** dialog box; *Balloon Material* is assigned to *Balloon*.

14. Make sure *Balloon* is selected and then choose the **Modify** tab in the **Command Panel**. In the **Mesh Select Parameters** rollout, choose the **Face** button.

15. In the Front viewport, select faces of bottom three rows on *Balloon*, as shown in Figure 11-12.

Figure 11-12 Selecting faces of bottom three rows

16. Set the **Set ID** to **1** in the **Polygon Material ID's** rollout of the **Modify** panel.

17. Make sure the Front viewport is active. Next, select faces of middle two rows on *Balloon*, as shown in Figure 11-13.

18. Set the **Set ID** to **2** in the **Polygon Material ID's** rollout of the **Modify** panel.

19. Select the remaining faces of top three rows on *Balloon*, as shown in Figure 11-14.

20. Set the **Set ID** to **3** in the **Polygon Material ID's** rollout of the **Modify** panel.

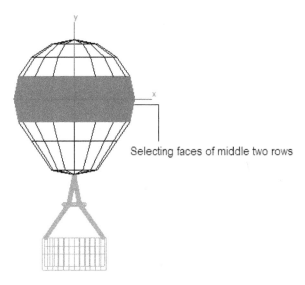

Figure 11-13 Selecting faces of middle two rows

Figure 11-14 Selecting faces of top three rows

Assigning Material to Balloon

In this section, you will assign materials that as been created for the balloon. This can be accomplished by using the **Material Editor** dialog box.

1. In the **Material Editor** dialog box, make sure the *Balloon Material* is selected. Next, choose the first submaterial button with ID 1; the parameters for the blue material are displayed.

2. Enter the name of submaterial as **Blue** in the material name drop-down list located below the material sample slots and then press the ENTER key.

3. In the **Shader Basic Parameters** rollout, select **Phong** from the drop-down list.

4. In the **Specular Highlights** area of the **Phong Basic Parameters** rollout, set the value **50** in the **Specular Level** spinner and **20** in the **Glossiness** spinner.

5. Choose the **Go to Parent** button to return to the root level of the material. Next, choose the second submaterial button with ID 2; the parameters for the red material are displayed.

6. Select **Phong** from the drop-down list of the **Shader Basic Parameters** rollout and then using the same process, rename the second submaterial as **Red**. Set the value **50** in the **Specular Level** spinner and **20** in the **Glossiness** spinner.

7. Choose the **Go to Parent** button to return to the root level of the material. Next, choose the third submaterial button with ID 3; the parameters for the yellow material are displayed.

8. Select **Phong** from the drop-down list of the **Shader Basic Parameters** rollout and then rename the third submaterial as **Yellow**. Set the value **50** in the **Specular Level** spinner and **20** in the **Glossiness** spinner.

9. At *Yellow* submaterial level, select the **Color** check box in the **Self Illumination** area in the **Phong Basic Parameters** rollout; the spinner is replaced by a color swatch.

10. Choose the color swatch to display the **Color Selector: Self-Illum Color** dialog box. Change the color to dark red.

    The **Self-Illumination** color will help give the illusion of a gas burner inside *Balloon*.

11. Return to the parent material level and close the **Material Editor** dialog box.

12. Activate the Perspective viewport and invoke the **Render Production** tool from the **Main Toolbar**; the still image of *Balloon* is rendered in the **Rendered Frame** window.

Assigning Material to Ropes

In this section, you will assign the created materials to ropes to give them realistic look.

1. Select *Rope01*, *Rope02*, *Rope03*, and *Rope04* from the **Scene Explorer**.

2. Invoke the **Material Editor** tool from the **Main Toolbar**; the **Material Editor** dialog box is displayed. Next, select the second material sample slot.

3. Choose the **Get Material** button to display the **Material/Map Browser** dialog box.

4. In this dialog box, choose the **Material/Map Browser Options** button; a flyout is displayed. Next, select the **Open Material Library** option from this flyout, as shown in Figure 11-15; the **Import Material Library** dialog box is displayed.

Figure 11-15 Selecting the Open Material Library option

5. In this dialog box, select the **3dsmax.mat** file and then choose the **Open** button; the different materials available in the *3dsmax.mat* library are displayed.

6. Double-click on the material **Fabric_Tan_Carpet (Standard)** to load it into selected material sample slot of the **Material Editor** dialog box. Next, in the **Material Editor** dialog box, choose the **Assign Material to Selection** button. Close the **Material/Map Browser** dialog box and minimize the **Material Editor** dialog box.

7. Make sure the ropes are selected and choose the **Modify** tab in the **Command Panel**. In the **Modifier List** drop-down list, select **UVW Map** in the **OBJECT-SPACE MODIFIERS** section; the **UVW Map** modifier is applied to all ropes.

8. In the **Mapping** area of the **Parameters** rollout, clear the **Real-World Map Size** check box and make sure the **Planar** radio button is selected. In the **Alignment** area, select the **Y** radio button and then choose the **Fit** button.

9. Make sure the Perspective viewport is activated and then invoke the **Render Production** tool from the **Main Toolbar** to render the scene.

Assigning Material to Collar
In this section, you will assign the material to the collar.

1. Select **Collar** from the **Scene Explorer** to highlight it.

2. Restore the **Material Editor** dialog box and then select the third sample slot. Next, choose the **Get Material** button; the **Material/Map Browser** dialog box is displayed.

3. Double-click on the material **Fabric_Blue_Carpet (Standard)** to load it into the material sample slot of the **Material Editor** dialog box. Next, choose the **Assign Material to Selection** button in the **Material Editor** dialog box. Minimize the **Material Editor** dialog box and close the **Material/Map Browser** dialog box.

4. Make sure *Collar* is selected and choose the **Modify** tab in the **Command Panel**. In the **Modifier List** drop-down list, select **UVW Map** in the **OBJECT-SPACE MODIFIERS** section.

5. In the **Mapping** area of the **Parameters** rollout, clear the **Real-World Map Size** check box and select the **Cylindrical** radio button.

6. Set the values in the respective spinners as given next:

Length: **60**	Width: **60**	Height: **60**
U Tile: **0.3**	V Tile: **0.3**	W Tile: **0.3**

Assigning Material to Basket

In this section, you will assign the material to the basket.

1. Select *Basket01* from the **Scene Explorer** to highlight it.

2. Restore the **Material Editor** dialog box. Select the fourth sample slot in the **Material Editor** dialog box to make it active.

3. Choose the **Get Material** button; the **Material/Map Browser** dialog box is displayed. Double-click on the material **Wood-Cedfence (Standard)** to load it into the material sample slot in the **Material Editor** dialog box.

4. Choose the **Assign Material to Selection** button in the **Material Editor** dialog box. Close both the **Material/Map Browser** dialog box and the **Material Editor** dialog box.

5 Make sure the basket is selected and then choose the **Modify** tab in the **Command Panel**. In the **Modifier List** drop-down list, select **UVW Map** in the **OBJECT-SPACE MODIFIERS** area.

6. In the **Mapping** area of the **Parameters** rollout, clear the **Real-World Map Size** check box and select the **Box** radio button.

7. Set the values in the respective spinners as given next:

Length: **4000**	Width: **4000**	Height: **4000**

8. Render the Perspective viewport. Close the **Rendered Frame** window after viewing the image.

Adding Lights and Camera

In this section, you will add lights and camera in the viewports.

1. Invoke the **Zoom All** tool and zoom the objects such that they are displayed at about one-fourth of their original size.

2. Choose **Create > Lights** in the **Command Panel**. Change **Photometric** option to **Standard** option in the drop-down list below the **Lights** button. Next, invoke the **Omni** tool from the **Object Type** rollout.

3. In the Front viewport, place two omni lights; one in the upper right corner and the other in the upper left corner of the viewport. Invoke the **Zoom Extents All** tool to view the lights properly in all viewports.

4. Invoke the **Select and Move** tool. In the Top viewport, move omni lights to the bottom left and top right corners, refer to Figure 11-16.

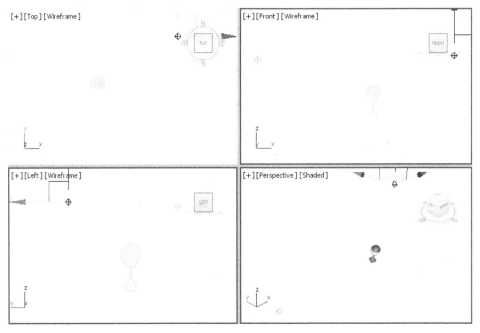

Figure 11-16 Adjusting Omni001 and Omni002 lights in the scene

5. Select the omni light in the lower left corner of the Top viewport and choose the **Modify** tab in the **Command Panel** to display various rollouts. In the **Shadows** area of the **General Parameters** rollout, clear the **On** check box. In the **Intensity/Color/Attenuation** rollout, set the value **0.4** in the **Multiplier** spinner.

6. Select omni light in the upper right corner of the Top viewport. Expand the **Intensity/ Color/Attenuation** rollout and set the value **0.8** in the **Multiplier** spinner. Expand the **Shadow Parameters** rollout and set the value **0.7** in the **Dens** spinner.

   This lightens the shadows cast by the omni light.

7. Choose **Create > Cameras** in the **Command Panel**. Next, invoke the **Target** tool from the **Object Type** rollout and place the camera in the Front viewport and position it in all viewports, as shown in Figure 11-17.

8. Activate the Perspective viewport and then press the C key to make it the Camera viewport.

Figure 11-17 The camera placed and positioned in the Front viewport

9. Make sure the **Select and Move** tool is invoked and then move the camera to get the desired view in the Camera viewport. In the Camera viewport, you can use the **Field-of-View** tool and other camera viewport tools to move the camera view closer and get a better view, refer to Figure 11-18. The **Zoom Region** tool is replaced by the **Field-of-view** tool when the Camera viewport is active.

10. Render the Camera viewport.

Setting the Background
In this section, you will set the background scene.

1. Choose **Rendering > Environment** from the menu bar; the **Environment and Effects** dialog box is displayed, as shown in Figure 11-19.

2. Choose the **None** button in the **Background** area of the **Common Parameters** rollout; the **Material/Map Browser** dialog box is displayed.

3. In this dialog box, expand the **Maps** rollout, if it is not expanded already and then select the **Bitmap** option from it. Now, choose the **OK** button; the **Select Bitmap Image File** dialog box is displayed, as shown in Figure 11-20.

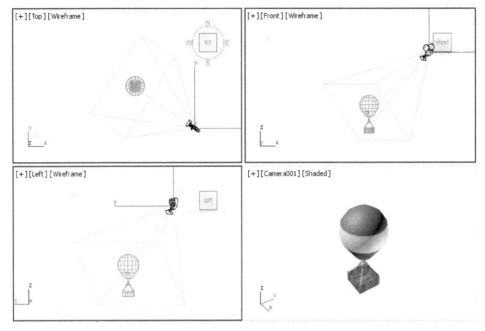

Figure 11-18 *The view adjusted using the* **Field-of-View** *tool*

Figure 11-19 *The* **Environment and Effects** *dialog box*

Figure 11-20 *The Select Bitmap Image File dialog box*

As the project folder is already set, the *images* folder of this project is displayed in the **Look in** drop-down list.

4. Select **Background_Falls.jpg** and choose the **Open** button; the *Background_Falls.jpg* replaces the **None** label in the **Environment and Effects** dialog box.

5. Make sure the **Use Map** check box is selected in the **Environment and Effects** dialog box. Next, close this dialog box and invoke the **Material Editor** dialog box.

6. In the **Material Editor** dialog box, select the fifth sample slot.

7. Choose the **Get Material** button; the **Material/Map Browser** dialog box is displayed. Next, scroll down and open the **Scene Materials** rollout.

8. Double-click on **Map # (Background_Falls.jpg)[Environment]** in the list to load it into the **Material Editor** dialog box, refer to Figure 11-21. Now, close the **Material/Map Browser** dialog box.

9. In the **Material Editor** dialog box, make sure the **Environ** radio button is selected in the **Coordinates** rollout and also make sure **Screen** is selected in the **Mapping** drop-down list. Also, make sure **0.0** is entered in the **Blur offset** spinner.

10. Close the **Material Editor** dialog box and render the Camera001 viewport; the rendered view of the balloon with the *Background_Falls.jpg* is displayed, as shown in Figure 11-22.

Figure 11-21 *Loading* **Map# (Background_Falls.jpg)[Enviornment]** *in the material sample slot*

Figure 11-22 *The final rendered scene*

Self-Evaluation Test

Answer the following questions and then compare them to those given at the end of this chapter:

1. Which of the following modifiers is used to apply mapping coordinates to an object?

    (a) **UVW Map**   (b) **Extrude**
    (c) **Edit Mesh**   (d) **Mesh Select**

2. You can change the intensity of the omni light by changing the value in the _____ spinner of the **Intensity/Color/Attenuation** rollout.

3. The _____ dialog box is used to set the background scene for an object.

4. The **Assign Material to Selection** button in the **Material Editor** dialog box is used to display the materials on the objects in the viewport. (T/F)

Review Questions

Answer the following questions:

1. The **Get Material** button in the **Material Editor** dialog box is used to display the _____ dialog box.

2. You can apply mapping coordinates to an object by applying the _____ modifier.

3. The _____ button in the **Material Editor** dialog box is used to assign material to an object.

4. You can use the **Multi/Sub Object** material to assign different materials to different portions of an object. (T/F)

EXERCISE

The rendered output of the model used in the following exercise can be accessed by downloading the *c11_3dsmaxdesign_2015_exr.zip* from *www.cadcim.com*. The path of the file is as follows: *Textbooks > Animation and Visual Effects > 3ds Max Design > Autodesk 3ds Max Design 2015: A Tutorial Approach*

Exercise 1

Extract the contents of the *c11_3dsmaxdesign_2015_exr.zip* and then open *c11_exr01_start.max*. Next, apply materials to the model of the table, as shown in Figure 11-23.

(Expected time: 20 min)

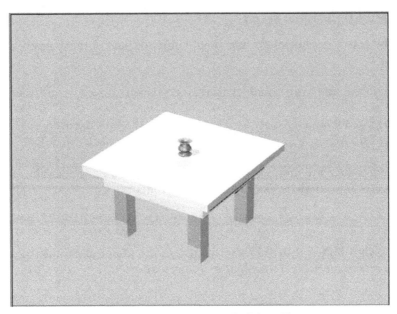

Figure 11-23 *The model of the table*

Chapter *12*

Interior Lighting-I

Learning Objectives

After completing this chapter, you will be able to:
• *Create the night interior scene*
• *Create the daylight interior scene*

INTRODUCTION

Lights are used to illuminate a scene and make it look more realistic. In Autodesk 3ds Max Design, there are two main categories of lights: Standard and Photometric. These categories can be further classified into different types. You can select one or more lights based on the requirement of a scene. In this chapter, you will learn to illuminate an interior scene using the standard lights.

TUTORIALS

Before starting the tutorials, you need to download the *c12_3dsmaxdesign_2015_tut.zip* file from *www.cadcim.com*. The path of this file is as follows: *Textbooks > Animation and Visual Effects > 3ds Max Design > Autodesk 3ds Max Design 2015: A Tutorial Approach*

Extract the contents of the zip file and save them in the *Documents* folder.

Tutorial 1

In this tutorial, you will illuminate a night interior scene using standard lights, refer to Figure12-1.   **(Expected time: 45 min)**

Figure 12-1 *The illuminated night interior scene*

The following steps are required to complete this tutorial:

a. Create the project folder.
b. Open the file.
c. Create the roof lights.
d. Create wall lights.
e. Create lamp lights.
f. Save and render the scene.

Creating the Project Folder

Create the project folder with the name *c12_tut1* in the *3dsmaxdesign 2015* folder, as discussed in earlier chapters.

Opening the File

1. Open Windows Explorer and then browse to *\Documents\c12_3dsmaxdesign_2015_tut*. Next, copy all files to *\Documents\3dsmaxdesign 2015\c12_tut1\sceneassets\images*.

2. Choose **Open** from the **Application** menu; the **Open File** dialog box is displayed. In this dialog box, browse to the location *\Documents\c12_3dsmaxdesign_2015_tut* and select the **c12_tut1_start.max** file from it. Choose the **Open** button to open the file, refer to Figure 12-2.

Figure 12-2 The c12_tut1_start.max file

3. Choose **Save As** from the **Application** menu; the **Save File As** dialog box is displayed. Browse to the location *\Documents\3dsmaxdesign 2015\c12_tut1\scenes*. Save the file with the name *c12tut1.max* at this location.

Creating the Roof Lights

In this section, you will create roof lights using the **Omni** tool.

1. Activate the Top viewport. Choose **Create > Lights** in the **Command Panel**. By default, the **Photometric** option is displayed in the drop-down list located below it. Select **Standard** from the drop-down list and then invoke the **Omni** tool from the **Object Type** rollout; various rollouts are displayed in the **Command Panel**. Next, click at the center of the room; the omni light is displayed in the viewport with the name *Omni001*.

2. Invoke the **Select and Move** tool and align *Omni001* in all viewports, as shown in Figure 12-3.

Figure 12-3 Omni001 aligned in all viewports

3. In the **Name and Color** rollout, enter the name as **roof Light1**.

4. Choose the **Modify** tab. Now, in the **General Parameters** rollout, make sure the **On** check box is selected in the **Shadows** area. Next, select **Ray Traced Shadows** from the drop-down list below this check box, if it is not selected.

5. Expand the **Intensity/Color/Attenuation** rollout and set the value **0.5** in the **Multiplier** spinner.

   Next, you will lighten the shadow color.

6. Expand the **Shadow Parameters** rollout and choose the color swatch next to the **Color** parameter in the **Object Shadows** area; the **Color Selector: Shadow Color** dialog box is displayed. In this dialog box, set the values of **Red**, **Green**, and **Blue** spinners to **52** and then choose the **OK** button.

7. Activate the Left viewport. Make sure *roof light1* is selected and create a copy of it. Now, align it in the position, as shown in Figure 12-4.

Figure 12-4 *The copy of roof light1 aligned in all viewports*

8. Set the angle of view in the Perspective viewport and render the Perspective viewport by invoking the **Render Production** tool from the **Main Toolbar**. The rendered image is displayed, refer to Figure 12-5.

Creating Wall Lights

In this section, you will create the wall lights using the **mr Area Spot** and **Omni** tools.

1. Maximize the Left viewport. Choose **Create > Lights** in the **Command Panel**. Make sure **Standard** is selected in the drop-down list. Next, invoke the **mr Area Spot** tool from the **Object Type** rollout. Next, click at the point and drag the cursor downwards. Next, release the left mouse button; a spot light and its target is created, as shown in Figure 12-6.

2. In the **Name and Color** rollout, enter **spot light 1**. Next, invoke the **Select and Move** tool and align *spot Light 1* and *spot light 1.Target* in all viewports, as shown in Figure 12-7.

3. Select *spot Light 1* and choose the **Modify** tab in the **Command Panel**.

4. In the **General Parameters** rollout, clear the **On** check box in the **Shadows** area.

Figure 12-5 *The rendered image*

Figure 12-6 *The spot light created*

Figure 12-7 The spot light 1 and spot light 1.Target aligned

5. Expand the **Intensity/Color/Attenuation** rollout and set the value in the **Multiplier** spinner to **30**. Next, choose the color swatch next to this spinner; the **Color Selector: Light Color** dialog box is displayed. In this dialog box, set the values of the **Red**, **Green**, and **Blue** spinners to **169**, **164**, and **23**, respectively and then choose the **OK** button to close the dialog box.

6. In the **Decay** area, select **Inverse Square** from the **Type** drop-down list. Next, set **33.777** in the **Start** spinner. Also, set the values in the **Start** and **End** spinners under the **Near Attenuation** and **Far Attenuation** areas, as shown in Figure 12-8.

Attenuation is the effect of the light intensity that decreases with the distance.

7. Expand the **Spotlight Parameters** rollout and set the value of the **Hotspot/Beam** and **Falloff/Field** spinners to **34** and **40**, respectively. Make sure the **Show Cone** check box is selected in the **Light Cone** area of the **Spotlight Parameters** rollout.

8. Set the angle of view in the Perspective viewport and render the Perspective viewport by invoking the **Render Production** tool from the **Main Toolbar**; the rendered image is displayed, refer to Figure 12-9.

Figure 12-8 The parameters in the Intensity/Color/Attenuation rollout

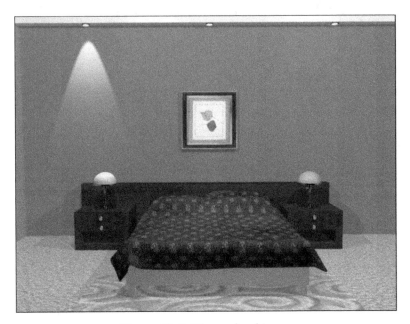

Figure 12-9 *The rendered image*

Now, you will use the omni light to show the glow at the source of the spot light.

9. Activate the Top viewport. Choose **Create > Lights** in the **Command Panel**. Make sure **Standard** is displayed in the drop-down list located below it. Next, invoke the **Omni** tool from the **Object Type** rollout; various rollouts are displayed in the **Command Panel**. Next, click in the viewport; the omni light is displayed in the viewport. Enter **glow light 1** in the **Name and Color** rollout.

10. Invoke the **Select and Move** tool and align *glow light 1* in all viewports, refer to Figure 12-10.

11. Make sure *glow light 1* is selected in the viewport and choose the **Modify** tab in the **Command Panel**. In the **General Parameters** rollout, clear the **On** check box in the **Shadows** area.

12. Expand the **Intensity/Color/Attenuation** rollout and set the value in the **Multiplier** spinner to **3**. Next, choose the color swatch next to this spinner; the **Color Selector: Light Color** dialog box is displayed. In this dialog box, make sure the values of the **Red**, **Green**, and **Blue** spinners are set to **169**, **164**, and **23**, respectively and then choose the **OK** button to close the dialog box.

13. In the **Decay** area, select **Inverse Square** from the **Type** drop-down list and set the value **15** in the **Start** spinner located below it. Also select the **Show** check box in this area. Make sure that the **Use** and **Show** check boxes in the **Far Attenuation** and **Near Attenuation** areas are clear.

Figure 12-10 The glow light 1 aligned

14. Set the angle of view in the Perspective viewport and then invoke the **Render Production** tool from the **Main Toolbar**; the rendered image is displayed, refer to Figure 12-11.

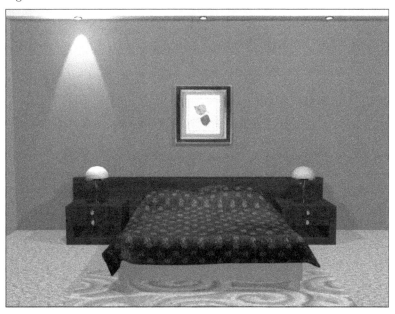

Figure 12-11 The rendered image

Next, you need to create two copies of both *spot light 1* and *glow light 1*.

15. Activate the Left viewport. Select *glow light 1*, *spot light 1*, and *spot light 1.Target* from the **Scene Explorer**. Next, press and hold the SHIFT key and drag the cursor to *light fixture 001*. Release the left mouse button; the **Clone Options** dialog box is displayed. In this dialog box, make sure the **Instance** radio button is selected. Set **2** in the **Number of Copies** spinner and choose the **OK** button; two copies of both *spot light 1* and *glow light 1* are created in all viewports, as shown in Figure 12-12.

Figure 12-12   *The copies of spot light 1 and glow light 1 created*

 Note
*If you select the **Instance** radio button in the **Clone Options** dialog box, the copy of the object created will be the instance of the original object which means that the changes made in the parameters of one object will automatically reflect in the other object.*

16. Set the angle of view in the Perspective viewport and render it by invoking the **Render Production** tool from the **Main Toolbar**; the rendered image is displayed, refer to Figure 12-13.

Figure 12-13 *The rendered image*

Creating Lamp Lights

In this section, you will create lamp lights for bed side lamps.

1. Maximize the Left viewport. Choose **Create > Lights** in the **Command Panel**. Next, invoke the **mr Area Spot** tool from the **Object Type** rollout and click at the point and drag the cursor downwards. Now, release the left mouse button; a spot light and its target is created.

2. In the **Name and Color** rollout, enter **lamp light 1** as the name of the light. Next, invoke the **Select and Move** tool and align the *lamp light 1* and *lamp light 1.Target* in all viewports, as shown in Figure 12-14.

3. Select *lamp light 1*. In the **Intensity/Color/Attenuation** rollout, set the value **1** in the **Multiplier** spinner. Next, choose the color swatch next to this spinner; the **Color Selector: Light Color** dialog box is displayed. In this dialog box, make sure the values of the **Red**, **Green**, and **Blue** spinners are set to **169**, **164**, and **23**, respectively and then choose the **OK** button to close the dialog box.

4. In the **Far Attenuation** area, select the **Use** and **Show** check boxes and set the values of the **Start** and **End** spinners to **30.243** and **32.323**, respectively.

5. In the **Spotlight Parameters** rollout, set the value of the **Hotspot/Beam** and **Falloff/Field** spinners to **90** and **98**, respectively.

Figure 12-14 *The lamp light 1and lamp light 1.Target aligned*

6. Set the angle of view in the Perspective viewport and render it by invoking the
    Render Production tool from the **Main Toolbar**; the rendered image is displayed,
    refer to Figure 12-15.

Figure 12-15 *The rendered image*

Next, you need to add an omni light to simulate the glow of *lamp light 1*.

7. Activate the Top viewport. Choose **Create > Lights** in the **Command Panel**. Next, invoke the **Omni** tool from the **Object Type** rollout; various rollouts are displayed in the **Command Panel**. Next, click in the viewport; the omni light is displayed in the viewport. Enter **lamp glow light 1** in the **Name and Color** rollout.

8. Invoke the **Select and Move** tool and align *lamp glow light 1* in all viewports, as shown in Figure 12-16.

Figure 12-16 *The lamp glow light 1 aligned*

9. Make sure *lamp glow light 1* is selected in the viewport and choose the **Modify** tab in the **Command Panel**. In the **General Parameters** rollout, clear the **On** check box in the **Shadows** area.

10. In the **Intensity/Color/Attenuation** rollout, set the value **200** in the **Multiplier** spinner and set the color swatch to yellow color.

11. In the **Decay** area, make sure **Inverse Square** is selected from the **Type** drop-down list and set the value **6** in the **Start** spinner located below it. Also, make sure the **Show** check box in this area is selected.

12. In the **Shadows** area of the **General Parameters** rollout, choose the **Exclude** button; the **Exclude/Include** dialog box is displayed. In this dialog box, select *lamp top 2* from the list displayed on the left of this dialog box. Next, choose the **>>** button and also select the **Include** radio button; *lamp top 2* is displayed on the right of this dialog box. Next, choose the **OK** button to close the dialog box.

Note
*The options in the **Exclude/Include** dialog box are used to exclude or include some of the scene objects from the light's illumination, shadow casting, or both.*

13. Set the angle of view in the Perspective viewport and render it by invoking the **Render Production** tool from the **Main Toolbar**; the rendered image is displayed, refer to Figure 12-17.

Figure 12-17 The rendered image

Next, you need to create the copy of *lamp light 1* and *lamp glow light 1* for other bed side lamp.

14. Activate the Left viewport. Select *lamp glow light 1, lamp light 1, and lamp light 1.Target*. Next, press and hold the SHIFT key and drag the cursor to *lamp top 1*. Release the left mouse button; the **Clone Options** dialog box is displayed. In this dialog box, select the **Copy** radio button. Make sure the value **1** is set in the **Number of Copies** spinner and then choose the **OK** button; a copy of *lamp light1, lamp light1.Target* and *lamp glow light 1* is created. Next, invoke the **Select and Move** tool and align these lights in all viewports as shown in Figure 12-18.

15. Select *lamp glow light 002* light and choose the **Modify** tab in the **Command Panel**. Next, in the **Shadows** area of the **General Parameters** rollout, choose the **Exclude** button; the **Exclude/Include** dialog box is displayed. In this dialog box, select **lamp top 1** from the list displayed on the left of this dialog box. Next, choose the **>>** button and also select the **Include** radio button; *lamp top 1* is displayed on the right of this dialog box. Next, choose the **OK** button to close the dialog box.

Figure 12-18 The copy of lamp light 1, lamp light1.Target, lamp glow light 1 aligned

Saving and Rendering the Scene

In this section, you will save the scene that you have created and then render it. You can also view the final rendered image of this model by downloading the *c12_3dsmaxdesign_2015_rndr.zip* file from *www.cadcim.com*. The path of the file is as follows: *Textbooks > Animation and Visual Effects > 3ds Max Design > Autodesk 3ds Max Design 2015: A Tutorial Approach*

1. Choose **Save** from the **Application** menu.

2. Activate the Perspective viewport. Next, invoke the **Render Production** tool from the **Main Toolbar**; the rendered image is displayed, refer to Figure 12-19.

Figure 12-19 *The rendered image*

Tutorial 2

In this tutorial, you will create a daylight interior scene using the target direct light, as shown in Figure 12-20.   **(Expected Time: 20 min)**

The following steps are required to complete this tutorial:

a.   Create the project folder.
b.   Open the file.
c.   Create lights.
d.   Save and render the scene.

Creating the Project Folder
Create the project folder with the name *c12_tut2* in the *3dsmaxdesign 2015* folder, as discussed in earlier chapters.

Opening the File
1.   Open Windows Explorer and then browse to *\Documents\c12_3dsmaxdesign_2015_tut*. Next, copy all jpeg files to *\Documents\ 3dsmaxdesign 2015\c12_tut2\sceneassets\images*.

2.   Choose **Open** from the **Application** menu; the **Open File** dialog box is displayed. In this dialog box, browse to the location *\Documents\c12_3dsmaxdesign_2015_tut* and open the **c12_tut2_start.max** file, refer to Figure 12-21.

Figure 12-20 *The daylight interior scene*

Figure 12-21 *The c12_tut2_start file*

3.   Choose **Save As** from the **Application** menu; the **Save File As** dialog box is displayed. Browse to the location *Documents**3dsmaxdesign 2015**c12_tut2**scenes*. Save the file with the name *c12tut2.max* at this location.

Creating Lights

In this section, you will use the **Omni** and **Target Direct** tools to create the daylight effect.

1.   Activate the Top viewport. Choose **Create > Lights** in the **Command Panel**. By default, the **Photometric** option is displayed in the **Command Panel**. Select **Standard** from the drop-down list and then invoke the **Omni** tool from the **Object Type** rollout; various rollouts are displayed in the **Command Panel**. Next, click at a point in the room; the omni light is created in the viewport with the name *Omni001*. Next, align it as shown in Figure 12-22.

Figure 12-22 *The omni 001 light aligned in all viewports*

2.   Make sure *Omni001* is selected. Next, choose the **Modify** tab in the **Command Panel**.

3.   In the **General Parameters** rollout, make sure the **On** check box is selected in the **Shadows** area and select the **Ray Traced Shadows** option in the drop-down list. Next, choose the **Exclude** button; the **Exclude/Include** dialog box is displayed. In this dialog box, select *window grid 1* from the list displayed on the left of this dialog box. Next, choose the **>>** button and also make sure the **Exclude** radio button is selected; *window grid 1 is* displayed on the right of this dialog box. Next, choose the **OK** button to close the dialog box; *window grid 1* is excluded from *Omni001*.

4. Expand the **Intensity/Color/Attenuation** rollout and set the value of the **Multiplier** spinner to **0.7**. Next, choose the color swatch next to this spinner; the **Color Selector: Light Color** dialog box is displayed. In this dialog box, make sure the values of the **Red**, **Green**, and **Blue** spinners are set to **255**, **255**, and **255**, respectively and then choose the **OK** button to close the dialog box.

5. Expand the **Shadow Parameters** rollout and set the value **0.8** in the **Dens** spinner. Next, select the color swatch next to the **Color** parameter; the **Color Selector: Shadow Color** dialog box is displayed. In this dialog box, set the values of the **Red**, **Green**, and **Blue** spinners to **50** and then choose the **OK** button to close the dialog box.

6. Similarly, create another omni light as created in step 1 with the name *Omni 002*. Next, align it in all viewports, as shown in Figure 12-23.

Figure 12-23 The omni 002 aligned

7. Make sure *Omni 002* is selected in the viewport. Choose the **Modify** tab in the **Command Panel**. In the **General Parameters** rollout, make sure the **On** check box is selected in the **Shadows** area and **Ray Traced Shadows** option is selected in the drop-down list. Next, choose the **Exclude** button; the **Exclude/Include** dialog box is displayed. In this dialog box, select *window grid 1* from the list displayed on the left of this dialog box. Next, choose the **>>** button and also make sure the **Exclude** radio button is selected; *window grid 1* is displayed on the right of this dialog box. Next, choose the **OK** button to close the dialog box; *window grid 1* is excluded from *Omni002*.

8. Expand the **Intensity/Color/Attenuation** rollout and set the value of the **Multiplier** spinner to **0.5**.

9. Expand the **Shadow Parameters** rollout and make sure the value is set to **0.8** in the **Dens** spinner.

    Next, you will use a direct light to simulate the sunlight coming from the window of the room.

10. Invoke the **Render Production** tool from the **Main Toolbar** to view the rendered scene.

11. Activate the Left viewport. Invoke the **Target Direct** tool from **Create > Lights > Standard > Object Type** rollout in the **Command Panel**. Move the cursor on the right side of the viewport. Next, press and hold the left mouse button to specify the location of the light and drag the cursor near the front portion of *wall001* to locate the target of the light. Release the left mouse button; the light is displayed in all viewports and it is automatically named as *Direct001*.

12. Choose the **Modify** tab in the **Command Panel**; various rollouts are displayed to modify *Direct001*.

13. Expand the **General Parameters** rollout and select the **On** check box in the **Shadows** area, if it is not selected.

14. In the **Intensity/Color/Attenuation** rollout and set the value of the **Multiplier** spinner to **0.8**. Next, choose the color swatch next to this spinner; the **Color Selector: Light Color** dialog box is displayed. In this dialog box, set the values for the **Red**, **Green**, and **Blue** spinners to **235**, **209**, and **182**, respectively and then choose the **OK** button to close the dialog box.

15. Expand the **Directional Parameters** rollout, select the **Rectangle** radio button and set the values in the respective spinners as given next:

    Hotspot/Beam: **47**   Falloff/Field: **49**

16. Invoke the **Select and Move** tool and align *Direct001*, *Direct 001.Target* light in all viewports, as shown in Figure 12-24.

17. Render the scene to view the rendered output.

18. Select *Direct001*. Expand the **Atmospheres & Effects** rollout and choose the **Add** button; the **Add Atmosphere or Effect** dialog box is displayed. Select the **Volume Light** option and then choose the **OK** button; the **Volume Light** option is displayed in the text area of the **Atmospheres & Effects** rollout.

Figure 12-24 *The Direct 001, Direct 001.Target aligned*

Next, you need to modify the parameters of the **Volume Light**.

19. Select the **Volume Light** option in the **Atmospheres & Effects** rollout and choose the **Setup** button; the **Environment and Effects** dialog box is displayed. In this dialog box, the **Environment** tab is chosen by default.

20. In the **Atmosphere** rollout, make sure that the **Volume Light** option is selected in the **Effects** area. Set the value **0.05** in the **Density** spinner of the **Volume** area in the **Volume Light Parameters** rollout. Use the default values for other options and close the **Environment and Effects** dialog box.

Note
*You can also use different settings in the **Volume Light Parameters** rollout to apply different effects in the scene.*

21. Render the scene.

Saving and Rendering the Scene

In this section, you will save the scene that you have created and then render it. You can also view the final rendered image of this model by downloading the *c12_3dsmaxdesign_2015_rndr.zip* file from *www.cadcim.com*. The path of the file is as follows: *Textbooks > Animation and Visual Effects > 3ds Max Design > Autodesk 3ds Max Design 2015: A Tutorial Approach*

1.   Choose **Save** from the **Application** menu.

2. Activate the Perspective viewport. Next, invoke the **Render Production** tool from the **Main Toolbar**; the rendered image is displayed, refer to Figure 12-25.

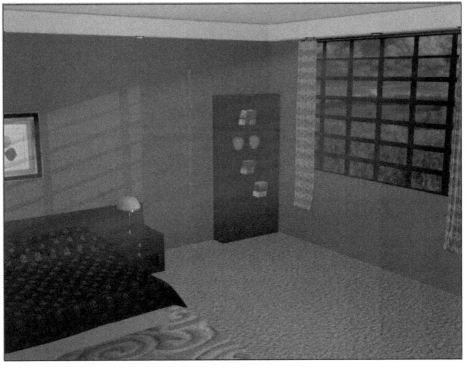

Figure 12-25 *The rendered image*

Self-Evaluation Test

Answer the following questions and then compare them to those given at the end of this chapter:

1. Which of the following tools is used to create standard lights?

    (a) **Target Direct**   (b) **Target Light**
    (c) **Free Light**   (d) All of these

2. Which of the following tools is used to create the area spot light?

    (a) **Target Spot**   (b) **mr Area Spot**
    (c) **mr Area Omni**   (d) All of these

3. The _____ check box in the **General Parameters** rollout is selected to view the shadow of a light.

4. The options in the _____ rollout are used to assign special effects to the environment such as fog and glow on rendering.

5. The **Exclude** button in the **General Parameters** rollout is used to define a number of objects in the scene that will be affected by the light on rendering. (T/F)

Review Questions

Answer the following questions:

1. Which of the following spinners is used to specify the intensity of the light in the **Intensity/Color/Attenuation** rollout?

   (a) **Start**   (b) **Color**
   (c) **Multiplier**   (d) None of these

2. Which of the following tools is used to create a light that illuminates the scene in all directions?

   (a) **mr Sky Portal**   (b) **Omni**
   (c) **Free Spot**   (d) None of these

3. The parameters in the _____ rollout are used to control the properties of the spotlight.

4. The parameters in the _____ rollout are used to control the properties of the shadow.

5. Attenuation is the effect of light intensity that decreases with the distance. (T/F)

EXERCISE

The rendered output of the scene used in the following exercise can be accessed by downloading the *c12_maxdesign_2015_exr.zip* from *www.cadcim.com*. The path of the file is as follows: *Textbooks > Animation and Visual Effects > 3ds Max Design > Autodesk 3ds Max Design 2015: A Tutorial Approach*

Exercise 1

Extract the contents of the *c12_3dsmaxdesign_2015_exr.zip* and then open *c12_exr01_start.max*. Next, illuminate the scene using omni and spot lights, as shown in Figure 12-26.

(Expected time: 20 min)

Figure 12-26 The illuminated scene

Chapter *13*

Interior Lighting-II

Learning Objectives

After completing this chapter, you will be able to:
- *Use photometric lights for interior lighting*
- *Use IES files*

INTRODUCTION

In the last chapter, you learned to use standard lights to illuminate interior scene. In this chapter, you will learn to use photometric lights to illuminate an interior scene. Photometric lights are more complex than the standard lights but provide more realistic lighting effects.

Additionally, you will create special lighting patterns by using the standard IES (Illuminating Engineering Society) files.

TUTORIALS

Before starting the tutorials, you need to download the *c13_3dsmaxdesign_2015_tut.zip* file from *www.cadcim.com*. The path of the file is as follows: *Textbooks > Animation and Visual Effects > 3ds Max Design > Autodesk 3ds Max Design 2015: A Tutorial Approach*

Extract the contents of the zip file and save them in the *Documents* folder.

Tutorial 1

In this chapter, you will illuminate a night interior scene using photometric lights, refer to Figure 13-1.   **(Expected time: 30 min)**

Figure 13-1 The illuminated night interior scene

The following steps are required to complete this tutorial:

a.   Create the project folder.
b.   Open the file.
c.   Create the roof light.
d.   Create wall lights.
e.   Save and render the scene.

Creating the Project Folder

Create a project folder with the name *c13_tut1* in the *3dsmaxdesign 2015* folder, as discussed in Tutorial 1 of Chapter 2.

Opening the File

1.   Open Windows Explorer and then browse to *\Documents\c13_3dsmaxdesign_2015_tut*. Next, copy all jpeg files to *\Documents\3dsmaxdesign 2015\c13_tut1\sceneassets\images*. Also copy *1.IES* file to *\Documents\3dsmaxdesign 2015\c13_tut1\sceneassets\photometric*.

2.   Choose **Open** from the **Application** menu; the **Open File** dialog box is displayed. In this dialog box, browse to the location *\Documents\c13_3dsmaxdesign_2015_tut* and select the **c13_tut1_start.max** file from it. Choose the **Open** button to open the file, refer to Figure 13-2.

Figure 13-2 The c13_tut1_start.max file

3.   Choose **Save As** from the **Application** menu; the **Save File As** dialog box is displayed. Browse to the location *\Documents\3dsmaxdesign 2015\c13_tut1\scenes*. Save the file with the name *c13tut1.max* at this location.

Creating the Roof Light

In this section, you will create the roof light by using the **Free Light** tool.

1. Invoke the **Maximize Viewport Toggle** tool to view the four viewports and activate the Top viewport. Choose **Create > Lights** in the **Command Panel**. By default, the **Photometric** option is displayed in the drop-down list below it.

2. Invoke the **Free Light** tool from the **Object Type** rollout; the **Photometric Light Creation** message box is displayed, as shown in Figure 13-3. Next, choose **Yes** from this message box. Also, various rollouts are displayed in the **Command Panel**.

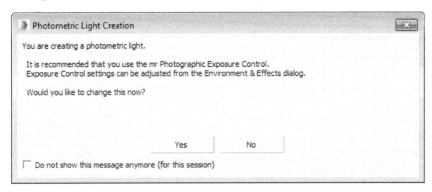

*Figure 13-3 The **Photometric Light Creation** message box*

3. Click at the center of the room; the free light is created with the name *PhotometricLight001*. Enter **rooflight1** in the **Name and Color** rollout.

4. Invoke the **Select and Move** tool and align *rooflight1* in all viewports, as shown in Figure 13-4.

    Next, you will modify the shape of *rooflight1*.

5. Choose the **Modify** tab in the **Command Panel.** Next, in the **Emit Light from (Shape)** area of the **Shape/Area Shadows** rollout, select the **Sphere** option from the drop-down list; the shape of the light changes in the viewport and the **Radius** spinner is displayed in the **Emit Light from (Shape)** area. Also, the **Shadow Samples** drop-down list is added to the **Rendering** area located below it.

6. Set the value **77.37** in the **Radius** spinner to increase the spread of the light; the shape of *rooflight1* is modified, as shown in Figure 13-5.

    Next, you will modify the parameters of *rooflight1* to lit the room with proper intensity, colors, and shadows.

Figure 13-4 *The rooflight1 aligned in all viewports*

Figure 13-5 *The shape of rooflight1 changed*

7. In the **General Parameters** rollout, make sure the **On** check box is selected in the **Shadows** area. Next, select **Ray Traced Shadows** in the drop-down list below this check box.

8. Make sure the **Uniform Spherical** option is selected in the drop-down list located in the **Light Distribution (Type)** area.

   The **Uniform Spherical** option is used to spread light in all directions.

9. Select the radio button located near the **Kelvin** Spinner; the **Kelvin** spinner is activated.

10. Set the value **6372** in the **Kelvin** spinner; the color swatch located next to the **Kelvin** spinner is changed to white. Next, choose the **Filter Color** color swatch located below it; the **Color Selector: Filter Color** dialog box is displayed. In this dialog box, make sure the value in the **Red**, **Green**, and **Blue** spinners is set to **255** and then choose the **OK** button to close the dialog box.

 Note
   *The value in the **Kelvin** spinner and the color in the **Filter Color** color swatch together define the color shade of the light being created. You can use different combinations of the spinner value and color shade in the color swatch to achieve variety of light color shades.*

   Next, you will set the intensity of *rooflight1*.

11. In the **Intensity** area of the **Intensity/Color/Attenuation** rollout, select the **lm** radio button; the value in the first spinner located below the **lm** radio button changes and displays the intensity of the light in Lumen. Next, set the value **700** in this spinner; the intensity of the light is changed.

   Now, you will render the scene to view the effect of modifying rooflight parameters in the scene.

12. Activate the Perspective viewport and adjust its view. Next, invoke the **Render Production** tool from the **Main Toolbar**; the rendered image is displayed, refer to Figure 13-6.

   You will notice the grains in the rendered image. Next, you will remove grains in the image by using higher shadow samples.

13. In the **Rendering** area of the **Shape/Area Shadows** rollout, select **256** from the **Shadow Samples** drop-down list.

 Note
   *If you select higher values for sampling shadows from the **Shadow Samples** drop-down list, the quality of the render is improved but the rendering time also increases.*

14. Render the Perspective viewport again as discussed earlier. The rendered image is displayed, refer to Figure 13-7.

Figure 13-6 *The rendered image with grains*

Figure 13-7 *The rendered image without grains*

Creating Wall Lights

In this section, you will create wall lights by using the **Target Light** tool. You will also use IES file to achieve a specific light pattern.

1. Switch from the Left viewport to the Right viewport. Now, activate the Front viewport. Choose **Create > Lights** in the **Command Panel**. Next, invoke the **Target Light** tool from the **Object Type** rollout; various rollouts are displayed in the **Command Panel**.

2. Click at a point and drag the cursor downwards. Next, release the left mouse button; a target light is created. In the **Name and Color** rollout, enter **spot light1**. Next, invoke the **Select and Move** tool and then select *spot light1* and *spot light1.Target*. Now, align them in all viewports, as shown in Figure 13-8. You may need to invoke the **Zoom Extents All** tool to view the lights in all viewports.

Figure 13-8 The spot light1 and spot light1.Target aligned in all viewports

Next, you need to modify the parameters of *spot light1*.

3. Choose the **Modify** tab in the **Command Panel**. In the **General Parameters** rollout, make sure the **On** check box is selected in the **Shadows** area. Next, select the **Photometric Web** option in the drop-down list from the **Light Distribution (Type)** area; a **Distribution (Photometric Web)** rollout is displayed in the **Command Panel**.

    Now, you will use a standard photometric IES file to create a specific lighting pattern. These IES files are standard files provided by light manufacturers and are available on the internet for free download.

4. In the **Emit Light from (Shape)** area of the **Shape/Area Shadows** rollout, make sure the **Point** option is selected in the drop-down list.

5. Choose the **< Choose Photometric File >** button from the **Distribution (Photometric Web)** rollout; the **Open a Photometric Web File** dialog box is displayed. As the project folder is already set, the *photometric* folder of this project is displayed in the **Look in** drop-down list. Next, select the **1.ies** file from this dialog box and then choose the **Open** button; label of the button is replaced by the name of the selected file. Also, the lighting pattern is displayed in the window located above this button.

    Next, you need to set the intensity and color of *spot light1*.

6. Select the radio button located near the **Kelvin** Spinner; the **Kelvin** spinner is activated.

7. Choose the **Filter Color** color swatch located below it; the **Color Selector: Filter Color** dialog box is displayed. In this dialog box, set the value in the **Red**, **Green**, and **Blue** spinners as given next:

    Red: **243**   Green: **240**   Blue: **146**

    Choose the **OK** button to close the dialog box; the color in the **Filter Color** color swatch is changed to yellow.

8. In the **Intensity** area of the **Intensity/Color/Attenuation** rollout, select the **lm** radio button; the value in the first spinner located below this radio button changes and displays the intensity of the light in Lumen. Next, set the value **600** in this spinner; the intensity of the light is increased.

    At this stage, you may render the scene to view the effect of modifying *spot light1* parameters in the scene. Next, you will set the parameters in the **Far Attenuation** area to attenuate *spot light1*.

9. In the **Far Attenuation** area, select the **Use** and **Show** check boxes. Next, set the value **0** and **60** in the **Start** and **End** spinners, respectively.

10. Activate the Perspective viewport. Next, invoke the **Render Production** tool from the **Main Toolbar**; the rendered image is displayed, refer to Figure 13-9.

    Next, you will add glow to the source of *spot light1*.

11. Activate the Top viewport. Choose **Create > Lights** in the **Command Panel**. Next, invoke the **Free Light** tool from the **Object Type** rollout.

12. Next, click at a point, refer to Figure 13-10; the free light is displayed with the name *PhotometricLight001*. Enter **glowlight1** in the **Name and Color** rollout.

13. Invoke the **Select and Move** tool and align *glowlight1* in all viewports, as shown in Figure 13-10.

Next, you need to set the intensity and color of *glowlight1*.

Figure 13-9 *The rendered image*

Figure 13-10 *The glowlight1 aligned in all viewports*

14. Choose the **Modify** tab in the **Command Panel.** Next, in the **Light Distribution (Type)** area of the **General Parameters** rollout, make sure **Uniform Spherical** is selected in the drop-down list.

15. In the **Color** area of the **Intensity/Color/Attenuation** rollout, make sure the **D65 Illuminant (Reference White)** is selected in the drop-down list. Next, choose the **Filter Color** color swatch located below it; the **Color Selector: Filter Color** dialog box is displayed. In this dialog box, make sure the values in the **Red**, **Green**, and **Blue** spinners are as given next:

Red: **243** Green: **240** Blue: **146**

Choose the **OK** button to close the dialog box; the color in the **Filter Color** color swatch is set to yellow.

16. In the **Intensity** area of the **Intensity/Color/Attenuation** rollout, select the **lm** radio button; the value in the first spinner located below it changes to show the intensity of the light in Lumen. Next, set the value **30** in this spinner; the intensity of the light is decreased.

17. Activate the Perspective viewport. Next, invoke the **Render Production** tool from the **Main Toolbar**; the rendered image is displayed, refer to Figure 13-11.

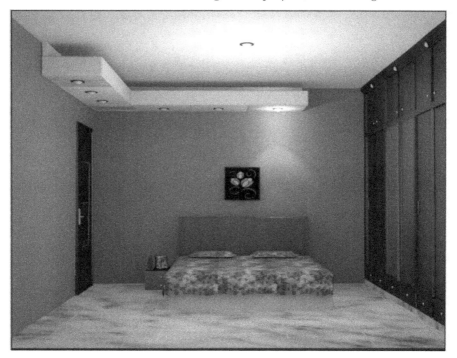

Figure 13-11 *The rendered image*

Next, you will make two copies of *spot light1* and *glowlight1* and place them at the other two spotlights located at its left.

18. Activate the Right viewport. Next, select *spot light1*, *spot light1.Target*, and *glowlight1*. Next, press and hold the SHIFT key and drag the cursor to *new lamp holder001*. Release the left mouse button; the **Clone Options** dialog box is displayed. In this dialog box, select the **Copy** radio button. Set the value **2** in the **Number of Copies** spinner and choose the **OK** button; two copies of *spot light1*, *spot light1.Target*, and *glowlight1* are created in all viewports. Next, invoke the **Select and Move** tool and align these lights in all viewports, as shown in Figure 13-12.

Figure 13-12 Copies of spot light1, spot light1.Target, and glowlight1 aligned in all viewports

19. Similarly, you can create copies of *spot light1*, *spot light1.Target*, and *glowlight1* and place them at the remaining spot lights of the false ceiling.

Saving and Rendering the Scene

In this section, you will save the scene that you have created and then render it. You can also view the final rendered image of this model by downloading the *c13_3dsmaxdesign_2015_rndr.zip* file from *www.cadcim.com*. The path of the file is as follows: *Textbooks > Animation and Visual Effects > 3ds Max Design > Autodesk 3ds Max Design 2015: A Tutorial Approach*

1. Choose **Save** from the **Application** menu.

2. Activate the Perspective viewport. Next, invoke the **Render Production** tool from the **Main Toolbar**; the rendered image is displayed, refer to Figure 13-13.

Figure 13-13 *The rendered image*

Tutorial 2

In this tutorial, you will create false ceiling lights, as shown in Figure 13-14 using the **Free Light** tool. **(Expected time: 20 min)**

Figure 13-14 *The scene with false ceiling lights*

The following steps are required to complete this tutorial:

a.   Create the project folder.
b.   Open the file.
c.   Create the false ceiling lights.
d.   Save and render the scene.

Creating the Project Folder

Create the project folder with the name *c13_tut2* in the *3dsmaxdesign 2015* folder, as discussed in earlier chapters.

Opening the File

1.   Open Windows Explorer and then browse to *\Documents\c13_3dsmaxdesign_2015_tut*. Next, copy all jpeg files to *\Documents\3dsmaxdesign 2015\c13_tut2\sceneassets\images*.

2.   Choose **Open** from the **Application** menu; the **Open File** dialog box is displayed. In this dialog box, browse to the location *\Documents\c13_3dsmaxdesign_2015_tut* and select the **c13_tut2_start.max** file from it. Next, choose the **Open** button to open the file, refer to Figure 13-15.

You will notice that one light is already there in the scene.

Figure 13-15 *The c13_tut2_start.max file*

3.   Choose **Save As** from the **Application** menu; the **Save File As** dialog box is displayed. Browse to the location *\Documents\3dsmaxdesign 2015\c13_tut2\scenes*. Save the file with the name *c13tut2.max* at this location.

Creating the False Ceiling Lights

In this section, you will create false ceiling lights using the **Free Light** tool.

1. Activate the Top viewport and then choose **Create > Lights** in the **Command Panel**. By default, the **Photometric** option is displayed in the **Command Panel**.

2. Invoke the **Free Light** tool from the **Object Type** rollout; if the **Photometric Light Creation** message box is displayed, choose the **Yes** button from this message box. Now, click at a point; the free light is displayed with the name *PhotometricLight001*. Enter **fceilinglight1** in the **Name and Color** rollout.

3. Choose the **Modify** tab. Now, in the **General Parameters** rollout, make sure the **On** check box is selected in the **Shadows** area and the **Ray Traced Shadows** option is selected in the drop-down list.

4. In the **Emit light from (Shape)** area of the **Shape/Area Shadows** rollout, select the **Line** option from the drop-down list; the shape of the light changes in the viewport and the **Length** spinner is added to the **Emit Light from (Shape)** area.

5. Set the value **53** in the **Length** spinner to increase the spread of the light; the shape of *fceilinglight1* is changed to a line shape.

6. Invoke the **Select and Move** tool and align *fceilinglight1* in all viewports, as shown in Figure 13-16.

Figure 13-16 The fceilinglight1 aligned in all viewports

Make sure that you align *fceilinglight1* close to the wall behind the bed and close to the false ceiling.

Next, you will modify the parameters of *fceilinglight1* to achieve the desired lighting effect.

7. Select the radio button located near the **Kelvin** spinner; the **Kelvin** spinner is activated.

8. Set the value **3386** in the **Kelvin** spinner; the color in the color swatch located next to it is changed.

9. Choose the **Filter Color** color swatch located below it; the **Color Selector: Filter Color** dialog box is displayed. In this dialog box, set the values in the **Red**, **Green**, and **Blue** spinners as given next:

   Red: **223**   Green: **13**   Blue: **28**

   Choose the **OK** button to close the dialog box; the color in the **Filter Color** color swatch is changed.

10. In the **Intensity** area of the **Intensity/Color/Attenuation** rollout, select the **lm** radio button; the value in the first spinner located below this radio button changes and displays the intensity of the light in Lumen. Next, set the value **2** in this spinner; the intensity of the light is decreased.

    Next, you will render the scene to view the effect of *fceilinglight1* in the scene.

11. Activate the Perspective viewport and adjust the view, refer to Figure 13-17. Next, invoke the **Render Production** tool from the **Main Toolbar**; the rendered image is displayed, as shown in Figure 13-17.

    Next, you need to copy *fceilinglight1* and place the copy at the other side of false ceiling.

12. Activate the Top viewport and select *fceilinglight1*. Now, press and hold the SHIFT key and drag the cursor. Next, release the left mouse button; the **Clone Options** dialog box is displayed. In this dialog box, select the **Copy** radio button. Set the value **1** in the **Number of Copies** spinner and choose the **OK** button; a copy of *fceilinglight1* is created in all viewports with the name *fceilinglight002*. Next, align it in all viewports using the **Select and Move** and **Select and Rotate** tools, as shown in Figure 13-18.

    Make sure that you align *fceilinglight002* close to the wall and also close to the false ceiling.

13. Choose the **Modify** tab in the **Command Panel**. In the **Emit Light from (Shape)** area of the **Shape/Area Shadows** rollout, set the value **46** in the **Length** spinner.

Figure 13-17 The rendered image

Figure 13-18 The fceilinglight002 aligned in all viewports

Note
You can set different length, color, and intensity values of false ceiling lights to achieve different lighting effects.

Saving and Rendering the Scene

In this section, you will save the scene that you have created and then render it. You can also view the final rendered image of this model by downloading the *c13_3dsmaxdesign_2015_rndr.zip* file from *www.cadcim.com*. The path of the file is as follows: *Textbooks > Animation and Visual Effects > 3ds Max Design > Autodesk 3ds Max Design 2015: A Tutorial Approach*

1. Choose **Save** from the **Application** menu.

2. Activate the Perspective viewport. Next, invoke the **Render Production** tool from the **Main Toolbar**; the rendered image is displayed, as shown in Figure 13-19.

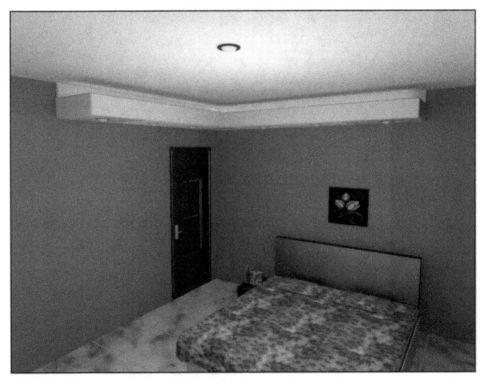

Figure 13-19 The rendered image

Self-Evaluation Test

Answer the following questions and then compare them to those given at the end of this chapter:

1. Which of the following tools is used to create photometric lights?

   (a) **Omni**   (b) **Target Spot**
   (c) **Free Light**   (d) All of these

2. Which of the following options in the **Light Distribution (Type)** area of the **General Parameters** rollout is used to spread the light in all directions?

   (a) **Uniform spherical**   (b) **Uniform Distribution**
   (c) **Photometric Web**   (d) All of these

3. You can create specific lighting patterns by using the standard _____ files.

4. Higher the value you specify in the **Shadow Samples** drop-down list, more will be the rendering time. (T/F)

5. The **On** check box in the **General Parameters** rollout of the spot light can be selected to view the shadow of a light. (T/F)

Review Questions

Answer the following questions:

1. Which of the following areas of the **Intensity/Color/Attenuation** rollout is used to attenuate the spotlight?

   (a) **Dimming**   (b) **Far Attenuation**
   (c) **Intensity**   (d) None of these

2. The options in the _____ area are used to change the shape of the light.

3. The value in the _____ spinner and the color in the _____ color swatch together define the color shade of the light being created.

4. Photometric Lights are more complex than standard lights. (T/F)

5. You can improve the quality of rendering by changing the options in the **Shadow Samples** drop-down list. (T/F)

EXERCISE

The rendered output of the scene used in the following exercise can be accessed by downloading the *c13_maxdesign_2015_exr.zip* from *www.cadcim.com*. The path of the file is as follows: *Textbooks > Animation and Visual Effects > 3ds Max Design > Autodesk 3ds Max Design 2015: A Tutorial Approach*

Exercise 1

Extract the contents of the *c13_3dsmaxdesign_2015_exr.zip* and then open the *c13_exer1_start* file from it. Next, illuminate the scene using the photometric spot lights, as shown in Figure 13-20.   **(Expected time: 25 min)**

Figure 13-20 *The illuminated scene*

Chapter **14**

Animation Basics

Learning Objectives

After completing this chapter, you will be able to:

- *Adjust the number of frames in an animation*
- *Modify object pivot points*
- *Create keyframes*
- *Create hierarchical links between the child and parent objects*
- *Adjust the tracking and key info*

INTRODUCTION

A computer animation is created by defining the transformation of an object at key points during the animation. These defined points are known as keyframes or keys. The computer fills in the information between these keys to complete the animation. The final animation consists of a series of frames. Each frame of the series has the objects in different positions. When the frames are played quickly, the objects in the viewport appears moving. The greater the number of frames, the longer the animation lasts. A computer typically plays frames at the rate of 24 frames per second (1,440 frames per minute). If you want the animation to last for 5 minutes, you need to have 7200 frames (24 frames/second × 60 second/minute × 5 minutes).

TUTORIALS

Before starting the tutorials, you need to download the *c14_3dsmaxdesign_2015_tut.zip* file from *www.cadcim.com*. The path of the file is as follows: *Textbooks > Animation and Visual Effects > 3ds Max Design > Autodesk 3ds Max Design 2015: A Tutorial Approach*

Extract the contents of the zip file and save them in the *Documents* folder.

Tutorial 1

In this tutorial, you will create simple objects and add basic materials to them. You will also impart motion to the objects and save the animation to a file. Figure 14-1 shows the animated scene at frame 12.   **(Expected time: 25 min)**

Figure 14-1 Animated scene at frame 12

The following steps are required to complete this tutorial:

a. Create the project folder.
b. Create the shaft.
c. Create and move the bearing.

d. Create and move the ball.
e. Assign materials.
f. Add lights.
g. Add cameras.
h. Add animation to the scene.
i. Save and render the animation.

Creating the Project Folder

Create the project folder with the name *c14_tut1* in the *3dsmaxdesign 2015* folder, as discussed in previous chapters.

Creating the Shaft

In this section, you will create the shaft by using the **Tube** tool.

1. Choose **Create > Geometry** in the **Command Panel** and then invoke the **Tube** tool from the **Object Type** rollout; various rollouts related to the **Tube** tool are displayed in the **Command Panel**.

2. In the **Parameters** rollout, set the value **20** in the **Sides** spinner and make sure the **Smooth** check box is selected.

3. Expand the **Keyboard Entry** rollout. Next, set the values **50** in the **Inner Radius** spinner, **80** in the **Outer Radius** spinner, and **300** in the **Height** spinner. Next, choose the **Create** button in the **Keyboard Entry** rollout; a tube is created and displayed in the viewport.

4. In the **Name and Color** rollout, enter **Shaft** and choose the color swatch; the **Object Color** dialog box is displayed.

5. In this dialog box, select green color and then choose the **OK** button.

6. Invoke the **Zoom Extents All** tool so that *Shaft* is zoomed to its extents, refer to Figure 14-2.

Creating and Moving the Bearing

In this section, you will create the bearing by using the **Torus** tool.

1. Restore the four viewport configuration. Activate the Top viewport and then choose **Create > Geometry** in the **Command Panel**. Next, invoke the **Torus** tool from the **Object Type** rollout.

2. Expand the **Keyboard Entry** rollout and set the value **100** in the **Major Radius** spinner and **20** in the **Minor Radius** spinner. Next, choose the **Create** button.

3. In the **Name and Color** rollout, enter **Bearing** and choose the color swatch; the **Object Color** dialog box is displayed. Select blue color from it. Next, choose the **OK** button to close the dialog box.

Figure 14-2 The Shaft zoomed

4. Invoke the **Zoom Extents All** tool; the objects are zoomed to their extents, as shown in Figure 14-3.

Figure 14-3 The objects zoomed to their extents

Bearing is created at the bottom of *Shaft*. You need to move it upwards.

5. Invoke the **Select and Move** tool from the **Main Toolbar**.

6. Activate the Front viewport. Drag *Bearing* up until the Y coordinate in the coordinate display reads almost 150 and release the mouse button; *Bearing* is placed in the middle of *Shaft*, as shown in Figure 14-4.

Figure 14-4 *Bearing placed near the middle of Shaft*

Creating and Moving the Ball

In this section, you will create the ball using the **Sphere** tool and then move it.

1. Activate the Top viewport and then choose **Create > Geometry** in the **Command Panel**. Next, invoke the **Sphere** tool from the **Object Type** rollout.

2. In the **Parameters** rollout of the **Command Panel**, set the value **30** in the **Segments** spinner and make sure that the **Smooth** check box is selected.

3. Expand the **Keyboard Entry** rollout and set **50** in the **Radius** spinner. Next, choose the **Create** button; the sphere is created near the bottom of *Shaft*.

4. In the **Name and Color** rollout, enter **Ball01**. Next, assign red color to *Ball01*, as done earlier.

5. Activate the Left viewport and invoke the **Select and Move** tool.

6. Make sure *Ball01* is selected in the viewport. Now, drag it down until the Y coordinate in the coordinate display reads about –125; *Ball01* moves down along the Y axis, as shown in Figure 14-5.

Figure 14-5 Ball01 created and moved down the Y axis

Next, you will copy the ball.

7. Make sure the Left viewport is activated and *Ball01* is selected.

8. Press and hold the SHIFT key and move *Ball01* up until the Y coordinate in the coordinate display reads about 550, and then release the mouse button; the **Clone Options** dialog box is displayed.

9. In this dialog box, enter **Ball02** in the **Name** text box and select the **Copy** radio button. Next, choose the **OK** button; a copy of *Ball01* is created and placed at the selected location, as shown in Figure 14-6.

10. Invoke the **Zoom Extents All** tool to zoom the objects to their extents.

Assigning Materials

In this section, you will assign materials to all objects in the scene.

1. Navigate to the *\Documents\c14_3dsmaxdesign_2015_tut* folder and copy the *Wood1*, *Masonry_Stone1.jpg*, and *Metal1* files to *\Documents\3dsmaxdesign 2015\c14_tut1\sceneassets\ images*.

2. Select *Shaft* from the **Scene Explorer**. Next, choose **Rendering > Material Editor > Compact Material Editor** from the menu bar; the **Material Editor** dialog box is displayed. In this dialog box, select the first sample slot.

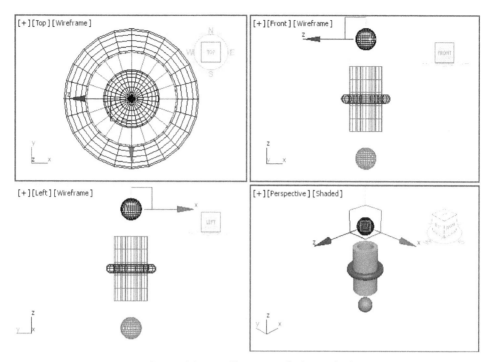

Figure 14-6 Ball02 created above Shaft

3. Choose the **Arch & Design** button to change the material type; the **Material/Map Browser** dialog box is displayed. In this dialog box, select **Standard** from **Materials > Standard** rollout and then choose the **OK** button; the **Arch & Design** material is replaced by the **Standard** material in the **Material Editor** dialog box.

4. In the **Blinn Basic Parameters** rollout of the **Material Editor** dialog box, choose the **Diffuse** button; the **Material/Map Browser** dialog box is displayed again.

5. In this dialog box, select the **Bitmap** map from **Maps > Standard** rollout and choose the **OK** button; the **Select Bitmap Image File** dialog box is displayed.

6. In this dialog box, make sure **All Formats** is selected in the **Files of type** drop-down list. As the project folder is already set, the *images* folder of this project is displayed in the **Look in** text box. Select the **wood1.jpg** file and choose the **Open** button; the image file is loaded and the parameters are displayed for the map in the **Material Editor** dialog box.

7. Choose the **Assign Material to Selection** button in the **Material Editor** dialog box. Next, choose the **Show Shaded Material in Viewport** button to display the assigned material in the viewport; the material **wood1.jpg** is assigned to *Shaft*.

8. Move to one level up and enter **Shaft** in the material name drop-down list located below the material sample slots.

9. Choose the **Modify** tab in the **Command Panel**. In the **Parameters** rollout, clear the **Real-World Map Size** check box.

   Next, you will assign material to *Bearing*.

10. Select **Bearing** from the **Scene Explorer**.

11. Select the second sample slot in the **Material Editor** dialog box and change the **Arch & Design** to **Standard**, as discussed earlier.

12. In the **Blinn Basic Parameters** rollout, choose the **Diffuse** button; the **Material/Map Browser** dialog box is displayed.

13. In this dialog box, select the **Bitmap** map from **Maps > Standard** rollout. Next, choose the **OK** button; the **Select Bitmap Image File** dialog box is displayed. As the project folder is already set, the *images* folder of this project is displayed in the **Look in** drop-down list of this dialog box.

14. Select the file **Masonry_Stone1.jpg** and choose the **Open** button; the image file is loaded and the parameters are displayed for the map in the **Material Editor** dialog box.

15. Choose the **Assign Material to Selection** button in the **Material Editor** dialog box. Also, choose the **Show Shaded Material in Viewport** button; the material is assigned to *Bearing*.

16. Enter **Bearing** in the material name drop-down list located below the material sample slots.

   Next, you will assign material to balls.

17. Select *Ball01* and *Ball02* in the viewport.

18. In the **Material Editor** dialog box, select the third sample slot and change the material **Arch & Design** to **Standard,** as discussed earlier.

19. In the **Blinn Basic Parameters** rollout, choose the **Diffuse** button; the **Material/Map Browser** dialog box is displayed.

20. Select the **Bitmap** map from the **Maps > Standard** rollout from the **Material/Map Browser** dialog box. Next, choose the **OK** button; the **Select Bitmap Image File** dialog box is displayed. As the project folder is already set, the *images* folder of this project is displayed in the **Look in** drop-down list.

21. Select the file **metal1.jpg** and choose the **Open** button; the image file is loaded and the parameters are displayed for the map in the **Material Editor** dialog box.

22. Choose the **Assign Material to Selection** button in the **Material Editor** dialog box. Next, choose the **Show Shaded Material in Viewport** button to display the assigned material in the viewport; the material is assigned to *Ball01* and *Ball02*.

23. Move one level up and enter **Ball** in the drop-down list located below the material sample slots.

24. Close the **Material Editor** dialog box.

Adding Lights

In this section, you will create and position two omni lights in the scene. The lights should be positioned away from the object to prevent hot spots. For this reason, you may need to zoom out to create more space around the objects.

1. Invoke the **Zoom** tool. Next, zoom out in the Top viewport until the objects are displayed about one-third of their original size.

2. Choose the **Lights** button in the **Create** tab of the **Command Panel**.

3. Select **Standard** from the drop-down list located below it. Invoke the **Omni** tool from the **Object Type** rollout.

4. Click at a point in the lower-left corner of the Top viewport to place a light; an omni light is placed at the selected point.

5. Click at a point near the upper-right corner of the Top viewport to place another omni light; an omni light is placed at the selected point.

6. Invoke the **Zoom Extents All** tool to zoom the objects in viewports to their extents and invoke the **Select and Move** tool.

7. In the Front viewport, select the light at the left and move it up to a position near the upper left corner of the viewport.

8. Select the light at the right and move it up to a position in the upper right corner of the viewport.

9. Invoke the **Zoom Extents All** tool; the two omni lights are displayed in all viewports, as shown in Figure 14-7.

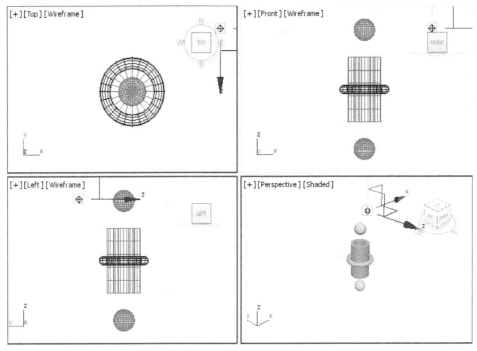

Figure 14-7 The two omni lights displayed in all viewports

Adding Camera

In this section, you will add camera to the scene. By adding a camera to the scene, you can look at the object from any direction and from any distance.

1. Activate the Top viewport. Choose **Create > Cameras** in the **Command Panel**. Next, invoke the **Target** tool from the **Object Type** rollout.

2. Click in the lower-right corner of the viewport to position the camera. Next, press and hold the left mouse button and drag the cursor to the center of the objects, and then release the left mouse button.

    The second point defines the target point for the camera.

3. Activate the Perspective viewport and press the C key to change the viewport to the camera view. Also, press the G key to turn off the grid; the Perspective viewport becomes the Camera viewport.

4. Activate the Left viewport and invoke the **Select and Move** tool.

5. Select the camera (not its target) and drag it up and select a point that gives you the desired view of the objects in the Camera viewport.

    As you move the camera, the Camera viewport is dynamically updated.

6. Activate the Camera viewport and invoke the **Truck Camera** tool in the viewport navigation controls.

7. Move the cursor to place the objects in the center of the Camera viewport, as shown in Figure 14-8. Right-click to exit the tool.

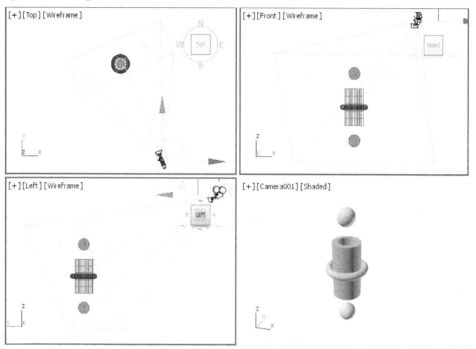

Figure 14-8 *Placing the objects at the center of the Camera viewport*

8. Invoke the **Render Production** tool from the **Main Toolbar**; the rendered image is displayed in the **Rendered Frame** window, refer to Figure 14-9. Close this window.

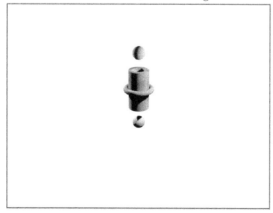

Figure 14-9 *The rendered image*

Creating Animation

In this section, you will create animation for balls and bearing. When you create objects and position lights and camera, you create the first animation scene (frame 0). You can arrange the objects, lights, and camera and create additional keyframes. The frames in between the previous frame and the new frame are automatically created.

1.   Choose the **Display** tab in the **Command Panel**.

2.   In the **Hide by Category** rollout, select the check boxes for **Lights** and **Cameras**; both lights and the camera are hidden in the viewports.

     While creating an animation, arranging objects is often easier if the display of lights and cameras is turned off.

3.   Invoke the **Zoom Extents All** tool; the viewports are zoomed to their extents. The camera and lights are still not included in the zoom.

     Next, you will create position and scale keys for *Bearing*.

4.   Activate the Front viewport. Next, choose the **Toggle Auto Key Mode** button; it turns red indicating that you are in the auto key animation mode.

5.   Move the time slider to frame 25. You can either drag the slider bar or you can use the **Next Frame** button to change the frame. Alternatively, you can enter the frame number in the **Current Frame (Go to Frame)** spinner.

6.   Invoke the **Select and Move** tool from the **Main Toolbar**.

7.   Select **Bearing** from the **Scene Explorer**. Move *Bearing* straight up so that its top edge touches the top edge of *Shaft*.

8.   Invoke the **Select and Uniform Scale** tool.

9.   Make sure *Bearing* is selected. Now, drag the cursor until the coordinate display reads 125%; *Bearing* is scaled up to 125%.

10. Move to frame 75 and scale *Bearing* down to 80% of its current size.

11. Invoke the **Select and Move** tool and move *Bearing* straight down until its bottom edge touches the bottom edge of *Shaft*.

12. Move to frame 100 and move *Bearing* up until it is in the middle of the tube (its original position).

13. Choose the **Toggle Auto Key Mode** button to exit the auto key animation mode.

14. Activate the Camera viewport.

15. Choose the **Play Animation** button; the animation is previewed in the Camera viewport.

    The **Play Animation** button is replaced by the **Stop Animation** button once the animation is started.

16. Choose the **Stop Animation** button to stop the playback.

    Next, you will create the position keys for *Ball01*.

17. Activate the Front viewport and invoke the **Zoom** tool. Drag the cursor down such that the objects are displayed in half of their original size, and then invoke the **Maximize Viewport Toggle** tool.

18. Choose the **Display** tab in the **Command Panel** and then choose the **Hide by Name** button in the **Hide** rollout; the **Hide Objects** dialog box is displayed, as shown in Figure 14-10.

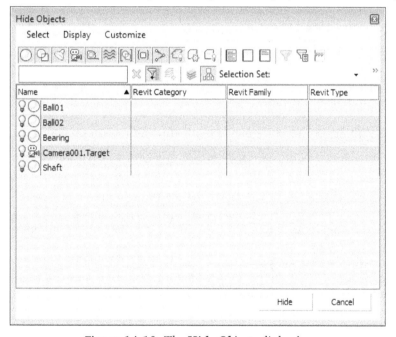

*Figure 14-10 The **Hide Objects** dialog box*

19. Select **Ball02** from the list and then choose the **Hide** button; the dialog box is closed and *Ball02* is hidden.

20. Choose the **Toggle Auto Key Mode** button to activate the auto key animation mode. `Auto Key`

21. Move to frame 15. Next, invoke the **Select and Move** tool. Select *Ball01* in the viewport and lock the selection set. Move *Ball01* down and to the right. Figure 14-11 shows the suggested paths for the two balls.

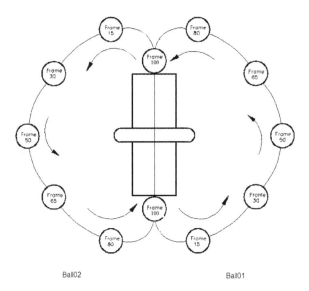

Figure 14-11 *The image showing the suggested paths for the two balls*

22. Move to frame 30 and move the sphere a little up and right.

23. Move to frame 50. Again, move *Ball01* a little toward the right and up so that it is in line with the middle of the tube.

24. Move to frame 65 and move *Ball01* a little up and toward the left.

25. Move to frame 80 and move *Ball01* a little more up and left.

26. Move to frame 100 and move *Ball01* so that it touches the top of *Shaft*.

27. Choose the **Toggle Auto Key Mode** button to exit the animation mode.

28. Activate the Camera viewport and choose the **Play Animation** button to check the motion of *Ball01*. Choose the **Stop Animation** button to stop and then choose the **Go to Start** button to go back to frame 0. Now, unlock the selection set.

 Note
The locations of balls are approximate. You can use your own paths or the ones shown in Figure 14-11.

Next, you will create position keys for *Ball02*. You will also change the background color to white.

29. Choose the **Display** tab in the **Command Panel**. Next, choose the **Unhide All** button in the **Hide** rollout.

30. Choose the **Hide by Name** button in the **Hide** rollout; the **Hide Objects** dialog box is displayed.

31. Select **Ball01** in the list and choose the **Hide** button.

32. Choose the **Toggle Auto Key Mode** button to enter the auto key animation mode and move to frame 15.

33. Make sure *Ball02* is selected and then lock the selection set.

34. Activate the Front viewport. Move *Ball02* up and left, refer to Figure 14-11.

35. Move to frame 30 and move *Ball02* a little down and left.

36. Move to frame 50 and move *Ball02* a little to the left and down so that it is in line with the middle of the tube.

37. Move to frame 65 and move *Ball02* a little down and to the right.

38. Move to frame 80 and move *Ball02* a little more down and right.

39. Move to frame 100 and move *Ball02* so that it touches the bottom of the shaft.

40. Choose the **Toggle Auto Key Mode** button to exit the auto key animation mode.

41. Activate the Camera viewport and choose the **Play Animation** button to check the motion of *Ball02*. Next, choose the **Stop Animation** button.

42. In the **Display** tab of the **Command Panel**, choose the **Unhide All** button available under the **Hide** rollout; *Ball01* is displayed.

43. Choose the **Play Animation** button; the full animation is played.

44. Choose the **Stop Animation** button to exit the playback. You can then choose the **Go to Start** button to move to frame 0 or you can simply drag the time slider to frame 0. Now, unlock the selection set.

45. Choose **Rendering > Environment** from the menu bar; the **Environment and Effects** dialog box is displayed.

46. In this dialog box, choose the **Color** swatch in the **Background** area; the **Color Selector: Background Color** dialog box is displayed. Set the color to white and then choose the **OK** button to close this dialog box. Also, close the **Environment and Effects** dialog box.

 Note

*If all objects are not displayed during animation, invoke the **Field-of-View** tool. Use it* *in the Camera viewport to increase the field of view so that all objects are easily displayed in the Camera viewport.*

Saving and Rendering the Animation

In this part of the tutorial, you will render the animation to a file. Next, you will play the rendered animation.

1. Choose **Save** from the **Application** menu.

2. Make sure the Camera viewport is activated and invoke the **Render Setup** tool; the **Render Setup: NVIDIA mental ray** dialog box is displayed, as shown in Figure 14-12.

Figure 14-12 The Render Setup: NVIDIA mental ray dialog box

3. In the **Time Output** area, select the **Active Time Segment** radio button.

4. In the **Render Output** area, choose the **Files** button; the **Render Output File** dialog box is displayed, as shown in Figure 14-13. As the project folder is already set, the *renderoutput* folder of this project is displayed in the **Save in** text box. Select **AVI File (*.avi)** from the **Save as type** drop-down list.

Figure 14-13 The Render Output File dialog box

5. In the **File name** text box, enter **c14tut1render** and choose the **Save** button; the path of the file is displayed in the **Render Output** area of the **Render Setup** dialog box.

    If the **AVI File Compression Setup** dialog box is displayed, choose the **OK** button to close it.

6. Make sure that the **Save File** check box is selected in the **Render Output** area. Now, choose the **Render** button to render the animation and close the **Render Setup** dialog box.

    It will take several minutes to render the animation frame by frame. After the rendering is complete, close the render window.

7. Choose **Rendering > View Image File** from the menu bar; the **View File** dialog box is displayed, refer to Figure 14-14.

Figure 14-14 The View File dialog box

8. Select **c14tut1render.avi** and choose the **Open** button; the AVI file is played in Windows Media Player.

Tutorial 2

In this tutorial, you will create the animation of a folding bed in a cabinet. Next, you will animate objects using the parent-child relationship. In addition to this, you will adjust the tracking and key info of the objects, refer to Figure 14-15.   **(Expected time: 30 min)**

Figure 14-15 Animated scene at frame 39

The following steps are required to complete this tutorial:

a. Create the project folder.
b. Open the file.
c. Define pivot points.
d. Animate the objects.
e. Adjust the track info.
f. Adjust the left door movement.
g. Adjust the right door movement.
h. Link objects together.
i. Adjust the link info.
j. Add animation keys.
k. Save and render the animation.

Creating the Project Folder

Create the project folder with the name *c14_tut2* in the *3dsmaxdesign 2015* folder, as discussed in previous chapters.

Opening the File

1. Choose **Open** from the **Application** menu; the **Open File** dialog box is displayed. In this dialog box, browse to the location *\Documents\c14_3dsmaxdesign_2015_tut* and select the **c14_tut2_start.max** file from it. Choose the **Open** button to open the file, refer to Figure 14-16.

Figure 14-16 *The c14_tut2_start.max file*

2. Choose **Save As** from the **Application** menu; the **Save File As** dialog box is displayed. Browse to the location *Documents\3dsmaxdesign 2015\c14_tut2\scenes*. Save the file with the name *c14tut2.max* at this location.

Defining Pivot Points

Like the hinge on a door, all objects that will rotate in the animation need a pivot point to define the base point of their rotation. The base point for each object to be rotated in an animation should be adjusted before adding an animation key. In this section, you will first set the number of frames and then you will define pivot points for the objects.

1. By default, the time slider is at frame 0. Drag the time slider from the left to the right.

    3ds Max Design cycles through the default 100 frames of animation. Currently there are no animation keys created, so there is no movement.

2. Choose the **Time Configuration** button in the lower-right corner of the interface; the **Time Configuration** dialog box is displayed, as shown in Figure 14-17.

*Figure 14-17 The **Time Configuration** dialog box*

3. In the **Animation** area, set **80** in the **Length** spinner. Next, choose the **OK** button; the total number of frames in the animation are set to 80.

4. Make sure the time slider is set at frame 0.

5. Choose the **Hierarchy** tab in the **Command Panel** and make sure the **Pivot** button is chosen.

The **Adjust Pivot**, **Adjust Transform**, **Working Pivot**, and **Skin Pose** rollouts are displayed in the **Command Panel**.

The **Adjust Pivot** rollout allows the pivot point or object to be selected for adjustment.

6. Choose the **Affect Pivot Only** button; it turns blue.

   Move and rotate transformations will now affect only the object's pivot point.

7. Select **Door-Left** from the **Scene Explorer**. Activate the Top viewport and zoom in if required.

8. Invoke the **Select and Move** tool and move the cursor over the pivot point, hold down the left mouse button, and drag the pivot point to the left corner of *Door-Left*, refer to Figure 14-18; the pivot point moves to the new location.

Figure 14-18 *The Pivot point of the Door-Left object*

 Note
*You may use the **Align** tool while aligning pivot points.*

The pivot points for the other objects that will be animated need to be positioned as well. Next, you will define the Pivot Points for other objects.

9. Select **Door-Right** from the **Scene Explorer**.

   As the **Affect Pivot Only** button is still active, the pivot point for the right door is displayed.

10. In the Top viewport, move the pivot point to the right corner of *Door-Right*; the pivot point moves to the new location.

Note
If you observe in the Front viewport, the pivot points for both door objects are located in the vertical center of the door. This is correct since the doors rotate only about the vertical axis.

11. Select **Frame** from the **Scene Explorer**; *Frame* is selected and its pivot point is displayed.

12. In the Left viewport, move the pivot point to the lower-right corner of *Frame*; the pivot point moves to the new location.

13. Select **Leg-Left** from the **Scene Explorer**; *Leg-Left* is selected and the pivot point axis is displayed.

14. In the Left viewport, move the pivot point to the upper-left corner of *Leg-Left*; the pivot point moves to the new location.

15. Select **Leg-Right** from the **Scene Explorer**; *Leg-Right* is selected and its pivot point is displayed.

16. In the Left viewport, move the pivot point to the upper-left corner of *Leg-Right*; the pivot point moves to the new location.

17. Choose the **Affect Pivot Only** button again to deactivate it.

Note
*To change the object's pivot point at any time while animating, set the current frame to 0, choose the **Affect Pivot Only** button, and transform the pivot point as needed.*

Animating the Objects

In this section, you will animate the objects in the scene. To create an animation, a series of keys are created. 3ds Max Design then fills in the animation between the keys.

1. Drag the time slider to frame 20.

   You can also set **20** in the spinner at the left of the **Time Configuration** button to move to frame 20.

2. Invoke the **Select and Rotate** tool. Next, activate the Top viewport and select **Door-Left.**

3. Press the SPACEBAR key to lock the selection.

   Pressing the SPACEBAR key activates the **Selection Lock Toggle** button and locks the selected objects (selection set) so that only those objects can be transformed. Choosing the **Selection Lock Toggle** button (located at the bottom of the interface)

will also lock and unlock the selection set. A locked object (or set of objects) can be transformed by clicking anywhere on the screen.

4. Choose the **Toggle Auto Key Mode** button.

   When the **Toggle Auto Key Mode** button is active (red), any transformation creates an animation key on the current frame. If this button is inactive, the transformation is applied to frame zero, regardless of the current frame.

5. Make sure the **Angle Snap** tool is activated.

   The **Angle Snap** tool assists in rotating objects to an exact angle.

6. In the Top viewport, rotate the object –135 degrees about the local Z axis; a key is created at frame 20 where *Door-Left* is rotated –135 degrees and then press the SPACEBAR key to unlock the selection.

7. Select *Door-Right*. Make sure the Top viewport is activated.

   Note
   *If you use the H key or the **Select by Name** tool, you do not need to unlock the current selection set before selecting the new objects. The old selection set is replaced with the new one, but remains locked.*

8. Rotate *Door-Right* 135 degrees about the local Z axis; a key is created at frame 20 for *Door-Right*.

9. Choose the **Toggle Auto Key Mode** button to exit the animation mode.

   Drag the time slider from left to right to play the animation. You will notice that 3ds Max Design automatically adjusts the required movement of the doors from their starting position on frame 0 to the rotated position on frame 20.

   Next, you will create the additional keys.

10. Drag the time slider to frame 60.

11. Make sure *Door-Right* is selected and then choose the **Motion** tab in the **Command Panel**; the **Assign Controller**, **PRS Parameters**, and **Key Info** rollouts are displayed, as shown in Figure 14-19.

12. Expand the **PRS Parameters** rollout. The **PRS Parameters** rollout contains several sets of the **Position**, **Rotation**, and **Scale** buttons.

13. Choose the **Rotation** button in the **Create Key** area of the rollout; a key is created at frame 60 for *Door-Right*. This key contains the rotation value or "state" of the object for the current frame (60). At frame 60, the door is rotated.

14. Unlock the selection and select *Door-Left*. Next, lock the selection again. Remember, if you use the H key or the **Select by Name** tool, you do not need to unlock the selection; *Door-Left* is selected.

15. Choose the **Rotation** button in the **Create Key** area of the rollout; a key is created at frame 60 for *Door-Left*.

*Figure 14-19 The **Motion** tab displayed for the Door-Right object*

Adjusting the Track Info

In the **Track View - Dope Sheet** window, 3ds Max Design displays the animation keys associated with each object in the scene. The individual keys can be adjusted, moved, copied, or deleted to edit the animation. In this section, you will copy the keys using the **Track View - Dope Sheet** window

1. Choose **Graph Editors > Track View - Dope Sheet** from the menu bar; the **Track View - Dope Sheet** window is displayed, as shown in Figure 14-20.

*Figure 14-20 The **Track View -Dope Sheet** window*

2. In this window if the entry is not already expanded, select the plus sign (**+**) on the left side of **Door-Left** in the tree and then click on the plus sign (**+**) on the left side of **Transform**. **Track View - Dope Sheet** window displays the animation keys for *Door-Left*. Across the bottom of the window are the frame numbers. On the left side, the types of animation being tracked are listed. At frame 0, the object has a key for its default rotation. Since you rotated the object at frame 20 and frame 60, there are keys in the rotation track containing the rotation values. Now, the doors should close at frame 80. Instead of dragging the time slider to frame 80 and creating a rotation key, you can use **Track View - Dope Sheet** window to copy the rotation key at frame 0 (door closed) to frame 80.

3. Make sure the **Move Keys** button on the left of the **Track View - Dope Sheet** window is activated.

4. Press and hold the SHIFT key, drag the rotation key from frame 0 to frame 80; a copy of the frame 0 rotation key at frame 80 is created, thus specifying that *Door-Left* should return to its original position (closed) at frame 80. Unlock the selection if it is locked.

5. Select **Door-Right** from the **Scene Explorer**. Make sure the selection is locked.

6. In the **Track View - Dope Sheet** window, click on the plus sign (**+**) on the left side of **Door-Right** in the tree and then click on the plus sign (**+**) on the left side of **Transform**; the animation keys for *Door-Right* are displayed in the **Track View - Dope Sheet** window.

7. Press and hold the SHIFT key, drag the rotation key from frame 0 to frame 80 for *Door-Right*; the rotation key at frame 0 is copied, thus specifying that *Door-Right* should return to its original position at frame 80.

8. Close the **Track View - Dope Sheet** window and unlock the selection set.

    Drag the time slider to left and right to view the animation. You will notice the required movement of the doors.

Adjusting the Left Door Movement

The doors do not stay at the exact rotation point that you applied to them. As you drag the time slider, you will notice the doors "float" past the assigned rotation. In this section, you will use the **Track View - Dope Sheet** window to correct the door movement.

1. Select *Door-Left* in the viewport. Next, choose **Graph Editors > Saved Track Views > Track View - Dope Sheet** from the menu bar; the **Track View - Dope Sheet** window is displayed with the previous settings.

2. In this window, right-click on the rotation key at frame 0 for **Door-Left**; the **Door-Left\ Rotation** dialog box is displayed, as shown in Figure 14-21.

3. Set **0** in the **Continuity** spinner, if it is not already 0; the rotation appears mechanical. You will also notice the change in the graph, as shown in Figure 14-22.

Figure 14-21 *The **Door-Left\Rotation** dialog box*

Figure 14-22 *The **Door-Left\Rotation** dialog box*

4. Choose the right arrow button at the top of the dialog box to move to key 2.

5. Set **0** in the **Continuity** spinner.

6. Choose the right arrow button to move to key number 3.

7. Set **0** in the **Continuity** spinner.

8. Choose the right arrow button to move to key number 4.

9. Set **0** in the **Continuity** spinner.

10. Close the **Door-Left\Rotation** dialog box and the **Track View - Dope Sheet** window.

   Now, drag the time slider left and right to view the animation. Notice how the left door has a mechanical or linear movement and the right door floats through the rotation keys.

Adjusting the Right Door Movement

In this section, you will adjust the continuity settings of *Door-Right* so that it also rotates with a mechanical movement.

1. Select *Door-Right* and Choose **Graph Editors > Saved Track Views > Track View - Dope Sheet** from the menu bar; the **Track View - Dope Sheet** window is displayed.

2. Scroll up in the list and right-click on the rotation key at frame 0 for *Door-Right*.

3. Set **0** in the **Continuity** spinner of the **Door-Right\Rotation** dialog box, if it is not already zero.

4. Choose the right arrow button at the top of the dialog box to move to key number 2.

5. Set **0** in the **Continuity** spinner.

6. Choose the right arrow button to move to key number 3.

7.   Set the value **0** in the **Continuity** spinner.

8.   Choose the right arrow button to move to key number 4.

9.   Set the value **0** in the **Continuity** spinner.

10. Close the **Door-Right\Rotation** dialog box and **Track View - Dope Sheet** window.

Linking Objects Together

One object can be linked to another object to create a parent-child relationship. The transformation of the child object is controlled by the transformation of the parent object. This link is one-way; the child object follows its parent object, but the parent object does not follow the child. In this section, you will link frame with *Bed, Leg-Left,* and *Leg-Right.* The frame of the bed will be the parent object and will control the bed and the left and right legs. If the frame rotates down, the bed and legs will follow it and will not have to be rotated individually.

1.   Drag the time slider to frame 40.

2.   Make sure the **Select and Rotate** tool is invoked.

3.   Activate the Left viewport and select *Frame.*

     The pivot point is already in the correct location, which is the bottom-right corner of *Frame* in the Left viewport.

4.   Choose the **Toggle Auto Key Mode** button.

5.   Right-click on the **Select and Rotate** tool; the **Rotate Transform Type-In** dialog box is displayed. Set the value **-90** in the **Z** spinner of the **Offset: Screen** area; a key is created at frame 40 where *Frame* is rotated 90 degrees. Close this dialog box.

6.   Choose the **Toggle Auto Key Mode** button to exit the animation mode.

     Drag the time slider to the left and then back to the right to replay the animation.

7.   Select *Bed* and drag the time slider to frame 0.

     The objects need to be linked on frame 0 so that the parent-child relationship is based on the relative starting positions of objects.

8.   Invoke the **Select and Link** tool from the **Main Toolbar**.

9.   Invoke the **Select by Name** tool; the **Select Parent** dialog box is displayed.

     This dialog box is the same as the **Select From Scene** dialog box.

10. In this dialog box, select *Frame* and choose the **Link** button.

11. Invoke the **Select Object** tool to exit the tool.

12. Drag the time slider left and right to replay the animation.

Bed has been designated as a child object of *Frame* and automatically rotates to follow its parent object. You will notice that no animation keys have been created for *Bed*

 Note
Links are active over the entire length of an animation, regardless of the Frame on which the objects are linked. However, the child object will maintain the position it had relative to the parent object at the Frame in which the objects were linked. Also, the linking and unlinking of objects cannot be animated.

Next, you will link the left leg with *Frame*.

13. Select *Leg-Left* and drag the time slider to frame 0.

14. Invoke the **Select and Link** tool from the **Main Toolbar**.

15. Invoke the **Select by Name** tool; the **Select Parent** dialog box is displayed.

16. In this dialog box, select *Frame* and choose the **Link** button. Invoke the **Select Object** tool to exit the tool; *Leg-Left* is a child object of *Frame* and automatically rotates to follow its parent object.

17. Repeat the process to link *Leg-Right* to *Frame*. Make sure you invoke the **Select Object** tool to exit the link tool.

Adjusting the Link Info

In this section, you will control the movement of linked objects by adjusting their link info.

1. Select *Leg-Left* in the viewport and choose the **Hierarchy** tab in the **Command Panel**.

2. Choose the **Link Info** button, as shown in Figure 14-23; the **Locks** and **Inherit** rollouts are displayed.

The **Inherit** rollout allows you to limit the axes on which the move, rotate, and scale transformations are inherited.

3. In the **Inherit** rollout, clear the **X** check box in the **Rotate** area, if it is selected; this turns off the link between the child and parent for rotation on the X axis. The leg will not inherit the rotation of the frame on the X axis.

4. Select *Leg-Right*. Next, in the **Inherit** rollout, clear the **X** check box in the **Rotate** area if it is selected; the link between the child and parent for rotation on the X axis is turned off.

5. Drag the time slider to left and right to replay the animation.

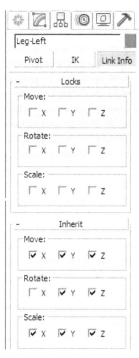

*Figure 14-23 The **Link Info** button in the **Hierarchy** tab*

Notice how the legs follow the frame down without rotating.

6.   Drag the time slider to frame 0.

Adding Animation Keys

Currently, as the door frame opens, it hits the doors of the chest. *Frame* needs additional animation keys to keep it from hitting the doors. In this section, you will add these animation keys.

1.   Make sure *Frame* is selected. Next, choose **Graph Editors > Saved Track Views > Track View - Dope Sheet** from the menu bar; the **Track View - Dope Sheet** window is displayed.

2.   In this window, scroll up in the list and expand the tree to display the animation tracks for *Frame*; the animation keys for *Frame* are displayed in the window.

3.   Choose the **Move Keys** button, if it is not chosen; you are now able to move animation keys along the track.

4.   Press and hold the SHIFT key, drag the rotation key from frame 0 to frame 25; a copy of the selected key is created at frame 25.

5.   Press and hold the SHIFT key and drag the rotation key from frame 0 to frame 55; this creates animation keys that keep the frame from hitting the door as it opens and rotates the frame back into the closed position.

6. Right-click on the rotation key for *Frame* at frame 0; the **Frame\Rotation** dialog box is displayed.

7. Set the value **0** in the **Continuity** spinner and then choose the right arrow button at the top of the dialog box to move to key 2.

8. Set the value **0** in the **Continuity** spinner and then choose the right arrow button to move to key 3.

9. Set the value **0** in the **Continuity** spinner and then choose the right arrow button to move to key 4.

10. Set the value **0** in the **Continuity** spinner and then close the **Frame\Rotation** dialog box and **Track View- Dope Sheet** window.

Saving and Previewing the Animation

In this section, you will save and preview the scene.

1. Make sure the Camera-Bedroom viewport is activated.

2. Choose **Tools > Preview-Grab Viewport > Create Preview Animation** from the menu bar; the **Make Preview** dialog box is displayed, as shown in Figure 14-24.

*Figure 14-24 The **Make Preview** dialog box*

3. In the **Overlay** area, select the **Frame Numbers** check box, if it is not already selected; a frame number is rendered for each frame of the animation.

4. Choose the **Create** button; if the **Video Compression** dialog box is displayed, choose the **OK** button to accept the default settings.

When the animation is completed, it is played in the Windows Media Player.

5. To save the preview animation, choose **Tools > Preview - Grab Viewport > Save Preview Animation As** from the menu bar. The animation is saved and played in Windows Media Player.

Self-Evaluation Test

Answer the following questions and then compare them to those given at the end of this chapter:

1. Which of the following tabs in the **Command Panel** is used to adjust a pivot point of an object?

    (a) **Hierarchy**   (b) **Modify**
    (c) **Display**   (d) None of these

2. You can press the _____ key to change to the Camera viewport.

3. Computer animation is created by defining _____, and then calculating the movement that occurs between those frames.

4. All objects that need to be rotated in an animation require a properly placed _____ to define the base point of their rotation.

5. Pressing the _____ key locks the selected objects, making them the only objects that can be transformed.

6. In the _____ window, 3ds Max Design displays the animation keys associated with each object in a scene.

7. The _____ tool creates a relationship between objects in such a way that one object is controlled by the movement of another object.

8. You can adjust the camera to view an object from any direction and from any distance. (T/F)

9. Autodesk 3ds Max Design automatically creates the frames in between two keyframes. (T/F)

10. The **Play Animation** button is replaced by the **Stop Animation** button once you start playing the animation. (T/F)

Review Questions

Answer the following questions:

1. Which of the following buttons in the **Command Panel** is used to create keyframes automatically?

    (a) **Time Configuration**   (b) **Toggle Auto Key Mode**
    (c) **Set Keys**   (d) None of these

2. The **Hide By Category** rollout is available in the _____ tab of the **Command Panel**.

3. The _____ key is used to activate the **Selection Lock Toggle** button.

4. The default range available in 3ds Max Design for animation is _____ frames.

5. Animation keys cannot be adjusted, moved, copied, or deleted once they are created. (T/F)

EXERCISES

The rendered sequence of the scenes used in the following exercises can be accessed by downloading the *c14_3dsmaxdesign_2015_exr.zip* from *www.cadcim.com*. The path of the file is as follows: *Textbooks > Animation and Visual Effects > 3ds Max Design > Autodesk 3ds Max Design 2015: A Tutorial Approach*

Exercise 1

Extract the contents of the *c14_3dsmaxdesign_2015_exr.zip* and then open *c14_exr01_start.max*. Next, animate a chest with a lid and double doors shown in Figures 14-25 through 14-28.

(Expected time: 25 min)

Figure 14-25 Animation at frame 15

Figure 14-26 Animation at frame 30

Figure 14-27 *Animation at frame 45*   **Figure 14-28** *Animation at frame 60*

Exercise 2

Open *c14_exr02_start.max* and animate the company logo, refer to Figures 14-29 through 14-31.   (**Expected time: 25 min**)

Figure 14-29 *Animation at frame 0*   **Figure 14-30** *Animation at frame 10*

Figure 14-31 *Animation at frame 30*

Exercise 3

Open *c14_exr03_start.max* and animate the computer disk holder, refer to Figures 14-32 through
14-35.   (**Expected time: 20 min**)

Figure 14-32 *Animation at frame 0*

Figure 14-33 *Animation at frame 30*   *Figure 14-34* *Animation at frame 40*

Answers to Self-Evaluation Test
1. a, **2.** C, **3.** keyframes, **4.** pivot point, **5.** SPACEBAR, **6.** Track View Dope - Sheet, **7.** Select and Link,
8. T, **9.** T, **10.** T

Chapter **15**

Complex Animation

INTRODUCTION

In this chapter, you will learn to animate the objects using the dummy objects. Dummy objects are used to control the movement of other objects by linking them. If several objects are linked to a dummy object, the dummy can be used to move all objects simultaneously. The objects linked to the dummy can also to be moved individually without affecting the dummy object or any other object linked to the dummy object.

TUTORIAL

Before starting the tutorial, you need to download the *c15_3dsmaxdesign_2015_tut.zip* file from *www.cadcim.com*. The path of the file is as follows: *Textbooks > Animation and Visual Effects > 3ds Max Design > Autodesk 3ds Max Design 2015: A Tutorial Approach*

Extract the contents of the zip file and save them in the *Documents* folder.

Tutorial 1

In this tutorial, you will create the animation of a steel manufacturing process. You will create dummy objects to assist in movement during animation, refer to Figure 15-1.

(Expected time: 30 min)

Figure 15-1 *Animation at frame 43*

The following steps are required to complete this tutorial:

a. Create the project folder.
b. Open the file.
c. Create dummy objects.
d. Link the objects.
e. Set continuity value.
f. Animate the hook and cauldron.
g. Add a position key.
h. Create a snapshot.

i. Hide the object during animation.
j. Hide the object using object properties.
k. Preview the animation.
l. Animate the camera.
m. Animate the camera target.
n. Save and preview the animation.

Creating the Project Folder

Create the project folder with the name *c15_tut1* in the *3dsmaxdesign 2015* folder, as discussed in earlier chapters.

Opening the File

1. Choose **Open** from the **Application** menu; the **Open File** dialog box is displayed. In this dialog box, browse to the location *\Documents\c15_3dsmaxdesign_2015_tut* and select the **c15_tut1_start.max** file from it. Choose the **Open** button to open the file, refer to Figure 15-2.

Figure 15-2 *The c15_tut1_start file*

2. Choose **Save As** from the **Application** menu; the **Save File As** dialog box is displayed. Browse to the location *\Documents\3dsmaxdesign 2015\c15_tut1\scenes*. Save the file with the name *c15tut1.max* at this location.

Creating Dummy Objects

In this section, you will set the number of frames in the animation and create the dummy object.

1. Choose the **Time Configuration** button from the animation playback controls; the **Time Configuration** dialog box is displayed, as shown in Figure 15-3.

*Figure 15-3 The **Time Configuration** dialog box*

2. In the **Animation** area, set **150** in the **Length** spinner and choose the **OK** button; the total number of frames for the animation is set to 150.

3. Choose **Create > Helpers** in the **Command Panel**. Next, invoke the **Dummy** tool from the **Object Type** rollout.

4. Restore the four viewports configuration and activate the Front viewport by clicking on it.

5. Click at a point below *Cauldron* and drag the mouse to create a small cube. Next, move the cube in the Left viewport to position it below *Cauldron*; a dummy object is created, as shown in Figure 15-4.

    The size of the cube does not matter. This cube is the dummy object and will not be visible in the rendered animation. Resize the cube so that you can select it easily, yet not so large that it interferes with the selection of other objects in your scene.

6. Enter **Cal-Dummy** in the **Name and Color** rollout.

7. Invoke the **Dummy** tool again from the **Object Type** rollout. In the Front viewport, click at a point below *Base* and drag the cursor to create another small cube. Adjust the position of the cube in the Left viewport to position it below *Base*, as shown in Figure 15-5.

8. Enter **Base-Dummy** in the **Name and Color** rollout.

Figure 15-4 *A dummy object created*

Figure 15-5 *Adjusting the position of the cube below Base*

9. Activate the Top viewport. Next, use the **Align** tool from the **Main Toolbar** to center
    Base-Dummy with the center of the Base object along the X and Y axes. Also, align
    the center of *Cal-Dummy* with the center of *Cauldron* along the X and Y axes.

Linking the Objects

In this section, you will link the objects in the scene. Linking more than one object to a dummy
object simplifies the animation process and allows individual movement later in the animation.

1. Invoke the **Select and Link** tool from the **Main Toolbar**.

2. Click *Cauldron* and drag the cursor to *Cal-Dummy* and then release the left mouse button,
    refer to Figure 15-6. Invoke the **Select Object** tool to exit the tool.

Figure 15-6 Linking Cauldron with Cal-Dummy

When the first object is selected, the link cursor appears. On dragging the mouse button
and releasing it on the second object, the two objects will be linked. *Cauldron* becomes a
child of *Cal-Dummy* and will follow its movement.

3. Make sure the **Select and Link** tool is invoked. Next, click *Hook*, drag the cursor to
    Cal-Dummy, and release the left mouse button. Invoke the **Select Object** tool to exit the
    tool; *Hook* becomes a child of *Cal-Dummy* and will follow its movement.

4. Make sure the **Select and Link** tool is invoked. Next, click *Base*, drag the cursor to
    Base-Dummy, and release the left mouse button; *Base* becomes a child of *Base-Dummy*. Now,
    invoke the **Select Object** tool to exit the tool.

Setting Continuity Value

In this section, you will set the continuity value using the **Set Controller Defaults** dialog box. Continuity controls an object's movement through animation keys, creates the appearances of life-like motion, or creates the appearances of mechanical motion. The objects in this animation should have mechanical motion. A continuity default value can be set before creating animation keys so that each key does not have to be individually adjusted later.

1. Choose **Customize > Preferences** from the menu bar; the **Preference Settings** dialog box is displayed. Next, choose the **Animation** tab in the **Preference Settings** dialog box.

2. In the **Controller Defaults** area, choose the **Set Defaults** button; the **Set Controller Defaults** dialog box is displayed, as shown in Figure 15-7.

3. In this dialog box, select **TCB Float** from the list and then choose the **Set** button; the **TCB Default Key Values** dialog box is displayed, as shown in Figure 15-8.

Figure 15-7 The Set Controller Defaults
dialog box

Figure 15-8 The TCB Default Key Values
dialog box

4. In this dialog box, set the value **0** in the **Continuity** spinner and then choose the **OK** button.

5. Choose **OK** in the **Set Controller Defaults** dialog box. Next, choose **OK** in the **Preference Settings** dialog box.

Animating the Hook and Cauldron

In this section, you will animate *Hook* and *Cauldron*. To create an animation, a series of keys are defined.

1. Choose the **Toggle Auto Key Mode** button to turn the animation mode on (red). ![Auto Key]

    When the **Toggle Auto Key Mode** button is chosen (red), any transformation creates an animation key on the current frame. If this button is off, the transformation is applied to frame 0, regardless of the current frame.

2. Drag the time slider to frame 25. Alternatively, you can set the value **25** in the spinner at the left side of the **Time Configuration** button.

3. Activate the Front viewport and click *Cal-Dummy*. Next, right-click on the **Select and Move** tool; the **Move Transform Type-In** dialog box is displayed, refer to Figure 15-9.

*Figure 15-9 The **Move Transform Type-In** dialog box*

4. Set the value **300** in the **X** spinner of the **Offset:Screen** area and press the ENTER key; *Cauldron* is now centered over *Base*.

5. Drag the time slider to frame 50.

6. Make sure *Cal-Dummy* is selected. In the **Move Transform Type-In** dialog box, set **–300** in the **Y** spinner of the **Offset:Screen** area and press the ENTER key; *Cauldron* is placed on *Base*, refer to Figure 15-10.

Figure 15-10 The Cauldron placed on the circular Base

7. Close the **Move Transform Type-In** dialog box and exit the animation mode by choosing the **Toggle Auto Key Mode** button.

Adding a Position Key

If the movement of *Hook* is animated, the movement would begin at frame 0 and would end at the active frame was current when *Hook* was moved. As a result, *Hook* would gradually drift away from its parent object. To prevent this, *Hook* needs a position key added at frame 50. The position key locks the *Hook's* position at frame 50. Any movement applied to *Hook* affects only frames between frame 50 and the current frame. In this section, you will use the different frame settings in the **Track View - Dope Sheet** window to create the position key.

1. Select all objects in the viewport. Next, choose **Graph Editors > Track View - Dope Sheet** from the menu bar; the **Track View - Dope Sheet** window is displayed.

2. In this window, click on the plus sign at the left of **Hook**. Notice that currently there are no animation keys for *Hook*.

3. Choose the **Add Keys** button on the upper left of the **Track View - Dope Sheet** window.

4. Click on the **Position** track for *Hook* at frame 50; a position key for *Hook* is created at frame 50, refer to Figure 15-11. Next, close the **Track View - Dope Sheet** window.

*Figure 15-11 The new key added to the Hook's **Position** track*

5. Drag the time slider to frame 55 and choose the **Toggle Auto Key Mode** button.

6. Select *Hook* in the Front viewport. Move *Hook* –60 units on the X axis and –60 units on the Y axis; *Hook* is detached from *Cauldron*.

7. Drag the time slider to frame 70. Next, move *Hook* 300 units on the Y axis.

8. Choose **Graph Editors > Saved Track Views > Track View - Dope Sheet** from the menu bar; the **Track View-Dope Sheet** window is displayed with the previous settings active.

9. Choose the **Add Keys** button on the upper left of the **Track View-Dope Sheet** window.

10. Zoom in the window and add a key in the **Position** track at frame 90 for *Hook*. Next, close the **Track View-Dope Sheet** window; the current position of *Hook* is recorded in a key at frame 90.

11. Drag the time slider to frame 105. Next, in the Front viewport, move *Hook* –300 units on the Y axis.

12. Drag the time slider to frame 110. Next, move *Hook* 60 units on the X axis and 60 units on the Y axis; *Hook* is reattached to *Cauldron*.

13. Choose **Graph Editors > Saved Track Views > Track View-Dope Sheet** from the menu bar; the **Track View-Dope Sheet** window is displayed. Next, select *Cal-Dummy* in the viewport and click on the plus sign on the left of **Cal-Dummy** and then **Transform** in the **Track View-Dope Sheet** window.

14. Choose the **Add Keys** button and add a key in the **Position** track at frame 110 for *Cal-Dummy*. Next, close the **Track View-Dope Sheet** window.

15. Drag the time slider to frame 130.

16. In the Front viewport, move *Cal-Dummy* 300 units on the Y axis; *Cal-Dummy*, *Hook*, and *Cauldron* move.

17. Drag the time slider to frame 150.

18. Move *Cal-Dummy* –300 units on the X axis.

19. Choose the **Toggle Auto Key Mode** button to exit the animation mode. Next, drag the time slider to left and right to replay the animation. Alternatively, choose the **Play Animation** button to see the animation in the viewport.

Creating a Snapshot

The **Snapshot** tool duplicates an object in its current state, but unlike the **Copy** tool, it does not copy any animation keys associated with the object. The snapshot copy can then be used for complex animation sequences. In this section, you will create a snapshot of *Cauldron* and rotate it by 45 degrees.

1. Drag the time slider to frame 50. Next, select *Cauldron*.

2. Choose **Tools > Snapshot** from the menu bar; the **Snapshot** dialog box is displayed, as shown in Figure 15-12.

3. Make sure the **Single** radio button is selected in the **Snapshot** area. Also, select the **Copy** radio button in the **Clone Method** area, and then choose **OK** to close the dialog box.

   A duplicate copy of *Cauldron* is created at the same location as the original. Therefore, the copy of *Cauldron* had to be moved to frame 50. The copy is named as *Cauldron001*.

*Figure 15-12 The **Snapshot** dialog box*

 Note
*The **Snapshot** dialog box allows you to create multiple copies over a range of frames using the **Range** radio button or a single copy using the **Single** radio button.*

4. Drag the time slider to frame 0.

    There are now two cauldrons in the scene: the original and the copy located at the original's position at frame 50 when the snapshot was made.

5. Invoke the **Select and Link** tool from the **Main Toolbar**.

6. Click and drag *Cauldron001* to *Base Dummy,* as shown in Figure 15-13. Release the left mouse button and invoke the **Select Object** tool to exit the tool; *Cauldron001* is now the child of *Base Dummy* and will follow its movement.

7. Select *Base Dummy* in the viewport.

8. Choose **Graph Editors > Saved Track Views > Track View-Dope Sheet** from the menu bar; the **Track View-Dope Sheet** window is displayed. Next, click on the (**+**) plus sign at the left of **Base-Dummy** and **Transform**.

9. Make sure the **Add Keys** button is activated and add a key in the **Rotation** track at frame 70 for *Base Dummy*. Next, close **Track View - Dope Sheet** window.

10. Drag the time slider to frame 80. Choose the **Toggle Auto Key Mode** button to enter the animation mode.

11. In the Front viewport, rotate *Base Dummy* object – 45 degrees on the Z axis, as shown in Figure 15-14.

12. Drag the time slider to frame 90. In the Front viewport, rotate *Base Dummy* +45 degrees on the Z axis, as shown in Figure 15-15.

Figure 15-13 *Linking Cauldron with Base-Dummy*

Figure 15-14 *Rotating Base-Dummy -45 degrees on the Z axis*

Figure 15-15 *Rotating Base-Dummy +45 degrees on the Z axis*

13. Choose the **Toggle Auto Key Mode** button to exit the animation mode. Next, drag the time slider to left and right to replay the animation.

Hiding the Object During Animation

All parts of the animation are now complete, but there are two cauldrons visible during the animation. You must turn off the visibility, or hide the cauldrons during different segments of the animation. In this section, you will hide object using the **Track View-Dope Sheet** window. There are two ways to do this. You can use the **Track View -Dope Sheet** window or modify the object's properties.

1. Select *Cauldron* in the viewport. Next, choose **Graph Editors > Saved Track Views > Track View-Dope Sheet** from the menu bar; the **Track View-Dope Sheet** window is displayed.

2. Select **Cauldron** in the **Track View-Dope Sheet** window. Click on the (**+**) plus sign at the left of *Cauldron*.

3. Choose **Edit > Visibility Tracks > Add** from the menu bar in the **Track View - Dope Sheet** window; a visibility track is added for **Cauldron**.

4. Choose the **Add Keys** button and add a key in the **Visibility** track at frame 0 for *Cauldron*, refer to Figure 15-16.

5. Right-click on the new key; the **Cauldron/Visibility** dialog box is displayed. In this dialog box, make sure **1.0** is set in the **Value** spinner. Also, set the **In** and **Out** image tiles to the square mechanical transition, refer to Figure 15-17. Do not close the **Cauldron/Visibility** dialog box; *Cauldron* is fully visible at frame 0.

Figure 15-16 *Adding a new key in the* **Visibility** *track at frame 0*

Figure 15-17 *The* **Cauldron/Visibility** *dialog box*

6. Add a key in the **Visibility** track at frame 50 for *Cauldron*.

7. In the **Cauldron/Visibility** dialog box, set the value **0** in the **Value** spinner. Also, set the **In** and **Out** image tiles to the square mechanical transition; *Cauldron* is invisible at frame 50. Close the **Cauldron/Visibility** dialog box.

8. Add a key in the **Visibility** track at frame 90 for *Cauldron*.

9. Right-click on the new key; the **Cauldron/Visibility** dialog box is displayed. In this dialog box, set the value **1.0** in the **Value** spinner. Also, set the **In** and **Out** image tiles to the square mechanical transition; *Cauldron* is fully visible at frame 0. Next, close the **Cauldron/Visibility** dialog box and the **Track View-Dope Sheet** window.

Hiding the Object Using Object Properties

In this section, you will hide the objects using the object properties.

1. Drag the time slider to frame 0.

2. Select *Cauldron001* in any viewport. Right-click in the viewport; the quad menu is displayed. Choose **Object Properties** from the lower-right quadrant of the quad menu; the **Object Properties** dialog box is displayed, as shown in Figure 15-18.

Figure 15-18 The **Object Properties** dialog box

3. In this dialog box, choose the **By Layer** button from the **Rendering Control** area; the **By Layer** button is replaced by the **By Object** button. Also, the options in this area are activated.

4. Set the value **0** in the **Visibility** spinner. Next, choose the **OK** button to close the **Object Properties** dialog box; *Cauldron001* is invisible at this frame (frame 0). This also adds a visibility track in the **Track View - Dope Sheet** window.

5. Drag the time slider to frame 50 and then choose the **Toggle Auto Key Mode** button to enter the animation mode.

6. Make sure *Cauldron001* is selected. Next, right-click in the viewport; the quad menu is displayed. Next, choose **Object Properties** from the quad menu; the **Object Properties** dialog box is displayed.

7. Set the value **1.0** in the **Visibility** spinner of the **Object Properties** dialog box.

   You will notice that the corners of the spinner turn red. This indicates that the parameter is animated.

8. Choose the **OK** button to close the **Object Properties** dialog box; *Cauldron001* becomes visible at frame 50.

9. Drag the time slider to frame 90. Make sure *Cauldron001* is selected Next, right-click in the viewport; the quad menu is displayed. Next, choose **Object Properties** from the quad menu.

10. Set **0** in the **Visibility** spinner of the **Object Properties** dialog box. Next, choose the **OK** button to close the **Object Properties** dialog box; *Cauldron001* is invisible at frame 90.

11. Choose the **Toggle AutoKey Mode** button to exit the animation mode. Drag the time slider left and right to replay the animation.

   You will notice that *Cauldron001* fades in and out. Therefore, you need to adjust the transition in the **Track View - Dope Sheet** window.

12. Choose **Graph Editors > Saved Track Views > Track View-Dope Sheet** from the menu bar; the **Track View-Dope Sheet** window is displayed. In this window, click on the plus sign on the left of **Cauldron001** to expand the tree, if it is not already expanded.

13. Right-click on the first key in the **Visibility** track; the **Cauldron001/Visibility** dialog box is displayed. In this dialog box, set the **In** and **Out** image tiles to the square mechanical transition.

14. Repeat this for the visibility keys at frame 50 and frame 90. Close the **Cauldron/Visibility** dialog box and the **Track View-Dope Sheet** window.

15. Drag the time slider left and right to preview the animation or choose the **Play Animation** button.

   Notice that *Cauldron001* no longer fades in and out. The visibility changes for both cauldron objects are instantaneous, providing the illusion that there is only one cauldron in the scene.

Previewing the Animation

In this section, you will preview the animation. The preview animation is a low resolution/low color format used to quickly verify that the animation is working correctly.

1. Make sure the Camera-Lift viewport is activated.

2. Choose **Tools > Preview - Grab Viewport > Create Preview Animation** from the menu bar; the **Make Preview** dialog box is displayed, as shown in Figure 15-19.

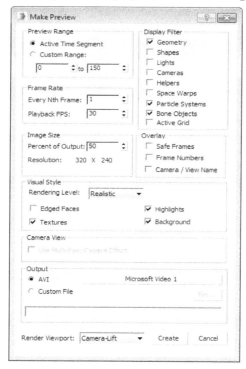

Figure 15-19 *The* **Make Preview** *dialog box*

3. In this dialog box, select the **Frame Numbers** check box in the **Overlay** area. Next, choose the **Create** button. If the **Video Compression** dialog box is displayed, choose **OK** to accept the default settings.

   When the animation is completed, it is played in Windows Media Player. Notice that the invisible cauldrons will not appear clearly. This is just a representation in the preview rendering. In the final animation, the cauldrons are completely invisible.

Animating the Camera

In this section, you will animate the camera. The camera can be animated just like any other object in the scene. When a camera is animated, both the camera target and camera body may need to be moved or rotated.

1. Choose the **Display** tab in the **Command Panel**.

2. In the **Hide by Category** rollout, clear the **Cameras** check box; the camera named *Camera-Lift* is displayed in the scene.

3. Invoke the **Zoom Extents All** tool; the scene is zoomed out in the viewports so that the camera and target fit on the screen.

4. Drag the time slider to frame 75.

5. Invoke the **Select and Move** tool. Next, choose the **Toggle Auto Key Mode** button to enter the animation mode.

6. Select the camera in the Top viewport and move it –1300 units on the X axis and 1300 units on the Y axis (to the left and up).

7. Make sure the **Display** tab is chosen in the **Command Panel**. In the **Display Properties** rollout, select the **Trajectory** check box; the path that the camera follows is displayed.

    The dots along the path represent individual frames in the animation. The white boxes represent frames that have animation keys in them for the camera.

8. Drag the time slider to frame 32.

9. Select the camera in the Top or Front viewport and move it 600 units on the X axis and 600 units on the Y axis (to the right and up). Invoke the **Zoom Extents All** tool, refer to Figure 15-20. Next, choose the **Toggle Auto Key Mode** button again to exit the animation.

Figure 15-20 Adjusting the camera position in the viewport

Next, you will preview the animation to view the effect of moving the camera.

10. Make sure the Camera-Lift viewport is activated.

11. Choose **Tools > Preview - Grab Viewport > Create Preview Animation** from the menu bar; the **Make Preview** dialog box is displayed.

12. In this dialog box, choose the **Create** button. If the **Video Compression** dialog box is displayed, choose the **OK** button to accept the default settings.

When the animation is completed, it is played in Windows Media Player.

Animating the Camera Target

The camera target can be animated to follow the movement of an object during animation. A camera target can be linked as a child to the object being followed in the animation to simplify the process.

1. Drag the time slider to frame 0. Also, make sure the **Toggle Auto Key Mode** button is deactivated (not red).

2. Invoke the **Select and Move** tool. Next, invoke the **Zoom Extents All** tool.

3. Select *Camera-Lift.target* and drag it to the center of *Cauldron* in the Top and Left viewports, as shown in Figure 15-21; the camera target is now centered on *Cauldron*.

Figure 15-21 *Adjusting the Camera-Lift.target to the center of Cauldron in the Top and Left viewports*

4. Invoke the **Select and Link** tool from the **Main Toolbar**.

5. In the Front viewport, select *Camera-Lift.target*, drag the cursor to *Cal-Dummy*, and then release it. Invoke the **Select Object** tool to exit the tool; *Camera-Lift.target* is now the child of *Cal-Dummy* and will follow its movement.

 Note
If the camera represents a person walking through a scene, it is better to create a dummy object and link both the camera target and the person to the dummy object. In this way, only the dummy object will be animated.

Saving and Previewing the Animation

In this section, you will create a quick preview of the updated animation to show the movement of the camera target.

1. Change the background color of the scene to white by following the steps, as given in Tutorial 1 of Chapter 2.

2. Choose **Save** from the **Application** menu.

3. Make sure the Camera-Lift viewport is activated.

4. Choose **Tools > Preview - Grab Viewport > Create Preview Animation** from the menu bar; the **Make Preview** dialog box is displayed.

5. Choose the **Create** button. If the **Video Compression** dialog box is displayed, choose the **OK** button to accept the default settings.

    When the animation is completed, it is played in the Windows Media Player.

Self-Evaluation Test

Answer the following questions and then compare them to those given at the end of this chapter:

1. Which of the following tools is used to duplicate an object in its current state, but does not copy any animation keys associated with the object?

    (a) **Copy**   (b) **Dummy**
    (c) **Snapshot**   (d) None of these

2. An object can be _____ to a dummy object, and it will then follow the movement of the dummy object.

3. A dummy object will not be visible on _____.

4. The _____ window can be used to create a position key.

5. While adjusting the key information of a key in an object's visibility track, a setting of _____ in the **Value** spinner will make the object completely visible.

6. An object can be made invisible by creating a visibility track in **Track View - Dope Sheet** window, or by adjusting the object's _____.

7. When a camera is animated, both _____ and _____ can be moved or rotated.

8. On selecting _____ in the **Display Properties** rollout of the **Command Panel**, camera's path is displayed in the viewport.

9. Frames that have animation keys for the camera are indicated in the trajectory by white boxes. (T/F)

Review Questions

Answer the following questions:

1. Which of the following dialog boxes is used to set the total number of frames in animation?

    (a) **Set Controller Defaults**   (b) **Time Configuration**
    (c) **Object Properties**   (d) None of these

2. The _____ objects are used to control the movement of other objects by linking them, but are not rendered.

3. The _____ tool is used to link one object with another object.

4. The _____ button is used to add keys in **Track View - Dope Sheet**.

5. The _____ option verifies the current state of animation.

6. The **Snapshot** tool is similar to the **Copy** command. (T/F)

EXERCISE

The rendered sequence of the scene used in the following exercise can be accessed by downloading the *c15_maxdesign_2015_exr.zip* from *www.cadcim.com*. The path of the file is as follows: *Textbooks > Animation and Visual Effects > 3ds Max Design > Autodesk 3ds Max Design 2015: A Tutorial Approach*

Exercise 1

Extract the contents of the *c15_3dsmaxdesign_2015_exr.zip* and then open *c15_exr01_start.max*. Next, animate the vise, refer to Figures 15-22 through 15-25.

Figure 15-22 Animation at frame 50

Figure 15-23 Animation at frame 75

Figure 15-24 Animation at frame 125

Figure 15-25 Animation at frame 150

Answers to Self-Evaluation Test

1. c, **2.** linked, **3.** rendering, **4. Track View - Dope Sheet**, **5.** 1.0, **6.** properties, **7.** camera, target, **8. Trajectory**, **9.** T

Chapter 16

Rendering

Learning Objectives

After completing this chapter, you will be able to:
- *Create an animation for preview*
- *Define the current segment of an animation*
- *Render all frames, a single frame, a segment, or a range of an animation*
- *Render a single frame as a bitmap file*
- *Render the final animation*

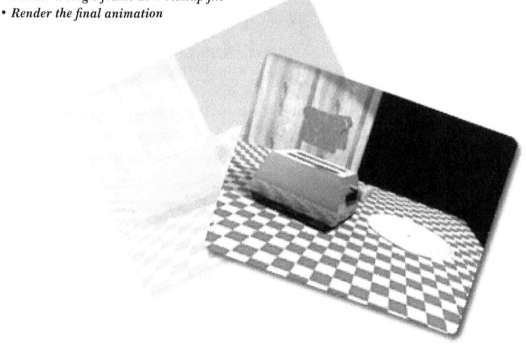

INTRODUCTION

3ds Max Design allows you to create a rendered preview in low resolution. The rendered preview animation allows you to check the result of an animation before you go for the final rendering. Rendering a final animation can take a long time and if there is an error in the animation, it needs to be completely re-rendered after the rectification the error.

TUTORIAL

Before starting the tutorial, you need to download the *c16_3dsmaxdesign_2015_tut.zip* file from *www.cadcim.com*. The path of the file is as follows: *Textbooks > Animation and Visual Effects > 3ds Max Design > Autodesk 3ds Max Design 2015: A Tutorial Approach*

Extract the contents of the zip file and save them in the *Documents* folder.

Tutorial 1

In this tutorial, you will render the animation for preview by using various options available. You will render single frame and also a range of frames of an animation, refer to Figure 16-1.

(Expected time: 25 min)

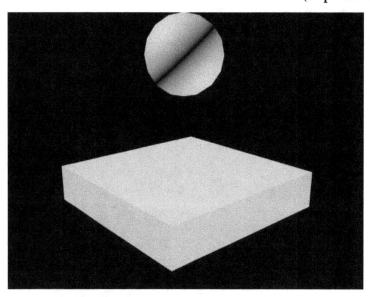

Figure 16-1 *The rendered animation for preview*

The following steps are required to complete this tutorial:

a. Create the project folder.
b. Open the file.
c. Preview an animation.
d. Define an active time segment.
e. Reset the active segment to the entire animation.
f. Preview a range of frames

g. Render a single frame as an image.
h. Render and save the final animation.
i. Render the second camera view.
j. Merge two animations together.

Creating the Project Folder

Create the project folder with the name *c16_tut1* in the *3dsmaxdesign 2015* folder, as discussed in earlier chapters.

Opening the File

1. Choose **Open** from the **Application** menu; the **Open File** dialog box is displayed. In this dialog box, browse to the location *\Documents\c16_3dsmaxdesign_2015_tut* and select the **c16_tut1_start.max** file from it. Choose the **Open** button to open the file, refer to Figure 16-2.

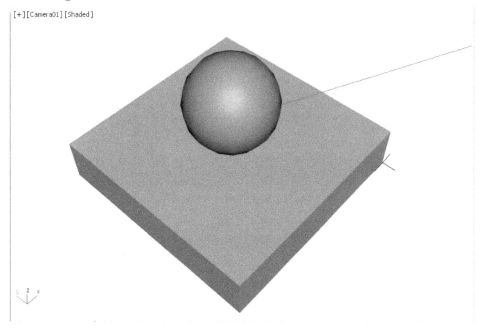

Figure 16-2   *The c16_tut1_start.max file*

2. Choose **Save As** from the **Application** menu; the **Save File As** dialog box is displayed. Browse to the location *\Documents\3dsmaxdesign 2015\c16_tut1\scenes*. Save the file with the name *c16tut1.max* at this location.

Previewing an Animation

1. Make sure the Camera01 viewport is activated.

2. Choose **Tools > Preview - Grab Viewport > Create Preview Animation** from the menu bar; the **Make Preview** dialog box is displayed, as shown in Figure 16-3.

*Figure 16-3 The **Make Preview** dialog box*

All the settings in this dialog box can be modified so that the required information needed can be made active while rendering the preview animation.

3. In the **Preview Range** area, make sure the **Active Time Segment** radio button is selected.

The active time segment in the animation is currently set to all frames (frame 0 to 30).

4. Choose the **Create** button at the bottom of this dialog box; the **Video Compression** dialog box is displayed. In this dialog box, use the default values and then choose the **OK** button; the animation is rendered and automatically played in Windows Media Player, refer to Figure 16-4.

5. To view the animation again, choose **Tools > Preview - Grab Viewport > Play Preview Animation** from the menu bar or press SHIFT+V; the animation is played.

Figure 16-4 *The preview animation played in Windows Media Player*

Defining an Active Time Segment

The longer an animation is, the more will be the number of frames to be managed. To make this process easier, you can define an active time segment. A time segment is a group of sequential frames in the animation. The active time segment is the group of frames currently accessible with the time slider. The active time segment can be rendered as a preview or final animation.

1. Choose the **Time Configuration** button in the animation playback controls area; the **Time Configuration** dialog box is displayed, as shown in Figure 16-5.

2. In the **Animation** area of this dialog box, set the value **10** in the **Start Time** spinner and **20** in the **End Time** spinner. Next, choose the **OK** button to close this dialog box.

   Frames 10 to 20 have been set as the current active time segment.

3. Make sure the Camera01 viewport is activated and then choose **Tools > Preview - Grab Viewport > Create Preview Animation** from the menu bar; the **Make Preview** dialog box is displayed.

4. In this dialog box, make sure the **Active Time Segment** radio button is selected in the **Preview Range** area.

5. Choose the **Create** button; the preview is rendered, starting at frame 10 and ending at frame 20, and played in Windows Media Player.

Figure 16-5 *The **Time Configuration** dialog box*

Previewing a Range of Frames

A range of frames can be previewed without setting it as the active time segment. However, that range must be a subset of the frames available in the active time segment.

1. Choose the **Time Configuration** button in the animation playback controls area; the **Time Configuration** dialog box is displayed. In the **Animation** area of this dialog box, set the value **0** in the **Start Time** spinner and **30** in the **End Time** spinner. Next, choose the **OK** button to close this dialog box.

2. Make sure the Camera01 viewport is activated. Next, choose **Tools > Preview - Grab Viewport > Create Preview Animation** from the menu bar; the **Make Preview** dialog box is displayed.

3. In the **Preview Range** area of this dialog box, select the **Custom Range** radio button.

4. Make sure 10 and 20 are set in the first and second fields, respectively. Next, choose the **Create** button; the preview is rendered from frame 10 to 20 only.

    However, notice that the active time segment is still from frame 0 to frame 30, as indicated in the time slider at the bottom of the 3ds Max Design screen.

Rendering a Single Frame as an Image

Frames in an animation can be rendered individually as individual bitmap file. These image files can be used as backgrounds or texture maps in 3ds Max Design. They can also be used as graphics on web pages, or illustrations in reports or slide shows. The rendered image files can be saved in several common formats.

The following example uses the JPEG format because it allows to set the amount of file compression increases, the file size and quality of the image decreases. If the amount of file compression decreases, the image quality improves, and the size of the image files also increases.

1. Make sure the Camera01 viewport is active. Now, press the C key; the **Select Camera** dialog box is displayed, as shown in Figure 16-6. Select the **Camera02** option and then choose the **OK** button to make the Camera02 viewport active.

*Figure 16-6 The **Select Camera** dialog box*

2. Choose **Rendering > Render Setup** from the menu bar or invoke the **Render Setup** tool from the **Main Toolbar**; the **Render Setup: NVIDIA mental ray** dialog box is displayed, as shown in Figure 16-7.

3. In the **Time Output** area of the **Common Parameters** rollout, select the **Frames** radio button to make it active. Next, type **25** in the text box next to the radio button.

    Only the frame(s) listed in the text box will be rendered.

4. In the **Output Size** area of this dialog box, make sure the **640×480** button is chosen; the image is set to be rendered at a resolution of 640 × 480 pixels. Also, make sure the values 640 and 480 are set in the **Width** and **Height** spinners, respectively.

5. In the **Render Output** area of this dialog box, choose the **Files** button; the **Render Output File** dialog box is displayed, as shown in Figure 16-8. As the project folder is already set, the folder *renderoutput* of this project is displayed in the **Save in** drop-down list.

6. Enter **c16tut1** in the **File name** text box.

*Figure 16-7 The **Render Setup: NVIDIA mental ray** dialog box displayed*

7. Select the **JPEG File** from the **Save as type** drop-down list and choose the **Save** button; the **JPEG Image Control** dialog box is displayed if this file type has not been saved during the current drawing session.

Note
*The **JPEG Image Control** dialog box lets you adjust the quality, size, and smoothing. If the image is to be used in a presentation, choose a better image quality. If the image is to be used on a web page, choose a smaller file size so that the image can be downloaded faster.*

This dialog box allows you to adjust the quality, size, and smoothing of the image.

*Figure 16-8 The **Render Output File** dialog box*

8. Choose the **OK** button to accept the default JPEG settings.

    You will notice that the **Save File** check box is selected and the path and file name
    are displayed in the **Render Output** area of the **Render Setup** dialog box.

9. Choose the **Render** button in the **Render Setup: NVIDIA mental ray** dialog box;
    the **Rendered Frame** window and the **Rendering** dialog box are displayed to show
    the status of rendering.

10. After the rendering is complete, close the render window and the **Render Setup:
    NVIDIA mental ray** dialog box.

Rendering the Final Animation

In most cases, a final animation is the ultimate goal of all the work that is done in 3ds Max
Design. The final animation contains all the movement and is rendered with colors, textures,
and shadows. This process can take some time, depending on the speed of the processor in
the computer and the length, complexity, and resolution of the animation.

1. Make the Camera01 viewport active by pressing the C key.

2. Invoke the **Render Setup** tool from the **Main Toolbar**; the **Render Setup: NVIDIA
    mental ray** dialog box is displayed.

3. In the **Time Output** area, select the **Active Time Segment** radio button to make it active.

This sets all the active frames in the animation to be rendered.

Note

*By selecting the **Range** radio button and using the spinners in the **Time Output** area of the **Render Setup** dialog box, you can specify the range of frames to be rendered for the final animation. When specifying the range of frames in the **Render Setup** dialog box, the selected range of frames is not required to fall within the active time segment.*

4. In the **Output Size** area of the dialog box, choose the **320x240** button; this sets the resolution of the animation to be rendered to 320 × 240 pixels. The higher the resolution, the longer it will take to render the animation and the file will also be a larger in size. To save time and hard drive space, render the animation at 320 × 240 resolution.

5. In the **Render Output** area of the dialog box, choose the **Files** button; the **Render Output File** dialog box is displayed. As the project folder is already set, the folder *renderoutput* of this project is displayed in the **Save in** drop-down list.

6. Type **Tut16a** in the **File name** text box.

7. Select the **AVI File** from the **Save as type** drop-down list and then choose the **Save** button; the **AVI File Compression Setup** dialog box is displayed if this file type has not been saved during the current drawing session.

This dialog box allows you to adjust the quality and keyframe rate of the animation.

8. Choose the **OK** button to accept the default AVI settings.

You will notice that the **Save File** check box is selected in the **Render Output** area of the **Render Setup** dialog box and the path and file name are displayed.

Note

*If the **Save File** check box is not selected, the animation will only be rendered on the screen. You will not be able to replay the animation.*

9. Choose the **Render** button in the **Render Setup: NVIDIA mental ray** dialog box; the **Rendered Frame** window and the **Rendering** dialog box are displayed.

When the rendering of the animation is complete, the **Rendering** dialog box will be closed and the last frame of the animation is displayed. The animation has been saved to the disk and must be viewed to see the results.

10. Close the **Rendered Frame** window and the **Render Setup: NVIDIA mental ray** dialog box.

11. Choose **Rendering > View Image File** from the menu bar; the **View File** dialog box is displayed.

12. Select *Tut16a.avi* and choose the **Open** button; the animation file is opened and played in Windows Media Player.

Rendering the Second Camera View

This scene has two cameras. Two viewports display the two different camera views. You just rendered and saved the animation in the first camera view. Now, render the animation in the second camera view and save it to a file as well.

1. Make the Camera02 viewport active and open the **Render Setup: NVIDIA mental ray** dialog box.

2. In the **Time Output** area, make sure the **Active Time Segment** radio button is selected.

3. In the **Output Size** area of the dialog box, make sure the **320×240** button is chosen. Also, make sure the values 320 and 240 are set in the **Width** and **Height** spinners, respectively. Next, in the **Render Output** area of this dialog box, choose the **Files** button; the **Render Output File** dialog box is displayed. As the project folder is already set, the *renderoutput* folder of this project is displayed in the **Save in** drop-down list of this dialog box.

4. Enter **Tut16b** in the **File name** text box.

5. Make sure the **AVI File** option is selected in the **Save as type:** drop-down list and then choose the **Save** button to save this file.

6. Choose the **Render** button in the **Render Setup: NVIDIA mental ray** dialog box; the **Rendered Frame** window and the **Rendering** dialog box are displayed.

7. After the rendering is complete, close the **Rendered Frame** window and the **Render Setup** dialog box.

8. Choose **Rendering > View Image File** from the menu bar; the **View File** dialog box is displayed.

9. Select *Tut16b.avi* and choose the **Open** button; the avi file is opened and played in the Windows Media Player.

Merging Two Animations Together

Now that the two animations have been created, they can be merged together. 3ds Max Design does not have the capability to merge two rendered avi files together. This can be done with Windows Movie Maker. Use Windows Help and Support for information on how to use Windows Movie Maker.

Self-Evaluation Test

Answer the following questions and then compare them to those given at the end of this chapter:

1. In which of the following areas, you can set the start time and end time in the **Time Configuration** dialog box?

   (a) **Animation**   (b) **Key Steps**
   (c) **Playback**   (d) **Frame Rate**

2. Which of the following shortcut keys is used to activate the Camera viewport?

   (a) V   (b) C
   (c) M   (d) H

3. In which of the following areas, the **Time Configuration** tool is located?

   (a) **Command Panel**   (b) Menu bar
   (c) Animation playback controls   (d) **Main Toolbar**

4. Which of the following dialog boxes is used to specify an active time segment for rendering?

   (a) **Time Configuration**   (b) **Unit Setups**
   (c) **Render Setup**   (d) **Preference Settings**

5. A single frame of an animation can be rendered as image (or bitmap) file. (T/F)

6. While rendering a scene to a JPEG file, increasing the amount of file compression decreases the file size and quality of the rendered image. (T/F)

7. If the **Save File** check box is not selected in the **Render Setup** dialog box, the scene will not be rendered. (T/F)

8. The _____ render contains all movements and is rendered with colors, textures, and shadows.

9. While rendering an animation, increasing the _____ will increase the rendering time and the file size of the final rendered animation.

10. By selecting the _____ radio button and using spinners in the **Time Output** area of the **Render Setup** dialog box, you can specify the range of frames to be rendered for the final animation.

Review Questions

Answer the following questions:

1. Which of the following map types is displayed in rendered preview?

   (a) **Diffuse Color**   (b) **Specular Color**
   (c) **Filter Color**   (d) **Ambient Color**

2. The _____ dialog box allows you to adjust the quality size and smoothing of the image.

3. 3ds Max Design allows you to create a _____ after rendering in low resolution.

4. In 3ds Max Design, you can merge two rendered movie files together. (T/F)

5. In 3ds Max Design, the rendered image files can be used as backgrounds or texture maps. (T/F)

6. The longer an animation is, lesser will be the number of frames to be managed. (T/F)

EXERCISE

The rendered sequence of the scene used in the following exercises can be accessed by downloading *c16_3dsmaxdesign_2015_exr.zip* from *www.cadcim.com*. The path of the file is as follows: *Textbooks > Animation and Visual Effects > 3ds Max Design > Autodesk 3ds Max Design 2015: A Tutorial Approach*

Exercise 1

Extract the contents of *c16_3dsmaxdesign_2015_exr.zip* and then open *c16_exr01_start.max*. Render the preview animation, still image, and final animation of the toaster, as shown in Figure 16-9.   **(Expected time: 35 min)**

Figure 16-9 *The toaster*

Chapter *17*

Creating Walkthrough

Learning Objectives

After completing this chapter, you will be able to:

- *Create a motion path for the camera to follow*
- *Modify the motion path*
- *Assign a path constraint controller to the position track of an object*
- *Adjust camera parameters and animate the camera*
- *Animate 3ds Max Design AEC objects*
- *Render the preview and final walkthrough*

INTRODUCTION

A walkthrough is created by defining a path of the walk by drawing a line from the start point to the end point. The camera is created and assigned to the path which records the animation along the path. A path constraint controller is assigned to the position track of the camera so that the camera follows the path. The path is modified to allow precise control over the animation. In addition, the camera rotation is animated, as it is the movement of 3ds Max Design AEC objects, such as doors and windows. Then, a preview is created before the final animation is rendered.

TUTORIAL

Before starting the tutorial, you need to download the file *c17_3dsmaxdesign_2015_tut.zip* from *www.cadcim.com*. The path of the file is as follows: *Textbooks > Animation and Visual Effects > 3ds Max Design > Autodesk 3ds Max Design 2015: A Tutorial Approach*

Extract the contents of the zip file and save them in the *Documents* folder.

Tutorial 1

In this tutorial, you will create a walkthrough in an architectural setting. You will draw a path and make a camera follow the path. The final animation will contain all movements and will be rendered with colors, textures, and shadows, refer to Figure 17-1. (**Expected time: 45 min**)

Figure 17-1 *The final walkthrough at frame 70*

The following steps are required to complete this tutorial:

a. Create the project folder.
b. Open the file.
c. Create the motion path.
d. Refine the motion path.
e. Define the length of the animation.
f. Use the walkthrough assistant.
g. Adjust the head tilt angle.
h. Add a camera and a path constraint controller.
i. Assign a path constraint controller.
j. Adjust the camera.
k. Animate objects in the scene.
l. Preview the animation.
m. Render and save the final animation.

Creating the Project Folder

Create a project folder with the name *c17_tut1* in the *3dsmaxdesign 2015* folder, as discussed in earlier chapters.

Opening the File

1. Choose **Open** from the **Application** menu; the **Open File** dialog box is displayed. In this dialog box, browse to the location *\Documents\c17_3dsmaxdesign_2015_tut* and select the **c17_tut1_start.max** file from it. Choose the **Open** button to open the file, refer to Figure 17-2.

Figure 17-2 The c17_tut1_start file

2. Choose **Save As** from the **Application** menu; the **Save File As** dialog box is displayed. Browse to the location *Documents\3dsmaxdesign_2015\c17_tut1\scenes*. Save the file with the name *c17tut1.max* at this location.

Creating the Motion Path

This animation will simulate the view of a person walking through a building. A line will be created to represent the path of the motion. The path will be followed precisely by a camera representing a person's line of site. The path will need to have round corners to represent the naturally smooth path a person takes as he walks. Also, the path must not lie too close to any of the walls and must pass through the center of door openings.

1. Activate the Top viewport and maximize it by invoking the **Maximize Viewport Toggle** tool.

2. Invoke the **Zoom Extents All** tool to zoom into the viewports.

3. Choose **Create > Shapes** in the **Command Panel** and make sure **Splines** is selected in the drop-down list below the **Shapes** button, if it is not already selected.

4. Invoke the **Line** tool from the **Object Type** rollout.

    The 2D objects (shapes) available are listed in the **Object Type** rollout. Shapes are used to construct objects such as lofts, or are used as motion paths.

5. Select the **Smooth** radio button in the **Initial Type** area from the **Creation Method** rollout.

    A smooth curve will be formed when points are selected.

6. Use the cones as a guide to create a line, starting from the bottom cone, as shown in Figure 17-3.

    The line will be used as a motion path for a camera.

7. Right-click to end the command. In the **Name and Color** rollout, enter the name of the spline as **Walkthrough-Path**.

 Note
If the line created is not exactly as you want, it can be further modified. Each of the vertices in the line can be moved and the path will change to flow through the modified vertices. You can also add new vertices, if they are not enough, by refining the line. Since the line is a 2D object, it does not go up the stairs as it enters the building. You can modify the line to follow the stairs into the building.

[+][Top][Wireframe]

Figure 17-3 A line created to be used as a path

Refining the Motion Path

If the starting vertex of the line was moved down to the level of the first stair, the motion path would bend to fit through the moved vertex. Since the second vertex is well inside the building, the path would pass through the steps and floor of the building. To prevent this, the line needs to be refined. The line will now be modified and follow the stairs into the house.

1. With the line selected, choose the **Modify** tab in the **Command Panel**.

2. In the **Selection** rollout, choose the **Vertex** button to activate the vertex sub-object mode to display each individual vertex of the path.

3. Choose the **Refine** button in the **Geometry** rollout.

4. Add a new vertex where the path enters the building by clicking on the line at that point; a new vertex appears on the path, as shown in Figure 17-4.

5. Invoke the **Select and Move** tool and select the newly added vertex and move it such that it is centered in the doorway.

6. Invoke the **Maximize Viewport Toggle** tool. Activate the Left viewport and maximize it.

7. Move the first vertex down so that it is at the same level as the bottom of the house, as shown in Figure 17-5.

Figure 17-4 *A new vertex added to the path*

Figure 17-5 *The first vertex moved down*

The motion path is modified such that it can follow the stairs into the building.

8. Choose the **Vertex** button in the **Selection** rollout to exit the vertex sub-object mode.

9. Move *Walkthrough-Path* 66.0 units on the Y axis.

The motion path is moved to the height of an average person's line of sight.

Defining the Length of the Animation

Walkthrough animations need a large number of frames. If less number of frames are used for the animation, the camera will appear turning at the corners very quickly. In addition, it will appear as if the person is running through the scene instead of walking. More the number of frames in the animation, smoother the final motion will be.

1. Choose the **Time Configuration** button in the animation controls; the **Time Configuration** dialog box is displayed.

2. Set the value **1000** is set in the **Length** spinner in the **Animation** area of this dialog box.

The total number of frames in the animation is set to 1000. This represents a little over 30 seconds of animation.

3. Choose the **OK** button to close the dialog box.

Using the Walkthrough Assistant

The **Walkthrough Assistant** automates the process of creating a camera and making it follow the path you created. It provides settings for the camera height and head angles.

1. Choose **Animation > Walkthrough Assistant** from the menu bar; the **Walkthrough Assistant** dialog box is displayed, as shown in Figure 17-6. It does not really matter which viewport is active.

2. In the **Camera Creation** area of the **Main Controls** rollout, make sure the **Free** radio button is selected. Next, choose the **Create New Camera** button; a free camera is automatically created with the name *Walkthrough_Cam001*. Now, the camera must be moved to the start of the path.

3. In the **Path Control** area, select the **Move Path to Eye level** check box. Next, choose the **Pick Path** button and select the line created as the path.

The camera is positioned and oriented along the path. The camera and motion path are automatically set at average person's eye level. This setting can be switched by changing the value in the **Eye Level** spinner.

4. In the **Advanced Controls** rollout, set the value **75** in the **Field of View** spinner and make sure **160** is entered in the **Target Distance** spinner of the **Camera Controls** area.

This sets the accurate camera view.

*Figure 17-6 The **Walkthrough Assistant** dialog box*

5. In the **Render Preview** rollout of the **Walkthrough Assistant** dialog box, choose the **Click to Render Preview** button; the current frame *Walkthrough_Cam001* view is rendered and appears in place of the button.

6. To work on the animation, make the Front viewport active. Change the display to *Walkthrough_Cam001* view by pressing the C key. Right-click on the viewport label and choose **Shaded** from the shortcut menu.

   With this viewport active, you will be able to watch modifications in the final animation as they occur instead of using the preview animation area in the **Walkthrough Assistant** dialog box for each frame.

7. Drag the time slider to the right and left to replay the animation of the camera following the motion path.

   If the animation seems not correct, you need to check it and remove the flaw. You may need to close the **Walkthrough Assistant** dialog box and delete the camera. You can then start over again by opening the **Walkthrough Assistant** dialog box and creating a new camera.

Adjusting the Head Tilt Angle

As the camera follows the motion path up toward the stairs, it tilts up to follow the path. A person walking up to the stairs usually does not tilt his head in this manner. The **Walkthrough Assistant** has a setting that allows the head tilt angle to be modified as the camera moves along the path.

1. Drag the time slider bar to frame 0.

2. Open the **Walkthrough Assistant** dialog box, if it is not already open. Scroll down and set the value **–45** in the **Head Tilt Angle** spinner in the **View Controls** rollout.

    The camera's line of sight is slightly below horizontal in frame 0 of the animation.

3. Choose the **Toggle Auto Key Mode** button to turn on the animation mode.

4. Drag the time slider to the frame in your animation where the camera is halfway through the doorway (about frame 134).

5. Set the value **–10** in the **Head Tilt Angle** spinner.

6. Choose the **Toggle Auto Key Mode** button to turn off the animation mode. Next, drag the time slider bar to frame 0.

7. Make sure the *Walkthrough_Cam001* viewport is activated. And, close the **Walkthrough Assistant** dialog box.

8. Choose the **Play Animation** button in the animation playback controls; the animation begins to play in the active viewport.

9. Choose the **Stop Animation** button to stop the animation replay.

10. Select *Walkthrough_Cam001* in any viewport. Right-click on the Camera; a quad menu is displayed. Choose **Hide Selection** from this menu.

11. Restore the viewport settings from [Walkthrough_Cam001][Shaded] to [Front] [Wireframe].

> **Note**
>
> *Although the **Walkthrough Assistant** makes adding and animating a camera quick and easy, it is important to understand how to accomplish the same task manually. The following section explains how to manually add and animate a camera for a walkthrough animation. Please note the following procedure is an alternative to using the **Walkthrough Assistant**, and is not necessary if the **Walkthrough Assistant** is used to add and animate a camera.*

Adding a Camera and a Path Constraint Controller

The camera used for a walkthrough animation is usually a **Free** camera. Using a **Free** camera eliminates the need to animate both the camera and the camera target.

1. Create a **Free** camera at the starting point of the path in the Front viewport and align it in all viewports, refer to Figure 17-7.

Figure 17-7   *Creating a Free camera*

2. Choose the **Modify** tab in the **Command Panel**. In the **Stock Lenses** area of the **Parameters** rollout, choose the **24mm** button.

   A camera is placed in the viewport. The camera does not need to be positioned exactly on the motion path. The camera will be automatically aligned when the path constraint controller is added.

3. Activate the Perspective viewport. Press the C key to turn this viewport into Camera001 viewport.

Assigning a Path Constraint Controller

A path constraint is a controller assigned to an object that makes the object follow a selected path. You will assign a path constraint controller to the free camera. Then, you will specify the path you created as the motion path for the controller.

1. Select *Camera001*, if it is not already selected.

2. Choose the **Motion** tab in the **Command Panel**. Expand the **Assign Controller** rollout. In this rollout, a hierarchy tree which appears similar to **Track View** is displayed.

3. Click the plus sign (**+**) on the left side of the **Transform: Position/Rotation/Scale** to expand the tree, if it is not already expanded.

4. Select **Position: Position XYZ** in the hierarchy. Next, choose the **Assign** 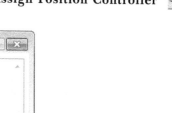 **Controller** button at the top of the rollout; the **Assign Position Controller** dialog box is displayed, as shown in Figure 17-8.

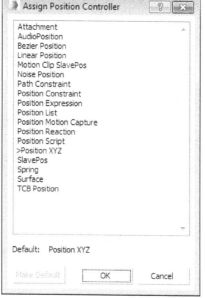

Figure 17-8 The *Assign Position Controller* dialog box

5. In the **Assign Position Controller** dialog box, select **Path Constraint** from the list. Then, choose the **OK** button to close the dialog box.

The **Path Parameters** rollout now appears in the **Motion** tab in the **Command Panel**.

6. In the **Command Panel**, choose the **Add Path** button in the **Path Parameters** rollout. Next, select the *Walkthrough-Path* in any viewport.
The camera will now move along the path.

7. Select the **Follow** check box in the **Path Options** area of the **Path Parameters** rollout.

8. The camera may rotate on the path. If required, select the **Y** radio button in the **Axis** area of the **Path Parameters** rollout so that the camera looks down the path.

Adjusting the Camera

In this section, you will adjust the camera view in the Perspective viewport.

1. Make sure the camera is selected in the Left viewport and then right-click on the **Select and Rotate** button; the **Rotate Transform Type-In** dialog box is displayed.

2   In the **Absolute:World** area of this dialog box, set the values in the spinners, as given next:

    X: **80**   Y: **0**   Z: **0**

    The camera is given a more natural line of sight and is squared up with the viewports.

3. Activate animation mode by choosing the **Toggle Auto Key Mode** button and drag the time slider to the frame in your animation where the camera is halfway through the doorway (about frame 134).

4. In the **Absolute:World** area of the **Rotate Transform Type-In** dialog box, set the values in the spinners as given next:

    X: **80**   Y: **0**   Z: **0**

5. Close the **Rotate Transform Type-In** dialog box.

Animating Objects in the Scene

The doors and windows in this scene were created with the 3ds Max Design AEC objects. These objects have predefined pivot points and animation paths that can be accessed using the **Modify** tab in the **Command Panel**. Currently, the entrance door does not open and the camera moves right through it as it follows the motion path. The door needs to be opened before the camera reaches it and it must remain open as the camera passes through.

1. Drag the time slider to frame 50.

    This is the frame where the door should begin to open.

2. Choose the **Graph Editors > Track View - Dope Sheet** from the menu bar.

3. Select the **Entrance Door** in the viewport. In the **Track View - Dope Sheet** window, click on the plus sign (**+**) on the left side of the **Entrance Door** and then on the **Object (PivotDoor)** to expand the tree.

    The **Track View - Dope Sheet** window displays the **Open (degrees)** track for the **Entrance Door** object, as shown Figure 17-9.

4. Choose the **Add Keys** button on the top of the **Track View-Dope Sheet** window.

Figure 17-9 The Track View - Dope Sheet window

5. Choose the **Open (degrees)** track at frame 50 for the **Entrance Door**.

   A key for the **Entrance Door** is created at frame 50. The value of this key is 0 which means the door is closed. This key sets the frame where the door begins to open.

6. Close the **Track View-Dope Sheet** window.

7. Drag the time slider to frame 100 and activate the animation mode, if it is not already active.

8. Make sure the **Entrance Door** is selected in any viewport.

9. Choose the **Modify** tab in the **Command Panel**.

10. In the **Parameters** rollout, set the value **90** in the **Open** spinner; the **Entrance Door** is opened 90 degrees at frame 100, as shown Figure 17-10.

11. Choose **Graph Editors > Saved Track Views > Track View - Dope Sheet** from the menu bar; the **Track View - Dope Sheet** window is displayed with the previous settings active.

12. Choose the **Add Keys** button on the top of the **Track View - Dope Sheet** window.

13. Choose the **Open (degrees)** track at frame 225 for the **Entrance Door**.

14. Right-click on the new key; the **Entrance Door\Open (degrees)** dialog box for the new key is displayed, as shown in Figure 17-11.

Figure 17-10 The **Entrance Door** *is opened 90 degrees at frame 100*

Figure 17-11 The **Entrance Door\Open (degrees)** *dialog box*

15. Make sure 90 is selected as the value in the **Value** spinner.

    A value of 90 degrees sets the **Entrance Door** to the fully open position.

16. Close the **Entrance Door\Open (degrees)** dialog box and **Track View - Dope Sheet** window.

17. Drag the time slider to frame 275.

18. Make sure the **Toggle Auto Key Mode** button is chosen, set the value **0** in the **Open** spinner in the **Parameters** rollout.

The **Entrance Door** is closed at frame 275.

19. Choose the **Toggle Auto Key Mode** button to exit the animation mode.

20. Make the Camera001 viewport active and choose the **Play Animation** button in the animation controls to play the animation.

21. When the animation has finished, choose the **Stop Animation** button in the animation controls to stop the animation.

Previewing the Animation

Now, you can view the animation you have created by rendering a quick preview. The animation will give you a good idea of whether the animation is working correctly. Before the animation is rendered, hide any object that you do not want to be visible in the preview or the final animation.

1. Invoke the **Select Object** tool from the **Main Toolbar** and select the *Walkthrough-Path* in any viewport; the motion path becomes the active object.

2. Right-click in the viewport to display the quad menu. Choose **Hide Selection** from the upper-right quadrant of this quad menu; the path is hidden and will not be visible in the animation.

3. Make the Camera001 viewport active, if it is not already active.

4. Choose **Tools > Preview - Grab Viewport > Create Preview Animation** from the menu bar; the **Make Preview** dialog box is displayed.

5. In this dialog box, choose the **Create** button to accept the default settings and render the preview.

   The preview is generated and then played in Windows Media Player.

Rendering the Final Animation

Now that the animation has been completed and verified with a preview animation, it is time to render the final animation. The final animation contains all movements and is rendered with colors, textures, and shadows. This process can take some time, depending on the speed of the computer's processor and the length, complexity, and resolution of the animation.

1. Activate the Camera001 viewport and then invoke the **Render Setup** tool from the **Main Toolbar**; the **Render Setup: NVIDIA mental ray** dialog box is displayed.

2. In the **Time Output** area, select the **Active Time Segment** radio button.

   This sets all the active frames in the animation to be rendered.

3. In the **Output Size** area of the dialog box, choose the **320×240** button.

This sets the animation to be rendered at a resolution of 320 × 240 pixels. This animation does not need to be of high resolution. The higher the resolution, the longer it will take to render the animation and the larger the file will be.

4. In the **Render Output** area of this dialog box, choose the **Files** button; the **Render Output File** dialog box is displayed. As the project folder is already set, the *renderoutput* folder of this project is displayed in the **Save in** drop-down list.

5. Select **AVI File (*.avi)** from the **Save as type** drop-down list. In the **File name** text box, enter **c17tut1Render** and choose the **Save** button; the path of the file is displayed in the **Render Output** area of the **Render Setup** dialog box.

    The **AVI File Compression Setup** dialog box is displayed, if this file type has not been saved during the current drawing session. This dialog box allows you to adjust the quality and keyframe rate of the animation.

6. Choose the **OK** button to accept the default AVI settings.

Note

*If the **Save File** check box is not selected, the animation will only be rendered to the screen. You will not be able to replay the animation.*

7. Choose the **Render** button in the **Render Setup: NVIDIA mental ray** dialog box; the **Rendered Frame** window and the **Rendering** dialog box are displayed. When the rendering is complete, the **Rendering** dialog box will be closed and the last frame of the animation will be displayed. The animation has been saved to the disk and must be viewed to see the results.

8. Close the **Rendered Frame** window and the **Render Setup: NVIDIA mental ray** dialog box.

9. Choose **Rendering > View Image File** from the menu bar; the **View File** dialog box is displayed. As the project folder is already set, the *renderoutput* folder of this project is displayed in **Look in** drop-down list.

10. Choose the **Open** button; the animation file is opened and played in Windows Media Player. Now, save the scene.

Self-Evaluation Test

Answer the following questions and then compare them to those given at the end of this chapter:

1. Which of the following buttons is used to toggle the animation mode on/off ?

   (a) **Toggle Set Key Mode**   (b) **Toggle Auto Key Mode**
   (c) **Isolate Selection Toggle**   (d) **Selection Lock Toggle**

2. Which of the following buttons is used to create new keys in the **Track View - Dope Sheet** window?

   (a) **Add Keys**   (b) **Edit Keys**
   (c) **Slide Keys**   (d) **Show Selected Key Stats**

3. Which of the following cameras is automatically created with the name *Walkthrough_Cam001* while creating a walkthrough?

   (a) **Target**   (b) **Free**
   (c) Both (a) and (b)   (d) None of these

4. Which of the following is the default renderer in Autodesk 3ds Max Design 2015?

   (a) **Scanline**   (b) **VUE File**
   (c) **NVIDIA mental ray**   (d) **Quicksilver Hardware**

5. A _____ can be used as a motion path.

6. The path is followed precisely by using the _____ to represent a person's line of sight.

7. If there are not enough vertices in a line, it can be _____ to add more vertices.

8. A walkthrough animation is created by defining the path of the walk by drawing a line from the start point to end point. (T/F)

9. Walkthrough animations need a large number of frames to make the animation smooth. (T/F)

10. The **Walkthrough Assistant** has a setting that allows the head tilt angle to be modified as the camera moves along the path. (T/F)

Review Questions

Answer the following questions:

1. Which of the following dialog boxes is used to set the length of the animation within defined frames?

    (a) **Time Configuration**   (b) **Walkthrough Assistant**
    (c) **Make Preview**   (d) **Render Setup**

2. The _____ button is used to add new vertices to the existing spline.

3. The _____ is a controller assigned to an object to make the object follow a selected path.

4. The vertices in a spline cannot be modified. (T/F)

5. The camera used for a walkthrough assistant is usually a **Target** camera. (T/F)

EXERCISE

The rendered sequence of the scene used in the following exercise can be accessed by downloading the *c17_3dsmaxdesign_2015_exr.zip* from *www.cadcim.com*. The path of the file is as follows: *Textbooks > Animation and Visual Effects > 3ds Max Design > Autodesk 3ds Max Design 2015: A Tutorial Approach*

Exercise 1

Extract the contents of *c17_3dsmaxdesign_2015_exr.zip* and then open *c17_exr01_start.max*. Create a walkthrough for the lobby, as shown in Figure 17-12.   **(Expected time: 30 min)**

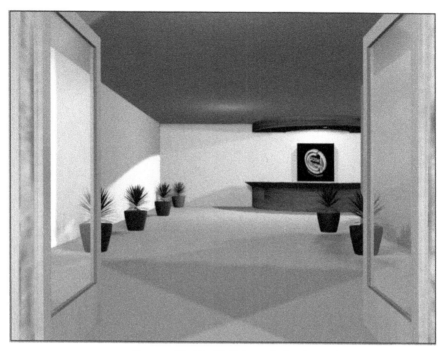

Figure 17-12 *Walkthrough for the lobby*

Answers to Self-Evaluation Test
1. b, **2.** a, **3.** b, **4.** c, **5.** line(Spline), **6.** free camera, **7.** refined, **8.** T, **9.** T, **10.** T

Project 1

Creating a Windmill

PROJECT DESCRIPTION

In this project, you will create the model of a windmill, as shown in Figure P1-1. You will apply materials to the windmill, animate the blades of the windmill, and then render the animation for the final output.

Figure P1-1 *The model of the windmill*

Creating the Project Folder

Create a new project folder with the name *Prj_1* at *\Documents\3dsmaxdesign 2015* and then save the file with the name *Prj1*, as discussed in Tutorial 1 of Chapter 2.

Downloading the Files

Before starting the project, you need to download the *prj1_3dsmaxdesign_2015.zip* file from *www.cadcim.com*. The path of the file is given next: *Textbooks > Animation and Visual Effects > 3ds Max Design > Autodesk 3ds Max Design 2015: A Tutorial Approach*

Extract the contents of the zip file to *Documents*. Open Windows Explorer and then browse to *\Documents\prj1_3dsmaxdesign_2015* and then copy all files to *\Documents\3dsmaxdesign2015\Prj1\sceneassets\images*.

Creating the Base of the Windmill

In this section, you will create the base structure of the windmill by using the **NGon** tool.

1. Invoke the **Maximize Viewport Toggle** tool to display all four viewports.

2. Make sure the **Wireframe** option is chosen in the Shaded viewport label in the Top, Front, and Left viewports. Turn the grid off in all viewports by using the G key.

3. Activate the Top viewport and then choose **Create > Shapes** in the **Command Panel**. Next, invoke the **NGon** tool from the **Object Type** rollout; various rollouts are displayed in the **Command Panel**.

4. In the **Parameters** rollout, make sure the **Inscribed** radio button is selected. Next, set the value **8** in the **Sides** spinner and then press the ENTER key.

5. Expand the **Keyboard Entry** rollout and set the value **100** in the **Radius** spinner. Now, choose the **Create** button; the shape is created with the name *NGon001*, as shown in Figure P1-2.

6. Invoke the **3D Snap Toggle** tool from the **Snaps Toggle** flyout to activate 3D snapping.

7. Activate the Front viewport and make sure the **Shapes** button is activated in the **Command Panel**. Invoke the **Line** tool from the **Object Type** rollout.

8. Expand the **Keyboard Entry** rollout and choose the **Add Point** button to create the first point of the line. Next, set the value **150** in the **Y** spinner and then choose the **Add Point** button; a line of 150 units in length is displayed in the viewports. Right-click in the viewport to exit the tool.

9. Select *NGon001* and right-click on the **Select and Rotate** tool; the **Rotate Transform Type-In** dialog box is displayed. In this dialog box, set the value **22.5** in the **Z** spinner in the **Absolute World** area and then press the ENTER key; *NGon001* rotates, as shown in Figure P1-3. Now, close the dialog box and exit the **Select and Rotate** tool.

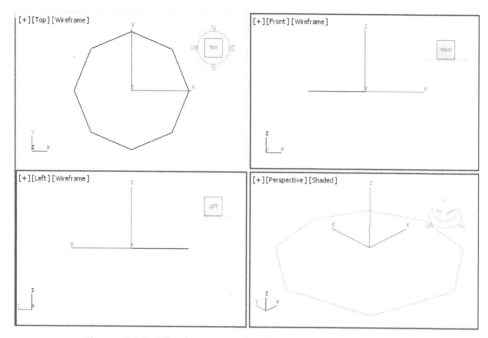

Figure P1-2 *The shape created with the name NGon001*

Figure P1-3 *Rotating NGon001 in the Top viewport*

10. Make sure *NGon001* is selected in any of the viewports. Choose **Create > Geometry** in the **Command Panel** and select **Compound Objects** in the drop-down list.

11. Invoke the **Loft** tool from the **Object Type** rollout. Clear the **Smooth Width** check box in the **Surface Parameters** rollout. Next, set the value **0** in the **Shape Steps** spinner of the **Skin Parameters** rollout.

12. Choose the **Get Path** button in the **Creation Method** rollout and then select the line in the viewport; *NGon001* is lofted along the line to create *Loft001*, as shown in Figure P1-4.

13. Invoke the **Zoom Extents All** tool to view the objects properly in all viewports.

14. Make sure *Loft001* is selected and then choose the **Modify** tab in the **Command Panel**. Next, expand the **Deformations** rollout and choose the **Scale** button; the **Scale Deformation(X)** dialog box is displayed.

15. Maximize the **Scale Deformation(X)** dialog box. Make sure the **Move Control Point** button is chosen and select the right end control point. Move it down so that **90.0** is displayed in the right text field at the bottom of the dialog box, as shown in Figure P1-5.

16. Close the **Scale Deformation(X)** dialog box; the lofted object is tapered at its top, as shown in Figure P1-6.

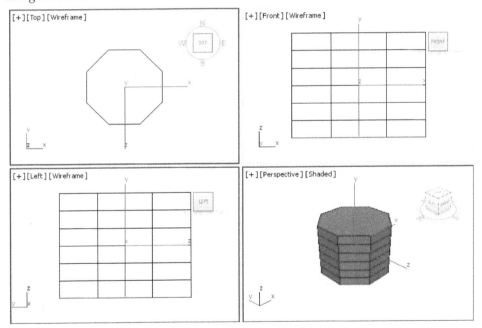

Figure P1-4 *NGon001 lofted along the line in all viewports*

17. Make sure *NGon001* is selected in the viewport.

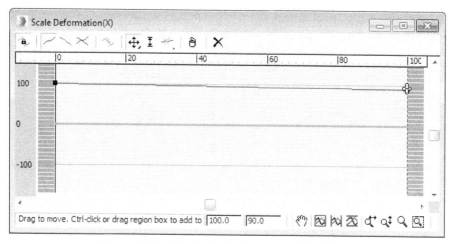

Figure P1-5 *The Scale Deformation(X) dialog box*

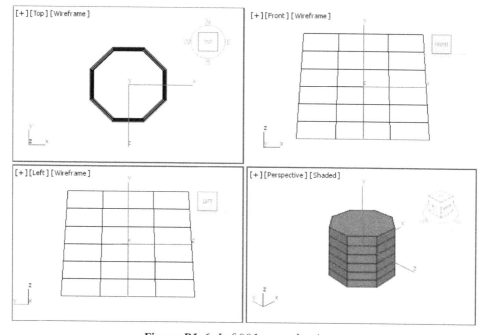

Figure P1-6 *Loft001 tapered at its top*

18. Choose **Edit > Clone** from the menu bar; the **Clone Options** dialog box is displayed. In this dialog box, select the **Copy** radio button in the **Object** area of this dialog box. Next, enter **Floor_lo** in the **Name** text box and choose the **OK** button to close this dialog box; a copy of *NGon001* is created with the name *Floor_lo* at the same location as the original.

19. Make sure *Floor_lo* is selected in the viewport. Expand the **Parameters** rollout and set the value **99** in the **Radius** spinner. Next, select **Extrude** in the **Modifier List** drop-down list under the **OBJECT-SPACE MODIFIERS** section.

20. Set the value **5** in the **Amount** spinner of the **Parameters** rollout for the **Extrude** modifier. Select the **Generate Mapping Coords** check box and clear the **Real-World Map Size** check box; a floor with a thickness of five units is created, as shown in Figure P1-7.

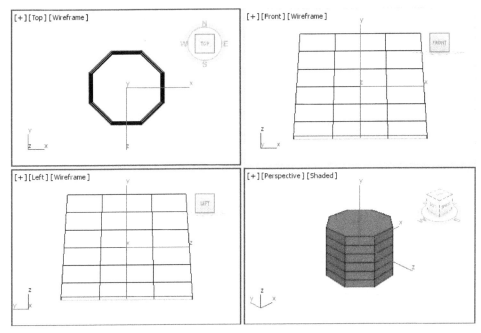

Figure P1-7   *Floor created with a thickness of five units*

21. Select *Loft001* in any viewport. Choose **Edit > Clone** from the menu bar; the **Clone Options** dialog box is displayed. Make sure the **Copy** radio button is selected in this dialog box and the name *Loft002* is displayed in the **Name** text box. Now, choose the **OK** button; a copy of *Loft001* is created with the name *Loft002*.

22. Make sure *Loft002* is selected in the viewport. Also, make sure the **Modify** tab is chosen in the **Command Panel**. Choose the **Scale** button in the **Deformations** rollout; the **Scale Deformation(X)** dialog box is displayed.

23. In this dialog box, make sure the **Move Control Point** button is chosen and move the right-hand control point down two lines to **80**. You will notice that the value 80 is displayed in the right text box at the bottom of this dialog box. Similarly, move the left-hand point down to **90**; the deformation is applied to *Loft002*. Now, close the **Scale Deformation(X)** dialog box.

24. Select *Loft001* from the **Scene Explorer** or in any viewport. Choose **Create > Geometry** in the **Command Panel** and select **Compound Objects** in the drop-down list, if it is not selected. Next, invoke the **Boolean** tool from the **Object Type** rollout. Make sure the **Subtraction (A-B)** radio button is selected in the **Operation** area of the **Parameters** rollout.

25. Choose the **Pick Operand B** button in the **Pick Boolean** rollout and select *Loft002* in any viewport; *Loft002* is subtracted from *Loft001*, leaving the walls for the base of the windmill, as shown in Figure P1-8.

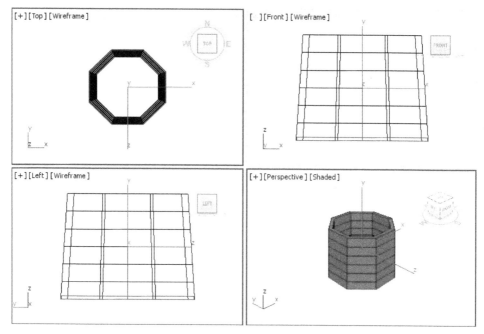

Figure P1-8 *Loft001 displayed after performing the Boolean operation*

26. Invoke the **Select Object** tool from the **Main Toolbar** to exit the Boolean operation.

27. Enter **Base_lo** as the name of the object in the **Name and Color** rollout.

Creating the Middle Structure of the Windmill
In this section, you will create the middle structure of the windmill.

1. Make sure the Front viewport is selected. Invoke the **Pan View** tool to pan the viewport down so that only the top of *Base_lo* is displayed. Make sure the subgrid is displayed.

2. Choose **Create > Shapes** in the **Command Panel**. Invoke the **Line** tool from the **Object Type** rollout to activate it.

3. Create a vertical line **150** units in length starting from the top-center of *Base_lo*. Now, right-click to exit the **Line** tool.

4. Select *NGon001* in any viewport. Choose **Edit > Clone** from the menu bar; the **Clone Options** dialog box is displayed. Make sure the **Copy** radio button is selected in this dialog box and enter **NGon003** in the **Name** text box. Next, choose the **OK** button; the dialog box is closed and a copy of *NGon001* is created with the name *NGon003*.

5. Invoke the **Align** tool and align *NGon003* with the top of *Base_lo*.

6. Make sure *NGon003* is selected and then choose **Create > Geometry** in the **Command Panel**. Select the **Compound Objects** in the drop-down list, if it is not selected. Next, invoke the **Loft** tool from the **Object Type** rollout to activate it.

7. Clear the **Smooth Width** check box in the **Surface Parameters** rollout. Next, in the **Creation Method** rollout, choose the **Get Path** button and then select the line drawn on the top of *Base_lo*; *NGon003* is lofted along the line and named *Loft001*, refer to Figure P1-9. This name is used because the original *Loft001* was renamed.

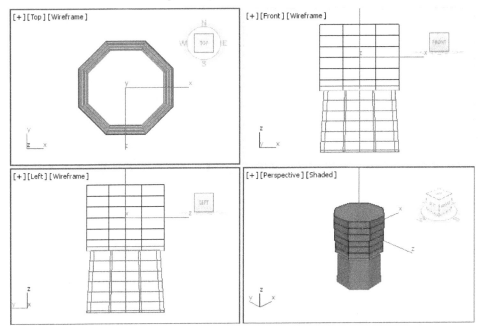

Figure P1-9 *NGon003 lofted along the line*

8. Invoke the **Zoom Extents All** tool to zoom the viewports to their extents.

9. Make sure the new *Loft001* is selected and then choose the **Modify** tab of the **Command Panel**. Expand the **Skin Parameters** rollout and make sure the value **0** is entered in both the **Shape Steps** and **Path Steps** spinners in the **Options** area.

10. In the **Deformations** rollout, choose the **Scale** button; the **Scale Deformation(X)** dialog box is displayed.

11. In the **Scale Deformation(X)** dialog box, choose the **Insert CornerPoint** button and insert a point at **30** on the horizontal scale. Next, choose the **Move Control Point** button and move the point down to **75**.

Note
You can specify the exact values in the text boxes at the bottom of the dialog box. The value entered in the text box on the left is used for positioning the control point in relation to the horizontal scale. The value entered in the text box on the right positions the control point in relation to the vertical scale.

12. Similarly, insert a point at **60** and move it down horizontally to **60**, insert a point at **80** and move it down horizontally to **53**, and move the right corner (**100**) down horizontally to **50**, as shown in Figure P1-10.

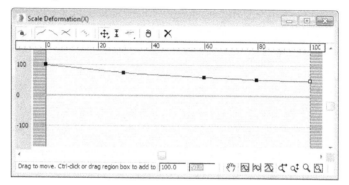

Figure P1-10 *Inserting and moving the control points in the* **Scale Deformation(X)** *dialog box*

13. Close the **Scale Deformation(X)** dialog box and invoke the **Zoom Extents All** tool to view the objects in all viewports.

14. Create a copy of *Loft001* and assign it the name **Loft002**.

15. Make sure *Loft002* is selected. Also, make sure the **Modify** tab is chosen in the **Command Panel**. Choose the **Scale** button in the **Deformations** rollout; the **Scale Deformation(X)** dialog box is displayed. Maximize this dialog box and move all control points down to two lines (**–5** units) on the vertical scale. This can be accomplished by selecting the control points one at a time and subtracting **5** from the value displayed in the right-hand text box at the bottom of the dialog box.

16. Close the **Scale Deformation(X)** dialog box and select *Loft001* in any viewport to activate it.

17. Choose **Create > Geometry** in the **Command Panel**. Select the **Compound Objects** in the drop-down list, if it is not selected. Next, invoke the **Boolean** tool from the **Object Type** rollout.

18. Make sure the **Subtraction (A-B)** radio button is selected in the **Operation** area of the **Parameters** rollout. Choose the **Pick Operand B** button in the **Pick Boolean** rollout and select *Loft002* in any viewport: the walls for the middle structure of the windmill are created, as shown in Figure P1-11.

19. Invoke the **Select Object** tool to exit the boolean operation.

Figure P1-11 *Walls created for the middle structure of the windmill*

20. Enter **Base_mid** in the **Name and Color** rollout and save the changes.

Creating the Top Structure of the Windmill

In this section, you will create the top structure of the windmill. You will then alter the top structure to give it a dome shape.

1. Select *NGon001* and create a copy with the name **NGon002**.

2. Move *NGon002* up in the Front viewport until it is at level with the top of *Base_mid*.

3. Choose the **Modify** tab in the **Command Panel**. In the **Parameters** rollout, set the value **60** in the **Radius** spinner.

4. Zoom in the Front viewport to display the subgrid. Then, pan the viewport down so that only the upper portion of *Base_mid* is visible.

5. Choose **Create > Shapes** in the **Command Panel**. Invoke the **Line** tool from the **Object Type** rollout. Next, create a vertical line of length **80** units from the top-center of *Base_mid*. Right-click to exit the **Line** tool.

6. Select *NGon002* in any viewport. Choose **Create > Geometry** in the **Command Panel** and select **Compound Objects** in the drop-down list, if it is not selected. Next, invoke the **Loft** tool from the **Object Type** rollout.

7. Choose the **Get Path** button in the **Creation Method** rollout, and then select the line object you just created; *NGon002* is lofted along the line, as shown in Figure P1-12.

Figure P1-12 *NGon002 lofted along the line*

8. Enter **Base_top** in the **Name and Color** rollout.

9. Create a copy of *Base_top* and name it as **Top_drill**.

10. Make sure *Top_drill* is selected and then choose **Hierarchy > Pivot** in the **Command Panel**. Choose the **Affect Pivot Only** button in the **Move/Rotate/Scale** area of the **Adjust Pivot** rollout. Next, move the pivot so that it is aligned with the bottom of *Top_drill*. Choose the **Affect Pivot Only** button to exit the pivot adjustment mode.

 Note
The pivot point may already be in the correct location and may not require any adjustment.

11. Invoke the **Select and Uniform Scale** tool. Also, invoke the **Percent Snap Toggle** tool to turn on the percentage snaps.

12. In the Front viewport, scale *Top_drill* until the coordinate display shows 90.0 in each of the **X**, **Y**, and **Z** spinners; *Top_drill* is scaled uniformly, as shown in Figure P1-13. You can also use the **Scale Transform Type-In** dialog box to scale the *Top_drill*, if you prefer.

13. Make sure *Top_drill* is selected in the viewport and then choose the **Modify** tab in the **Command Panel**. Clear the **Smooth Width** check box in the **Smoothing** area of the **Surface Parameters** rollout. Choose the **Scale** button in the **Deformations** rollout; the **Scale Deformation(X)** dialog box is displayed.

Figure P1-13 *Top_drill scaled uniformly*

14. Maximize the **Scale Deformation(X)** dialog box, if required. Choose the **Insert Corner Point** button and insert points at **40, 80**, and **90** on the top scale. Next, choose the **Scale Control Point** button and move these points to **90, 60**, and **40**, respectively. Also, move the right control point to **0**, as shown in Figure P1-14.

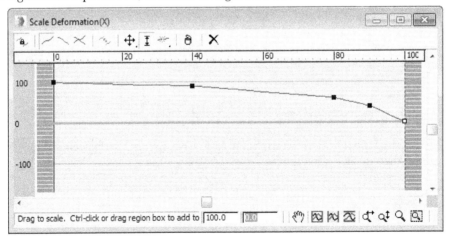

Figure P1-14 *Top_drill modified using the **Scale Deformation(X)** dialog box*

15. Close the **Scale Deformations(X)** dialog box.

The shape of drill is altered to a dome shape. However, *Base_top* needs to be changed too.

16. Select *Base_top* and choose the **Modify** tab in the **Command Panel**. Clear the **Smooth Width** check box in the **Surface Parameters** rollout and choose the **Scale** button in the **Deformations** rollout; the **Scale Deformation(X)** dialog box is displayed.

17. In the **Scale Deformation(X)** dialog box, insert and scale the points at the same positions as done for *Top_drill*. Refer to step 14. Now, close the **Scale Deformation(X)** dialog box.

18. Select *NGon002*, which was used to make the top of the building. Create a copy with the name **Floor_top**.

19. Make sure *Floor_top* is selected in the viewport. Also, make sure the **Modify** tab is chosen in the **Command Panel**. Set the value **58** in the **Radius** spinner in the **Parameters** rollout. Select **Extrude** in the **Modifier List** drop-down list under the **OBJECT-SPACE MODIFIERS** section.

20. Make sure the value 5 is set in the **Amount** spinner of the **Parameters** rollout; *Floor_top* is extruded, as shown in Figure P1-15.

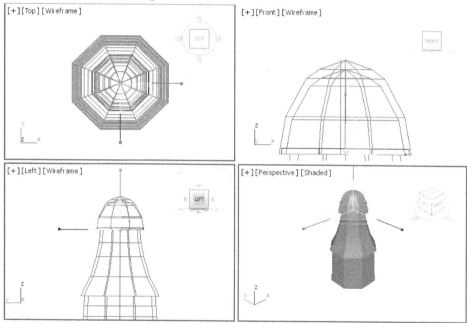

Figure P1-15 *Floor_top extruded*

Creating the Top Structure of the Windmill

In this section, you will create the top structure of the windmill. You will then modify it to a dome shape and make it smooth.

1. Select *Base_top, Top_drill,* and *Floor_top*.

2. Choose the **Display** tab in the **Command Panel**. Invoke the **Hide Selected** tool in the **Hide** rollout; the top portion of the building is hidden.

Note

An alternative method of hiding the objects would be to select the objects, right-click in the viewport, and choose **Hide Selection** *from the quad menu.*

3. Make sure the Front viewport is active and choose **Create > Shapes** in the **Command Panel**. Invoke the **Line** tool from the **Object Type** rollout.

4. Expand the **Keyboard Entry** rollout and enter the following values in the **X**, **Y**, and **Z** spinners. You need to choose the **Add Point** button after every XYZ coordinate entry:

X: 0	Y: 380	Z: 0
X: −20	Y: 370	Z: 0
X: −30	Y: 350	Z: 0
X: −40	Y: 300	Z: 0
X: 40	Y: 300	Z: 0
X: 30	Y: 350	Z: 0
X: 20	Y: 370	Z: 0

5. After the last entry, choose the **Close** button to add the last segment and create a closed line; a dome shape is created. In the **Name and Color** rollout, enter **Ext01**. Right-click to exit the tool.

6. Make sure *Ext01* is selected in the viewport and then choose the **Modify** tab in the **Command Panel**. Choose the **Vertex** button in the **Selection** rollout to enter the **Vertex** sub-object mode. Drag a selection window around the top five vertices and then right-click on one of the selected vertices; the quad menu is displayed, as shown in Figure P1-16.

Figure P1-16 The quad menu displayed

7. Choose **Smooth** from the upper-left quadrant; the dome shape becomes smooth, refer to Figure P1-17.

Figure P1-17 Ext01 line smoothened

8. Choose the **Vertex** button again to exit the **Vertex** sub-object mode.

9. Select **Extrude** in the **Modifier List** drop-down list under the **OBJECT-SPACE MODIFIERS** section. Set the value **80** in the **Amount** spinner of the **Parameters** rollout for the **Extrude** modifier; *Ext01* is extruded, as shown in Figure P1-18.

10. Create a copy of *Ext01* and name it **Drill02**.

11. Make sure *Drill02* is selected in the viewport and then set the value **100** in the **Amount** spinner of the **Parameters** rollout for the **Extrude** modifier of the **Modify** tab in the **Command Panel**.

12. Choose the **Hierarchy** tab in the **Command Panel** and make sure the **Pivot** button is chosen. In the **Adjust Pivot** rollout, choose the **Affect Pivot Only** button in the **Move/Rotate/Scale** area. In the Front viewport, move the pivot point so that it is aligned with the bottom of *Drill02*, as shown in Figure P1-19. Now, choose the **Affect Pivot Only** button to exit the adjustment mode.

13. In the Front viewport, scale *Drill02* to **90%** by using the **Select and Uniform Scale** tool.

 Tip: *You can also scale the object precisely by using the **Scale Transform Type-In** dialog box.*

Figure P1-18 *Ext01 line extruded*

Figure P1-19 *The pivot point aligned at the bottom of Drill02*

14. Choose the **Display** tab in the **Command Panel** and then choose the **Unhide All** button in the **Hide** rollout; the hidden objects are now displayed.

15. Select *Base_top* and choose **Create > Geometry** in the **Command Panel**. Select **Compound Objects** in the drop-down list, if it is not selected.

16. Invoke the **Boolean** tool from the **Object Type** rollout and then select the **Union** radio button in the **Operation** area of the **Parameters** rollout.

17. Choose the **Pick Operand B** button in the **Pick Boolean** rollout. Now, select *Ext01* in any viewport; the two objects are joined together. Invoke the **Select Object** tool to exit the Boolean operation.

18. Make sure *Base_top* is selected in the viewport and then invoke the **Boolean** tool from the **Object Type** rollout. Select the **Subtraction (A-B)** radio button in the **Operation** area of the **Parameters** rollout.

19. Choose the **Pick Operand B** button from the **Pick Boolean** rollout and select *Top_drill* in any viewport. Invoke the **Select Object** tool to exit the Boolean operation.

20. Make sure *Base_top* is selected in the viewport and then invoke the **Boolean** tool in the **Object Type** rollout. Make sure the **Subtraction (A-B)** radio button is selected in the **Parameters** rollout.

21. Choose the **Pick Operand B** button in the **Pick Boolean** rollout. Then, select *Drill02* in any viewport; *Base_top* gets hollowed out and leaves walls for the top section, as shown in Figure P1-20. Invoke the **Select Object** tool to exit the Boolean operation.

Creating the Second Level Deck

In this section, you will create the deck and its multiple copies at the top of windmill. This deck will be placed on the base structure and will serve as a stand for the middle structure of the windmill.

1. Select *Base_mid* and choose the **Display** tab in the **Command Panel**. In the **Hide** rollout, choose the **Hide Unselected** button; the middle section of the building remains visible.

2. Invoke the **Zoom Extents All** tool to zoom the viewports to their extents.

3. Choose **Create > Shapes** in the **Command Panel**. Invoke the **Line** tool from the **Object Type** rollout.

4. In the Top viewport, draw an isosceles triangle starting at (**0,0,0**), through points (**50,-120,0**) and (**-50,-120,0**), and back to (**0,0,0**), and then choose the **Close** button to close the spline. In the **Name and Color** rollout, enter **Deck01**.

 Note
If you are using the cursor to draw the line, you may need to first zoom in to display the subgrid.

Figure P1-20 Base_top hollowed out

5. Make sure *Deck01* is selected and then choose the **Modify** tab in the **Command Panel**. Next, select **Extrude** in the **Modifier List** drop-down list under the **OBJECT-SPACE MODIFIERS** section. Set the value **–5.0** in the **Amount** spinner of the **Parameters** rollout for the **Extrude** modifier; the *Deck01* is extruded, as shown in Figure P1-21. Now, select **Cap Holes** in the **Modifier** drop-down list under the **OBJECT-SPACE MODIFIERS** section, refer to Figure P1-21.

6. In the **Modifier List** drop-down list, select **UVW Map** under the **OBJECT-SPACE MODIFIERS** section. Clear the **Real-World Map Size** check box in the **Mapping** area of the **Parameters** rollout.

7. Activate the Front viewport and invoke the **Zoom Extents** tool so that the triangle is visible in the viewport.

8. Move *Deck01* up in the Front viewport until it is even with the bottom of *Base_mid* refer to Figure P1-21.

9. Make sure the **Box** radio button is selected, then set the values as given next:

    Length: **50**   Width: **100**   Height: **100**

    This adds a **UVW Map** modifier to the object so that the material appears correct when it is added later. Since the object is going to be arrayed, it is more appropriate to apply the modifier one time to the original object, rather than to select and apply the modifier to each of the copies once the array is created.

Figure P1-21 *Deck01 extruded in all viewports*

10. Activate the Top viewport. Invoke the **Use Transform Coordinate Center** tool from the Pivot Point flyout. Next, select **World** in the **Reference Coordinate System** drop-down list. Select *Deck01*, if it is not already selected.

These settings will cause all transformations to be centered on the origin.

11. Choose **Tools > Array** from the menu bar; the **Array** dialog box is displayed, as shown in Figure P1-22.

Figure P1-22 *The Array dialog box*

12. Choose the **Reset All Parameters** button in the **Array** dialog box. Set the value **45** in the **Incremental Z** spinner in the **Rotate** row. In the **Array Dimensions** area, make sure the **1D** radio button is selected and set the value **8** in the **Count** spinner. Select the **Copy** radio button in the **Type of Object** area and choose the **OK** button to create the array, as shown in Figure P1-23. However, there may be a small overlap of the objects that need to be adjusted in order to get a perfect shape.

Figure P1-23 *The array created*

Note

If time permits, you may need to reposition the UVW map modifier gizmo for each of the Deck objects so that each deck segment has a slightly different material pattern. This will add to the realism of the model.

13. Select only the decks and choose the **Display** tab in the **Command Panel**. In the **Hide** rollout, choose the **Hide Unselected** button; only the decks are visible.

14. Activate the Top viewport. Choose **Create > Geometry** in the **Command Panel** and select **Standard Primitives** in the drop-down list.

15. Invoke the **Box** tool from the **Object Type** rollout. Expand the **Keyboard Entry** rollout and set the values as given next:

Length: **250**   Width: **5**   Height: **10**

16. In the **Parameters** rollout, clear the **Real-World Map Size** check box.

17. Choose the **Create** button in the **Keyboard Entry** rollout; the box is created. Enter **DeckBeam01** in the **Name and Color** rollout. Next, exit the **3D Snap Toggle** tool and the **Percent Snap** tool from the **Main Toolbar**.

18. Activate the Left viewport and invoke the **Zoom Extents** tool. Move *DeckBeam01* up until its top is aligned with the bottom of the deck edge, as shown in Figure P1-24.

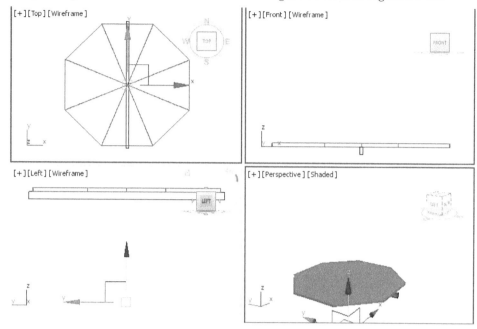

Figure P1-24   *DeckBeam01 created and aligned*

19. Select the **View** option in the **Reference Coordinate System** drop-down list. Also, invoke the **Use Pivot Point Centre** tool from the **Main Toolbar**.

20. Activate the Top viewport and rotate *DeckBeam01* –22.5° about the Z axis using its pivot point as the center of transformation. The default pivot point should be at 0,0,0.

21. Choose **Tools > Array** from the menu bar; the **Array** dialog box is displayed. Choose the **Reset All Parameters** button. Enter the value **45** in the **Incremental Z** spinner in the **Rotate** row. In the **Array Dimensions** area, select the **1D** radio button and enter the value **4** in the **Count** spinner. Select the **Copy** radio button in the **Type of Object** area and then choose the **OK** button; the copies of *DeckBeam01* is created, as shown in Figure P1-25.

22. Make sure the Top viewport is active and then choose **Create > Geometry** in the **Command Panel**. Invoke the **Box** tool from the **Object Type** rollout.

23. Enter the following values in the **Keyboard Entry** rollout:

X:	**40**
Y:	**-120**
Z:	**144**
Length:	**40**
Width:	**3**
Height:	**6**

Figure P1-25 *The clones of DeckBeam01 created*

24. Clear the **Real-World Map Size** check box in the **Parameters** rollout. Choose the **Create** button in the **Keyboard Entry** rollout and enter **DeckBoard01** in the **Name and Color** rollout.

25. Enter the values given next in the **Keyboard Entry** rollout to create two more boxes in the Top viewport. For each box, clear the **Real-World Map Size** check box in the **Parameters** rollout and then choose the **Create** button from the **Keyboard Entry** rollout. Next, rename each box in the **Name and Color** rollout.

Name and Color:	DeckBoard02	DeckBoard03
X:	20	0
Y:	–95	–70
Z:	144	144
Length:	90	140
Width:	3	3
Height:	6	6

26. Select *DeckBoard01* and *DeckBoard02* in the Top viewport. Invoke the **Use Selection Center** tool from the Pivot Point flyout on the **Main Toolbar**. Make sure the **Screen** option is selected in the **Reference Coordinate System** drop-down list. Next, invoke the **Mirror** tool; the **Mirror: Screen Coordinates** dialog box is displayed.

27. Make sure the **X** radio button in the **Mirror Axis** area is selected and set the value **– 60** in the **Offset** spinner. Select the **Copy** radio button in the **Clone Selection** area and choose the **OK** button to mirror the objects, refer to Figure P1-26.

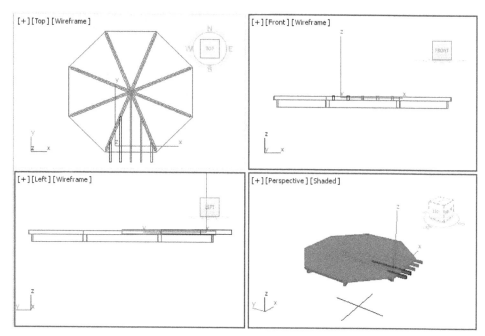

Figure P1-26 *The first set of DeckBeam01 created*

Two more deck boards are created on the left of *DeckBoard03*, refer to Figure P1-26.

28. Select all the five deck board objects. Choose **Group > Group** from the menu bar; the **Group** dialog box is displayed. Enter **DeckBoard_Group01** in the **Group name** text box and choose the **OK**; the dialog box is closed and the five deckboards are grouped together.

29. Invoke the **Use Transform Coordinate Center** tool from the Pivot Point flyout. Also, select **World** from the **Reference Coordinate System** drop-down list.

Note

By default, the ***View*** *option is selected in the* ***Reference Coordinate System*** *drop-down list. If you want to rotate objects about the world origin, the* ***Reference Coordinate System*** *setting may need to be changed to* ***World*** *if the viewport is not centered on the origin. After rotating the objects, you may need to set the* ***Reference Coordinate System*** *back to* ***View*** *to avoid confusion.*

30. Choose **Tools > Array** from the menu bar; the **Array** dialog box is displayed. Choose the **Reset All Parameters** button and set the value **45** in the **Incremental Z** spinner in the **Rotate** row. In the **Array Dimensions** area, select the **1D** radio button, if it is not selected and set the value **8** in the **Count** spinner. Select the **Copy** radio button in the **Type of Object** area and then choose the **OK** button; the dialog box is closed and the array is created, as shown in Figure P1-27.

*Figure P1-27 The array of deck support boards created using the **Array** tool*

Creating the Deck Rails

In this section, you will create the deck rails by using the **Line** tool.

1. Activate the Front viewport and maximize it to zoom in on the right side of the objects.

2. Choose **Create > Shapes** in the **Command Panel**. Invoke the **Line** tool from the **Object Type** rollout.

3. Expand the **Keyboard Entry** rollout and set the values in the spinners as given next. Make sure you choose the **Add Point** button after entering each set of XYZ coordinates.

X: **120**	Y: **155**	Z: **0**
X: **130**	Y: **190**	Z: **0**
X: **135**	Y: **190**	Z: **0**
X: **130**	Y: **170**	Z: **0**
X: **140**	Y: **150**	Z: **0**
X: **135**	Y: **150**	Z: **0**
X: **130**	Y: **160**	Z: **0**
X: **125**	Y: **150**	Z: **0**
X: **120**	Y: **150**	Z: **0**

4. Close the shape and enter **DeckRail03** in the **Name and Color** rollout.

5. Make sure *DeckRail03* is selected and then choose the **Modify** tab in the **Command Panel**. Select **Extrude** in the **Modifier List** drop-down list under the **OBJECT-SPACE MODIFIERS** section. In the **Parameters** rollout for the extrude modifier, enter **2** in the **Amount** spinner.

6. Select **UVW Map** in the **Modifier List** drop-down list under the **OBJECT-SPACE MODIFIERS** section. In the **Mapping** area of the **Parameters** rollout, clear the **Real-World Map Size** check box and select the **Box** radio button.

7. In the **Parameters** rollouts, set the values in the spinners as given next:

    Length: **20**   Width: **20**   Height: **20**

8. Select the **X** radio button in the **Alignment** area of the **Parameters** rollout; the **UVW Map** modifier is added to the object so that it appears correctly when the material is added later.

9. Activate the Top viewport. Zoom in and move *DeckRail03* up **1.0** unit on the local Y axis so that it is in the middle of the deck board.

10. Create a copy of *DeckRail03* with the name **DeckRail02**. Move *DeckRail02* up **20** units on the local Y axis so that it is placed on the next deck board.

     Tip: *You can also move the deck rail objects by using the **Move Transform Type-In** dialog box.*

11. Create a copy of *DeckRail02* with the name **DeckRail01**. Move it up **20** units to place it on the next deck board.

12. Create a copy of *DeckRail01* with the name **DeckRail04** and move it down **–60** units on the local Y axis so that it is placed on the lower deck board.

13. Create a copy of *DeckRail04* with the name **DeckRail05** and move it down **–20** units so that it is placed on the next lower deck board.

14. Invoke the **Zoom Extents All** tool to view the objects properly in all viewports.

15. Select all the five deck rail objects and choose **Group > Group** from the menu bar; the **Group** dialog box is displayed. Enter **DeckRail_Group01** in the **Group name** text box and choose the **OK** button; the group of *DeckRails* is created, as shown in Figure P1-28.

16. Invoke the **Use Transform Coordinate Center** tool from the Pivot Pointflyout.

17. Choose **Tools > Array** from the menu bar; the **Array** dialog box is displayed. Choose the **Reset All Parameters** button in it. Set the value **45** in the **Incremental Z** spinner in the **Rotate** row. In the **Array Dimensions** area, select the **1D** radio button, if it is not selected and set the value **8** in the **Count** spinner. Select the **Copy** radio button in the **Type of Object** area. Next, choose the **OK** button; the dialog box is closed and the array of *DeckRails* is created to create the array, as shown in Figure P1-29.

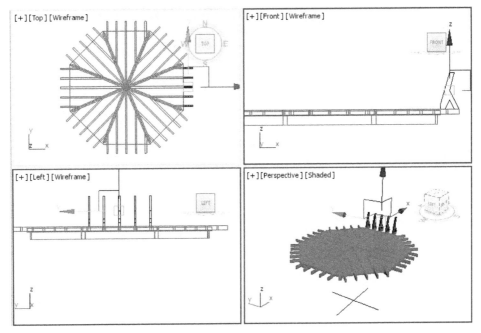

Figure P1-28 *DeckRail_Group01 created in all viewports*

Figure P1-29 *The set of DeckRail_Group objects created*

Creating the Handrails and Deck Braces

In this section, you will create the handrails and deck braces by using the **NGon** tool.

1. Choose the **Display** tab in the **Command Panel**. In the **Hide** rollout, choose the **Unhide by Name** button; the **Unhide Objects** dialog box is displayed. Select *NGon001* from the list and choose the **Unhide** button; *NGon001* is displayed in the viewports; the other hidden objects remain hidden.

2. Select *NGon001* and create a copy of *NGon001* with the name **NGon004**.

3. In the **Display** tab, choose the **Hide by Name** button; the **Hide Objects** dialog box is displayed. Select *NGon001* from this dialog box and then choose the **Hide** button to hide *NGon001*.

4. Activate the Front viewport and invoke the **Zoom Extents** tool to zoom the objects to their extents. Move *NGon004* up **190** units, refer to Figure P1-30.

5. Make sure *NGon004* is selected in the viewport and then choose the **Modify** tab in the **Command Panel**. In the **Parameters** rollout, set the value **145** in the **Radius** spinner; *NGon004* will get attached to the deck rails.

6. Choose **Create > Shapes** in the **Command Panel**. Invoke the **Circle** tool from the **Object Type** rollout.

Figure P1-30 NGon004 created and positioned

7. Expand the **Keyboard Entry** rollout, set the value **3** in the **Radius** spinner, and then choose the **Create** button to create a circle.

8.   Enter **Circle01** in the **Name and Color** rollout. Right-click to exit the **Circle** tool.

9.   Select *NGon004* in any viewport. Next, choose **Create > Geometry** in the **Command Panel**. Select **Compound Objects** in the drop-down list and invoke the **Loft** tool from the **Object Type** rollout.

10. In the **Smoothing** area of the **Surface Parameters** rollout, make sure the **Smooth Length** and **Smooth Width** check boxes are selected. In the **Mapping** area, select the **Apply Mapping** check box. Set the values in the **Length Repeat** spinner to **8** and the **Width Repeat** spinner to **2**. Make sure the value **0** is entered in the **Shape Steps** spinner of the **Skin Parameters** rollout.

11. Choose the **Get Shape** button in the **Creation Method** rollout. Select *Circle01* in any viewport; *Circle01* is lofted along *NGon004* path to create a handrail, as shown in Figure P1-31. In the **Name and Color** rollout, assign the name **Handrail** to the loft object.

Figure P1-31 Handrail created in viewports

12. Choose the **Display** tab in the **Command Panel**. In the **Hide** rollout, choose the **Unhide by Name**; the **Unhide Objects** dialog box is displayed. Select *Base_lo* from the list and choose the **Unhide** button to unhide *Base_lo*.

13. Activate the Left viewport. Choose **Create > Geometry** in the **Command Panel**. Select **Standard Primitives** in the drop-down list. Next, invoke the **Box** tool from the **Object Type** rollout.

14. Expand the **Keyboard Entry** rollout, enter the values in the spinners as given next:

    X: **115**
    Y: **115**
    Z: **–2**
    Length: **70**
    Width: **6**
    Height: **4**

15. Choose the **Create** button to create the box and enter **DeckBrace01** in the **Name and Color** rollout.

16. Choose the **Modify** tab in the **Command Panel**. Select **UVW Map** in the **Modifier List** drop-down list under the **OBJECT-SPACE MODIFIERS** section. In the **Mapping** area of the **Parameters** rollout, clear the **Real-World Map Size** check box.

17. Select the **Box** radio button, and enter the values in the spinners as given next:

    Length: **70**   Width: **70**   Height: **70**

18. Maximize the Left viewport. Make sure that *DeckBrace01* is selected. Next, choose the **Hierarchy** tab in the **Command Panel** and choose the **Pivot** button, if it is not already chosen. Now, choose the **Affect Pivot Only** button in the **Move/Rotate/Scale** area of the **Adjust Pivot** rollout.

19. Move the pivot point to the top right corner of *DeckBrace01*, as shown in Figure P1-32. Choose the **Affect Pivot Only** button to exit the adjustment mode.

Figure P1-32 The pivot point of DeckBrace01 moved to the top right corner

20. Invoke the **Zoom Extents** tool to zoom the objects to their extents in the viewport.

21. Invoke the **Select and Rotate** tool and rotate *DeckBrace01* by 26.3 about the local X axis, as shown in Figure P1-33. Use the object's pivot point as the center of rotation and make sure that **View** is selected in the **Reference Coordinate System** drop-down list.

Figure P1-33 *DeckBrace01 rotated in the Left viewport*

22. Invoke the **Maximize Viewport Toggle** tool to return to the four viewport configuration. Make sure the **Use Transform Coordinate Center** tool in the Pivot Point flyout is activated. Next, select **World** in the **Reference Coordinate System** drop-down list.

23. Activate the Top viewport. Make sure *DeckBrace01* is selected and choose **Tools > Array** from the menu bar; the **Array** dialog box is displayed. Choose the **Reset All Parameters** button. Set the value **45** in the **Incremental Z** spinner in the **Rotate** row. In the **Array Dimensions** area, select the **1D** radio button, if it is not selected and set the value **8** in the **Count** spinner. Now, select the **Copy** radio button in the **Type of Object** area and then choose the **OK** button; the copies of *DeckBrace01* are created, as shown in Figure P1-34.

Creating the Windmill Blades

In this section, you will create the blades of windmill by using the **Cylinder** tool.

1. Select all objects in any viewport and right-click; a quad menu is displayed. Choose **Hide Selection** from the quad menu; all objects are hidden.

2. Invoke the **Use Pivot Point Center** tool from the Pivot Point flyout. Also, select **View** from the **Reference Coordinate System** drop-down list.

Figure P1-34 *The clones of DeckBrace01 created*

3. Activate the Front viewport and then choose **Create > Geometry** in the **Command Panel**. Select **Standard Primitives** in the drop-down list.

4. Invoke the **Cylinder** tool from the **Object Type** rollout. Enter the values given next in the **Keyboard Entry** rollout:

X:	**0**
Y:	**340**
Z:	**–40**
Radius:	**5**
Height:	**130**

5. Choose the **Create** button to create a cylinder. In the **Name and Color** rollout, enter **Shaft01**.

6. Invoke the **Box** tool from the **Object Type** rollout. Enter the values given next in the **Keyboard Entry** rollout:

X:	**0**
Y:	**340**
Z:	**90**
Length:	**20**
Width:	**20**
Height:	**20**

7. Choose the **Create** button to create a box. In the **Name and Color** rollout, enter **Hub01**.

8. Select *Shaft01* and choose **Create > Geometry** in the **Command Panel**. Select **Compound Objects** in the drop-down list. Invoke the **Boolean** tool from the **Object Type** rollout.

9. In the **Operation** area of the **Parameters** rollout, select the **Union** radio button. In the **Pick Boolean** rollout, choose the **Pick Operand B** button. Next, select *Hub01* in any viewport. Invoke the **Select Object** tool to exit the Boolean operation.

10. Invoke the **Zoom Extents All** tool to see the objects properly in all viewports.

11. In the Front viewport, zoom out and pan the viewport up. Next, choose **Create > Shapes** in the **Command Panel**. Invoke the **Line** tool from the **Object Type** rollout.

12. Draw a **130** unit line vertically down from the center of the hub's lower edge. Use snaps as needed.

13. Invoke the **Rectangle** tool from the **Object Type** rollout. Draw a 10-unit square anywhere in the Front viewport, as shown in Figure P1-35.

Figure P1-35 A line and a square created

14. Select the line and choose **Create > Geometry** in the **Command Panel**. Select **Compound Objects** from the drop-down list. Invoke the **Loft** tool from the **Object Type** rollout.

15. In the **Creation Method** rollout, choose the **Get Shape** button. Next, select the sqaure in any viewport; the square is lofted along the line. In the **Name and Color** rollout, enter **MainRib01**.

16. Make sure the loft object is selected in the viewport and then choose the **Modify** tab in the **Command Panel**. Expand the **Deformations** rollout and choose the **Scale** button; the **Scale Deformation(X)** dialog box is displayed. Now, move the right hand vertex down to **50**. Close the dialog box.

17. Activate the Left viewport and invoke the **Zoom Extents** tool. Move *MainRib01* to the right so that it is centered on the hub. Choose the **Display** tab of the **Command Panel**. In the **Hide** rollout, choose the **Unhide by Name** button; the **Unhide Objects** dialog box is displayed. Select *Base_top* from this dialog box and then choose the **Unhide** button; the hidden objects are displayed, as shown in Figure P1-36.

Figure P1-36 MainRib01 zoomed to its extents

18. Invoke the **Zoom Extents All** tool to zoom the objects to their extents, refer to Figure P1-36.

19. Activate the Front viewport. Choose **Create > Geometry** in the **Command Panel**. Select **Standard Primitives** in the drop-down list.

20. Invoke the **Box** tool from the **Object Type** rollout. Set the values as given next in the **Keyboard Entry** rollout:

X:	**10**
Y:	**260**
Z:	**99.5**
Length:	**118**
Width:	**2**
Height:	**1**

21. Choose the **Create** button; a box is created. Enter **Rib01** in the **Name and Color** rollout.

22. Create a copy of *Rib01* and name it as **Rib02**. In the Front viewport, move *Rib02* to the right by **10** units. Two vertical ribs are created, on which you will place the horizontal ribs, as shown in Figure P1-37.

Figure P1-37 *Rib01 and Rib02 created in viewports*

23. Invoke the **Box** tool from the **Object Type** rollout. Make sure the Front viewport is active. In the **Keyboard Entry** rollout, set the values as given next:

X:	**15**
Y:	**310**
Z:	**99.5**
Length:	**2**
Width:	**28**
Height:	**1**

24. Choose the **Create** button; a box is created. In the **Name and Color** rollout, enter **Rib03**; a horizontal rib is created on the vertical ribs.

25. Right-click in the Front viewport to exit the **Box** tool.

26. With *Rib03* selected, choose **Tools > Array** from the menu bar; the **Array** dialog box is displayed.

27. Choose the **Reset All Parameters** button. Set the value **–10** in the **Incremental Y** spinner in the **Move** row. In the **Array Dimensions** area, select the **1D** radio button, if it is not selected and set the value **11** in the **Count** spinner. Select the **Copy** radio button from the **Type of Object** area. Choose the **OK** button; the array is created, as shown in Figure P1-38.

Figure P1-38 *The horizontal ribs are created*

28. Select *Rib01*. Choose **Create > Geometry** in the **Command Panel**. Select **Compound Objects** from the drop-down list.

29. Invoke the **Boolean** tool from the **Object Type** rollout. In the **Operation** area of the **Parameters** rollout, make sure the **Union** radio button is selected. In the **Pick Boolean** rollout, choose the **Pick Operand B** button and then select *Rib02* in any viewport and invoke the **Select Object** tool to exit the Boolean operation.

30. Invoke the **Boolean** tool from the **Object Type** rollout again. Choose the **Pick Operand B** button in the **Pick Boolean** rollout and select *Rib03* in any viewport. Similarly, group all the ribs together to create one object. Invoke the **Select Object** tool to exit the Boolean tool.

31. Activate the Top viewport and select *MainRib01*. Rotate it through an angle of –45 degrees about the local Z axis using the object's pivot point as the center.

32. With *MainRib01* selected, invoke the **Boolean** tool from the **Object Type** rollout. Make sure the **Union** radio button is selected in the **Operation** area of the **Parameters** rollout and then choose the **Pick Operand B** button in the **Pick Boolean** rollout and select *Rib01* in any viewport. The first blade of the windmill is created.

33. Invoke the **Select Object** tool to exit the Boolean command.

34. Make sure *MainRib01* is selected in the viewport and then choose the **Hierarchy** tab in the **Command Panel**. Choose the **Affect Pivot Only** button and move the pivot point to the center of *Shaft01* in the Front viewport. Choose the **Align to World** button in the **Alignment** area of the **Adjust Pivot** rollout, and then choose the **Affect Pivot Only** button to exit the adjustment mode.

35. Make sure the Front Viewport is active. With *MainRib01* selected, choose **Tools > Array** from the menu bar; the **Array** dialog box is displayed. Choose the **Reset All Parameters** button.

36. Set the value **90** in the **Incremental Z** spinner in the **Rotate** row. In the **Array Dimensions** area, select the **1D** radio button, if it is not selected and set the value **4** in the **Count** spinner.

37. Select the **Copy** radio button in the **Type of Object** area and choose the **OK** button; the blades of the windmill are created, as shown in Figure P1-39.

Figure P1-39 The blades of the windmill created

38. Invoke the **Zoom Extents All** tool to zoom the objects to their extents.

39. Choose the **Display** tab in the **Command Panel**. In the **Hide** rollout, choose the **Unhide All** button; all hidden objects are displayed, as shown in Figure P1-40.

40. Invoke the **Zoom Extents All** tool to zoom all objects to their extents, refer to Figure P1-40.

Figure P1-40 *All objects of the windmill displayed*

Applying Materials

In this section, you will assign the materials to all objects you have created.

1. Select *MainRib01, MainRib002, MainRib003, MainRib004,* and *Shaft01*.

2. Choose **Rendering > Material Editor > Compact Material Editor** from the **Main Toolbar**; the **Material Editor** dialog box is displayed.

3. Choose the **Arch & Design** button to change the material type; the **Material/Map Browser** dialog box is displayed. Select **Standard** from the **Materials > Standard** rollout and then choose the **OK** button; the **Arch & Design** material is replaced by the **Standard** material. Also, various rollouts are displayed in the **Material Editor** dialog box to modify the **Standard** material.

4. Select **Blinn** from the drop-down list in the **Shader Basic Parameters** rollout, if it is not already selected.

5. Expand the **Maps** rollout. Next, choose the **Diffuse Color** map button which is currently labeled as **None**; the **Material/Map Browser** dialog box is displayed showing the types of maps that can be added.

6. Select the **Bitmap** map from the **Maps > Standard** rollouts and choose the **OK** button; the **Material/Map Browser** dialog box is closed and the **Select Bitmap Image File** dialog box is displayed. As the project folder is already set, the *images* folder of this project is displayed in the **Look in** drop-down list of this dialog box.

7. Select the file **WoodMaterial.jpg** and then choose the **Open** button; the image file is loaded in the first material sample slot and the parameters are displayed for the map in the **Material Editor** dialog box.

8. In the **Material Editor** dialog box, choose the **Assign Material to Selection** button. Next, choose the **Show Shaded Material in Viewport** button; the material is applied to the selected objects.

9. Choose the **Modify** tab in the **Command Panel**. Select **UVW Map** in the **Modifier List** drop-down list under the **OBJECT-SPACE MODIFIERS** section. In the **Mapping** area of the **Parameters** rollout, clear the **Real-World Map Size** check box. Select the **Box** radio button.

10. Set the values in the spinners as given next:

    Length: **220**   Width: **220**   Height: **220**

    The **UVW Map** modifier is applied to all selected objects.

11. Enter the name **WoodMaterial** in the material name drop-down list to rename the first material sample slot in the **Material Editor** dialog box.

Note

*By grouping the objects together and applying single **UVW Map** modifier, the map is spread out across those objects. This is an easy way to apply materials to cloned objects so that each object has a slightly different appearance.*

12. Similarly, apply map and materials to the objects in the scene as explained next:

•   All Decks(*Deck01, Deck002* through *Deck008*) — Create a new standard material and name it **Old_Floor**. Use a **Mix** procedural map for the diffuse color map. For **Color #1** of the mix, use **CEDFENCE.jpg** that you have downloaded from *www.cadcim.com*. For **Color #2** of the mix, use **GRYPLANK.JPG** that you have downloaded from *www.cadcim.com*. Set the value in the **Mix Amount** spinner to **25** to give the material a weathered appearance. Assign the material to the *Deck* objects.

•   *Floor_top* — Apply the material **Old_Floor**. Apply a **UVW Map** modifier. Clear the **Real-World Map Size** check box. Select the **Box** radio button.

    Set the values in the spinners as given next:

    Length: **90**   Width: **90**   Height: **90**
    U Tile: **1**   V Tile: **1**   W Tile: **1**

    In the Top viewport, rotate the **UVW Map** gizmo **–22.5°** around the local Z axis.

- *Base_lo* — Apply the map **StoneMaterial.jpg** that you have downloaded from *www.cadcim.com*. Apply the **UVW Map** modifier. Make sure the **Real-World Map Size** check box is selected. Select the **Cylindrical** radio button. Next, select the **X** radio button in the **Alignment** area of the **Parameters** rollout. Also, choose the **Fit** button.

- *Base_mid* — Apply the map **DarkBrownStone.jpg** that you have downloaded from *www.cadcim.com*. Apply the **UVW Map** modifier and select the **Box** radio button in the **Mapping** area of the **Parameters** rollout. Make sure the **Real-World Map Size** check box is selected.

- *Base_top* — Apply the map **DarkBrownStone.jpg** that you have downloaded from *www.cadcim.com*. Apply the **UVW Map** modifier and select the **Box** radio button in the **Mapping** area of the **Parameters** rollout. Make sure the **Real-World Map Size** check box is selected.

  In the **Alignment** section of the **Parameters** rollout, select the **X** radio button.

- On all *DeckBeam*, *DeckBoard*, *DeckRail*, and *Handrail* objects — Apply the map **Pine.jpg** that you have downloaded from *www.cadcim.com*.

- On all *DeckBrace* objects — Apply the map **Wood.Red Oak.jpg** that you have downloaded from *www.cadcim.com*.

- *Floor_lo* — Apply the map **StoneMaterial.jpg** that you have downloaded from *www.cadcim.com*. Apply the **UVW Map** modifier and select the **Box** radio button in the **Mapping** area of the **Parameters** rollout. Make sure the **Real-World Map Size** check box is selected. Next, select the **Y** radio button in the **Alignment** area of the **Parameters** rollout. Next, close the **Material Editor** dialog box.

Adding Lights and Camera

In this section, you will add lights and camera in the scene.

1. Invoke the **Zoom Extents All** tool to zoom the objects to their extents.

2. Choose **Create > Lights** in the **Command Panel**. Select the **Standard** option in the drop-down list. Invoke the **Omni** tool from the **Object Type** rollout.

3. In the Left viewport, click at any point on the right side of the viewport midway up *Base_mid* to place the first omni light; an omni light (*Omni001*) is placed at the selected point.

4. Click at any point on the left side of *Base_mid*; an omni light (*Omni002*) is placed at the selected point. Zoom out of the Left viewport to get more space.

5. Click at any point on the far right, approximately at twice the height of the windmill; an omni light (*Omni003*) is placed at the selected point, refer to Figure P1-41.

6. Choose **Create > Cameras** in the **Command Panel**. Invoke the **Target** tool from the **Object Type** rollout.

7. Create the camera and position it, as shown in Figure P1-41.

Figure P1-41 *Lights and Camera created and positioned in the scene*

8. Activate the Perspective viewport and press the C key; the Perspective viewport becomes the Camera viewport.

9. With the Camera viewport active, use the **Truck Camera** and **Field-of-View** tools to place the objects in the center of the viewport. Right-click to exit each command. Also, move the camera in the other viewports so that you can see an angled view of the windmill.

Rendering a Still Image

In this section, you will render the still image for the final output. Before rendering, you need to change the background color of the scene to white, refer to Tutorial 1 of Chapter 2.

1. Make sure the Camera viewport is active. If possible, rotate the image to render it in an appropriate direction.

2. Invoke the **Render Production** tool from the **Main Toolbar**; the rendered image is displayed in the render window, as shown in Figure P1-42.

Figure P1-42 *The scene displayed after rendering at frame 1*

3. Close the render window.

4. Move the lights and adjust their intensity as required.

5. Save the scene.

Adding Animation in the Windmill
In this section, you will add animation in the windmill.

1. Choose the **Display** tab of the **Command Panel**. In the **Hide by Category** rollout, select the **Shapes**, **Lights**, and **Cameras** check boxes. Next, invoke the **Zoom Extents All** tool to zoom the objects to their extents; the camera, all lights, and all shapes are hidden in all viewports.

2. Select *MainRib01, MainRib002, MainRib003, and MainRib004* from the **Scene Explorer**. Next, right-click in the **Scene Explorer** to display the quad menu. Choose **Add Selected To > New Parent (Pick)** from the quad menu; Now, select *Shaft01* from the **Scene Explorer** to link all ribs.

3. Activate the Front viewport and select *Shaft01*. Next, choose the **Toggle Auto Key Mode** button to enter the animation mode. Press the SPACEBAR key to lock the selection set.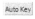

4. Drag the time slider to frame **100**.

5. Using the **Select and Rotate** tool, rotate *Shaft01* **-720** degrees about the local Z axis using its pivot point as the center. If the pivot point on *Shaft01* is not at the center of the shaft, exit the animation mode and adjust the pivot before applying the animation.

6. Exit the animation mode and activate the Camera001 viewport. Also, press the SPACEBAR key to unlock the selection set.

7. Choose the **Play Animation** button; the animation is played in the Camera001 viewport. The windmill blades and shaft rotate two complete turns over the length of the animation.

8. Choose the **Stop Animation** button to stop playback.

9. Save the scene.

Rendering the Animation
In this section, you will play the animation in the Windows Media Player.

1. With the Camera viewport active, choose the **Render Setup** button; the **Render Setup** dialog box is displayed.

2. In the **Time Output** area of the **Common Parameters** rollout, select the **Active Time Segment** radio button. In the **Render Output** area, choose the **Files** button; the **Render Output File** dialog box is displayed.

   As the project folder is already set, the *renderoutput* folder of this project is displayed in the **Save in** drop-down list of this dialog box.

3. In the **Render Output File** dialog box, select **AVI File (*.avi)** from the **Save as type** drop-down list. In the **File name** text box, enter the name **Project01**. Next, choose the **Save** button; the **AVI File Compression Setup** dialog box is displayed.

4. Choose the **OK** button in the **AVI File Compression Setup** dialog box.

5. Make sure the **Save File** check box is selected in the **Render Output** area of the **Render Setup** dialog box and then choose the **Render** button in the dialog box.

   It may take several minutes to render the animation. After rendering is complete, close the **Rendered Frame** window and the **Render Setup** dialog box.

6. Choose **Rendering > View Image File** from the menu bar; the **View File** dialog box is displayed. Select the **Project01.avi** and choose the **Open** button; the animation is played in Windows Media Player.

Project 2

Creating a Diner

PROJECT DESCRIPTION

In this project, you will create a scene of the diner, as shown in Figure P2-1. The scene consists of floor, walls, booths, tables with pedestals, and hanging lamps. You will create a window in the wall, a set of blinds in front of the window, and add animation to the blinds. To add a realistic effect to the scene, you will set up and adjust lights and camera, create glasses and plates on the tables, create text on the window, and assign materials to various objects. Lastly, you will make necessary adjustments and render the scene for the final output.

Figure P2-1 *The scene of the diner*

Creating the Project Folder

Create a new project folder with the name *Prj_2* at *\Documents\3dsmaxdesign 2015* and then save the file with the name *Prj2*, as discussed in Tutorial 1 of Chapter 2.

Downloading the Files

Before starting the project, you need to download the *prj2_3dsmaxdesign_2015.zip* file from *www.cadcim.com*. The path of the file is as follows: *Textbooks > Animation and Visual Effects > 3ds Max Design > Autodesk 3dsMax Design 2015: A Tutorial Approach*

Extract the contents of the zip file to *Documents*. Open Windows Explorer and then browse to *\Documents\prj2_3dsmaxdesign_2015*. Next, copy all files to *\Documents\3dsmaxdesign2015\Prj2\ sceneassets\images*.

Creating the Floor

In this section, you will create the floor by using the **Box** tool and then you will apply material to the floor to give it a realistic look.

1. Activate the Top viewport and choose **Create > Geometry** in the **Command Panel**. Then, invoke the **Box** tool from the **Object Type** rollout.

2. Expand the **Keyboard Entry** rollout and set the values in the spinners as given next:

    Length: **100**   Width: **130**   Height: **1**

3. Choose the **Create** button; the floor is created. In the **Name and Color** rollout, enter **Floor**.

4. Choose **Rendering > Material Editor > Compact Material Editor** from the menu bar; the **Material Editor** dialog box is displayed. Select the first material sample slot. Choose the **Arch & Design** button to change the material type; the **Material/Map Browser** dialog box is displayed.

5. In this dialog box, select **Standard** from the **Materials > Standard** rollout and then choose the **OK** button; the **Material/Map Browser** dialog box is closed and the **Arch & Design** material is replaced by the **Standard** material. Also, various rollouts are displayed in the **Material Editor** dialog box to modify the **Standard** material.

6. Select **Blinn** from the drop-down list in the **Shader Basic Parameters** rollout, if it is not already selected.

7. Expand the **Maps** rollout. Next, choose the **Diffuse Color** button which is currently labeled as **None**; the **Material/Map Browser** dialog box is displayed showing the types of maps that can be added.

8. Select the **Bitmap** map from the **Maps > Standard** rollout and choose the **OK** button; the **Material/Map Browser** dialog box is closed and the **Select Bitmap Image File** dialog box is displayed. As the project folder is already set, the *images* folder of this project is displayed in the **Look in** drop-down list.

9. Select the file **Floor.RedTiles.jpg** and choose the **Open** button.

10. In the **Coordinates** rollout, make sure the **Use Real-World Scale** check box is selected.

    You may need to resize the tile map so that the seams between tile squares align with the edges of *Floor* and the red diamond pattern is centered in *Floor*.

11. Choose the **Assign Material to Selection** button; the tile material is assigned to *Floor*.

12. Choose the **Show Shaded Material in Viewport** button; the applied material is displayed in the Perspective viewport. Next, rotate the Perspective viewport to set an angle of view, as shown in Figure P2-2.

13. Close the **Material Editor** dialog box and invoke the **Zoom Extents All** tool to display *Floor* to its extent.

Figure P2-2 Floor created and a material assigned to it

Creating Walls

In this section, you will create the walls by using the **Box** tool.

1. Activate the Front viewport and then choose **Create > Geometry** in the **Command Panel**. Invoke the **Box** tool from the **Object Type** rollout.

2. Expand the **Keyboard Entry** rollout and set the values in the spinners as given next, if these values are not there:

   Length: **100**   Width: **130**   Height: **1**

3. Choose the **Create** button; the wall is created. Enter **Wall01** in the **Name and Color** rollout.

4. Use the **Select and Move** tool or the **Align** tool to move *Wall01* upward so that the lower edge and the upper edge of *Floor* have the same level.

5. In the Left viewport, use the **Select and Move** tool or the **Align** tool to move *Wall01* toward left so that it is aligned with the end of *Floor*.

6. Make sure *Wall01* is selected and then choose **Edit > Clone** from the menu bar; the **Clone Options** dialog box is displayed. In this dialog box, select the **Copy** radio button and enter **Wall02** in the **Name** text box. Choose **OK** in this dialog box; a copy of *Wall01* is created with the name *Wall02*.

7. Make sure *Wall02* is selected and then choose the **Modify** tab of the **Command Panel**. In the **Parameters** rollout, set the value **100** in the **Width** spinner.

8. Invoke the **Select and Rotate** tool and rotate *Wall02* by 90 degrees in the Top viewport.

9. Align *Wall02* and move it such that its left edge is aligned with the left edge of *Floor* and its bottom edge is aligned with the bottom edge of *Floor*, as shown in Figure P2-3.

Figure P2-3 *Setting the Perspective viewport*

10. Invoke the **Zoom Extents All** tool to zoom the objects to their extents.

11. Press and hold the CTRL key and select both the walls in the viewport.

12. Choose **Rendering > Material Editor > Compact Material Editor** from the menu bar; the **Material Editor** dialog box is displayed. In this dialog box, select the second material sample slot. Choose the **Arch & Design** button to change the material type; the **Material/Map Browser** dialog box is displayed.

13. Select **Standard** from the **Materials > Standard** rollout and then choose the **OK** button; the **Arch & Design** material is replaced by the **Standard** material. Also, various rollouts are displayed in the **Material Editor** dialog box to modify the **Standard** material.

14. Select **Blinn** from the drop-down list in the **Shader Basic Parameters** rollout, if it is not already selected.

15. Expand the **Maps** rollout. Next, choose the **Diffuse Color** map button which is currently labeled as **None**; the **Material/Map Browser** dialog box is displayed showing the types of maps that can be added.

16. Select the **Bitmap** map from the **Maps > Standard** rollout and choose the **OK** button; the **Material/Map Browser** dialog box is closed and the **Select Bitmap Image File** dialog box is displayed. As the project folder is already set, the *images* folder of this project is displayed in the **Look in** drop-down list.

17. Select the file **WoodBoard.jpg** and choose the **Open** button.

18. In the **Coordinates** rollout, make sure the **Use Real-World Scale** check box is selected. Next, make sure the values are set to **0** in the **Width: Offset** and the **Height: Offset** spinners. Now, set the value **130** in the **Width: Size** and **Height: Size** spinners.

The material is adjusted and its appearance becomes consistent on objects of different sizes. Additionally, the value in the **Width: Offset** spinner is adjusted such that the dark boards will not appear adjacent to each other when the material is applied to the two walls.

Note
*The **Use Real-World Scale** option is useful if the objects in the scene are drawn to scale, or if the material is to be assigned to multiple objects of different sizes. The values in the **Width: Size** and **Height: Size** spinners determine the size of the map in drawing units. Since the map is of same size regardless of the size of the object it is assigned to, there is no need to adjust the tiling on individual objects in order to maintain a consistent pattern across different objects.*

19. In the **Material Editor** dialog box, choose the **Go To Parent** button to move one level up. Now, choose the **Assign Material to Selection** button to assign the material on the object.

20. Choose the **Show Shaded Material in Viewport** button to display the assigned material in the viewport, as shown in Figure P2-4. Close the **Material Editor** dialog box.

***Figure P2-4** The material assigned to Wall01 and Wall02 displayed in the viewport*

Creating the Booth

In this section, you will create the profile of the booth by using the **Line** tool.

1. Right-click on the **Snaps Toggle** tool from the **Main Toolbar**; the **Grid and Snap Settings** dialog box is displayed. In this dialog box, choose the **Home Grid** tab and set the value **2** in the **Grid Spacing** spinner. Next, clear the **Inhibit Grid Subdivision Below Grid Spacing** check box and close the dialog box.

2. Activate the Front viewport and invoke the **Maximize Viewport Toggle** tool to maximize it. Zoom in on the lower-left portion of the viewport.

3. Choose **Create > Shapes** in the **Command Panel**. Invoke the **Line** tool from the **Object Type** rollout. Expand the **Keyboard Entry** rollout and set the following values in the **X**, **Y**, and **Z** spinners. After entering the value for every x, y, z point, choose the **Add Point** button:

X: **–64**	Y: **1**	Z: **0**
X: **–64**	Y: **49**	Z: **0**
X: **–62**	Y: **49**	Z: **0**
X: **–62**	Y: **21**	Z: **0**
X: **–46**	Y: **21**	Z: **0**
X: **–46**	Y: **1**	Z: **0**

4. Choose the **Close** button; the shape is created. Enter **booth** as name of the shape; the profile of *booth* is created. Right-click to exit the tool. Zoom out if needed to see the entire shape. Now, you need to create the seat for *booth*.

5. Make sure the Front viewport is activated. Invoke the **Line** tool again. Expand the **Keyboard Entry** rollout and set the values in the **X**, **Y**, and **Z** spinners as given next. After entering the value for every x, y, z point, choose the **Add Point** button:

X: **–62**   Y: **49**   Z: **0**
X: **–58**   Y: **49**   Z: **0**
X: **–58**   Y: **25**   Z: **0**
X: **–42**   Y: **25**   Z: **0**
X: **–42**   Y: **19**   Z: **0**
X: **–46**   Y: **19**   Z: **0**
X: **–46**   Y: **21**   Z: **0**
X: **–62**   Y: **21**   Z: **0**

6. Choose the **Close** button to close the shape; the profile of the seat is created, as shown in Figure P2-5. Enter **Seat** as name of the shape in the **Name and Color** rollout. Right-click to exit the tool.

[+] [Front] [Wireframe]

Figure P2-5 *The profile of seat created*

7. Make sure *Seat* is selected. Next, choose the **Modify** tab in the **Command Panel**. In the **Selection** rollout, choose the **Vertex** button; the **Vertex** sub-object mode is activated.

8. Right-click on the top-right vertex of *Seat*; the quad menu is displayed. Select **Bezier** from the upper-left quadrant; the bezier handles are displayed on the vertex and one segment adjoining the vertex is curved.

9. Using the **Select and Move** tool, move the bezier handles to form a curve for the back. Similarly, modify the middle-right vertex of *Seat*, as shown in Figure P2-6. Choose the **Vertex** button in the **Selection** rollout to exit the **Vertex** sub-object mode.

[+][Front][Wireframe]

Figure P2-6 *The vertices of Seat modified using the bezier handles*

10. Invoke the **Maximize Viewport Toggle** tool to shift the display back to the four-viewport display.

11. Select both *Booth* and *Seat* in any viewport and make sure the **Modify** tab of the **Command Panel** is selected.

12. In the **Modifier List** drop-down list, select **Extrude** in the **OBJECT-SPACE MODIFIERS** section; the **Extrude** modifier is applied to both the shapes.

13. In the **Parameters** rollout, set the value **40** in the **Amount** spinner; both line profiles are extruded.

14. Activate the Top viewport and move both the extruded objects to the top-left corner of the walls. Next, activate the Perspective viewport and rotate and zoom the *Booth* and *Seat* for better visualization. *Booth* and *Seat* are positioned, as shown in Figure P2-7.

15. Select *Booth* and open the **Material Editor** dialog box by pressing the M key. Select the third material sample slot.

16. Change the **Arch & Design** material type to **Standard** as discussed earlier. Next, choose the **Diffuse** button from the **Blinn Basic Parameters** rollout; the **Material/Map Browser** dialog box is displayed.

17. Select the **Bitmap** map from the **Maps > Standard** rollout and choose the **OK** button. Now, load the map **FabricValvet.jpg**, as discussed earlier; the material is displayed in the third sample slot.

Figure P2-7 *Booth and Seat created in the viewport*

18. In the **Coordinates** rollout, make sure the **Use Real-World Scale** check box is selected. Set the value of the **Width: Size** and **Height: Size** spinners to **36**. Assign the material to *Booth*, as discussed earlier and close the **Material/Map Browser** dialog box.

19. Select *Seat* and make sure the **Material Editor** dialog box is invoked. Next, select the fourth sample slot in the **Material Editor** dialog box. Next, load the map **FabricPlaid.jpg**, as discussed earlier; the material is displayed in the selected sample slot.

20. In the **Coordinates** rollout, make sure the **Use Real-World Scale** check box is selected and the values are set to **48** in the **Width: Size** and the **Height: Size** spinners.

21. Make sure *Seat* is selected and then choose the **Assign Material to Selection** and **Show Shaded Material in Viewport** buttons. Close the **Material Editor** and **Material/Map Browser** dialog boxes.

22. Activate the Top viewport and select *Booth* and *Seat*. Choose **Group > Group** from the menu bar; the **Group** dialog box is displayed. In this dialog box, enter **Booth01** in the **Group name** textbox and then choose the **OK** button.

    Now, the group can be transformed or modified as a single object.

23. Activate the Front viewport. With the group selected, make sure the **Use Selection Center** tool is invoked in the Pivot Point flyout from the **Main Toolbar**.

24. Invoke the **Mirror** tool from the **Main Toolbar**; the **Mirror: Screen Coordinates** dialog box is displayed. In the **Clone Selection** area of this dialog box, select the **Copy** radio button. In the **Mirror Axis** area, select the **X** radio button and set the value **40** in the **Offset** spinner. Next, choose the **OK** button; a mirror image is created at an offset of 40 units to the right of *Booth01*, as shown in Figure P2-8.

Figure P2-8 *Mirror image created 40 units to the right of Booth01*

25. Enter the name of the mirror image as **Booth02** in the **Name and Color** rollout.

26. Invoke the **Zoom Extents All** tool to zoom the objects to their extents in the viewports.

Creating the Table

In this section, you will create the table. You will also create the base for the table by using the **Cone** tool. Next, you will create the pedestal for the table by using the **Cylinder** tool. The pedestal will be placed on the base of the table. Finally, you will create the table top which will be placed on the top of the pedestal.

1. Activate the Top viewport and then choose **Create > Geometry** in the **Command Panel**. Invoke the **Cone** tool from the **Object Type** rollout. Expand the **Keyboard Entry** rollout, and set the values of the parameters as given next.

    Radius 1: **6**   Radius 2: **3**   Height: **4**

2. Choose the **Create** button. Then, enter the name **Base** in the **Name and Color** rollout; a cone is created, which will become the base of the table.

3. In the **Object Type** rollout, invoke the **Cylinder** tool. In the **Keyboard Entry** rollout, set the value **3** in the **Radius** spinner and **28** in the **Height** spinner.

4. Choose the **Create** button; a cylinder is created. Next, enter the name **Pedestal** in the **Name and Color** rollout.

    Pedestal is created on the base. Now, you will create a tabletop which will be placed on the top of *Pedestal*.

5. Select **Extended Primitives** from the drop-down list below the **Geometry** button. In the **Object Type** rollout, invoke the **ChamferBox** tool.

6. Expand the **Keyboard Entry** rollout and set the values in the spinners as given next:

Length: **40**   Width: **26**   Height: **2**   Fillet: **0.25**

7. Choose the **Create** button; a chamfer box is created. Next, enter the name **Top** in the **Name and Color** rollout; *Top* of the table is created, as shown in Figure P2-9.

Figure P2-9 Top of the table created

8. Maximize the Front viewport and zoom in on the three table objects until the subgrid is displayed. Use the **Select and Move** tool or the **Align** tool to move *Base* so that its lower edge is even with top of *Floor*.

9. Select *Pedestal* and use the **Select and Move** tool or the **Align** tool to move it upward so that its lower edge is even with the top edge of *Base*.

10. Select *Top* and use the **Select and Move** tool or the **Align** tool to move it upward so that its lower edge is even with the top edge of *Pedestal*.

11. Restore the four-viewport display. Maximize the Top viewport and zoom in to display the subgrid.

12. Select *Base*, *Pedestal*, and *Top* and move them such that they are centered between the two booths, as shown in Figure P2-10.

[+] [Top] [Wireframe]

Figure P2-10 *The table components aligned*

13. Select *Base & Pedestal* in any viewport. Choose **Rendering > Material Editor > Compact Material Editor** from the menu bar; the **Material Editor** dialog box is displayed. Next, select the next unused sample slot. Choose the **Arch & Design** button to change the material type; the **Material/Map Browser** dialog box is displayed.

14. Select **Standard** from the **Materials > Standard** rollout and then choose the **OK** button; the **Arch & Design** material is replaced by the **Standard** material. Also, various rollouts are displayed in the **Material Editor** dialog box to modify the **Standard** material.

15. Select **Blinn** from the drop-down list in the **Shader Basic Parameters** rollout, if it is not already selected.

16. Expand the **Maps** rollout. Next, choose the **Diffuse Color** map button which is currently labeled as **None**; the **Material/Map Browser** dialog box is displayed showing the types of maps that can be added.

17. Select the **Bitmap** map from the **Maps > Standard** rollout and choose the **OK** button; the **Material/Map Browser** dialog box is closed and the **Select Bitmap Image File** dialog box is displayed. As the project folder is already set, the folder *images* is displayed in the **Look in** drop-down list.

18. Select the file **WoodWhiteAsh.jpg** and choose the **Open** button.

19. Choose the **Assign Material to Selection** button to assign the material in the viewport. Now, choose the **Show Shaded Material in Viewport** button to display the material type in the viewport.

20. Select *Top* in any viewport. In the **Material Editor** dialog box, select the next unused sample slot. Next, load the map **WoodParquet.jpg** as discussed earlier; the material is displayed in the selected sample slot.

21. Choose the **Assign Material to Selection** button to assign the materials in the viewport. Next, choose the **Show Shaded Material in Viewport** button to display the material type in the viewport.

22. In the **Coordinates** rollout, make sure the **Use Real-World Scale** check box is selected and the value of the **Width: Size** spinner and the **Height: Size** spinner is **48**.

23. Close the **Material Editor** dialog box.

Creating the Lamp, Tube, and Target Light
In this section, you will create lights by using the various light tools to illuminate the diner.

1. Activate the Top viewport and then choose **Create > Shapes** in the **Command Panel**. Invoke the **Star** tool from the **Object Type** rollout. In the **Parameters** rollout, set the value **30** in the **Points** spinner.

2. In the **Keyboard Entry** rollout, set the value **10** in the **Radius 1** spinner and **12** in the **Radius 2** spinner. Then, choose the **Create** button; a star shape is created in the Top viewport with the name *Star001*. Right-click to exit the tool.

3. Maximize the Front viewport and zoom to display the subgrid. Invoke the **Line** tool from the **Object Type** rollout.

4. Draw a vertical line of 12 units length anywhere in the viewport. Right-click to exit the **Line** tool.

5. Make sure the line is selected. Next, choose **Create > Geometry** in the **Command Panel**. Select **Compound Objects** in the drop-down list. Invoke the **Loft** tool from the **Object Type** rollout.

6. In the **Skin Parameters** rollout, set the value **0** in both the **Shape Steps** and the **Path Steps** spinners. In the **Creation Method** rollout, choose the **Get Shape** button and select *Star001*; the star shape is lofted along the line, as shown in Figure P2-11.

7. Enter the name **Shade** in the **Name and Color** rollout.

8. Make sure the loft object is selected and then choose the **Modify** tab in the **Command Panel**. Expand the **Deformations** rollout and choose the **Scale** button; the **Scale Deformation(X)** dialog box is displayed.

9. In the **Scale Deformation(X)** dialog box, choose the **Insert Corner Point** button and then insert vertices at points 10 and 90.

After the vertices are inserted, they can be precisely positioned by entering a value in the text box at the bottom right of the dialog box.

Figure P2-11 *The lofted star shape*

10. Choose the **Move Control Point** button and move the right-hand vertex at point 100 and the vertex at point 90 to 30, as shown in Figure P2-12; the lamp shade is created. Close the **Scale Deformation(X)** dialog box.

Figure P2-12 *The vertices created and moved in the* **Scale Deformation**(X) *dialog box*

11. Choose **Edit > Clone** from the menu bar; the **Clone Options** dialog box is displayed. In this dialog box, make sure the **Copy** radio button is selected in the **Object** area and enter the name **Shade01** in the **Name** text box. Next, choose the **OK** button.

12. Make sure *Shade01* is selected. Choose the **Hierarchy** tab in the **Command Panel**. Make sure the **Pivot** button is chosen. Next, choose the **Affect Pivot Only** button in the **Move/Rotate/Scale:** area of the **Adjust Pivot** rollout. Move the pivot point in the Front

viewport so that it is aligned with the bottom-middle of *shade*. Choose the **Affect Pivot Only** button again to exit the pivot adjustment mode.

13. Make sure *Shade01* is selected. Next, invoke the **Select and Uniform Scale** and **Use Pivot Point Center** tools. Scale *Shade01* in the Front viewport to 90%, as indicated in the **X**, **Y**, and **Z** text boxes. Alternatively, you can use the **Scale Transformation Type-In** dialog box to scale *shade01*, which is displayed by right-clicking on the **Select and Uniform Scale** tool.

14. Select *Shade* in any viewport and then choose **Create > Geometry** in the **Command Panel**. Make sure the **Compound Objects** is selected in the drop-down list. Invoke the **Boolean** tool from the **Object Type** rollout.

15. In the **Operation** area of the **Parameters** rollout, make sure the **Subtraction (A-B)** radio button is chosen. In the **Pick Boolean** rollout, choose the **Pick Operand B** button and then select *Shade01* in any viewport. Invoke the **Select Object** tool to complete the Boolean operation; *Shade* is hollowed out.

16. Delete the star and line shapes that were used to create the lamp.

17. Invoke the **Zoom Extents All** tool. In the Front viewport, move *Shade* so that it is centered above the table. In the Top viewport, move and rotate *Shade* to the center of the table, as shown in Figure P2-13.

Figure P2-13 Shade moved into position

18. Choose **Rendering > Material Editor > Compact Material Editor** from the menu bar; the **Material Editor** dialog box is displayed. Select the next unused sample slot in it.

19. Choose the **Autodesk Solid Glass** button to change the material type; the **Material/Map Browser** dialog box is displayed again.

20. Select **Architectural** from the **Materials > Standard** rollout and then choose the **OK** button; the **Autodesk Solid Glass** material is replaced by the **Architectural** material. Also, various rollouts are displayed in the **Material Editor** dialog box to modify the **Architectural** material.

21. In the **Templates** rollout, select **Glass-Translucent** from the drop-down list.

22. In the **Physical Qualities** rollout, choose the **Diffuse Map** map button that is currently labeled as **None**; the **Material/Map Browser** dialog box is displayed. Next, load the map **Furnishings.Fabrics.Stripes.4.jpg**, as discussed earlier; the material is displayed in the selected sample slot.

23. Choose the **Assign Material to Selection** button. Next, choose the **Show Shaded Material in Viewport** button; the material is assigned to the shade.

24. Make sure *Shade* is selected and then choose the **Modify** tab in the **Command Panel**. From the **Modifier List** drop-down list, select **UVW Map** in the **OBJECT-SPACE MODIFIERS** section.

25. In the **Parameters** rollout for the modifier, clear the **Real-World Map Size** check box. Select the **Cylindrical** radio button and set the value **10** in the **Length**, and **Width** spinners. Next, set the value **0.5** in the **Height** spinner. In the **Alignment** area, select the **X** radio button.

26. Activate the Top viewport and choose **Create > Geometry** in the **Command Panel**. Select **Standard Primitives** in the drop-down list. Invoke the **Cylinder** tool from the **Object Type** rollout.

27. In the **Keyboard Entry** rollout, enter **0.5** in the **Radius** spinner, and **15** in the **Height** spinner. Next, choose the **Create** button; a cylinder is created.

28. In the Front viewport, move the cylinder so that its lower edge is aligned with the upper edge of *Shade*. In the Top viewport, place the cylinder at the center of *Shade*, as shown in Figure P2-14.

29. Assign the material **WoodWhiteAsh.jpg** to *Cylinder001*, as discussed earlier. Close the **Material Editor** dialog box.

30. Invoke the **Zoom Extents All** tool to zoom the objects to their extents.

31. Choose **Create > Lights** in the **Command Panel**. Select the **Standard** light type in the drop-down list. Next, invoke the **Target Spot** tool from the **Object Type** rollout.

32. In the **Spotlight Parameters** rollout, select the **Show Cone** check box. Also, set the value **80** in the **Hotspot/Beam** spinner and **100** in the **Falloff/Field** spinner. Then, set the value **0.4** in the **Multiplier** spinner of the **Intensity/Color/Attenuation** rollout.

33. In the Front viewport, click at some point in the middle of *Shade*, drag down, and place the target point on the tabletop.

Figure P2-14 *A suspension cylinder created*

You may need to zoom in on *Shade* and *Table*. Make sure the light is centered inside *Shade*.

34. In the Top viewport, make sure the **Use Pivot Point Center** tool from the Pivot Point flyout is selected. Now, move both *Spot001* and *Spot001.Target* to the center of *Shade*, as shown in Figure P2-15.

Figure P2-15 *A light placed inside the lamp shade*

Creating Glasses

In this section, you will create glasses by using the **Cone** tool. These glasses will be placed on the table top.

1. Make sure the Top viewport is active. Next, choose **Create > Geometry** in the **Command Panel**. In the **Object Type** rollout, invoke the **Cone** tool. In the **Parameters** rollout, set the value **1** in the **Height Segments** spinner.

2. Expand the **Keyboard Entry** rollout and enter the values in the spinners as given next:

   Radius 1: **1.5**   Radius 2: **2.5**   Height: **6**

3. Choose the **Create** button; a cone shape for the glass is created. Enter the name of the shape as **Glass01** in the **Name and Color** rollout and right-click on the viewport to exit the tool.

4. Zoom in on the glass in the Front viewport. Next, choose **Edit > Clone** from the menu bar; the **Clone Options** dialog box is displayed. In this dialog box, select the **Copy** radio button in the **Object** area and enter the name **Glass02** in the **Name** text box. Next, choose the **OK** button.

5. Make sure *Glass02* is selected and then choose the **Hierarchy** tab in the **Command Panel**. Make sure the **Pivot** button is chosen and then choose the **Affect Pivot Only** button. Move the pivot point to the top-center of the cone in the Front viewport. Choose the **Affect Pivot Only** button again to exit the pivot adjustment mode.

6. Invoke the **Select and Uniform Scale** and scale *Glass02* to 95%, as shown in the **X**, **Y**, and the **Z** spinners on the status bar.

7. Select *Glass01* and then choose **Create > Geometry** in the **Command Panel**. Select **Compound Objects** from the drop-down list. Invoke the **Boolean** tool from the **Object Type** rollout.

8. In the **Operation** area of the **Parameters** rollout, choose the **Subtraction (A-B)** radio button, if it is not selected. In the **Pick Boolean** rollout, choose the **Pick Operand B** button and then select *Glass02* in any viewport. Invoke the **Select Object** tool to exit the Boolean operation; *Glass01* is hollowed out.

9. Activate the Top viewport. Next, choose **Create > Geometry** in the **Command Panel** and select **Standard Primitives** from the drop-down list. In the **Object Type** rollout, invoke the **Cone** tool.

10. Expand the **Keyboard Entry** rollout and set the values in the spinners as given next:

    Radius 1: **1.4**   Radius 2: **2**   Height: **4**

11. Choose the **Create** button; the water level is created in *Glass01*, as shown in Figure P2-16. Next, enter the name **Water** in the **Name and Color** rollout and right-click on the viewport to exit the tool.

Figure P2-16 A glass with water created

12. Open the **Material Editor** dialog box and select the next unused sample slot. Change the **Autodesk Wall Paint** material type to **Standard** type, as discussed earlier.

13. In the **Shader Basic Parameters** rollout, select **Blinn** from the drop-down list. Select the **2-Sided** check box. In the **Blinn Basic Parameters** rollout, set the value **25** in the **Opacity** spinner. In the **Specular Highlights** area, set the value **45** in both the **Specular Level** and **Glossiness** spinners.

14. In the **Maps** rollout, choose the **Refraction** map button, currently labeled as **None**; the **Material/Map Browser** dialog box is displayed. In this dialog box, select the **Reflect/Refract** map type from the **Maps > Standard** rollout and choose the **OK** button. Assign it to *Water*.

15. Select *Glass01* in any viewport. In the **Material Editor** dialog box, select the next unused material sample. Change the **Autodesk Metal** material type to **Standard** type, as discussed earlier.

16. In the **Shader Basic Parameters** rollout, make sure **Blinn** is selected in the drop-down list and select the **2-Sided** check box. In the **Blinn Basic Parameters** rollout, set the value **25** in the **Opacity** spinner. In the **Specular Highlights** area, set the value **85** in the **Specular Level** spinner and **35** in the **Glossiness** spinner. Choose the **Ambient** color swatch; the **Color Selector: Ambient Color** dialog box is displayed. In this dialog box, set the values as given next:

Red: **0**   Green: **35**   Blue: **102**

17. Choose the Lock button between **Ambient** and **Diffuse** to turn it off.

    This enables you to assign a different color to the **Diffuse** color swatch.

18. Without closing the **Color Selector: Ambient Color** dialog box, choose the **Diffuse** color swatch in the **Material Editor** dialog box; the **Color Selector: Diffuse Color** dialog box is displayed. In this dialog box, set the values as given next:

    Red: **77**   Green: **96**   Blue: **237**

    Now, close the **Color Selector: Diffuse Color** dialog box.

19. In the **Maps** rollout, choose the **Bump** map button, currently labeled as **None**; the **Material/Map Browser** dialog box is displayed. In this dialog box, select the **Bitmap** from the **Maps > Standard** rollout and choose the **OK** button; the **Select Bitmap Image File** dialog box is displayed. In this dialog box, select the map **ConcreteExposed.jpg** and choose the **Open** button; the map is displayed in the selected material slot.

20. In the **Coordinates** rollout, make sure the **Use Real-World Scale** tool check box is cleared and the value in the **U Tiling** and **V Tiling** spinners is set to 1. Also, clear the **U Tile** and **V Tile** check boxes.

21. Choose the **Go to Parent** button to return to the **Maps** rollout. In the **Maps** rollout, set the value **120** in the **Bump** spinner.

22. Enter the name of the material as **Glass** in material drop-down list and assign it to *Glass01*. Close the **Material Editor** dialog box.

23. With *Glass01* selected, choose the **Modify** tab in the **Command Panel**. In the **Modifier List** drop-down list, select **UVW Map** in the **OBJECT-SPACE MODIFIERS** section.

24. In the **Mapping** area of the **Parameters** rollout for the modifier, make sure the **Real-World Map Size** check box is cleared and select the **Cylindrical** radio button.

25. Set the value **5** in the **Length**, **Width**, and **Height** spinners. Also, select the **Z** radio button, if it is not selected and then choose the **Fit** button in the **Alignment** area of the **Parameters** rollout.

26. Select *Glass01* and *Water*. Choose **Group > Group** from the menu bar; the **Group** dialog box is displayed. Enter the name **Drink01** in the **Group** dialog box. Choose the **OK** button; the glass and water are grouped together.

27. Activate the Front viewport and invoke the **Zoom Extents** tool.

28. Move *Drink01* to the top of the table so that its bottom edge is aligned with the upper edge of *Top*.

29. In the Top viewport, move *Drink01* upward and toward the left, so that it is placed just to the left of the centerline and 3/4 of the length of the table.

30. Activate the Front viewport and then make sure the **Select and Move** tool is invoked. Press and hold the left mouse button along with the SHIFT key and move *Drink01* toward the right of the table. Now, release the SHIFT key and the left mouse button; the **Clone Options** dialog box is displayed.

31. Make sure the **Copy** radio button is selected in this dialog box and enter **Drink02** in the **Name** textbox. Choose the **OK** button; the dialog box is closed and a copy of *Drink01* is created on the right side of the table.

32. Activate the Top viewport and align *Drink02* so that it is placed at the right of the center line and about ¼th of the length of the table, as shown in Figure P2-17.

Figure P2-17 *Drink02 created and positioned*

Creating the Plates

In this section, you will create plates by using the **Cone** tool and then place them on the table top along with glasses.

1. Make sure the Top viewport is activated and then choose **Create > Geometry** in the **Command Panel**. Select **Standard Primitives** in the drop-down list below the **Geometry** button, if it is not selected. Invoke the **Cone** tool from the **Object Type** rollout.

2. In the **Parameters** rollout, make sure the value is set to **1** in the **Height Segments** spinner.

3. Expand the **Keyboard Entry** rollout and set the values in the spinners as given next:

Radius 1: **2.5**   Radius 2: **5.0**   Height: **0.75**

4. Choose the **Create** button; a truncated cone is created. Enter the name **Plate01** in the **Name and Color** rollout and right-click on the viewport to exit the tool. Next, *Plate01* will be hollowed out to create a plate.

5. Create a copy of *Plate01,* as discussed earlier and name it as **Plate02**. Zoom in on the plates in the Front viewport.

6. Move the pivot point to the top-center of *Plate02* and scale *Plate02* from its pivot point to 95%, as discussed earlier.

7. Select *Plate01* and choose **Create > Geometry** in the **Command Panel**. Select **Compound Objects** in the drop-down list below the **Geometry** button. Next, invoke the **Boolean** tool from the **Object Type** rollout.

8. In the **Operation** area of the **Parameters** rollout, make sure the **Subtraction (A-B)** radio button is selected. In the **Pick Boolean** rollout, choose the **Pick Operand B** button. Next, select *Plate02* in any viewport. Invoke the **Select Object** tool to exit the Boolean operation.

9. In the Front viewport, zoom in so that the table and plate are displayed and then move *Plate01* such that it sits on top of the table.

10. In the Left viewport, move *Plate01* next to one glass, as shown in Figure P2-18.

Figure P2-18 *Plate01 created and positioned*

11. Choose **Rendering > Material Editor > Compact Material Editor** from the menu bar; the **Material Editor** dialog box is displayed. Select the next unused sample slot. Change the **Arch & Design** material type to **Standard** type, as discussed earlier.

12. Choose the **Diffuse Color** color swatch; the **Color Selector: Diffuse Color** dialog box is displayed. In this dialog box, set the values as given next:

Red: **223** Green: **235** Blue: **233**

13. Choose the **OK** button to close the **Color Selector: Diffuse Color** dialog box. Name the material as **Plate** and assign it to *Plate01*. Close the **Material Editor** dialog box.

Creating the Window

In this section, you will create a window by using the **Box** tool. This window will be positioned on the wall next to the diner.

1. Activate the Front viewport and invoke the **Zoom Extents All** tool. Choose **Create > Geometry** in the **Command Panel** and select **Standard Primitives** from the drop-down list below the **Geometry** button. Invoke the **Box** tool from the **Object Type** rollout.

2. Expand the **Keyboard Entry** rollout and set the values in the spinners as given next:

Length: **60** Width: **90** Height: **1.5**

3. Choose the **Create** button and enter the name **Frame01** in the **Name and Color** rollout.

4. Create another box by setting the value **60** in the **Length** spinner, **90** in the **Width** spinner, and **2.5** in the **Height** spinner. Choose the **Create** button and enter the name **FrameDrill** in the **Name and Color** rollout and right-click on the viewport to exit the tool.

5. Select *Frame01* and create its copy named **Frame02**. Make sure *Frame02* is selected and then choose the **Modify** tab in the **Command Panel**.

6. In the **Parameters** rollout, set the values in the spinners as given next:

Length: **53** Width: **80** Height: **2.5**

7. Select *Frame01* and choose **Create > Geometry** in the **Command Panel**. Select **Compound Objects** from the drop-down list below the **Geometry** button. Invoke the **Boolean** tool from the **Object Type** rollout.

8. In the **Operation** area of the **Parameters** rollout, make sure the **Subtraction (A-B)** radio button is selected. In the **Pick Boolean** rollout, choose the **Pick Operand B** button. Then, select *Frame02* in any viewport. Invoke the **Select Object** tool to exit the Boolean operation.

9. Choose the **Modify** tab in the **Command Panel**. In the **Modifier List** drop-down list, select **UVW Map** in the **OBJECT-SPACE MODIFIERS** section. In the **Mapping** area of the **Parameters** rollout for the modifier, make sure the **Real-World Map Size** is cleared and select the **Box** radio button.

10. Set the values in the spinners of the **Parameters** rollout as given next:

    U Tile: **0.75**   V Tile: **0.75**   W Tile: **0.75**

11. Choose the **Fit** button in the **Alignment** area.

12. Make sure the Front viewport is active, choose **Create > Geometry** in the **Command Panel** and select **Standard Primitives** in the drop-down list below the **Geometry** button. Invoke the **Box** tool from the **Object Type** rollout.

13. Expand the **Keyboard Entry** rollout and set the values in the spinners as given next:

    Length: **53**   Width: **80**   Height: **0.1**

14. Choose the **Create** button and then enter the name **Win-Glass** in the **Name and Color** rollout and right-click on the viewport to exit the tool.

15. Select *Frame01*, *FrameDrill*, and *Win-Glass*. In the Front viewport, move the selected objects to the upper-left corner of the wall and then move the selected objects downward by five units and toward the right by seven units.

    You can change the snap settings and the zoom level as needed.

16. In the Top viewport, move the selected objects so that they are vertically centered (approximately) on *Wall01*.

17. Select *Wall01* and then choose **Create > Geometry** in the **Command Panel** and select **Compound Objects** in the drop-down list. Invoke the **Boolean** tool from the **Object Type** rollout.

18. In the **Operation** area of the **Parameters** rollout, make sure the **Subtraction (A-B)** radio button is selected. In the **Pick Boolean** rollout, choose the **Pick Operand B** button.

19. Select *FrameDrill* in any viewport. Invoke the **Select Object** tool to complete the Boolean operation; the window is placed in the wall, as shown in Figure P2-19.

    If the **Material Attach Options** dialog box appears, choose the **OK** button.

20. Select *Frame01* and then open the **Material Editor** dialog box. Choose **Rendering > Material Editor > Compact Material Editor** from the menu bar; the **Material Editor** dialog box is displayed. Select the next unused sample slot. Change the **Arch & Design** material type to **Standard** type, as discussed earlier.

21. Choose the **Diffuse** button from the **Blinn Basic Parameters** rollout; the **Material/Map Browser** dialog box is displayed. Next, load the map **WoodWhiteAsh.jpg**, as discussed earlier.

Figure P2-19 *The window placed on the wall*

22. Choose the **Assign Material to Selection** button in the **Material Editor** dialog box; the material is assigned to *Frame01*. Now, invoke the **Show Shaded Material in Viewport** tool to display the material in the viewport.

23. Select the next unused sample slot in the **Material Editor**. Choose the **Material Type** button that is currently labeled as **Arch & Design**; the **Material/Map Browser** dialog box is displayed. Select the **Architectural** material from **Materials > Standard** and choose the **OK** button; the **Arch & Design** material is replaced by the **Architectural** material.

24. In the **Templates** rollout, select **Glass-Clear** from the drop-down list under the **Architectural** material type. Enter the name of material as **WindowGlass** in the materials drop-down list and assign it to *Win-Glass*. Next, invoke the **Show Shaded Material in Viewport** tool to display the material in the viewport.

25. Close the **Material Editor** dialog box.

Creating the Text Diner

In this section, you will create the text DINER by using the **Text** tool. This text will be positioned on the outer face of the wall.

1. Activate the Front viewport. Next, choose **Create > Shapes** in the **Command Panel**. Invoke the **Text** tool from the **Object Type** rollout.

2. In the **Parameters** rollout, select **Comic Sans MS Bold** from the text drop-down list. Set the value **20** in the **Size** spinner and in the **Text** area, highlight the current text and type the word DINER.

3. Click at a point at the center of *Win-Glass* in the Front viewport to place the text, as shown in Figure P2-20.

Figure P2-20 *The text for the sign created*

You may need to slightly reposition the text later in the modeling process.

4. Activate the Top viewport and move the DINER text to the outer (top) face of *Wall01*.

5. Make sure the text object is selected and then choose the **Modify** tab in the **Command Panel**. In the **Modifier List** drop-down list, select **Extrude** in the **OBJECT-SPACE MODIFIERS** section. In the **Parameters** rollout for the modifier, set the value **0.2** in the **Amount** spinner.

6. Make sure the Top viewport is activated. With the text object selected, invoke the **Mirror** tool; the **Mirror: Screen Coordinates** dialog box is displayed. Next, make sure the **No Clone** and **X** radio buttons are selected and then choose the **OK** button; the text appears reversed so that it can be read from outside the building.

7. Choose **Rendering > Material Editor > Compact Material Editor** from the menu bar; the **Material Editor** dialog box is displayed. Select the next unused sample slot.

8. Choose the **Material Type** button that is currently labeled as **Arch & Design**; the **Material/Map Browser** dialog box is displayed. Select the **Architectural** material from the **Materials > Standard** rollout and choose the **OK** button; the **Arch & Design** material is replaced by the **Architectural** material.

9. In the **Templates** rollout, select **Metal-Brushed** from the drop-down list under the **Architectural** material type. In the **Physical Qualities** rollout, choose the **Diffuse Color** color swatch and define a color of your choice. Enter the name of the material as **Sign** and assign it to the text object. Close the **Material Editor** dialog box.

10. Choose **Create > Lights** in the **Command Panel**. Make sure the **Standard** option is selected in the drop-down list. Next, invoke the **Omni** tool from the **Object Type** rollout. In the **Shadows** area of the **General Parameters** rollout, clear the **On** check box. Then, set the value **0.1** in the **Multiplier** spinner of the **Intensity/Color/Attenuation** rollout.

11. In the Front viewport, click in the middle of the text object to create the light. In the Top viewport, move the light slightly up, so that it is even with the bottom of *booth*, as shown in Figure P2-21.

Figure P2-21 Omni01 light created and positioned

Creating Blinds

In this section, you will create blinds for the window by using the **Box** tool.

1. Activate the Front viewport and then choose **Create > Geometry** in the **Command Panel** and select **Standard Primitives** from the drop-down list below the **Geometry** button. In the **Object Type** rollout, invoke the **Box** tool.

2. Expand the **Keyboard Entry** rollout and set the values in the spinners as given next:

   Length: **53**   Width: **4**   Height: **0.125**

3. Choose the **Create** button; a box is created. Enter the name **Blind01** in the **Name and Color** rollout.

4. In the Front viewport, move *Blind01* near the top-left corner of *Frame01*. To do so, you may need to zoom into the area around the top-left corner of *Frame01*.

5. Activate the Top viewport. Invoke the **Select and Rotate** and **Transform Gizmo Z Constraint** tools. Next, rotate *Blind01* at -20 degrees about the Z axis in the Top viewport.

6. In the Top viewport, move *Blind01* so that its top edge aligns with the bottom edge of *Frame01*. Zoom in to view *Blind01* properly, as shown in Figure P2-22.

Figure P2-22 *Blind01 created and positioned*

7. Select *Base*, *Booth01*, *Booth02*, *Top*, *Drink01*, *Drink02*, *Pedestal*, and *Plate01* from the **Scene Explorer**.

    These objects need to be moved slightly away from the wall to make room for the blinds.

8. Change the **Reference Coordinate System** to **World** from the **Main Toolbar**. Invoke the **Select and Move** tool and then right-click on it to open the **Move Transform Type-In** dialog box. In the **Offset:World** area, set the value **–2** in the **Y** spinner. Close the **Move Transform Type-In** dialog box.

    This moves the objects slightly away from the wall, so that the objects do not interfere with the blinds.

9. Select *Blind01* and then choose **Rendering > Material Editor > Compact Material Editor** from the menu bar; the **Material Editor** dialog box is displayed. Select the next unused sample slot. Next, change the **Arch & Design** material type to **Standard** type, as discussed earlier.

10. Choose the **Diffuse** color swatch; the **Color Selector:Diffuse Color** dialog box is displayed. Set the values as given next:

    Red: **255**   Green: **244**   Blue: **198**

11. Choose the **OK** button to close the **Color Selector:Diffuse Color** dialog box. Enter the name of the material as **Blinds** and assign it to *Blind01*. Next, close the **Material Editor** dialog box.

12. Make sure *Blind01* is selected and choose **Tools > Array** from the menu bar; the **Array** dialog box is displayed, as shown in Figure P2-23. Choose the **Reset All Parameters** button in this dialog box. Set the value **3.6** in the **Incremental X** spinner in the **Move** row. In the **Array Dimensions** area, make sure the **1D** radio button is selected and set the value **22** in the **Count** spinner. Next, select the **Copy** radio button in the **Type of Object** area and choose the **OK** button; 22 blinds are created extending across the window; as shown in Figure P2-24.

Figure P2-23 The Array dialog box

Figure P2-24 The blinds created using the Array tool

13. Invoke the **Zoom Extents All** tool to view the objects properly in all viewports and then save the scene.

Cloning Objects

In this section, you will create multiple copies of the objects by using the **Clone Options** dialog box.

1. Activate the Front viewport and select *Drink01*, *Drink02*, *Booth01*, *Booth02*, *Base*, *Pedestal*, *Plate01*, *Shade*, *Spot001*, *Spot001.Target*, *Top*, and *Cylinder001* from the **Scene Explorer**.

2. Make sure the **Select and Move** tool is invoked. Then, invoke the **Transform Gizmo X Constraint** tool. Press and hold the left mouse button along with the SHIFT key and move the selected objects to the right of the original objects. Release the SHIFT key and the left mouse button when the left edge of the copied booth lines up with the right edge of the original position; the **Clone Options** dialog box is displayed.

3. In this dialog box, enter the name **DinerSet** in the **Name** text box and select the **Copy** radio button. Now, choose the **OK** button; another set of selected objects is created, as shown in Figure P2-25.

Figure P2-25 *The selected objects copied and positioned*

Adding a Camera

In this section, you will create the camera to apply the angle of direction of the objects by using the **Target** tool.

1. Activate the Top viewport. Zoom out so that the objects are displayed with almost one-third of their original size.

2. Choose **Create > Cameras** in the **Command Panel**. Invoke the **Target** tool from the **Object Type** rollout. Click at a point at the bottom-middle of the viewport and a little toward the right of center. Pressing and holding the mouse button, drag the cursor and place the target near the right side of *Shade*.

3. Activate the Left viewport. Invoke the **Zoom Extents** tool. Move the camera upward such that it is at the same level as the shades. Next, move the target such that it is on the table.

4. Activate the Perspective viewport. Press the C key to display the Camera001 view.

5. Using the **Truck Camera** and **Dolly Camera** tools, adjust the camera in such a way that the edges of *walls* and *Floor* are not visible. Next, align the objects at the center of the Camera001 viewport, as shown in Figure P2-26.

Figure P2-26 *Aligning objects at the center of the Camera001 viewport*

Adding More Lights

In this section, you will create lights to illuminate the scene.

1. Activate the Front viewport. Zoom out until the objects are displayed about one-third of their original size.

2. Choose **Create > Lights** in the **Command Panel**. Make sure the **Standard** option is selected in the drop-down list. Invoke the **Omni** tool from the **Object Type** rollout.

3. In the Front viewport, click at a point at the upper-right corner of the viewport; another Omni light named *Omni002* is placed.

4. Activate the Top viewport and invoke the **Target Spot** tool from the **Object Type** rollout. In the Top viewport, click at a point near the lower-right corner of the viewport and then drag to place the target on the window. In the **Shadows** area of the **General Parameters** rollout, clear the **On** check box, if it is not cleared; another spotlight named *Spot003* is placed.

5. In the Left viewport, invoke the **Zoom Extents** tool. Next, move *Spot003* upward so that it is in level with the tabletop or slightly above it. Finally, move *Spot003.Target* and place it in the middle of the window, as shown in Figure P2-27.

Figure P2-27 *The Spot003.Target moved and placed in the middle of the window*

6. Change the intensity of both the lights to get the desired result.

Rendering the Still Image
In this section, you will render the still image.

1. Activate the Camera001 viewport. Invoke the **Render Production** tool from the **Main Toolbar**; a rendered view of the scene is displayed in the **Rendered Frame** window, as shown in Figure P2-28.

2. Close the **Rendered Frame** window.

3. Make the necessary adjustments in the lights in the scene, if required.

Animating the Scene
In this section, you will animate the scene.

1. Choose the **Display** tab of the **Command Panel**. In the **Hide by Category** rollout, select the **Lights** and **Cameras** check boxes; the lights and the camera are hidden in the viewports. Next, invoke the **Zoom Extents All** tool.

2. Click on the Shaded viewport label menu; the shortcut menu is displayed. Choose **Wireframe** from the shortcut menu.

    This will improve the system performance when previewing the animation in the viewport.

Figure P2-28 *The rendered view of the scene*

3. Activate and maximize the Top viewport. Zoom in on the blinds.

4. Choose the **Time Configuration** button to display the **Time Configuration** dialog box. In the **Animation** area, set the value **42** in the **Length** spinner. Choose the **OK** button; the number of frames in the active time segment changes to 42.

5. Make sure **World** is selected in the **Reference Coordinate System** drop down list from the **Main Toolbar**.

6. Drag the time slider to frame 0, if it is not at frame one and then choose the **Toggle Auto Key Mode** button to turn it on (red).

7. Select *Blind022* (the farthest-right blind) and right-click on the **Select and Move** tool; the **Move Transform-Type In** dialog box is displayed. In this dialog box, set the value **–2.7** in the **Offset World X** spinner; *Blind022* is moved to the left by 2.7 units. Then, close the **Move Transform Type-In** dialog box.

8. Move time slider to Frame 1 and select *Blind021* along with *Blind022*. Using the **Move Transform Type-In** dialog box, move these two blinds left by -2.7 units.

9. Move time slider to Frame 2 and select *Blind020* along with *Blind021* and *Blind022*. Using the **Move Transform Type-In** dialog box, move these three blinds left by -2.7 units.

10. Continue with this pattern until all the blinds are selected and moved except the last one (*Blind01*), as shown in Figure P2-29. The whole process will be completed in 20 frames.

Figure P2-29 *The blinds at the midpoint of the animation*

11. Move time slider to Frame 21 and start reversing the above process frame by frame. When you are done, choose the **Toggle Auto Key Mode** button to turn off the animation mode.

12. Display the four-viewport configuration and then activate the Camera viewport. Next, choose the **Play Animation** button; the animation is played in the Camera001 viewport.

13. Choose the **Stop Animation** button to stop the playback.

Setting the Background
Now, you need to set the background for the scene.

1. Choose **Create > Geometry** in the **Command Panel**. Invoke the **Plane** tool from the **Object Type** rollout.

2. In the Front viewport, create a plane and align it on the back of *Wall02* in the Left viewport, refer to Figure P2-30.

3. In the **Parameters** rollout, enter **140** in the **Length** spinner and **190** in the **Width** spinner. The proper length and width has been set to the plane.

4. Invoke the **Material Editor** dialog box and change the material type **Arch & Design** to **Standard** as discussed earlier.

5. In the **Blinn Basis Parameters** rollout, choose the **Diffuse** button; the **Material/Map Browser** dialog box is displayed. Next, choose the **Bitmap** map button from the **Maps > Standard** rollout and choose the **OK** button; the **Select Bitmap Image File** dialog box is displayed.

Figure P2-30 *The Plane created and aligned on back of Wall02*

6. In the **Select Bitmap Image File** dialog box, select the **Sunset.Jpg** file and choose the **Open** button to return to the **Material Editor** dialog box.

7. In the **Coordinates** rollout, make sure the **User Real-World Scale** check box is selected and enter the value **100** in the **Width: Size** and **Height: Size** spinners.

8. Choose the **Go To Parent** button to go one level up and unlock the **Diffuse** and **Ambient** color swatches. Next, set the **Ambient** color to white. Make sure the *Plane001* is selected in the viewport and assign this material to *Plane001*.

9. In the **Material Editor** dialog box, activate the *WindowGlass* material sample slot. In the **Physical Quantities** rollout, choose the **Diffuse Color** swatch; the **Color Selector: Diffuse** dialog box is displayed. Set the color to white and choose the **OK** button to close this dialog box.

Rendering the Animation
In this section, you will render the final animation.

1. Activate the Camera001 viewport. Then, invoke the **Render Setup** tool; the **Render Setup** dialog box is displayed.

2. In the **Time Output** area of the **Common Parameters** rollout, select the **Active Time Segment** radio button. In the **Render Output** area, choose the **Files** button; the **Render Output File** dialog box is displayed.

3. In the **Render Output File** dialog box, select **AVI File (*.avi)** from the **Save as type** drop-down list. In the **File name** text box, enter the name **Project02** and then choose the **Save** button; the **AVI File Compression Setup** dialog box is displayed. Choose the **OK** button in this dialog box.

4. Make sure the **Save File** check box is selected in the **Render Output** area of the **Render Setup** dialog box. Then, choose the **Render** button in the dialog box.

It may take several minutes to render the animation frame by frame. After rendering is complete, close the render window and the **Render Setup** dialog box.

5. Choose **Rendering > View Image File** from the menu bar; the **View File** dialog box is displayed. Select the **Project02.avi** and choose the **Open** button.

The animation is played once in Windows Media Player. Figure P2-31 shows the rendered frame at frame 42.

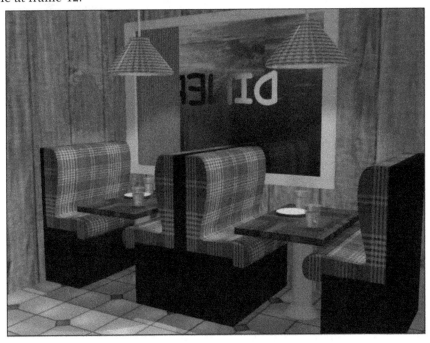

Figure P2-31 *The final animation rendered at frame 42*

Project 3

Architectural Project

PROJECT DESCRIPTION

This project guides you through the creation of the model of a residential garage, as shown in Figure P3-1. The procedures used in this project can be applied to any architectural project.

Figure P3-1 *The model of a residential garage*

Creating the Project Folder

Create a new project folder with the name *Prj_3* at *\Documents\3dsmaxdesign 2015* and then save the file with the name *Prj3*, as discussed in Tutorial 1 of Chapter 2.

Downloading the Files

Before starting the project, you need to download the *prj3_3dsmaxdesign_2015.zip* file from *www.cadcim.com*. The path of the file is as follows: *Textbooks > Animation and Visual Effects > 3ds Max Design > Autodesk 3ds Max Design 2015: A Tutorial Approach*

Extract the contents of the zip file to *Documents*. Open Windows Explorer and browse to *\Documents\prj3_3dsmaxdesign_2015* and then copy all files to *\Documents\3dsmaxdesign 2015\ Prj3\sceneassets\images*.

Changing the Units Setting

To start the project, you will change the units with which you are working. Since the units used in this project are in inches, you will set the units to decimal inches.

1. Choose **Customize > Units Setup** from the menu bar; the **Units Setup** dialog box is displayed.

2. In this dialog box, select the **US Standard** radio button in the **Display Unit Scale** area. Next, make sure the **Feet w/Fractional Inches** option is selected in the drop-down list below this radio button. In the right drop-down list, select 1/2, as shown in Figure P3-2. Choose the **OK** button to apply the settings and close the dialog box. If you want to work in the metric unit system, select the **Metric** radio button from the **Display Unit Scale** area of the **Units Setup** dialog box. Also, make sure the **Meters** option is selected in the drop-down list below the **Metric** radio button.

*Figure P3-2 The **Units Setup** dialog box*

3. Right-click on the **Snaps Toggle** tool from the **Main Toolbar**; the **Grid and Snap Settings** dialog box is displayed. Choose the **Home Grid** tab in this dialog box.

4. Set the value **1'0"(0.305m)** in the **Grid Spacing** spinner. Also, set the value **2** in the **Major Lines every Nth Grid Line** spinner. Next, select the **All Viewports** radio button. Close the **Grid and Snap Settings** dialog box to apply these changes.

Creating the Walls

In architectural projects, you can use 2D shapes as paths for lofting other shapes. The 2D shapes can also describe the outlines or elevation views of the walls. The outlines are then extruded to the required thickness or height.

1. Activate the Top viewport. Choose **Create > Shapes** in the **Command Panel**. Invoke the **Line** tool from the **Object Type** rollout.

2. In the **Creation Method** rollout, make sure the **Corner** radio button is selected in the **Initial Type** area.

3. Expand the **Keyboard Entry** rollout and enter the values in the **X**, **Y**, and **Z** spinners as given next. Choose the **Add Point** button after every XYZ coordinate entry:

X: **0'**	Y: **0'**	Z: **0'**
X: **0'**	Y: **22'(6.706m)**	Z: **0'**
X: **22'(6.706m)**	Y: **22'(6.706m)**	Z: **0'**
X: **22'(6.706m)**	Y: **0'**	Z: **0'**

4. After adding a point for the last entry, choose the **Finish** button. In the **Name and Color** rollout, enter the name **Wall Path**.

5. Invoke the **Zoom Extents All** tool to zoom the object to its extent.

   The exterior *Wall Path* is now visible.

Creating 3D Wall Objects

3ds Max Design allows you to automatically create 3D walls. The wall objects have height, width, and justification that need to be altered according to the project work. Door and window objects can be then added to the wall objects and the necessary openings in the wall are automatically created.

1. Choose **Create > Geometry** in the **Command Panel**. Next, select **AEC Extended** in the drop-down list. Invoke the **Wall** tool from the **Object Type** rollout.

2. In the **Parameters** rollout, set the value **0'6"(0.152m)** in the **Width** spinner and **8'0"(2.438m)** in the **Height** spinner. Select the **Left** radio button in the **Justification** area.

3. Expand the **Keyboard Entry** rollout. In this rollout, choose the **Pick Spline** button and then select *Wall Path* line in any viewport; a 3D wall object (Wall001) is created on top of the selected path, as shown in Figure P3-3.

Figure P3-3 The 3D Wall001 created on top of the selected path

Creating an Extruded Wall

In this section, you will create the front wall of the garage as a 2D outline or elevation view of the wall. The outline will be extruded to proper thickness matching with the walls, door, and windows.

1. Activate the Front viewport and then choose **Create > Shapes** in the **Command Panel**. Invoke the **Line** tool from the **Object Type** rollout.

2. Expand the **Keyboard Entry** rollout and enter the values in the **X**, **Y**, and **Z** spinners as given next. Choose the **Add Point** button after every XYZ coordinate entry:

X: **0'**	Y: **0'**	Z: **0'**
X: **0'**	Y: **8'(2.438m)**	Z: **0'**
X: **22'(6.706m)**	Y: **8'(2.438m)**	Z: **0'**
X: **22'(6.706m)**	Y: **0'**	Z: **0'**
X: **18'4"(5.588m)**	Y: **0'**	Z: **0'**
X: **18'4"(5.588m)**	Y: **7'4"(2.235m)**	Z: **0'**
X: **1'8"(0.508m)**	Y: **7'4"(2.235m)**	Z: **0'**
X: **1'8"(0.508m)**	Y: **0'**	Z: **0'**

3. After the last entry, choose the **Close** button to add the last segment; the front wall is created, as shown in Figure P3-4. In the **Name and Color** rollout, enter **Wall Front**.

4. Make sure *Wall Front* is selected and then choose the **Modify** tab in the **Command Panel**. In the **Modifier List** drop-down list, select **Extrude**. Next, in the **Parameters** rollout of the modifier, set the value **0'6"(0.152m)** in the **Amount** spinner. Also, select the **Generate Mapping Coords** check box at the bottom of the rollout.

Figure P3-4 *The front wall created*

Creating the Floor Slab

The floor of the garage is created as a standard 3D box primitive.

1. Activate the Top viewport. Choose **Create > Geometry** in the **Command Panel**. Select **Standard Primitives** from the drop-down list. Next, invoke the **Box** tool. In the **Parameters** rollout, make sure the **Generate Mapping Coords** check box is selected at the bottom of the rollout.

2. Expand the **Keyboard Entry** rollout and enter the values as given next:

    X: **11'(3.353m)**   Y: **10'9"(3.277m)**   Z: **0'**
    Length: **22'6"(6.858m)**   Width: **22'(6.706m)**   Height: **–6"(–0.152m)**

3. Choose the **Create** button; the floor and the walls are created, as shown in Figure P3-5. In the **Name and Color** rollout, enter **Floor Slab**.

Creating the Doors and Windows

3ds Max Design can automatically create 3D doors and windows. The door and window objects must be placed perfectly in the wall object for the required opening to be automatically created. You will create the side door that will be placed in the wall object with required settings.

1. Right-click on the **Snaps Toggle** tool in the **Main Toolbar**; the **Grid and Snap Settings** dialog box is displayed.

2. Select the **Edge/Segment** check box and close the dialog box; the cursor will now snap to the edges of objects.

Figure P3-5 *The floor and walls created*

3. Invoke the **2D Snap** tool from the **Snap Toggle** flyout to make 2D snaps active. Also, make sure the Top viewport is activated.

4. Choose **Create > Geometry** in the **Command Panel**. Next, select **Doors** from the drop-down list and then invoke the **Pivot** tool from the **Object Type** rollout.

5. In the **Creation Method** rollout, make sure the **Width/Depth/Height** radio button is selected.

6. In the **Frame** area of the **Parameters** rollout, make sure the **Create Frame** check box is selected. Also, select the **Generate Mapping Coords** check box at the bottom of the rollout.

7. Click and hold a point on the inside of the right wall near the bottom. Make sure the snap helper highlights the edge. With the mouse button held down, drag the door to any distance up along the inside of the wall to set the door width and then release the mouse button; an approximate door width is set. The width will be modified to the exact required dimension later.

8. Highlight and select the outside edge of the right wall; the door depth is set.

9. Highlight and select the outside top edge of the right wall at any point; an approximate door height is set. The door parameters can now be set to their exact required dimensions.

10. Make sure the door is selected and then choose the **Modify** tab in the **Command Panel**. In the **Parameters** rollout, set the values in the spinners as given below:

Height: **6'8"(2.032m)**   Width: **3'0"(0.914m)**   Depth: **0'6"(0.152m)**

11. In the **Parameters** rollout, enter the value **90** in the **Open** spinner.

Verify that the door is now open 90 degrees and there is an opening in the wall. Rotate the view in the Perspective viewport as needed to see the door. The door should open to the inside of the garage and toward the main garage door. If there is no door opening, then delete the door, verify that the 2D snaps are active, and create the door again.

12. In the **Parameters** rollout, select the **Flip Swing** and **Flip Hinge** check boxes, if they are not already selected. Rotate the Perspective viewport to set the angle of view. The door is created, as shown in Figure P3-6.

Figure P3-6 *The door created*

13. In the **Parameters** rollout, enter the value **0** in the **Open** spinner to close the door.

Next, you will create a window object that will be placed in the wall object with the required openings automatically created in the wall object.

14. Activate the Top viewport and then choose **Create > Geometry** in the **Command Panel**. Select **Windows** from the drop-down list. Then, invoke the **Sliding** tool from the **Object Type** rollout.

15. In the **Creation Method** rollout, make sure the **Width/Depth/Height** radio button is selected.

16. In the **Parameters** rollout, select the **Generate Mapping Coords** check box and make sure the **2D Snap** tool is invoked.

17. Click and hold a point on the inside of the left wall near the top. Make sure the snap helper highlights the edge. With the mouse button held down, drag the window to any distance down along the inside of the wall to set the width of the window and release the button; an approximate window width is set. The width will be modified to the required dimension later.

18. Highlight and select the outside edge of the left wall; the window depth has been set.

19. Highlight and select the top edge of the left wall at any point; an approximate window height is set. The window parameters can now be set to their exact required dimensions.

20. Make sure the window is selected and then choose the **Modify** tab in the **Command Panel**. In the **Parameters** rollout, enter the values in the spinners as given below:

    Height: **4'0"(1.219m)**   Width: **3'0"(0.914m)**   Depth: **0'6"(0.152m)**

21. Turn the snaps off and then make sure the **Select and Move** tool is invoked.

22. Activate the Left viewport. Invoke the **Align** tool and align the top of the window with the top of the door. You can also use the **Select and Move** tool for this step.

23. Set the value **100** in the **Open %** spinner in the **Open Window** area of the **Parameters** rollout.

    Verify that the window is now open and there is an opening in the wall. Rotate the view in the Perspective viewport to see the window properly. If the window opening is not there, delete the window, verify that 2D snaps are active, and create the window again.

24. Set the value **0** in the **Open %** spinner to close the window.

25. Create a similar window on the right-hand (with the door) wall, as shown in Figure P3-7. Ensure that there is a hole in the wall.

Creating the Overhead Door Frame and Overhead Door

In this section, you will create the overhead door frame and the overhead door as 2D outlines (shapes). The outlines will then be extruded to the proper thickness.

1. Activate the Front viewport and then choose **Create > Shapes** in the **Command Panel**. Next, invoke the **Line** tool from the **Object Type** rollout.

Figure P3-7 *The sliding windows created*

2. In the **Keyboard Entry** rollout, enter the following values. Choose the **Add Point** button after entering each set of coordinates:

X: **1'8"(0.508m)**   Y: **0'**   Z: **0'**
X: **1'8"(0.508m)**   Y: **7'4"(2.235m)** Z: **0'**
X: **18'4"(5.588m)**   Y: **7'4"(2.235m)** Z: **0'**
X: **18'4"(5.588m)**   Y: **0'**   Z: **0'**
X: **18'0"(5.486m)**   Y: **0'**   Z: **0'**
X: **18'0"(5.486m)**   Y: **7'0"(2.134m)** Z: **0'**
X: **2'0"(0.61m)**   Y: **7'0"(2.134m)** Z: **0'**
X: **2'0"(0.61m)**   Y: **0'**   Z: **0'**

3. Choose the **Close** button and enter the name **Overhead Door Frame** in the **Name and Color** rollout.

4. Make sure *Overhead Door Frame* is selected and then choose the **Modify** tab in the **Command Panel**. Select **Extrude** in the **Modifier List** drop-down list under the **OBJECT-SPACE MODIFIERS** section. In the **Parameters** rollout for the modifier, set the value **0'8"(0.203m)** in the **Amount** spinner. Also, make sure the **Generate Mapping Coords** check box is selected at the bottom of the rollout.

5. Activate the Top viewport and enter **0'1"(0.025)** in the **Y**-coordinate axis to move frame up so that it is centered on the wall; *Overhead Door Frame* is created and positioned, as shown in Figure P3-8.

Next, you will create the overhead door by using the **Line** tool.

Figure P3-8 Overhead Door Frame created and positioned

6. Activate the Front viewport and then choose **Create > Shapes** in the **Command Panel**. Next, invoke the **Line** tool from the **Object Type** rollout.

7. In the **Keyboard Entry** rollout, enter the following values. Choose the **Add Point** button after entering each set of coordinates:

    X: **2'0"(0.61m)**   Y: **0'**   Z: **0'**
    X: **2'0"(0.61m)**   Y: **7'0"(2.134m)**   Z: **0'**
    X: **18'0"(5.486m)**   Y: **7'0"(2.134m)**   Z: **0'**
    X: **18'0"(5.486m)**   Y: **0'**   Z: **0'**

8. Choose the **Close** button. In the **Name and Color** rollout, enter **Overhead Door**.

9. Make sure *Overhead Door* is selected and then choose the **Modify** tab in the **Command Panel**. Select **Extrude** in the **Modifier List** drop-down list under the **OBJECT-SPACE MODIFIERS** section. In the **Parameters** rollout for the modifier, set the value **0'4"(0.102m)** the **Amount** spinner. Also, make sure the **Generate Mapping Coords** check box is selected at the bottom of the rollout.

10. Activate the Top viewport and move *Overhead Door* down 0'1"(0.025m) so that it is centered on the wall. Alternatively, you can enter the same value in the **Y**-coordinate axis.

    Overhead Door is created and positioned, as shown in Figure P3-9.

Figure P3-9 *Overhead Door created and positioned*

Creating the Roof

The roof overhangs the garage walls by 1'0"(0.304m) on each side. The length of the flat edge of the roof is 24'0"(7.3152m) and the angled lines are both 12'0"(3.658m) in the X and Y axis. Since the garage is a square, one-quarter of the roof can be created and then copied by using the **Array** command.

1. Make sure the Top viewport is active and then invoke the **Zoom Extents** tool to zoom in the objects.

2. Choose **Create > Shapes** in the **Command Panel**. Invoke the **Line** tool from the **Object Type** rollout.

3. Expand the **Keyboard Entry** rollout and enter the following values. Choose the **Add Point** button after entering each set of coordinates:

    X: **–1'0"(–0.305m)**   Y: **–1'0"(–0.305m)**   Z: **8'0"(2.438m)**
    X: **11'0"(3.353m)**   Y: **11'0"(3.353m)**   Z: **8'0"(2.438m)**
    X: **23'0"(7.01m)**   Y: **–1'0"(–0.305m)**   Z: **8'0"(2.438m)**

4. Choose the **Close** button. In the **Name and Color** rollout, enter **Roof Section01**.

5. Make sure *Roof Section01* is selected and then choose the **Modify** tab in the **Command Panel**. Select **Extrude** in the **Modifier List** drop-down list under the **OBJECT-SPACE MODIFIERS** section. In the **Parameters** rollout for the modifier, enter the value **0'6"(0.152m)** in the **Amount** spinner. Also, make sure the **Generate Mapping Coords** check box is selected at the bottom of the rollout.

Roof Section01 is created, as shown in Figure P3-10.

Figure P3-10 *Roof Section01 created*

Next, you will add the slope to the roof to modify the vertices at the center of the roof. By moving these vertices straight up, the peak is added to the roof.

6. Make sure *Roof Section01* is selected and the **Modify** tab in the **Command Panel** is chosen. Select **Edit Mesh** in the **Modifier List** drop-down list under the **OBJECT-SPACE MODIFIERS** section.

7. In the **Selection** rollout for the modifier, choose the **Vertex** button; a **Vertex** sub-object mode is activated.

8. In the Top viewport, select the vertices at the center of the roof (top of the triangle) using the marque selection.

9. Right-click on the **Select and Move** tool; the **Move Transform Type-In** dialog box is displayed.

10. Set the value **4'0"(1.21m)** in the **Offset:Screen Z** text box in the **Move Transform Type-In** dialog box and press the ENTER key; the peak of the roof is moved, as shown in Figure 3-11.

11. In the **Selection** rollout, choose the **Vertex** button to exit the sub-object mode. Now, close the **Move Transform Type-In** dialog box.

Figure P3-11 *The peak of Roof Section01 moved*

The roof consists of a trim board or fascia running around the edge and it shingles on the top. You can apply two materials to create this effect in one of the two ways. Either you can use a multi/sub-object material and the material modifier or you can detach a face of the *Roof Section01* object so that different materials can be directly assigned to the roof and the detached face. You will use the second method in this section.

12. Make sure *Roof Section01* is selected and the **Modify** tab is chosen in the **Command Panel**.

13. In the **Selection** rollout, choose the **Polygon** button; the **Polygon** sub-object mode is activated. In this sub-object mode, you can detach faces.

14. Select the front face of *Roof Section01* in the Front viewport; it is displayed in red and the front face of *Roof Section01* is selected, as shown in Figure P3-12.

15. In the **Edit Geometry** rollout, choose the **Detach** button; the **Detach** dialog box is displayed, as shown in Figure P3-13. Enter the name **Fascia01** and choose the **OK** button.

The selected face is now a separate object in the scene.

16. In the **Selection** rollout, choose the **Polygon** button again to exit the sub-object mode.

Next, you will use the **Array** command to complete the roof. Before creating the array, you need to adjust the pivot point of the roof and fascia.

Figure P3-12 *The front face of the Roof Section01 selected*

17. Select *Roof Section01* and *Fascia01* in the Top viewport. Next, choose the **Hierarchy** tab in the **Command Panel**. Make sure the **Pivot** button is active and then choose the **Affect Pivot Only** button in the **Adjust Pivot** rollout.

Figure P3-13 *The **Detach** dialog box*

18. Invoke the **Align** tool and then select *Roof Section01*; the **Align Selection (Roof Section01)** dialog box is displayed.

19. In this dialog box, make sure the **Pivot Point** radio button is selected in the **Current Object** area. Also, in the **Target Object** area, make sure the **Maximum** radio button is selected. At the top of the dialog box, select the **Y Position** check box. Next, choose the **OK** button; the pivot point of each object is now at the top point of the roof.

20. Choose the **Affect Pivot Only** button again to exit the pivot mode.

21. Make sure the **Use Pivot Point Center** tool is activated in the Pivot Point flyout from the **Main Toolbar**.

22. Make sure *Roof Section01* and *Fascia01* are selected. Next, choose **Tools > Array** from the menu bar; the **Array** dialog box is displayed, as shown in Figure P3-14.

*Figure P3-14 The **Array** dialog box*

23. Choose the **Reset All Parameters** button to restore the default values in this dialog box.

24. In the **Incremental** area, set the value **90** in the **Z** column corresponding to the **Rotate** row. Make sure the **Re-Orient** check box located on the right of the **Rotate** row is selected.

25. In the **Array Dimensions** area, make sure the **1D** radio button is selected. Next, set the value **4** in the **Count** column. Also, make sure the **Instance** radio button in the **Type of Object** area is selected and then choose the **OK** button; the array is created to complete the roof, as shown in Figure P3-15.

Adding Lights and Camera

In this section, two spotlights and one omni light will be used to illuminate the scene. In addition to it, a camera will be used to control the movement of objects and set an angle of view in the Perspective viewport.

1. Activate the Top viewport and zoom out to make more space available for placing the lights and camera.

2. Choose **Create > Lights** in the **Command Panel**. Select **Standard** from the drop-down list and then invoke the **Omni** tool from the **Object Type** rollout.

3. Select a point outside and above the back wall of the garage, refer to Figure P3-16.

4. Invoke the **Target Spot** tool from the **Object Type** rollout. Select a point near the lower-right corner of the Top viewport and drag the target to the center of the garage.

Figure P3-15 *The array created to complete the roof*

5. Place another spotlight by selecting a point in the lower-left corner of the Top viewport and dragging the target to the center of the garage.

6. Activate the Front Viewport. Next, invoke the **Select and Move** tool and move the lights to their approximate positions, as shown in Figure P3-16.

Figure P3-16 *The lights displayed and positioned in all viewports*

7. Choose **Create > Cameras** in the **Command Panel**. Next, invoke the **Target** tool from the **Object Type** rollout.

8. In the Top viewport, click at some point near the lower-right corner to place the camera and drag the target to the center of the garage.

9. Activate the Perspective viewport and press the C key; the Perspective viewport switches to the Camera001 viewport.

10. Invoke the **Zoom Extents All** tool to zoom the objects to their extents.

11. Use the **Truck Camera**, **Orbit Camera**, and **Field-of-View** tools and move the camera until an appropriate view is displayed in the Camera001 viewport, as shown in Figure P3-17.

Figure P3-17 *The view displayed in the Camera001 viewport*

Creating Material Library

In this section, you will create a new material library. All materials that you create will be stored in the new material library.

1. Choose **Rendering > Material Editor > Compact Material Editor** from the **Main Toolbar**; the **Material Editor** dialog box is displayed.

2. Choose the **Get Material** button in the **Material Editor** dialog box; the **Material/Map** **Browser** dialog box is displayed.

3. Choose the **Material/Map Browser Options** button from the **Material/Map Browser** dialog box; the Material/Map Browser Options flyout is displayed.

4.   Choose **New Material Library** from the Material/Map Browser Options flyout; the **Create New Material Library** dialog box is displayed.

5.   Enter **Project03** as the new name for the material library and choose the **Save** button; the new material library **Project03** is created in the **Material/Map Browser**.

6.   Close the **Material/Map Browser** dialog box to return to the **Material Editor** dialog box.

Next, you will create frame and trim material.

Creating Frame and Trim Material

In this section, you will create frame and trim material by using the **Material Editor** dialog box.

1.   Make sure the first material sample slot is selected in the **Material Editor** dialog box.

2.   In this dialog box, choose the **Arch & Design** button; the **Material/Map Browser** dialog box is displayed. Select **Standard** from the **Materials > Standard** rollout and then choose the **OK** button; the **Arch & Design** material is replaced by the **Standard** material.

3.   Select **Blinn** from the drop-down list in the **Shader Basic Parameters** rollout, if it is not already selected.

This sets the rendering characteristics of the material being created.

4.   Choose the lock button between the **Ambient** and **Diffuse** color swatches to unlock
     colors.

The ambient and diffuse color settings can now be adjusted independently.

5.   Choose the **Ambient** color swatch in the **Material Editor** dialog box; the **Color Selector: Ambient Color** dialog box is displayed. Change the color settings as given next and choose the **OK** button to close this dialog box.

     Red: **50**   Green: **50**   Blue: **50**

6.   Choose the **Diffuse** color swatch in the **Material Editor** dialog box; the **Color Selector: Diffuse Color** dialog box is displayed. Change the color settings as given next and choose the **OK** button to close this dialog box.

     Red: **230**   Green: **230**   Blue: **230**

7.   Choose the **Specular** color swatch in the **Material Editor** dialog box; the **Color Selector: Specular Color** dialog box is displayed. Change the color settings as given next and choose the **OK** button to close this dialog box.

     Red: **255**   Green: **255**   Blue: **255**

8. In the **Specular Highlights** area of the **Blinn Basic Parameters** rollout, set the value **25** in the **Specular Level** spinner and **5** in the **Glossiness** spinner.

9. Enter the name **Frame and Trim** in the material name drop-down list located below the material sample slots and then press the ENTER key.

10. Choose the **Put to Library** button in the **Material Editor** dialog box; a flyout is displayed.

11. Choose **Project03.mat** from the flyout; the **Put To Library** dialog box is displayed and the name **Frame and Trim** appears in the text box of the **Put To Library** dialog box.

12. Choose the **OK** button; the current material is assigned the name *Frame and Trim* and added to the material library.

Next, you will create window glass material.

Creating Window Glass Material

In this section, you will create the window glass material for the window by using the **Material Editor** dialog box.

1. Select the next unused sample in the **Material Editor** dialog box and then enter the name **Glass** in the material name drop-down list.

2. Change the **Arch & Design** material to the **Standard** type, as discussed earlier.

3. Select **Blinn** from the drop-down list in the **Shader Basic Parameters** rollout, if it is not already selected.

4. Unlock the **Ambient** and **Diffuse** color swatches, if required.

5. Choose the **Ambient** color swatch; the **Color Selector: Ambient Color** dialog box is displayed. Change the color settings as given below:

   Red: **15**   Green: **15**   Blue: **15**

6. Choose the **Diffuse** color swatch; the **Color Selector: Diffuse Color** dialog box is displayed. Change the color settings as given below:

   Red: **146**   Green: **146**   Blue: **133**

7. Choose the **Specular** color swatch; the **Color Selector: Specular Color** dialog box is displayed. Change the color settings as given below:

   Red: **255**   Green: **255**   Blue: **255**

8. In the **Specular Highlights** area, set the value **75** in the **Specular Level** spinner and **85** in the **Glossiness** spinner.

9. In the **Blinn Basic Parameters** rollout, set the value **50** in the **Opacity** spinner; a very shiny dark glass material is created.

10. Choose the **Put to Library** button in the **Material Editor** dialog box; a flyout is displayed.

11. Choose **Project03.mat** from the flyout; the **Put To Library** dialog box is displayed.

12. Accept the name **Glass** and choose the **OK** button.

Creating Texture Map Material

In this section, you will create the texture map material that can turn flat walls into brick walls with mortar joints.

1. Select the third material sample and change the **Arch & Design** material to the **Standard** type, as discussed earlier.

2. In the material name drop-down list, enter the name **Brick**. Expand the **Maps** rollout below the **Blinn Basic Parameters** rollout.

3. Choose the **Diffuse Color** map button which is currently labeled as **None**; the **Material/ Map Browser** dialog box is displayed showing the types of maps that can be added.

4. Select the **Bitmap** map from the **Maps > Standard** rollout and choose the **OK** button; the **Material/Map Browser** dialog box is closed and the **Select Bitmap Image File** dialog box is displayed. As the project folder is already set, the *images* folder of this project is displayed in the **Look in** drop-down list.

5. Select the file **Brkwea.jpg** and then choose the **Open** button.

6. In the **Coordinates** rollout for the map, make sure the **Use Real-World Scale** check box is selected. Set the value **5'8"(1.727m)** in the **Width Size** spinner and **5'0"(1.524m)** in the **Height Size** spinner.

    Since the **Use Real-World Scale** option is being used, the map should be sized according to actual measurements. Standard bricks are 0'2"(0.0508m) high and 0'8"(0.203m) long with 0'1/2"(0.0127m) of mortar between bricks. The map depicts a patch of wall, 8 bricks wide and 24 bricks tall.

7. Choose the **Go To Parent** button in the **Material Editor** dialog box; you will return to the root level in the material definition.

8. In the **Maps** rollout and choose the **Bump** map button which is currently labeled **None**; the **Material/Map Browser** dialog box is displayed. Select **Bitmap** in the **Material/Map Browser** dialog box and then choose the **OK** button; the **Select Bitmap Image File** dialog box is displayed. As the project folder is already set, the *images* folder of this project is displayed in the **Look in** drop-down list.

9. Select the file **Brkwea_bump** and then choose the **Open** button.

10. Make sure the **Use Real-World Scale** check box is selected. In the **Coordinates** rollout, set the value **5'8"(1.727m)** in the **Width Size** spinner and **5'0"(1.524m)** in the **Height Size** spinner.

    The map chosen for the bump map is a black and white version of the diffuse map, and therefore, must have the same scaling.

11. Choose the **Go to Parent** button to go back to the parent level. In the **Maps** rollout, set the value **150** in the **Bump** spinner.

    This sets the intensity of the bump map.

12. Choose the **Show Shaded Material in Viewport** button in the **Material Editor** dialog box to display the material in the viewport.

13. Choose the **Put to Library** button in the **Material Editor** dialog box; a flyout is displayed. Choose **Project03.mat** from the flyout; the **Put To Library** dialog box is displayed. Accept the name **Brick** and choose the **OK** button in the **Put To Library** dialog box.

14. Repeat this procedure to create three more texture-mapped materials using the following information for the materials. Remember to name each material and put it in the material library when completed. Select the **Use Real-World Scale** check box in the **Coordinates** rollout for each material's diffuse map. Use an instance of the diffuse map for the bump map. After defining each material, choose the **Put to Library** button to add it to the material library:

Name	Diffuse Color and Bump Maps	Bump Amount	Width/Height Size
Concrete	*GRYCON.jpg* and *GRYCON_bump.jpg*	30	**22'6"/22'(6.858m/6.706m)**
Wood	*TUTASH.jpg* and *TUTASH_bump.jpg*	60	**0'4"/0'4"(0.101m/0.101m)**
Pro Materials	*Thermal&Moisture.jpg* and *Thermal&Moisture_bump.jpg*	150	**2'0"/3'0"(0.609m/0.914m)**

Creating Multi/Sub-Object Materials to the Walls

The multi/sub-object material type allows you to apply different types of materials to a single object. Material IDs are used to control which material should be applied to which face of the object. This is very useful for architectural projects where you want the inner and outer sides of the walls to be of different materials.

The first multi/sub-object material you will create is for the walls. Each wall is divided into five elements: vertical end caps, outside wall, inside wall, top of the wall, and bottom of the wall. Therefore, this material needs five different sub-materials.

1. In the **Material Editor** dialog box, select the next unused material sample slot.

    To display more unused material samples, you can use the scroll bar. However, you can also right-click on the active material sample and choose **6 × 4 Sample Windows** from the shortcut menu. This will display more samples (24) at one time and make it easier to create the multi/sub-object material.

2. Choose the **Autodesk Solid Glass** button in the **Material Editor** dialog box; the **Material/Map Browser** dialog box is displayed. In this dialog box, choose the **Material/map Browser options** button; a flyout is displayed. Next, select **Open Material Library** from the flyout; the **Import Material Library** dialog box is displayed.

    Navigate to *C:\Program Files\Autodesk\3ds Max Design 2015\materiallibraries*

3. Select the **AecTemplates** material library and then choose the **Open** button.

4. In the **Material/Map Browser** dialog box, select the **Wall-Template (Multi/Sub-Object)** material type and then choose the **OK** button; the **Replace Material** dialog box is displayed. Select the **Discard old material** radio button and choose the **OK** button. Rename the material as **Walls**.

    The **AecTemplates** material library contains five previously created multi/sub-object materials that can be assigned to objects in the scene. The material IDs and sub-material names are preset, as shown in Figure P3-18.

5. Make sure the material sample *Walls* is active and then press and hold the mouse button on *Brick* material sample, drag to the first (top) sub-material button in the **Multi/Sub-Object Basic Parameters** rollout, and then drop it; the **Instance (Copy) Material** dialog box is displayed. Next, make sure the **Instance** radio button is selected in this dialog box and then choose the **OK** button.

    By selecting **Instance**, any changes made to the original *Brick* material is also applied to the multi/sub-object material. *Brick* material is now part of the five elements of the new material and has 1 as material ID. All parts of an object to which the material is applied that have 1 as material ID will be rendered as bricks.

6. Similarly, drag the *Brick* material sample and drop it on the second, fourth, and fifth sub-material buttons. These sub-materials have material IDs as 2, 4, and 5 respectively.

    Make sure that after each drop, you select the **Instance** radio button in the **Instance (Copy) Material** dialog box and choose the **OK** button.

7. Drag *Frame and Trim* material sample and drop it on the third sub-material button, which corresponds to the material ID **3**. Select the **Instance** radio button in the **Instance (Copy) Material** dialog box and then choose the **OK** button.

Notice how each material sample in the **Multi/Sub-Object Basic Parameters** rollout reflects the sub-material. Also, notice how the main material sample reflects the sub-material.

8. Choose the **Put to Library** button in the **Material Editor** dialog box; a flyout is displayed. Choose **Project03.mat** from the flyout; the **Put To Library** dialog box is displayed. Accept the name *Walls* and choose the **OK** button in the **Put To Library** dialog box.

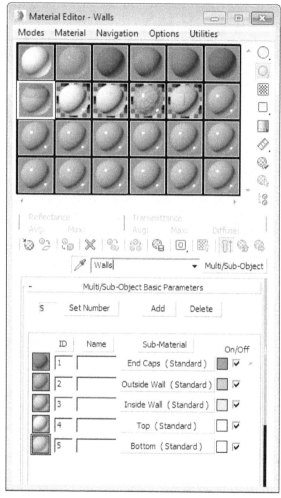

*Figure P3-18 The **Multi/Sub-Object** material created*

Creating Multi/Sub-Object Materials for the Windows

Each window is divided into five elements: front rails, back rails, panels, front frame, and back frame. Therefore, a multi/sub-object material is needed that contains five different sub-materials. This material will be created in the same way as the wall materials were created.

1. In the **Material Editor** dialog box, select the next unused material sample slot.

2. Choose the **Autodesk Ceramic** button; the **Material/Map Browser** dialog box is displayed.

3. In this dialog box, select the **Window-Template (Multi/Sub-Object)** material type from the **AecTemplates** material library and then choose the **OK** button; the **Replace Material** dialog box is displayed.

4. In the **Replace Material** dialog box, make sure the **Discard old material** radio button is selected and then choose the **OK** button.

5. Rename the material as **Windows**. With *Windows* material sample active, press and hold on *Frame and Trim* material sample, drag to the first sub-material button in the **Multi/Sub-Object Basic Parameters** rollout, and drop. The **Instance (Copy) Material** dialog box is displayed. Select the **Instance** radio button in this dialog box and then choose the **OK** button.

6. Similarly, drag *Frame and Trim* material sample and drop it on the second, fourth, and fifth sub-material buttons. These sub-materials have material IDs as 2, 4, and 5 respectively. After each drop, select the **Instance** radio button in the **Instance (Copy) Material** dialog box and then choose the **OK** button.

7. Drag *Glass* material sample and drop it on the third sub-material button, which corresponds to the material ID **3**. Select the **Instance** radio button in the **Instance (Copy) Material** dialog box and choose the **OK** button.

8. Choose the **Put to Library** button in the **Material Editor** dialog box; a flyout is displayed.

9. Choose **Project03** from the flyout; the **Put To Library** dialog box is displayed.

10. Accept the name **Windows** and choose the **OK** button in the **Put To Library** dialog box.

Creating Multi/Sub-Object Material for the Side Door

The side door is divided into five elements: front, back, inner bevel (panels), frame, and inner door. Therefore, a multi/sub-object material with five sub-materials will be created.

1. In the **Material Editor** dialog box, select the next unused material sample slot.

2. Choose the **Autodesk Wall Paint** button; the **Material/Map Browser** dialog box is displayed. In this dialog box, select **Door-Template (Multi/Sub-Object)** from the **AecTemplates** material library and then choose the **OK** button; the **Replace Material** dialog box is displayed.

3. In the **Replace Material** dialog box, make sure the **Discard old material** radio button is selected and then choose the **OK** button.

4. Rename the material as **Side Door**. Make sure *Side Door* material sample is active, press and hold the mouse button on *Wood* material sample, drag it to the first sub-material button in the **Multi/Sub-Object Basic Parameters** rollout, and drop it. The **Instance (Copy) Material** dialog box is displayed. In this dialog box, select the **Instance** radio button and then choose the **OK** button.

5. Similarly, drag *Wood* material sample and drop it on the second, third, and fifth sub-material buttons. Make sure that you select the **Instance** radio button after each drop in the **Instance (Copy) Material** dialog box and then choose the **OK** button.

6. Drag *Frame* and *Trim* material sample and drop it on the fourth sub-material button. Select the **Instance** radio button in the **Instance (Copy) Material** dialog box and choose the **OK** button.

7. Choose the **Put to Library** button in the **Material Editor**; a flyout is displayed. Choose **Project03.mat** from the flyout; the **Put To Library** dialog box is displayed.

8. Accept the name **Side Door** and choose the **OK** button in the **Put To Library** dialog box.

Saving the Material Library

The changes made in the material library must be saved or they will be lost when you exit 3ds Max Design. By saving the material library, the newly created materials will be available the next time you work in 3ds Max Design.

1. Choose the **Get Material** button in the **Material Editor** dialog box; the **Material/Map Browser** dialog box is displayed.

2. In this dialog box, right-click on the **Project03.mat** title bar; a flyout is displayed. Choose **Save** from the flyout, as shown in Figure P3-19. The material library is saved with the name **Project03**.mat.

3. Close the **Material/Map Browser** dialog box.

Applying the Materials

The materials have been created and the material library is saved. Now, the materials can be assigned to objects.

1. Select *Wall001* in any viewport and invoke the **Material Editor** dialog box from the **Main Toolbar**.

2. Make sure *Walls* material sample is active in this dialog box and then choose the **Assign Material to Selection** button.

3. Similarly, select *Wall Front* in any viewport. Make sure *Brick* material sample is active and then choose the **Assign Material to Selection** button to assign the materials on the objects in the viewport.

Figure P3-19 Saving the material library

4. Similarly, assign the following materials:

Material	Object(s)
Concrete	Floor Slab
Wood	Overhead Door
Side Door	PivotDoor001
Pro Materials	Fascia01
Frame and Trim	Roof Section01, Overhead Door Frame
Glass	SlidingWindow001, SlidingWindow002

5. Close the **Material Editor** dialog box.

Applying Mapping Coordinates

The mapping coordinates control the way the texture will appear on the object. In architectural projects, correct scaling of the texture is very important. The scale of the texture determines whether the materials (shingles or bricks, for example) look appropriate and are oversized, undersized, stretched, or squashed.

The real-world scaling option is useful in creating materials that are in proper scale to the model. With this option, you can determine the size (in drawing units) of a map. If the object on which the map is applied is larger than this size, the map appears on the object multiple times (is tiled). If the object is smaller than the size specified for the map, only a portion of the map will appear on the object. This greatly reduces the problems of poorly scaled materials. Since the materials in this model use real world scaling, they should appear realistic in the rendering.

1. Change the background color to white. Make sure the Camera01 viewport is active and then invoke the **Render Production** tool from the **Main Toolbar**; the Camera01 viewport is rendered. Since no warning dialog box appears, all objects have default mapping coordinates. However, the brick pattern on *Wall Front* needs to be properly aligned to the brick pattern on *Wall001*.

2. Close the render window. Zoom in the area where *Wall001* meets *Wall Front* in the Left viewport, as shown in Figure P3-20. Right-click on the Left viewport label and choose **Shaded** from the shortcut menu.

Figure P3-20 *Wall001 and Wall Front zoomed in the Left viewport*

3. Select *Wall Front* in the Front viewport and choose the **Modify** tab in the **Command Panel**. Select **UVW Map** in the **Modifier List** drop-down list under the **OBJECT-SPACE MODIFIERS** section.

4. In the **Alignment** area of the **Parameters** rollout, select the **Y** radio button. In the **Mapping** area, make sure the **Box** radio button is selected. Also, select the **U Tile: Flip** and **V: Tile Flip** check boxes. Render the Left viewport again.

    The brick patterns between *Wall001* and *Wall Front* are not lined up correctly, as shown in Figure P3-21. To fix this problem, the position of the **UVW Map Gizmo** must be adjusted. Adding the **UVW Map** modifier will fix the problem of the bricks at the edge of the wall.

Figure P3-21 *Pattern of Wall001 and Wall Front not lined up correctly*

5. Choose **Views > Set Active Viewport > Right** from the menu bar. Now, maximize the viewport.

6. Make sure *Wall Front* is selected and the **Modify** tab in the **Command Panel** is chosen. Expand **UVW Map** in the modifier stack by clicking on the plus sign on the left side. Select **Gizmo** in the modifier stack.

7. Invoke the **Select and Move** tool from the **Main Toolbar**. Next, look at the modifier stack. If the highlighted selection has jumped from **Gizmo** to **UVW Map**, select the **Gizmo** again. In the Right viewport, move the gizmo until the brick patterns on the two walls match up correctly, as shown in Figure P3-22. Select **Left** from the **Views** cascading menu to switch back to the Left view.

    The brick patterns displayed in the shaded viewport may get shifted slightly from the position displayed in rendering. For this reason, use the shaded viewport to get the gizmo close to the required location, and then render the Left viewport as required to precisely position the gizmo.

8. Select **UVW Map** in the modifier stack to deselect the gizmo. Right-click on the viewport label and select **Wireframe** from the shortcut menu.

9. Select the Camera001 viewport and then invoke the **Render Production** tool from the **Main Toolbar**; the **Rendered Frame** window is displayed. In this window, you will notice that all mapping coordinates in the scene now appear correct.

[+][Right][Shaded]

Brick pattern bewteen two walls match up correctly

Figure P3-22 *The brick pattern between two walls matched up correctly*

Adding Animation to the Scene

In this section, animation will be added to the scene by opening and closing the doors and one window. This will simulate the action of someone parking the car, opening the window, and leaving the garage through the side door. The first thing to be set in the animation is the number of frames.

1. Choose the **Time Configuration** button in the animation controls area; the **Time Configuration** dialog box is displayed.

2. In the **Animation** area, set the value **300** in the **Length** spinner and choose the **OK** button.

    This sets the total number of frames in the animation to 300, which is about ten seconds of animation.

Adding an Inside Light

You will now add a light inside the garage. This light will simulate the light on an automatic garage door opener. The light on the opener turns on as the door opens. Therefore, the light will be animated to appear as turning on and off.

1. Activate the Top viewport and then choose **Create > Lights** in the **Command Panel**. Make sure the **Standard** option is selected in the drop-down list. Next, invoke the **Omni** tool from the **Object Type** rollout.

2. Choose a point in the middle of the garage. In the **Name and Color** rollout, name the light as **Opener Light**. Move the light in the Front viewport upward so that it is aligned with the top of the walls, as shown in Figure P3-23.

Figure P3-23 *The light aligned on the top of walls*

3. Make sure *Opener Light* is selected and then choose the **Modify** tab in the **Command Panel**. Set the value **2** in the **Multiplier** spinner in the **Intensity/Color/Attenuation** rollout. Choose the color swatch next to the **Multiplier** spinner and set the values as given below and then choose the **OK** button:

Red: **255**   Green: **226**   Blue: **180**

The light is adjusted to give it a slight orange hue. This simulates incandescent lighting.

4. Choose **Graph Editors > Track View - Dope Sheet** from the menu bar; the **Track View-Dope Sheet** window is displayed.

5. Expand the tree for *Opener Light*. Choose the plus sign (**+**) on left side of the *Opener Light*. Next, expand the tree for the **Transform** and then **Object (Omni Light)**; you will notice that there are no animation keys in the **Track View - Dope Sheet** window.

6. Choose the **Add Keys** button on the left of the **Track View-Dope Sheet** window.

7. Choose the **Multiplier** track and insert keys at frames **0**, **65**, and **200**, refer to Figure P3-24.

8. Right-click on the first key (on frame 0); the **Opener Light\Multiplier** dialog box is displayed.

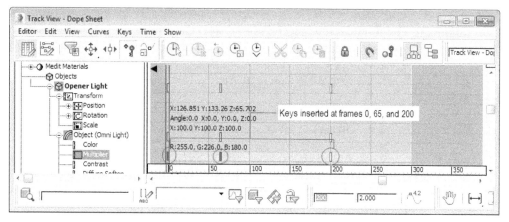

*Figure P3-24 Keys inserted at frames **0**, **65**, and **200** in the **Multiplier** track*

9. Set the value **0** in the **Value** spinner and select the square mechanical transition for the **In** and **Out** image tiles, as shown in Figure P3-25.

*Figure P3-25 The **Opener Light\Multiplier** dialog box*

10. Choose the right arrow button at the top of the **Opener Light\Multiplier** dialog box to move to the next key.

11. Make sure the **Value** spinner displays 2.0 and select the square mechanical transition for the **In** and **Out** image tiles.

12. Move to the next key (on frame **200**). Set the value **0** in the **Value** spinner and select the square mechanical transition for the **In** and **Out** image tiles.

13. Close the **Opener Light\Multiplier** dialog box and the **Track View - Dope Sheet** window.

Animating the Overhead Door

Now, the garage door opener light is created and set to turn on and off. The animation of the overhead door must work in conjunction with the light. The door should begin opening at frame 60, which is five frames before the light turns on. In addition, the door should open, pause fully opened, and then close at frame 150. In this case, the animation of door is a combination of motion and rotation. Before animation can be added, the overhead door's pivot point must be relocated.

1. Select *Overhead Door* in the Left viewport. Next, choose the **Hierarchy** tab in the **Command Panel**. Make sure the **Pivot** button is chosen. In the **Move/Rotate/Scale** area of the **Adjust Pivot** rollout, choose the **Affect Pivot Only** button.

   The pivot point is currently located in the middle of the door on the back (inside) surface.

2. Right-click on the **Select and Move** tool; the **Move Transform Type-In** dialog box is displayed.

3. In this dialog box, set the value **–3(–0.914m)** in the **Offset:Screen Y** spinner and press the ENTER key; the pivot axis is now 0'6"(0.153m) above the bottom of *Overhead Door*. Close the **Move Transform Type-In** dialog box.

4. Choose the **Affect Pivot Only** button in the **Adjust Pivot** rollout to exit the adjustment mode.

5. Choose **Graph Editors > Track View - Dope Sheet** from the menu bar; the **Track View - Dope Sheet** window is displayed.

6. In this window, choose the plus sign (**+**) on the left side of *Overhead Door* and then again choose the plus sign (**+**) on the left side of the **Transform** track; you will notice that there are no animation keys in the **Track View - Dope Sheet** window.

7. Choose the **Add Keys** button at the top of the **Track View** dialog box. Insert a key in the **Position** track at frame 60 and in the **Rotation** track at frame 60.

   These keys hold the same transform values for the door as on frame 0, or closed.

8. Close the **Track View - Dope Sheet** window.

9. Drag the time slider to frame 90 and choose the **Toggle Auto Key Mode** button to turn the animation mode on (red).

10. Make sure *Overhead Door* is selected and invoke the **Select and Rotate** tool. In the Left viewport, rotate the door 90 degrees about the local Z axis, as shown in Figure P3-26.

11. Invoke the **Select and Move** tool. In the Left viewport, move the door up 6'0"(1.82m) on the Y axis, as shown in Figure P3-27.

12. Drag the time slider to frame 150.

13. In the Left viewport, rotate the door –90° about the local Z axis. Also, move the door down –6'0"(–1.82m) on the Y axis.

14. Choose the **Toggle Auto Key Mode** button to exit the animation mode.   Auto Key

Figure P3-26 *The door rotated 90 degrees about the local Z axis*

Figure P3-27 *The door moved up 6'0"(1.82m) on the Y axis*

15. Make sure *Overhead Door* is selected. Now, select the key at frame 90 on the track bar below the time slider; the selected key turns white.

16. Hold down the SHIFT key and drag the key to frame 120. Next, release the key; the rotation key will be copied from frame 90 to frame 120.

17. Drag the time slider from the left to the right to preview the animation.

    Check if the door floats through the animation keys. Any float needs to be changed into mechanical movement.

18. Make sure *Overhead Door* is selected and then choose the **Motion** tab in the **Command Panel**. Expand the **Assign Controller** rollout. Select **Position: Position XYZ** in the tree and then choose the **Assign Controller** button at the top of the rollout; the **Assign Position Controller** dialog box is displayed.

19. Select **Linear Position** in the **Assign Position Controller** dialog box and choose the **OK** button; a linear position controller is assigned to *Overhead Door*.

20. Drag the time slider left and right to preview the animation.

    You will notice that the float in the door's movement is now corrected. Also, the door remains open from frame 90 to 120, as it should.

Animating the Window

Now, the window needs to be animated. Once the overhead door begins to close, you need to allow some time for the person to walk from the car to the window. The door begins closing at frame 121. Therefore, the window should begin opening on frame 150.

1. Select *SlidingWindow002* in any viewport and drag the time slider to frame **160**. Next, choose the **Toggle Auto Key Mode** button to turn the animation mode on (red).

2. Choose the **Modify** tab in the **Command Panel**. In the **Open Window** area of the **Parameters** rollout, set the value **100** in the **Open** spinner.

3. Choose the **Toggle Auto Key Mode** button again to exit the animation mode.

4. In the track bar below the time slider, choose the key at frame 0 and drag the key to frame 150. Next, release the key.

    Moving the key from frame 0 to frame 150 means the window will not begin to open until frame 150.

Animating the Side Door

You will now animate the side door. At this point, the person has parked the car, closed the overhead door, walked to the window, and opened it. Now, it will take some time to walk to the side door and begin opening it.

1. Select *PivotDoor001* in any viewport and drag the time slider to frame 180. Next, choose the **Toggle Auto Key Mode** button to turn the animation mode on (red).

This is the frame on which the side door should open completely.

2. Choose the **Modify** tab in the **Command Panel**, if it is not chosen. In the **Parameters** rollout, enter the value **90** in the **Open** spinner; the side door is now open 90 degrees.

3. Drag the **Time Slider** to frame 220.

4. In the **Parameters** rollout, enter the value **0** in the **Open** spinner; the side door is now closed.

5. Choose the **Toggle Auto Key Mode** button to exit the animation mode.

6. In the track bar below the time slider, choose the key at frame 0 and drag the key to frame 175. Next, release the key.

Moving the key means the door will not begin to open till frame 175.

Rendering the Animation

In this section, you will render the final animation to see the finished project. The final animation will show all materials, highlights, shadows, and lighting.

1. Make the Camera01 viewport active and choose **Rendering > Render Setup** from the menu bar or invoke the **Render Setup** tool from the **Main Toolbar**; the **Render Setup: NVIDIA mental ray** dialog box is displayed.

2. In the **Time Output** area of the **Common Parameters** rollout, select the **Active Time Segment** radio button to make it active.

This sets all the active frames in the animation to be rendered.

3. In the **Output Size** area of the dialog box, choose the **320×240** button.

This sets the animation to be rendered at a resolution of 320 × 240 pixels.

4. In the **Render Output** area of the dialog box, choose the **Files** button; the **Render Output File** dialog box is displayed. As the project folder is already set, the *renderoutput* folder of this project is displayed in the **Save as type** drop-down list.

5. Enter **Project03** in the **File name** text box.

6. Select **AVI File (*.avi)** from the **Save as type** drop-down list and choose the **Save** button; the **AVI File Compression Setup** dialog box is displayed if this file type has not been saved during the current drawing session. This dialog box allows you to adjust the quality and keyframe rate of the animation.

7. Choose the **OK** button to accept the default AVI settings and then choose the **Render** button to start rendering.

8. When the rendering of animation is done, close the render window and the **Render Setup:NVIDIA mental ray** dialog box. Figure P3-28 shows the rendered image at last frame.

Figure P3-28 *The rendered image at last frame*

9. Choose **Rendering > View Image File** from the menu bar; the **View File** dialog box is displayed.

10. Select the **Project03.avi** and choose the **Open** button; the animation file is opened and played in Windows Media Player.

11. Close Windows Media Player and save the completed scene.

Project 4

Corporate Design Project

PROJECT DESCRIPTION

This project guides you through the creation of the model of a logo. You will create the columns and floor slab. You will also create horn shapes and text. You will then apply materials to the objects to make them look realistic. In addition to this, you will create lights to illuminate the logo. Finally, you will animate the lights and render the animation, as shown in Figure P4-1. The procedures used can be applied to any corporate design project.

Creating the Project Folder

Create a new project folder with the name *Prj_4* at *\Documents\3dsmaxdesign 2015* and then save the file with the name *Prj4*, as discussed in Tutorial 1 of Chapter 2.

Downloading the Files

Before starting the project, you need to download the *prj4_3dsmaxdesign_2015.zip* file from *www.cadcim.com*. The path of the file is as follows: *Textbooks > Animation and Visual Effects > 3ds Max Design > Autodesk 3ds Max Design 2015: A Tutorial Approach*

Extract the contents of the zip file to *Documents*. Open Windows Explorer and browse to *\Documents\prj4_3dsmaxdesign_2015* and then copy all files to *\Documents\3dsmaxdesign 2015\ Prj4\sceneassets\images*.

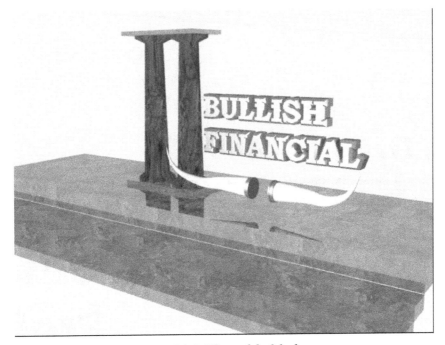

Figure P4-1 *The model of the logo*

Changing the Units Setting

In this section, you will change the units with which you are working. Since the measurement in this project is in inches, you will set the units to decimal inches.

1. Choose **Customize > Units Setup** from the menu bar; the **Units Setup** dialog box is displayed.

2. In the **Display Unit Scale** area, select the **US Standard** radio button and then select the **Decimal Inches** from the drop-down list below this radio button, as shown in Figure P4-2. Choose the **OK** button to apply the settings and close the dialog box. If you want to work in the metric unit system, select the **Metric** radio button from the **Display Unit Scale** area of the **Units Setup** dialog box. Also, make sure the **Meters** option is selected in the drop-down list below the **Metric** radio button.

3. Right-click on the **Snaps Toggle** tool; the **Grid and Snap Settings** dialog box is displayed. Choose the **Home Grid** tab in the dialog box.

4. In the **Grid Dimensions** area, set the value **1(0.3m)** in the **Grid Spacing** spinner. Next, select the **All Viewports** radio button from the **Dynamic Update** area and close the dialog box.

Figure P4-2 *The* **Units Setup** *dialog box*

Creating the Column

In many designs, 2D shapes are used as the building blocks for creating 3D objects in a scene. In this project, the column will be created as a shape to be lofted along a path to give it a proper height. You will first create the circle shape and then the line path.

1. Activate the Top viewport and then choose **Create > Shapes** in the **Command Panel**. Next, invoke the **Circle** tool from the **Object Type** rollout.

2. Expand the **Keyboard Entry** rollout and set the value **19(0.483m)** in the **Radius** spinner. Next, choose the **Create** button; the circle for the column is created. In the **Name and Color** rollout, enter **Column Shape**.

3. Invoke the **Line** tool from the **Object Type** rollout. Make sure the **Corner** radio button is selected in the **Initial Type** area of the **Creation Method** rollout.

4. Expand the **Keyboard Entry** rollout and set the values in the spinners as given next:

    X: **0**   Y: **0**   Z: **0**

5. Choose the **Add Point** button and set the values again in the spinners as given next:

    X: **0**   Y: **0**   Z: **140(3.556m)**

6. Choose the **Add Point** button and then choose the **Finish** button; the path for the column is created.

7. In the **Name and Color** rollout, enter **Column Path**.

Lofting the Column

Now that the path and shape are created, the column can be lofted. Once the loft object is created, a scale deformation will be added to control the shape of the column. To do so, the path needs more vertices. These extra vertices will be used to give the desired shape to the column.

1. Make sure *Column Path* is selected and then choose **Create > Geometry** in the **Command Panel**. Next, select **Compound Objects** in the drop-down list displayed below the **Geometry** button.

2. Invoke the **Loft** tool from the **Object Type** rollout. Expand the **Skin Parameters** rollout and set the value **10** in the **Shape Steps** spinner.

3. In the **Creation Method** rollout, choose the **Get Shape** button and select *Column Shape* in any viewport; a column is created. Next, in the **Name and Color** rollout, enter **Column01**.

4. Make sure *Column01* is selected and choose the **Modify** tab in the **Command Panel**. Expand the **Deformations** rollout and then choose the **Scale** button; the **Scale Deformation(X)** dialog box is displayed. In this dialog box, the line representing the scale of the column will be modified by adding points at different positions.

5. Choose the **Insert Corner Point** button at the top of the **Scale Deformation(X)** dialog box.

6. Insert points at 2, 5, 95, and 98. Next, choose the **Scale Control Point** button and move the point at 5 to 70% and the point at 95 to 50%, as shown in Figure P4-3. Close the **Scale Deformation(X)** dialog box.

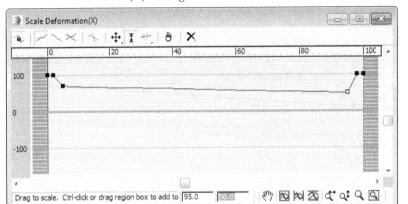

Figure P4-3   *The* **Scale Deformation(X)** *dialog box after scaling at different points*

The lofted object is scaled using the **Scale Deformation(X)** dialog box.

7. Invoke the **Zoom Extents All** tool to zoom the object to its extent. *Column01* is modified using the **Scale Deformation(X)** dialog box, as shown in Figure P4-4. The effects of the scale deformation on the column are clearly visible.

Figure P4-4   *Column01 modified using the* **Scale Deformation(X)** *dialog box*

Creating the Bottom and the Top for the Column

You will now create a box which will act as the base plate under the column. This box will be copied for the top plate of the column.

1. Make sure the Top viewport is activated and then choose **Create > Geometry** in the **Command Panel**. Select **Standard Primitives** in the drop-down list displayed below the **Geometry** button. Next, invoke the **Box** tool from the **Object Type** rollout.

2. Expand the **Keyboard Entry** rollout and set the values in the spinners as given next:

   Length: **45(1.143m)**   Width: **45(1.143m)**   Height: **–4(–0.102m)**

3. Choose the **Create** button; the base plate of the column is created. In the **Name and Color** rollout, enter **Column01Base**. Right-click to exit the tool.

4. Make sure *Column01Base* is selected and choose **Edit > Clone** from the menu bar; the **Clone Options** dialog box is displayed. In this dialog box, select the **Copy** radio button in the **Object** area. Enter **Column01Top** in the **Name** text box and choose the **OK** button; a copy of *Column01Base* is created with the name *Column01Top*.

5. Make sure *Column01Top* is selected. Next, invoke the **Align** tool from the **Main Toolbar**; the shape of the cursor changes. Now, select *Column01* in the Front viewport; the **Align Selection (Column 01)** dialog box is displayed. In this dialog box, select only the **Y Position** check box if it is not already selected. Select the **Minimum** radio button in the **Current Object** area and the **Maximum** radio button in the **Target Object** area. Next, choose the **OK** button; the bottom of *Column01Top* is aligned with the top of *Column01*, as shown in Figure P4-5.

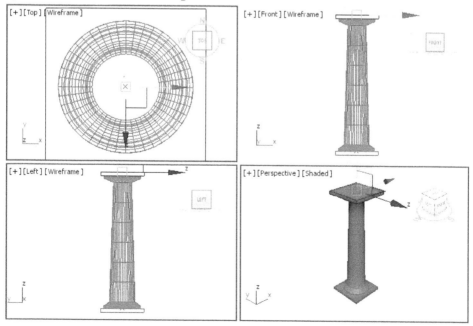

Figure P4-5 *Column01Top is aligned with the top of Column01*

Copying the Column

In this section, you will create and move a copy of the column assembly. To make this easier, you will group the first column with its base and top.

1. Select *Column01*, *Column01Base*, and *Column01Top* in any viewport.

2. Choose **Group > Group** from the menu bar; the **Group** dialog box is displayed. Enter **Column01Assembly** in the **Group name** text box. Next, choose the **OK** button.

3. Create a copy of *Column01Assembly* as discussed earlier. Rename it as **Column02 Assembly**.

4. Activate the Top viewport. Next, right-click on the **Select and Move** tool; the **Move Transform Type-In** dialog box is displayed.

5. In the **Offset: Screen** area of this dialog box, set the value **–45(–1.143)** in the **X** spinner; the edges of the column bases are aligned. Next, close the dialog box; *Column02 Assembly* is displayed, as shown in Figure P4-6. Invoke the **Zoom Extents All** tool to zoom the objects to their extents.

Figure P4-6 Column02 Assembly created

Creating the Horns

Now, you will create a horn by lofting a shape along a path. Next, you will mirror it to create the other horn.

1. Activate the Left viewport and choose **Create > Shapes** in the **Command Panel**. Next, invoke the **Circle** tool in the **Object Type** rollout.

2. Expand the **Keyboard Entry** rollout and set the value **8(0.203m)** in the **Radius** spinner. Choose the **Create** button; a circle is created, which is the cross-section for the horn. In the **Name and Color** rollout, enter **Horn Shape**.

3. Activate the Front viewport and then invoke the **Line** tool from the **Object Type** rollout.

4. Select the **Smooth** radio button in the **Initial Type** area of the **Creation Method** rollout.

5. Expand the **Keyboard Entry** rollout and set the values as given next. Choose the **Add Point** button after entering each set of XYZ coordinates.

X: **95(2.413m)**	Y: **15(0.381m)**	Z: **35(0.889m)**
X: **65(1.651m)**	Y: **15(0.381m)**	Z: **35(0.889m)**
X: **45(1.143m)**	Y: **15(0.381m)**	Z: **40(1.016m)**
X: **25(0.635m)**	Y: **25(0.635m)**	Z: **50(1.27m)**
X: **15(0.381m)**	Y: **45(1.143m)**	Z: **52(1.321m)**

6. Choose the **Finish** button; the path for the horn is created, as shown in Figure P4-7.

Figure P4-7 *The path created for the left-hand horn*

7. In the **Name and Color** rollout, enter **Horn Path**. Invoke the **Zoom Extents All Selected** tool to zoom the objects to their extents.

Lofting the Horn

After the path and shape are created, the first horn can be lofted. Once the loft object is created, its shape will be modified.

1. Make sure *Horn Path* is selected and choose **Create > Geometry** in the **Command Panel**. Next, select **Compound Objects** from the drop-down list. Invoke the **Loft** tool from the **Object Type** rollout.

2. Expand the **Skin Parameters** rollout and make sure the value **10** is entered in the **Shape Steps** spinner.

3. In the **Creation Method** rollout, choose the **Get Shape** button. Next, select *Horn Shape* in any viewport; the horn is lofted. In the **Name and Color** rollout, enter **Horn-Left**.

4. Make sure *Horn-Left* is selected and then choose the **Modify** tab in the **Command Panel**. In the **Deformations** rollout, choose the **Scale** button; the **Scale Deformation(X)** dialog box is displayed.

5. Make sure the **Move Control Point** button is chosen at the top of the **Scale Deformation(X)** dialog box.

6. Select (highlight) the control point at **100** (the right-hand control point). Enter **0** in the text box at the bottom right of the **Scale Deformation(X)** dialog box to move the control point down to 0%. Close the dialog box.

    Horn-Left is modified using the **Scale Deformation(X)** dialog box, refer to Figure P4-8.

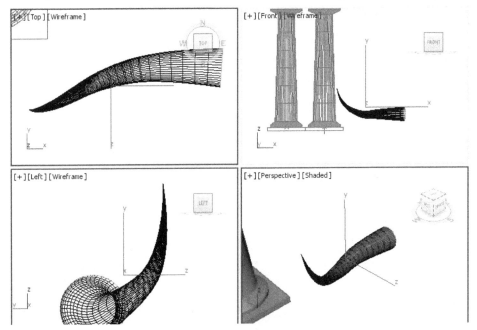

Figure P4-8 *Horn-Left modified using the **Scale Deformation(X)** dialog box*

7. Invoke the **Zoom Extents All** tool; the effects of the scale deformation on the horn are clearly visible.

Creating the Endcap for the Horn

You need to create two cylinders to represent the endcap for the horn. The parts for the endcap and the horn will be grouped together, so that they can be mirrored.

1. Activate the Left viewport and then choose **Create > Geometry** in the **Command Panel**.

2. Select **Standard Primitives** in the drop-down list below the **Geometry** button. Next, invoke the **Cylinder** tool from the **Object Type** rollout.

3. In the **Parameters** rollout, set the value **1** in the **Height Segments** spinner. Also, set the value **24** in the **Sides** spinner.

   Since the cylinder will not be modified, it should be created with a single height segment. This reduces the overall face count of the model. However, if modifiers are to be applied to the object, it may be necessary to increase the height segments to achieve the desired results.

4. Expand the **Keyboard Entry** rollout and set the values as given next:

   X: **35(0.889m)**   Y: **15(0.381m)**   Z: **–95(–2.413m)**
   Radius: **9(0.229m)**   Height: **–1(–0.025m)**

5. Choose the **Create** button; the cylinder is created. In the **Name and Color** rollout, enter **Cap-Left01**.

6. Create the second cylinder by setting the following values in the **Keyboard Entry** rollout:

   X: **35(0.889m)**   Y: **15(0.381m)**   Z: **–95(–2.413m)**
   Radius: **8.5(0.216m)**   Height: **3(0.076m)**

7. Choose the **Create** button; another cylinder is created. In the **Name and Color** rollout, enter **Cap-Left02**. Next, right-click to exit the tool.

8. Select *Horn-Left*, *Cap-Left01*, and *Cap-Left02*. Next, choose **Group > Group** from the menu bar; the **Group** dialog box is displayed. Enter **HornAssemblyLeft** in the **Group Name** text box. Then, choose the **OK** button; *HornAssemblyLeft* is created, as shown in Figure P4-9.

Figure P4-9 *HornAssemblyLeft created*

Mirroring the Horn Assembly

Now, you will mirror the left horn assembly to create the right horn assembly.

1. Activate the Front viewport.

2. Make sure *HornAssemblyLeft* is selected and then invoke the **Mirror** tool; the **Mirror:Screen Coordinates** dialog box is displayed.

3. In the **Mirror: Screen Coordinates** dialog box, select the **Copy** radio button in the **Clone Selection** area. Set the value **100(2.54m)** in the **Offset** spinner in the **Mirror Axis** area. Also, make sure the **X** radio button is selected in the **Mirror Axis** area. Next, choose the **OK** button to create the mirrored copy.

4. In the **Name and Color** rollout, enter **HornAssemblyRight**.

5. Invoke the **Zoom Extents All** tool to zoom the objects to their extents.

Creating the Text

The text is created as a 2D shape and it will be lofted along a straight line path. The text will be lofted, as opposed to extruded, so that its shape can be refined using a deformation.

1. Make sure the Front viewport is activated and then choose **Create > Shapes** in the **Command Panel**. Next, invoke the **Text** tool from the **Object Type** rollout.

2. In the **Parameters** rollout, select **Bookman Old Style Bold** from the list of available fonts in the drop-down list at the top of the rollout. Next, set the value **30(0.762m)** in the **Size** spinner.

3. Enter **BULLISH** in the **Text** text box. Press the ENTER key and then enter **FINANCIAL** in the second line.

4. Click anywhere in the Front viewport to place the text; the text is displayed as a single object, refer to Figure P4-10.

Figure P4-10 *The text displayed as a single object*

5. In the **Name and Color** rollout, enter **Text Shape**.

6. Activate the Top viewport and invoke the **Line** tool from the **Object Type** rollout.

7. In the **Initial Type** area of the **Creation Method** rollout, make sure the **Corner** radio button is selected.

8. Expand the **Keyboard Entry** rollout and set the value in the spinners as given next:

    X: **0**   Y: **0**   Z: **0**

9. Choose the **Add Point** button and set the values in the spinners as given next:

    X: **0**   Y: **16(0.406m)**   Z: **0**

10. Choose the **Add Point** button and then the **Finish** button; a line is created. In the **Name and Color** rollout, enter **Text Path**. Next, right-click in the viewport to exit the tool.

Lofting the Text

In this section, you will loft the text by using the lofting technique.

1. Select *Text Shape* in any viewport and then choose **Create > Geometry** in the **Command Panel**. Next, select **Compound Objects** in the drop-down list.

2. Invoke the **Loft** tool from the **Object Type** rollout. Next, expand the **Skin Parameters** rollout and set the value **0** in the **Shape Steps** spinner.

3. In the **Creation Method** rollout, choose the **Get Path** button. Select *Text Path* from the **Scene Explorer**; the logo text is lofted, as shown in Figure P4-11.

Figure P4-11 *The logo text lofted*

4. In the **Name and Color** rollout, enter **Logo Text**.

Modifying the Shape of the Text

In this section, you will add a bevel deformation to control the shape of the text.

1. Make sure *Logo Text* is selected and then choose the **Modify** tab in the **Command Panel**. In the **Deformations** rollout, choose the **Bevel** button; the **Bevel Deformation** dialog box is displayed.

2. Choose the **Insert Corner Point** button at the top of the **Bevel Deformation** dialog box and insert control points at 20 and 80.

3. Choose the **Move Control Point** button. Next, press and hold the CTRL key and select the newly inserted control points. Next, enter **–2.0** in the text box at the bottom right of the dialog box; the text is beveled, as shown in Figure P4-12.

Figure P4-12 A bevel deformation applied to Logo Text and the text centered over the horns

4. Close the dialog box and invoke the **Zoom Extents All** tool to zoom the objects to their extents.

Positioning the Text

In this section, you will move the text to a proper position.

1. Make sure the Front viewport is active. Invoke the **Select and Move** tool and then move the text so that it is placed approximately at the center in the space between the horns.

2. In the Top viewport, move the text so that it is centered above the portion of the horns that has the largest diameter.

3. Choose the **Display** tab in the **Command Panel**. Next, in the **Hide by Category** rollout, select the **Shapes** check box; the shapes are now hidden. Invoke the **Zoom** **Extents All** tool; the text is centered over the horns, refer to Figure P4-12.

Creating the Floor and Steps

In this section, you will create boxes to represent the floor and steps. A box will be created for the first step and then it will be copied to add the rest of the steps.

1. Choose **Create > Geometry** in the **Command Panel**.

2. Select **Standard Primitives** in the drop-down list below the **Geometry** button, if it is not selected. Next, invoke the **Box** tool from the **Object Type** rollout.

3. Expand the **Keyboard Entry** rollout and set the value **–4(–0.102m)** in the **Z** spinner. Next, set the values in other spinners as given next:

    Length: **150(3.81m)**   Width: **500(12.7m)**   Height: **–20(–0.508m)**

4. Next, choose the **Create** button; the box is created. In the **Name and Color** rollout, enter **Floor**.

5. Create another box, as discussed earlier. Expand the **Keyboard Entry** rollout and set the value **–85(–2.159m)** in the **Y** spinner and **–24(–0.61m)** in the **Z** spinner.

6. Next, set the values in other spinners as given next:

    Length: **20(0.508m)**   Width: **500(12.7m)**   Height: **10(0.254m)**

7. Choose the **Create** button; the first step is created. In the **Name and Color** rollout, enter **Stairs01**.

8. Create two copies of *Stairs01*, as discussed earlier, and name them **Stairs02** and **Stairs03**. Now, align the stairs in all viewports, as shown in Figure P4-13.

Figure P4-13 The floor and three stairs created and aligned

Assigning Materials

The creation of materials and texture maps will give this scene its needed detail. Texture mapping will turn the steps, base, and column into marble and the text into shiny gold. This project needs four materials, which will be stored in a new material library.

1. Choose **Rendering > Material Editor > Compact Material Editor** from the menu bar; the **Material Editor** dialog box is displayed.

2. In this dialog box, choose the **Get Material** button; the **Material/Map Browser** dialog box is displayed.

3. Choose the **Material/Map Browser Options** button from the **Material/Map Browser** dialog box; the **Material/Map Browser Options** flyout is displayed. Select **New Material Library** from the flyout; the **Create New Material Library** dialog box is displayed.

4. Enter **Project04** as the new name for the material library. Choose the **Save** button; the new material library *Project04.mat* is created and displayed in the **Material/Map Browser** dialog box.

5. Close the **Material/Map Browser** dialog box to return to the **Material Editor** dialog box.

Creating the Shiny Gold Material

In this section, you will create the shiny gold material for the objects by using the **Material Editor** dialog box.

1. Make sure the first material sample slot is active in the **Material Editor** dialog box. Next, choose the **Arch & Design** button to change the material type; the **Material/Map Browser** dialog box is displayed.

2. Select **Standard** from the **Materials > Standard** rollouts and then choose the **OK** button; the **Arch & Design** material is replaced by the **Standard** material. Also, various rollouts are displayed in the **Material Editor** dialog box to modify the **Standard** material.

3. In the **Shader Basic Parameters** rollout, select **Metal** from the drop-down list.

    This sets the rendering characteristics of the material being created.

4. In the **Metal Basic Parameters** rollout, choose the Lock button located between the **Ambient** and **Diffuse** color swatches to unlock the colors; the ambient and diffuse color settings can now be adjusted independently.

5. Choose the **Ambient** color swatch; the **Color Selector: Ambient Color** dialog box is displayed. In this dialog box, set the values as given next and then choose the **OK** button.

    Red: **25**   Green: **15**   Blue: **10**

6. Choose the **Diffuse** color swatch in the **Material Editor** dialog box; the **Color Selector: Diffuse Color** dialog box is displayed. In this dialog box, set the color values as given next and then choose the **OK** button.

   Red: **160**   Green: **135**   Blue: **30**

7. In the **Specular Highlights** area of the **Metal Basic Parameters** rollout, set the color value **80** in the **Specular Level** spinner. Set the value **75** in the **Glossiness** spinner.

8. In the **Material Name** drop-down list, enter **Gold** and press the ENTER key.

9. Choose the **Put to Library** button in the **Material Editor** dialog box; a flyout is displayed.

10. Choose **Project04.mat** from the flyout; the **Put to Library** dialog box is displayed and the name **Gold** appears in the **Name** text box. Choose the **OK** button; the current material is assigned the name *Gold* and added to the **Project04** material library.

Creating the Ivory Material

In this section, you will create the ivory material for the objects.

1. Select the next unused sample slot in the **Material Editor** dialog box. Choose the **Arch & Design** button to change the material type; the **Material/Map Browser** dialog box is displayed.

2. Select **Standard** from the **Materials > Standard** rollout and then choose the **OK** button; the **Arch & Design** material is replaced by the **Standard** material. Also, various rollouts are displayed in the **Material Editor** dialog box to modify the **Standard** material.

3. In the **Material Name** drop-down list, enter **Ivory** and press the ENTER key.

4. In the **Shader Basic Parameters** rollout, select **Blinn** in the drop-down list, if it is not already selected.

5. In the **Blinn Basic Parameters** rollout, unlock the **Ambient** and **Diffuse** color swatches.

6. Choose the **Ambient** color swatch; the **Color Selector: Ambient Color** dialog box is displayed. In this dialog box, set the values as given next:

   Red: **15**   Green: **16**   Blue: **0**

7. Choose the **Diffuse** color swatch; the **Color Selector: Diffuse color** dialog box is displayed. In this dialog box, set the values as given next:

   Red: **240**   Green: **240**   Blue: **220**

8. Choose the **Specular** color swatch; the **Color Selector: Specular color** dialog box is displayed. In this dialog box, set the values as given next:

Red: **255** Green: **255** Blue: **235**

Close the **Color Selector: Specular Color** dialog box.

9. In the **Specular Highlights** area, set the value **80** in the **Specular Level** spinner and **50** in the **Glossiness** spinner.

10. Choose the **Put to Library** button in the **Material Editor** dialog box; a flyout is displayed.

11. Choose **Project04.mat** from the flyout; the **Put to Library** dialog box is displayed; the name **Ivory** appears in the **Name** text box. Choose the **OK** button.

Creating the Bump Map Marble Material
In this section, you will create the bump map marble material.

1. Activate the third material sample slot in the **Material Editor** dialog box. Next, change the material **Arch & Design** to **Standard** type, as discussed earlier.

2. Expand the **Maps** rollout and then choose the **Diffuse Color** map button, currently labeled as **None**; the **Material/Map Browser** dialog box is displayed. This dialog box shows the types of maps that can be added.

3. Select the **Bitmap** map from **Maps > Standard** rollout and choose the **OK** button; the **Select Bitmap Image File** dialog box is displayed. As the project folder is already set, the *images* folder of this project is displayed in the **Look in** drop-down list of this dialog box.

4. Select the **BENEDETI.JPG** file and choose the **Open** button; the material is displayed in the sample slot.

5. In the **Coordinates** rollout, make sure the **Use Real-World Scale** check box is cleared. Also, make sure the **U: Tiling** and **V: Tiling** spinners are set to **1**.

6. Choose the **Go To Parent** button in the **Material Editor** dialog box to return to the root level.

7. In the **Maps** rollout, select the **Bump** check box and set the value **200** in the **Bump Amount** spinner to set the intensity of the bump map.

8. Choose the **Bump Map** button, currently labeled **None**; the **Material/Map Browser** dialog box is displayed.

9. Select the **Bitmap** map from **Maps > Standard** rollout and then choose the **OK** button; the **Select Bitmap Image File** dialog box is displayed. As the project folder is already set, the *images* folder of this project is displayed in the **Look in** drop-down list of this dialog box.

10. Select the **ConcreteMaterial.jpg** file and then choose the **Open** button; the material is displayed in the sample slot.

11. In the **Coordinates** rollout, make sure the **Use Real-World Scale** check box is cleared. Set the value **0.75** in the **U: Tiling** spinner and **1** in the **V: Tiling** spinner.

12. Choose the **Go To Parent** button in the **Material Editor** dialog box to return to the parent level.

13. Choose the **Put to Library** button in the **Material Editor** dialog box; a flyout is displayed. Choose **Project04.mat** from the flyout; the **Put to Library** dialog box is displayed.

14. In this dialog box, enter **Column Marble** in the **Name** text box and then choose the **OK** button.

Creating the Shiny Marble Material

Marble floors are shiny and reflect the other objects around them. Since the material defined for the columns is not reflective, a second material needs to be created for the floor and steps. This material will be very similar to the one you just created, but will appear highly polished.

1. In the **Material Editor** dialog box, click and hold the **Column Marble** material sample slot. Drag the sample to the next unused material sample slot. Then, rename the material as **Floor Marble**; a duplicate copy of the material is created.

2. Make sure the **Maps** rollout is expanded. Next, click and hold on any button labeled as **None**. Drag and drop the **None** button on top of the **Bump** map button; the bump map is cleared.

3. In the **Maps** rollout, choose the **Reflection** map button, currently labeled as **None**; the **Material/Map Browser** dialog box is displayed.

4. Select the **Reflect/Refract** map from the **Maps > Standard** rollout and choose the **OK** button.

5. Choose the **Go To Parent** button in the **Material Editor** dialog box. In the **Maps** rollout, set the value **30** in the **Reflection Amount** spinner.

6. Make sure the **Show Shaded Material in Viewport** button is chosen. Next, choose the **Put to Library** button in the **Material Editor** dialog box; a flyout is displayed.

7. Choose **Project04.mat** from the flyout; the **Put to Library** dialog box is displayed.

8. In the **Put To Library** dialog box, the name **Floor Marble** appears in the **Name** text box. Choose the **OK** button.

Saving the Material Library

The changes to the material library must be saved, else they will be lost when you exit 3ds Max Design. By saving the material library, the newly created materials will be available at the next time when you work in 3ds Max Design.

1. Choose the **Get Material** button in the **Material Editor** dialog box; the **Material/Map Browser** dialog box is displayed.

2. In this dialog box, right-click on the **Project04.mat** rollout; a flyout is displayed. Choose **Save** from the cascading menu, as shown in Figure P4-14

Figure P4-14 *Saving the material library*

3. Close the **Material/Map Browser** dialog box.

    The materials have been created and then saved in the material library.

Applying the Materials

In this section, the materials created will be assigned to objects. You need to render the scene in the Perspective viewport to view the materials assigned to objects.

1. Before assigning materials, you need to ungroup all grouped objects. Press the CTRL+A keys to select all objects in the scene. Next, choose **Group > Ungroup** from the menu bar.

   Next, you need to rename some objects since they are created as clones of the original groups and automatically named.

2. Select and rename the following objects:

Current Name	New Name
Column002	*Column02*
Column01Top001	*Column02Top*
Column01Base001	*Column02Base*
Horn-Left001	*Horn-Right*
Cap-Left003	*Cap-Right01*
Cap-Left004	*Cap-Right02*

3. Select *Column01* and *Column02* in any viewport. In the **Material Editor** dialog box, select the material sample slot named *Column Marble*. Next, choose the **Assign Material to Selection** button to assign the material.

4. Choose the **Show Shaded Material in Viewport** button in the **Material Editor** dialog box to display the material on *Column Marble* in the Perspective viewport.

5. Similarly, assign the following materials:

Material	Object
Gold	*Logo Text, Cap-Left01, Cap-Left02, Cap-Right01,* and *Cap-Right02*
Ivory	*Horn-Right* and *Horn-Left*
Floor Marble	*Column01Base, Column02Base, Column01Top, Column02 Top, Floor,* and *Stairs01 through 03.*

6. Close the **Material Editor** dialog box and save the scene.

Applying Mapping Coordinates

Before the scene can be rendered, appropriate mapping coordinates need to be applied to objects with texture-mapped materials. The mapping coordinates control the appearance of the texture on the object. The objects in the scene are created with default mapping coordinates. However, since the real-world scaling option is not being used on the mapped materials, the default mapping coordinates will have to be adjusted to account for the relative sizes of the objects.

1. Select *Floor* in the Top viewport. Choose the **Modify** tab in the **Command Panel**; the **Modifier List** drop-down list is displayed.

2. Select the **UVW Map** modifier from the **OBJECT-SPACE MODIFIERS** section in the **Modifier List** drop-down list; the **UVW Map** modifier is displayed in the modifier stack and the **Parameters** rollout is displayed in the **Modify** panel.

3. In the **Mapping** area of the **Parameters** rollout for the modifier, make sure the **Real-World Map Size** check box is cleared and then select the **Box** radio button.

4. Set the values in the spinners as given next:

   Length: **140 (3.556m)**   Width: **140 (3.556m)**   Height: **140(3.556m)**

   By setting the value in the spinners to 140(3.556m), the map repeats every 140 units in all directions. The columns are 140(3.556m) units tall, which will be used as the basis for all mappings.

5. Select *Stairs01* in the viewport and then choose the **Modify** tab in the **Command Panel**.

6. Select **UVW Map** from the **Modifier List** drop-down list.

7. In the **Mapping** area of the **Parameters** rollout, make sure the **Real-World Map Size** check box is cleared and then select the **Box** radio button.

8. Set the values in the spinners as given next:

   Length: **140(3.556m)**   Width: **140(3.556m)**   Height: **140(3.556m)**

9. Click on the plus sign [**+**] left side to the **UVW Map** modifier in the modifier stack. Select **Gizmo** in the modifier stack. Invoke the **Select and Move** tool from the **Main Toolbar**.

10. In the Top viewport, move the gizmo along the X and Y axes to a random location. Invoke the **Select and Rotate** tool from the **Main Toolbar**. Rotate the gizmo a random number of degrees about the Z axis. Next, choose **Gizmo** in the modifier stack again to exit the **Gizmo** sub-object mode.

    As you move and rotate the gizmo in the Top viewport, you can observe the changes in map in the Perspective viewport. You can minimize repeating patterns in the scene by adjusting each object's **UVW Map** modifier gizmo in this manner. This technique is also useful if you want to precisely align map patterns on different objects, such as brick patterns on adjacent walls.

11. Select *Stairs02* and apply a **UVW Map** modifier, as discussed earlier.

12. In the **Mapping** area of the **Parameters** rollout, make sure the **Real-World Map Size** check box is cleared and select the **Box** radio button.

13. Set the values in the spinners as given next:

    Length: **140(3.556m)**   Width: **140(3.556m)**   Height: **140(3.556m)**

14. Adjust the gizmo, as described in step 10.

15. Select *Stairs03* and apply the **UVW Map** modifier to it.

16. In the **Mapping** area of the **Parameters** rollout, make sure the **Real-World Map Size** check box is cleared and select the **Box** radio button.

17. Set the values in the spinners as given next:

    Length: **140 (3.556m)**   Width: **140 (3.556m)**   Height: **140 (3.556m)**

18. Adjust the gizmo, as described in step 10.

    The floor and each of the three steps will now have a slightly different appearance when rendered.

19. Select *Column01* and choose the **Modify** tab in the **Command Panel**; the **Modifier List** drop-down list is displayed.

20. Select **UVW Map** in the **Modifier List** drop-down list.

21. In the **Mapping** area of the **Parameters** rollout, clear the **Real-World Map Size** check box and select the **Cylindrical** radio button. In the **Alignment** area, make sure the **Z** radio button is selected, and then choose the **Fit** button.

22. Click on the plus sign [+] left side of the **UVW Map** modifier in the modifier stack. Select **Gizmo** in the modifier stack. Invoke the **Select and Rotate** tool from the **Main Toolbar**. Rotate the gizmo to some degrees about the Z axis. Choose **Gizmo** in the modifier stack again to exit the **Gizmo** sub-object mode.

23. Repeat the procedure followed in steps 19 through 22 for *Column02*.

    After rotating the **UVW Map** modifier gizmo, a different portion of the map is displayed on the front of the column. The two columns no longer look identical.

24. Select *Column01Base, Column02Base, Column01Top,* and *Column02Top* objects. With all the four objects selected, select **UVW Map** from the **OBJECT-SPACE MODIFIERS** section of the **Modifier List**. In the **Mapping** area of the **Parameters** rollout, make sure the **Real-World Map Size** check box is cleared. Next, select the **Box** radio button.

25. Set the values in the spinners as given next:

    Length: **140 (3.556m)**   Width: **140 (3.556m)**   Height: **140(3.556m)**

    The **UVW Map** modifiers are applied to all four objects at the same time. Each object has a different location in relation to the gizmo, and will therefore display a different section of the map. Since the two top objects are adjacent to each other, they will display adjacent areas of the map, giving them the illusion of being a single object. The same is true for the bases.

Note

When a modifier is applied to multiple objects, as described here, changing the position of the modifier gizmo of one object will automatically change the position of the gizmo for the other objects as well.

Adding Lights

Lighting plays a very important role in a scene. Excessive light may spoil the visibility of a scene, whereas insufficient light may hide the details that you want to make visible. Spotlights can be used to cast shadows that add realism to the scene, but it slows down the rendering time. Therefore, in this scene, you will limit the lights to two spotlights and an Omni light.

1. Activate the Top viewport and zoom out to make the space available for creating the lights.

2. Choose **Create > Lights** from the **Command Panel**. Next, select the **Standard** option in the drop-down list and then invoke the **Target Spot** tool from the **Object Type** rollout.

3. Click on a point at the lower-left corner of the Top viewport and drag it to the center of *floor* and then release it to place the target.

4. Invoke the **Select and Move** tool and move the spotlight in Left and Front viewports, as shown in Figure P4-15.

5. Invoke the **Target Spot** tool from the **Object Type** rollout. Place another spotlight by clicking at a point in the lower-center of the Top viewport. Drag the spotlight target to the center of the horns and release to place the target.

6. Move the spotlight in the Left and Front viewports so that it is pointing directly to the center of the horns, refer to Figure P4-16.

   The spotlight is used to highlight the text and horns so that they can stand out in the scene. The other objects will be excluded from the effect of light.

7. Make sure that *Spot002* light is selected. Next, choose the **Modify** tab in the **Command Panel**. Choose the **Exclude** button at the bottom of the **General Parameters** rollout; the **Exclude/Include** dialog box is displayed.

8. Select the names of all objects in the scene except the two horns, text and endcaps.

9. Choose the **>>** button to add the selected objects to the exclusion list. Choose the **OK** button to close the **Exclude/Include** dialog box.

10. Select the **On** and **Use Global Settings** check boxes in the **Shadows** area of the **General Parameters** rollout, if they are not already selected. Also, select **Ray Traced Shadows** from the drop-down list located below the rollout.

11. Repeat the procedure followed steps 7 to 10 for *Spot001* light and then save the scene.

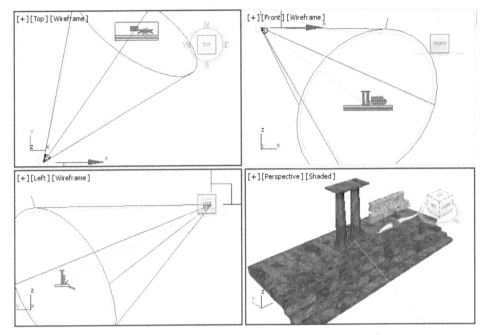

Figure P4-15 *The spotlights created and positioned*

12. Activate the Front viewport and then choose **Create > Lights** in the **Command Panel**.

13. Invoke the **Omni** tool from the **Object Type** rollout. Click on a point in front and to the right of the text to create the light. Align the light in the Front and Left viewports, as shown in Figure P4-16.

Figure P4-16 *The omni light positioned*

14. Make sure the **Omni** light is selected. Next, choose the **Modify** tab in the **Command Panel**. In the **Intensity/Color/Attenuation** rollout, set the value **1.5** in the **Multiplier** spinner. Next, choose the **Exclude** button at the bottom of the **General Parameters** rollout; the **Exclude/Include** dialog box is displayed.

15. Select the **Include** radio button and then select **Logo Text** from the **Scene Objects** area.

16. Choose the **>>** button in the **Exclude/Include** dialog box to add the selected objects to the inclusion list, as shown in Figure P4-17. Choose the **OK** button to close the **Exclude/Include** dialog box.

*Figure P4-17 The **Exclude/Include** dialog box*

17. Make sure the **On** and **Use Global Settings** check boxes are selected in the **Shadows** area of the **General Parameters** rollout. Also, make sure **Ray Traced Shadows** is selected in the drop-down list located below it.

Creating the Camera

You will now create a camera in the scene. Creating a camera will help you to view the scene properly.

1. Activate the Top viewport and then choose **Create > Cameras** in the **Command Panel**.

2. Invoke the **Target** tool from the **Object Type** rollout.

3. Click at a point in the lower-right corner of the Top viewport. Next, drag it to the center of the horns to place the target. Right-click to exit the tool.

4. Activate the Perspective viewport and press the C key; the Perspective viewport switches to Camera001 viewport.

5. Invoke the **Zoom Extents All** tool to zoom the objects to their extents.

6. Invoke the **Select and Move** tool and move the camera in all viewports until an appropriate view is displayed in the Camera001 viewport, as shown in Figure P4-18.

Figure P4-18 *The camera created and aligned*

When the Camera001 viewport is active, the **Field-of-View** and **Truck Camera** tools provide additional control of the view.

7. Choose **Rendering > Environment** from the menu bar; the **Environment and Effects** dialog box is displayed.

8. In the **Background** area of the **Environment and Effects** dialog box, choose the **Color** swatch; the **Color Selector: Background Color** dialog box is displayed. In this dialog box, set the values as given next:

Red: **255**   Green: **255**   Blue: **255**

This sets the background color to white. Since the marble material on the floor and steps is reflective, therefore changing the background color from black to white will lighten the scene and bring out detailing in the marble material.

9. In the **Global Lighting** area, choose the **Ambient** color swatch; the **Color Selector: Ambient Light** dialog box is displayed. In this dialog box, set the values as given next:

Red: **100**   Green: **100**   Blue: **100**

10. Close the **Environment and Effects** dialog box. Make the required adjustments to the lights and ambient lighting. Next, invoke the **Render Production** tool; the final rendered image is displayed, as shown in Figure P4-19.

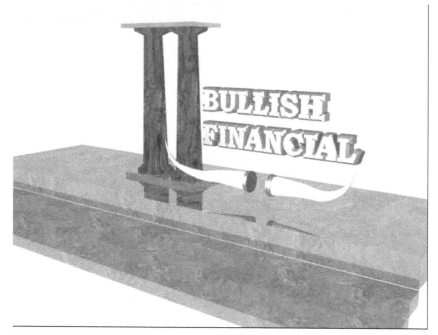

Figure P4-19 *The scene rendered after creating the lights and camera*

11. Save the scene.

Next, you will increase the animation range.

12. Choose the **Time Configuration** button in the animation playback controls; the **Time Configuration** dialog box is displayed.

13. In the **Animation** area, set the value **120** in the **Length** spinner and choose the **OK** button.

This sets the total number of frames in the animation at 120, which is about four seconds of animation.

Animating the Light Color

The color of a light source can be changed during an animation. By changing the color from black to white, an animated highlight can be created.

1. Select the **Omni** light in any of the viewports.

2. Choose **Graph Editors > Track View - Dope Sheet** from the menu bar; the **Track View - Dope Sheet** window is displayed.

3. Expand the tree for *Omni001* by clicking on the plus sign (**+**) on the left side of the *Omni001*. Also, expand the tree for **Transform** and then **Object (Omni Light)**. Notice that there is currently no animation key.

4. Choose the **Add Keys** button at the top of the **Track View-Dope Sheet** window.

5. Click on the **Color** track and add keys at frames 0, 5, 15, 110, and 120; five animation keys are created for the **Omni** light.

6. Right-click on the first key (on frame 0); the **Omni001\Color** dialog box is displayed, as shown in Figure P4-20.

*Figure P4-20 The **Omni001\Color** dialog box*

7. In the **Omni001\Color** dialog box, set the values in the spinners as given next:

     R: **0**   G: **0**   B: **0**

The color of the light is now black at frame 0.

8. Choose the right arrow button at the top of the **Omni001\Color** dialog box to move to the next key.

9. Set the values in the spinners as given next:

     R: **0**   G: **0**   B: **0**

The color of the light is set to black from frame 0 to frame 5.

10. Move to the next key. Set the value of the **R**, **G**, and **B** spinners to **255**, if they are not already set to this value.

From frame 5 to frame 15, the color of the light changes to white.

11. Move to the next key. Set the values in the spinners as given next:

   R: **255**   G: **255**   B: **255**

12. Move to the next key. Set the values in the spinners as given next:

   R: **0**   G: **0**   B: **0**

   From frame 110 to frame 120, the color of the light changes from white to black.

13. Close the **Omni001\Color** dialog box and save the scene.

Animating the Light

In this section, you will animate the light in the scene.

1. In the **Track View-Dope Sheet** window, expand the tree for the **Position** track and add a key in the Position track at frame 15 for *Omni001*. Then, close the **Track View-Dope Sheet** window.

   This key prevents the light from moving before frame 15.

2. Drag the time slider to frame 110 and then choose the **Toggle Auto Key Mode** button to turn the animation mode on.

3. Make sure *Omni001* is selected and then right-click on the **Select and Move** tool; the **Move Transform Type-In** dialog box is displayed.

4. Activate the Front viewport. Set the value **–300(–7.62m)** in the **X** spinner in the **Offset: Screen** area of the **Move Transform Type-In** dialog box and press the ENTER key.

5. Exit the animation mode by choosing the **Toggle Auto Key Mode** button, close the **Move Transform Type-In** dialog box, and save the scene.

Rendering the Animation

Render the final animation to see the completed project. The final animation will show all materials, highlights, shadows, and lighting.

1. Activate the Camera001 viewport. Choose **Rendering > Render Setup** from the menu bar or invoke the **Render Setup** tool from the **Main Toolbar**; the **Render Setup: NVIDIA mental ray** dialog box is displayed.

2. In the **Time Output** area, select the **Active Time Segment** radio button to make it active; the active frames will be set for rendering.

3. In the **Output Size** area of the dialog box, choose the **320×240** button; the animation to be rendered is set at a resolution of 320 × 240 pixels.

4. In the **Render Output** area of the dialog box, choose the **Files** button; the **Render Output File** dialog box is displayed.

5. As the project folder is already set, the *renderoutput* folder of this project is displayed in the **Save in** drop-down list of this project. Enter **Project04** in the **File name** text box.

6. Select **AVI File (*.avi)** from the **Save as type** drop-down list.

7. Choose the **Save** button; the **AVI File Compression Setup** dialog box is displayed.

8. Choose the **OK** button to close the **AVI File Compression Setup** dialog box.

9. Make sure the Camera001 viewport is activated and then choose the **Render** button in the **Render Setup** dialog box; the rendering begins.

    After the rendering is done, close the render window and the **Render Setup** dialog box.

10. Choose **Rendering > View Image File** from the menu bar; the **View File** dialog box is displayed.

11. Select **Project04.avi** in this dialog box and choose the **Open** button; the animation file is opened and played in Windows Media Player.

12. Close Windows Media Player and save the scene. Figure P4-21 shows the rendered output at frame 0.

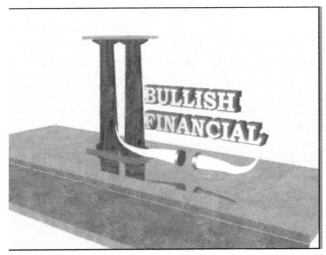

Figure P4-21 A rendered image of the final animation at frame 0

Project 5

Creating a Computer Center

PROJECT DESCRIPTION

In this project, you will create a computer center. You will then create workstations and computers inside the center. Also, you will create lights inside the center to illuminate the room. In addition to this, you will create exterior scene around the computer center. Finally, you will apply materials to these objects and create a walkthrough, as shown in Figure P5-1.

Figure P5-1 *Walkthrough towards the computer center*

Creating the Project Folder

Create a new project folder with the name *Prj_5* at *\Documents\3dsmaxdesign 2015* and then save the file with the name *Prj5*, as discussed in Tutorial 1 of Chapter 2.

Downloading the Files

Before starting the project, you need to download the *prj5_3dsmaxdesign_2015* from *www.cadcim.com*. The path of the file is as follows: *Textbooks > Animation and Visual Effects > 3ds Max Design > Autodesk 3ds Max Design 2015: A Tutorial Approach*

Extract the contents of the zip file to *Documents*. Open Windows Explorer and browse to *\Documents\prj5_3dsmaxdesign_2015* and then copy all files to *\Documents\3dsmaxdesign 2015\ Prj5\sceneassets\images*.

Changing the Units Setting

In this section, you need to change the current units you are working on. Since the units in this project are in inches, you will set the units to decimal inches.

1. Choose **Customize > Units Setup** from the menu bar; the **Units Setup** dialog box is displayed.

2. Select the **US Standard** radio button in the **Display Unit Scale** area. Next, select **Feet w/Fractional Inches** from the drop-down list below this radio button and make sure **1/2** is selected in the drop-down list on the right side. Also, make sure the **Feet** radio button is selected, as shown in Figure P5-2. Choose the **OK** button to apply the settings. If you want to work in the metric unit system, select the **Metric** radio button from the **Display Unit Scale** area of the **Units Setup** dialog box. Also, make sure the **Meters** option is selected in the drop-down list below the **Metric** radio button.

*Figure P5-2 The **Units Setup** dialog box*

Creating the Walls and Floor for the Room

In this section, you will create walls and floor for the computer center by using the **Wall** tool. Wall automates the creation of the walls. It belongs to a group of 3ds Max Design objects called AEC extended objects.

1. Switch to four viewport configuration. Activate the Top viewport and then choose **Create > Geometry** in the **Command Panel**. Select **AEC Extended** in the drop-down list. Next, invoke the **Wall** tool from the **Object Type** rollout.

2. In the **Parameters** rollout, set the value **9"(0.229m)** in the **Width** spinner and **10'(3.048m)** in the **Height** spinner.

3. In the **Keyboard Entry** rollout, set the following values in the spinners. Notice that the **Z** spinner is grayed out. Choose the **Add Point** button after specifying each set of coordinates:

    X: **0'**   Y: **0'**
    X: **13'(3.962m)**   Y: **0'**
    X: **13'(3.962m)**   Y: **23'6"(7.163m)**
    X: **0'**   Y: **23'6"(7.163m)**

4. Choose the **Close** button; the walls of the computer center are created, as shown in FigureP5-3. Right-click to exit the tool.

Figure P5-3 *Walls of the computer center*

5. In the **Name and Color** rollout, enter **Walls** and then invoke the **Zoom Extents All** tool to zoom the object to its extent.

6. Make sure the Top viewport is activated and then choose **Create > Geometry** in the **Command Panel**. Select **Standard Primitives** in the drop-down list. Next, invoke the **Box** tool from the **Object Type** rollout.

7. Expand the **Keyboard Entry** rollout and set the values as given next:

    X: **6'6"(1.981m)**   Y: **11'9"(3.581m)**   Z: **0'**
    Length: **24'3"(7.391m)**   Width: **13'9"(4.191m)**   Height: **–6"(–0.152m)**

8. Choose the **Create** button; the floor is created below *Walls*. In the **Name and Color** rollout, enter **Floor**. Right-click to exit the tool.

Adding Roof to the Building

The computer center has a flat roof. This will be created by first copying *Floor* and then modifying the parameters of *Floor*.

1. Select *Floor* in the Front viewport and then choose **Edit > Clone** from the menu bar; the **Clone Options** dialog box is displayed. Next, select the **Copy** radio button and enter the name as **Roof** in the **Name** text box. Now, choose the **OK** button; a copy of *Floor* is created in the viewport.

2. Make sure *Roof* is selected in the Front viewport and then right-click on the **Select and Move** tool; the **Move Transform Type-In** dialog box is displayed. Set the value **10'(3.048m)** in the **Y** spinner in the **Offset: Screen** area of this dialog box and press the ENTER key; the *Roof* moves up. Close the **Move Transform Type-In** dialog box.

3. Make sure *Roof* is selected. Now, choose the **Modify** tab in the **Command Panel**.

4. Expand the **Parameters** rollout and set the values in the spinners as given next:

    Length: **30'3"(9.22m)**   Width: **19'9"(6.02m)**   Height: **0'6"(0.152m)**

    There is now a 3'(0.914m) overhang all the way around the computer center and *Roof* extends 6"(0.152m) above *Walls*, as shown in Figure P5-4.

Creating the Entrance Door

You will now create the entrance door. The 3ds Max Design **Door** object creates the door, frame, and hole in the wall. Placement is important to make *Door* work correctly.

1. Select *Floor* and *Roof* in any viewport. Next, right-click anywhere in the viewport; a quad menu is displayed. Choose **Hide Selection** from the upper quadrant; the selected objects are hidden.

2. Invoke the **2D Snap Toggle** tool from the **Snaps Toggle** flyout to turn the snaps on. Next, right-click on the **2D Snap Toggle** tool; the **Grid and Snap Settings** dialog box is displayed.

Figure P5-4 Roof created and placed above Walls

3. In the **Snaps** tab, select only the **Edge/Segment** check box, if it is not already selected. Now, close the dialog box.

4. Choose **Create > Geometry** in the **Command Panel**. Next, select **Doors** in the drop-down list and choose the **Pivot** button from the **Object Type** rollout.

5. In the Top viewport, click on the inside of the right-hand wall near the bottom. Make sure the snap helper highlights the inner wall. Hold down the mouse button and drag the cursor straight up a short distance and release. Make sure the helper highlights the inner wall. Next, move the cursor outside wall and click, making sure the helper highlights the outside wall. Finally, move the cursor a short distance straight up and pick to set the height of the door. Right-click to exit the tool.

    The parameters will be set to the exact values in the next step.

6. Make sure the door is selected and then choose the **Modify** tab in the **Command** **Panel**. In the **Parameters** rollout, set the value **7'(2.134m)** in the **Height** spinner and **4'(0.919m)** in the **Width** spinner.

7. Set the value **90** in the **Open** spinner to open the door. Then, select the **Flip Swing** and **Flip Hinge** check boxes; the door opens out to the right. Also, verify that the opening in the wall has been created.

8. The door should be approximately **2'(0.609m)** from the edge of the building. If it is not, move it as needed in the Top viewport. Invoke the **Zoom Extents All** tool to zoom the objects to their extents. The door is created on the right wall, as shown in Figure P5-5. This position does not need to be exact.

Figure P5-5 *The door created on the right wall*

9. Set the value **0** in the **Open** spinner of the **Parameters** rollout; the door is closed.

Creating the Window

A window will now be placed at the end wall. Like the door, the window is created as a special 3ds Max Design object. The window object automates the creation and animation of windows. However, the window to be created will be fixed and will not be animated.

1. Choose **Create > Geometry** in the **Command Panel**. Select **Windows** from the drop-down list. Then, invoke the **Fixed** tool from the **Object Type** rollout.

2. In the Top viewport, click on the inside of the lower wall about 1/3 of the way inside from the left-hand side. Make sure the snap helper highlights the inner wall. Then, drag straight right to about 1/3 of the way inside from the right-hand side and click. Make sure the helper highlights the inner wall. Next, move the cursor outside wall and click, making sure the helper highlights the outside wall. Finally, move the cursor a short distance to the left and click to set the height of the window.

   The parameters will be set to the exact values in the next step.

3. Make sure the window is selected and then choose the **Modify** tab in the **Command Panel**. In the **Parameters** rollout, set the value **8'(2.438m)** in the **Height** and **Width** spinners.

4. Make the Top viewport active. Invoke the **Align** tool from the **Main Toolbar**. With the align tool active, select *Walls*; the **Align Selection (Walls)** dialog box is displayed. Select the **X Position** and **Z Position** check boxes and clear the **Y Position** check

box. Then, make sure the **Center** radio button is selected in the **Current Object** and **Target Object** areas of this dialog box. Choose the **OK** button; the window is precisely centered in the front wall, as shown in Figure P5-6.

Figure P5-6 *The alignment of the window on the front wall*

Creating a Computer Station

You will create one set of computer station which consists of computer table, monitors, and the chairs. Each computer station consists of a tabletop, two sides, and a partition. The tabletop and two sides are created as a single spline that is extruded. The partition is also a spline that is extruded. In this section, you will first start with computer station.

1. Activate the Left viewport and then choose **Create > Shapes** in the **Command Panel**. Next, invoke the **Line** tool from the **Object Type** rollout.

2. In the **Keyboard Entry** rollout, set the values as given next. Choose the **Add Point** button after specifying each set of XYZ coordinates:

X: –0'4 1/2"(–0.114m)	Y: 0'0"	Z: –0'4 1/2"(–0.114m)
X: –0'4 1/2"(–0.114m)	Y: 2'6"(0.762m)	Z: –0'4 1/2"(–0.114m)
X: –4'11 1/2"(–1.511m)	Y: 2'6"(0.762m)	Z: –0'4 1/2"(–0.114m)
X: –4'11 1/2"(–1.511m)	Y: 0'0"	Z: –0'4 1/2"(–0.114m)
X: –4'10 1/2"(–1.486m)	Y: 0'0"	Z: –0'4 1/2"(–0.114m)
X: –4'10 1/2"(–1.486m)	Y: 2'5"(0.737m)	Z: –0'4 1/2"(–0.114m)
X: –0'5 1/2"(–0.14m)	Y: 2'5"(0.737m)	Z: –0'4 1/2"(–0.114m)
X: –0'5 1/2"(–0.14m)	Y: 0'0"	Z: –0'4 1/2"(–0.114m)

3. After the last set of coordinates is entered, choose the **Close** button. In the **Name and Color** rollout, enter **Table01**.

4. Make sure *Table01* is selected and then choose the **Modify** tab in the **Command Panel**. In the **Modifier List** drop-down list, select **Extrude** in the **OBJECT-SPACE MODIFIERS** section.

5. In the **Parameters** rollout for the modifier, set the value **–2'9"(–0.838m)** in the **Amount** spinner; the top and sides of the first computer station are created inside the room near the window, as shown in Figure P5-7. You may need to rotate the Perpective viewport to set the angle of view for the table created.

Figure P5-7 *The top and sides of the first computer station*

Now, you need to create the partitions.

6. Activate the Perspective viewport and zoom in on *Table01*. Align *Table01* in the viewport. You may maximize the viewport.

7. Activate the Front viewport and choose **Create > Shapes** in the **Command Panel**. Next, invoke the **Line** tool from the **Object Type** rollout. Draw a triangle by entering the following coordinates in the **Keyboard Entry** rollout. Choose the **Add Point** button after entering the value of each set of coordinates.

X: **0'4 1/2"(0.114m)**	Y: **2'6"(0.762m)**	Z: **–4'11 1/2"(–1.511m)**
X: **0'4 1/2"(0.114m)**	Y: **4'0"(1.219m)**	Z: **–4'11 1/2"(–1.511m)**
X: **3'1 1/2"(0.952m)**	Y: **2'6"(0.762m)**	Z: **–4'11 1/2"(–1.511m)**

8. After the last set of coordinates is entered, choose the **Close** button. In the **Name and Color** rollout, enter **Side01**.

9. Make sure *Side01* is selected in the Front viewport and then choose the **Modify** tab in the **CommandPanel**. In the **Interpolation** rollout, select the **Adaptive** check box. In the **Selection** rollout, choose the **Vertex** button. Right-click on the top vertex; a quad menu is displayed and choose **Bezier Corner** from the quad menu. Similarly, change the right-hand vertex to the bezier corner type.

10. Invoke the **Select and Move** tool. Now, move the handles on the top and right-hand vertices to produce a shape similar to that in the Front viewport, as shown in Figure P5-8. Next, choose the **Vertex** button to exit the sub-object mode.

Figure P5-8 Side01 spline modified in Front viewport

11. Make sure *Side01* is selected. Next, in the **Modifier List** drop-down list, select **Extrude** in the **OBJECT-SPACE MODIFIERS** section. In the **Parameters** rollout for the modifier, set the value **1"(0.025m)** in the **Amount** spinner.

A side partition is created on the right-hand side of the computer station. Each station has a side partition only on the right side, which serves as the left-hand side partition for the next station.

Creating the Monitor

Now, a computer monitor will be created and placed on top of the computer station table. The monitor is created using three primitives: box, sphere, and chamfer box. These objects are modified to obtain the final shape.

1. Zoom in the computer station tabletop in the Top, Left, and Front viewports. Then, activate the Top viewport. Choose **Create > Geometry** in the **Command Panel**. Select **Standard Primitives** in the drop-down list. Invoke the **Box** tool from the **Object Type** rollout. It may be helpful to turn off the display of walls, door, and window.

2. In the **Parameters** rollout, set the value **2** in the **Width Segs** spinner. Next, in the **Keyboard Entry** rollout, set the values as given next:

   X: **1'9"(0.533m)**   Y: **2'8"(0.813m)**   Z: **2'6"(0.762m)**
   Length: **1'3"(0.381m)**   Width: **1'1"(0.33m)**   Height: **1'3"(0.381m)**

3. Choose the **Create** button; a box is created and placed on the top of the table.

4. Enter **Monitor CRT01** in the **Name and Color** rollout.

5. Activate the Left viewport and then choose **Create > Geometry** in the **Command Panel**. Select **Extended Primitives** in the drop-down list. Next, invoke the **ChamferBox** tool from the **Object Type** rollout.

   A chamfer box is similar to a box, but with rounded edges.

6. Expand the **Keyboard Entry** rollout and set the values as given next:

   X: **–2'8"(–0.813m)**   Y: **3'1 1/2"(0.952m)**   Z: **–2'4"(–0.711m)**
   Length: **1'0"(0.305m)**   Width: **1'0"(0.305m)**   Height: **0'1"(0.025m)**
   Fillet: **0'4 1/2"(0.114m)**

7. Choose the **Create** button; a chamfer box is created and is centered on the monitor, as shown in Figure P5-9. The chamfer box is also centered on the front of the monitor.

8. Enter **CRT Tube01** in the **Name and Color** rollout.

9. Activate the Top viewport and then choose **Create > Geometry** in the **Command Panel**. Select **Standard Primitives** in the drop-down list. Next, invoke the **Sphere** tool from the **Object Type** rollout.

10. In the **Parameters** rollout, set the value **0.75** in the **Hemisphere** spinner.

11. Expand the **Keyboard Entry** rollout and set the values as given next:

    X: **1'9"(0.533m)**   Y: **2'8"(0.813m)**   Z: **0'0"(0m)**   Radius: **0'8"(0.203m)**

12. Choose the **Create** button; the object is created.

13. Enter **Monitor Base01** in the **Name and Color** rollout.

14. Invoke the **Select and Move** tool from the **Main Toolbar**. Next, select **Monitor Base01** and move it such that the base will rest on the top of the computer station, refer to Figure P5-10.

Figure P5-9 *The chamfer box created and centered on the monitor*

Figure P5-10 *The shape of the monitor modified and the base created*

15. Select *Monitor CRT01* and *CRT Tube01* in the Top viewport and then right-click on the **Select and Move** tool; the **Move Transform Type-In** dialog box is displayed. Set the value **4"(0.101m)** in the **X** spinner in the **Offset: Screen** area; the objects are moved close to the front of the monitor.

16. Select the left side vertices in the Top viewport. Invoke the **Percent Snap Toggle** tool. Also, invoke the **Select and Uniform Scale** tool. Scale the vertices to 50%; the back of the monitor is tapered.

17. Choose the **Vertex** button to exit the sub-object mode.

18. Activate the Front viewport and select *Monitor CRT01* and *CRT Tube01*. Next, invoke the **Select and Rotate** tool. Make sure the **Use Selection Center** tool is invoked in the transform center flyout. Rotate both objects 10 degrees about the local Z axis.

19. Finally, move both objects up by **1"(0.025m)** on the local Y axis so that the bottom of *Monitor CRT01* is near the top of *Monitor Base01*. There will be a small amount of overlap.

20. Invoke the **Zoom Extents All Selected** tool to zoom the objects to their extents.

The shape of the monitor is modified and the base is created, as shown in Figure P5-10. The monitor is now complete.

Creating the Chair

In this section, you will now create the chair. A loft object is used as a frame and two chamfer boxes are used as seat and back of the chair. The loft object is created by lofting two shapes, star and circle along a path.

1. Activate the Front viewport and zoom in the computer station. Choose **Create > Shapes** in the **Command Panel**. Invoke the **Line** tool from the **Object Type** rollout. You may need to maximize the viewport.

2. Expand the **Keyboard Entry** rollout and set the values as given next:

X: 4'0"(1.219m)	Y: 0'0"(0m)	Z: –2'8"(–0.813m)
X: 4'0"(1.219m)	Y: 1'6"(0.457m)	Z: –2'8"(–0.813m)
X: 5'0"(1.524m)	Y: 1'6"(0.457m)	Z: –2'8"(–0.813m)
X: 5'0"(1.524m)	Y: 3'0"(0.914m)	Z: –2'8"(–0.813m)

3. Choose the **Add Point** button after setting the values in each set of XYZ coordinates.

4. Choose the **Finish** button; the path for the chair frame is created, as shown in Figure P5-11.

5. Enter **Chair Frame Path** in the **Name and Color** rollout.

6. Choose **Create > Shapes** in the **Command Panel**. Invoke the **Star** tool from the **Object Type** rollout.

7. In the **Parameters** rollout, set the value **5** in the **Points** spinner.

Figure P5-11 The path created for the chair frame

8. Expand the **Keyboard Entry** rollout and set the values as given next:

    Radius 1: **1'0"(0.305m)**   Radius 2: **0'1 1/2"(0.038m)**   Fillet Radius 1: **0'1"(0.025m)**
    Fillet Radius 2: **0'1"(0.025m)**

9. Choose the **Create** button; the shape is created.

10. Enter **Chair Base Shape** in the **Name and Color** rollout.

11. Choose **Create > Shapes** in the **Command Panel**. Invoke the **Circle** tool from the **Object Type** rollout.

12. Expand the **Keyboard Entry** rollout and set the value **1"(0.025m)** in the **Radius** spinner. Choose the **Create** button; the shape is created.

13. Enter **Chair Rail Shape** in the **Name and Color** rollout.

14. Select *Chair Frame Path* and then choose **Create > Geometry** in the **Command Panel**. Select **Compound Objects** in the drop-down list. Next, invoke the **Loft** tool from the **Object Type** rollout.

15. Expand the **Creation Method** rollout and choose the **Get Shape** button. Next, select *Chair Base Shape* in any viewport and enter **Chair Frame** in the **Name and Color** rollout.

    The frame will not look correct at this point since the star is lofted along the entire path.

16. Make sure *Chair Frame* selected is selected and then choose the **Modify** tab in the **Command Panel**. Expand the **Path Parameters** rollout and set the value **10** in the **Path** spinner.

17. Choose the **Get Shape** button in the **Creation Method** rollout. Finally, select *Chair Rail Shape* in any viewport; the frame is now correctly shaped, as shown in Figure P5-12.

Figure P5-12 *The Chair Frame created*

Next, you need to create the seat and back of the chair.

18. Activate the Top viewport. Choose **Create > Geometry** in the **Command Panel**. Next, select **Extended Primitives** in the drop-down list. Then, invoke the **Chamfer Box** tool from the **Object Type** rollout.

19. Expand the **Keyboard Entry** rollout and set the values as given next:

    X: **3'11"(1.194m)**   Y: **2'8"(0.813m)**   Z: **1'7"(0.483m)**   Length: **1'6"(0.457m)**
    Width: **1'6"(0.457m)** Height: **0'3"(0.076m)** Fillet: **0'1"(0.025m)**

20. Choose the **Create** button; the object is created. Enter **Seat01** in the **Name and Color** rollout.

21. Make sure the **Chamfer Box** tool is activated. Next, activate the Left viewport and then set the following values in the **Keyboard Entry** rollout:

    X: **–2'8"(–0.813m)**   Y: **3'0"(0.914m)**   Z: **–4'11"(–1.499m)** Length: **0'8"(0.203m)**
    Width: **1'3"(0.381m)** Height: **0'3"(0.076m)**   Fillet: **0'3"(0.076m)**

22. Choose the **Create** button; the chair is created, as shown in Figure P5-13.

Figure P5-13 *The chair created*

23. Enter **Back01** in the **Name and Color** rollout.

Creating the Ground

In this section, you will create the ground and a bed for plants. You will first create a quad patch for the ground in the scene and then you will create a box that will be used as a bed for plants in front of the window.

1. Activate the Top viewport. Choose **Create > Geometry** in the **Command Panel**. Select **Patch Grids** in the drop-down list. Choose the **Quad Patch** button from the **Object Type** rollout.

2. Expand the **Keyboard Entry** rollout and set the values as given next:

   X: **6'6"(1.981m)**   Y: **11'9"(3.581m)**   Z: **–0'6"(–0.152m)**
   Length: **150'(45.72m)**   Width: **225'(68.58m)**

3. Choose the **Create** button; the floor is placed on top of the ground inside the computer center.

   By setting the value **–0'6"(–0.152m)** for the Z coordinate, the floor is placed on top of the ground, thus creating a step into the computer center.

4. Enter **Ground** in the **Name and Color** rollout.

5. Make sure the Top viewport is activated and then choose **Create > Geometry** in the **Command Panel**. Select **Standard Primitives** in the drop-down list. Next, invoke the **Box** tool from the **Object Type** rollout.

6. Expand the **Keyboard Entry** rollout and set the values as given next:

    X: **6'6"(1.981m)**   Y: **–1'4 1/2"(–0.419m)**   Z: **–0'6"(–0.152m)**
    Length: **2'0"(0.61m)**   Width: **11'0"(3.353m)**   Height: **0'3"(0.076m)**

7. Choose the **Create** button. In the **Name and Color** rollout, enter **Flower Bed**.

Creating the Pathway

In this section, you will create a pathway leading to the computer center. The path is created as a spline that is modified and then extruded.

1. In the Top viewport, invoke the **Zoom Extents All** tool to zoom the objects to their extents.

2. Choose **Create > Shapes** in the **Command Panel**. Invoke the **Line** tool from the **Object Type** rollout.

3. Starting just off of the quad patch (Ground), draw a path that leads toward the window and then curves around the room to the door, as shown in Figure P5-14. Next, close the spline, refer to Figure P5-13. Enter the name of the spline as **Path**. To get the shape shown in Figure P5-14, you need to smoothen some of the vertices of *Path*.

Figure P5-14 *Path leading to computer center*

4. Make sure the vertex sub-object mode is activated and then move and curve the vertices as needed. The two vertices of the door should meet the floor. After modifying the spline, exit the sub-object mode.

5. Make sure *Path* is selected and then choose the **Modify** tab in the **Command Panel**. Select **Extrude** in the **Modifier List** drop-down list under the **OBJECT-SELECTION MODIFIERS** section. In the **Parameters** rollout for the modifier, set the value **1'(0.025m)** in the **Amount** spinner and press the ENTER key; *Path* is extruded, as shown in Figure P5-15.

Figure P5-15 *Path extruded*

6. In the Front viewport, move *Path* –6"(–0.152m) on the Y axis so that it sets on top of the ground.

Creating the Foliage

In this section, you will add foliage to the scene. 3ds Max Design has an automated foliage feature with several plants available in it. You will add two large trees and several small trees around the path.

1. Activate the Top viewport and invoke the **Zoom Extents** tool.

2. Choose **Create > Geometry** in the **Command Panel**. Select **AEC Extended** in the drop-down list. Invoke the **Foliage** tool from the **Object Type** rollout; various rollouts for foliage are displayed.

3. Expand the **Favorite Plants** rollout and scroll the image tiles down until the **American Elm** tile is displayed. Select the tile to highlight it.

4. Choose a point in the Top viewport near the rear-left of the building to place the **American Elm** tile. Similarly, place another **American Elm** foliage near the middle of the right side of the building.

5. With one of the trees selected, choose the **Modify** tab in the **Command Panel**. In the **Parameters** rollout, set the value **20'(6.096m)** in the **Height** spinner. Similarly, set the height of the other tree to **20'(6.096m)**.

6. In the Top viewport, move both trees so that the branches do not extend into the building.

7. Choose the **Display** tab in the **Command Panel** and then choose the **Unhide All** button in the **Hide** rollout to display *Roof* in the viewport.

8. Make sure the **Select and Move** tool is invoked and activate the Front viewport. Next, select *Roof* and align it on the top of *Walls*, if it is not aligned, as shown in Figure P5-16.

Figure P5-16 The roof aligned on the top of walls

9. In the Top viewport, zoom in on *Flower Bed* in front of the window.

10. Choose **Create > Geometry** in the **Command Panel**. Select **AEC Extended** in the drop-down list. Invoke the **Foliage** tool from the **Object Type** rollout.

11. Make sure the **Favorite Plants** rollout is expanded and scroll the image tiles down until the **Society Garlic** image tile is displayed. Select the tile to highlight it.

12. Choose a point near the center of *Flower Bed* to place a plant. Place four more plants, two on each side of the center plant.

13. With one of the plants selected, choose the **Modify** tab in the **Command Panel**. In the **Parameters** rollout, set the value **2'0"(0.61m)** in the **Height** rollout. Similarly, set the height of the other plants to **2'0"(0.61m)**, or as required.

You may change the plant heights slightly to create a more realistic appearance.

14. In the Left viewport, move the plants so that they do not overlap with the wall or window. Move *Flower Bed* so that it is centered underneath the plants. Finally, move the plants down so that the bottom of the plant objects is at the same level as the top of *Flower Bed*.

Next, you need to add more trees around the path to make the scene beautiful and realistic.

15. Expand the **Favorite Plants** rollout if it is not expanded and scroll the image tiles down until the **Scotch Pine** tile is displayed. Select the tile to highlight it.

16. Activate the Top viewport and place **8 Scotch Pine** tiles around *Path*, **4** on the left side and **4** on the right side.

17. With the trees selected, choose the **Modify** tab in the **Command Panel**. Expand the **Parameters** rollout and set the value **12'0"(3.658m)** in the **Height** spinner. Similarly, set the height of the remaining trees to **12'0"(3.658m)**.

18. In the Top viewport, align the trees around *Path*, as shown in Figure 5-17.

Figure P5-17 *The trees aligned around Path*

Creating and Applying Multi/Sub-Object Materials to the Walls

The materials applied to the walls of the building should look different from the interior of the building as compared to the exterior. You will create multi/sub-object materials for the walls. You will then make sub-object selections on the walls and change the sub-object material IDs to achieve the desired result.

1. Choose **Rendering > Material Editor > Compact Material Editor** from the menu bar; the **Material Editor** dialog box is displayed.

2. Select the first material sample slot and choose the **Arch & Design** button; the **Material/Map Browser** dialog box is displayed. Select **Standard** from the **Maps > Standard** rollout and choose the **OK** button; the **Arch & Design** button is changed to **Standard** type.

3. With the first material sample active, choose the **Diffuse** button from the **Blinn Basic Parameters** rollout; the **Material Map/Browser** dialog box is displayed.

4. Select **Bitmap** map from the **Maps > Standard** rollout. Next, choose the **OK** button; the **Select Bitmap Image File** dialog box is displayed. As the project folder is already set, the *images* folder is displayed in the **Look in** drop-down list.

5. Select the file **Stucco.Brown.Jpg** and then choose the **Open** button; the **Stucco.Brown** material is displayed in the first sample slot of the **Material Editor** dialog box.

6. In the **Coordinates** rollout, select the **Use Real-World Scale** check box, if it is not already selected. Set the value **5'(1.524m)** in the **Width: Size** and **Height: Size** spinners. Next, press the ENTER key.

7. Select next unused material sample slot in the **Material Editor** dialog box. Change the **Arch & Design** material type to **Standard** type as explained in step 2.

8. Choose the **Diffuse** button from the **Blinn Basic Parameters** rollout; the **Material/Browser** dialog box is displayed.

9. Select **Bitmap** map from the **Maps > Standard** rollout. Next, choose the **OK** button; the **Select Bitmap Image File** dialog box is displayed. As the project folder is already set, the *images* folder of this project is displayed in the **Look in** drop-down list.

10. Select the file **Finishes.Painting.Paint.jpg** and then choose the **Open** button; the **Finishes.Painting.Paint** material is displayed in the second sample slot of the **Material Editor** dialog box.

11. Choose the **Go to Parent** button. Next, choose the **Diffuse Color** swatch in the **Blinn Basic Parameters** rollout; the **Color Selector: Diffuse Color** dialog box is displayed.

12. Set the color values in the spinners as given next:

    Red: **192**   Green: **220**   Blue: **255**

13. Choose the **OK** button to close this dialog box.

14. Expand the **Maps** rollout and set the value **43** in the **Diffuse Color** spinner.

    This defines a light blue paint material that will be used on the interior walls of the building.

15. Select the next unused material sample in the **Material Editor** dialog box and choose the **Get Material** button; the **Material/Map Browser** dialog box is displayed. Choose the **Material/Map Browser Options** button from this dialog box; a flyout is displayed. Choose **Open Material Library** from the **Material/Map Browser Options** flyout; the **Import Material Library** dialog box is displayed.

16. Navigate to *C:\Program Files\Autodesk\3ds Max Design 2015\materiallibraries*.

17. Select the **AecTemplates.mat** material library and choose the **Open** button; the **Material/ Map Browser** dialog box is displayed.

18. In the **Material/Map Browser** window, double-click on the **Wall-Template (Multi/SubObject)** material.

19. With the **Wall-Template** material selected in the **Material Editor** dialog box, click and drag the **Stucco.Brown.Jpg** material to the first sub-material button in the **Walls-Template** material definition. Release the mouse button; the **Instance (Copy)** dialog box is displayed. Make sure the **Instance** radio button is selected and choose the **OK** button; an instance of the **Stucco.Brown.Jpg** material is assigned as the first sub-material in the **Walls-Template** material.

20. Replace the **Inside Wall**, **Top**, and **Bottom** sub-materials with instances of the **Stucco.Brown.Jpg** material using the drag-and-drop method described in the previous step. Also, replace the **Outside Wall** sub-material with an instance of the **Finishes.Painting. Paint** material.

21. In any viewport, select *walls* and then choose the **Assign Material to Selection** button in the **Material Editor** dialog box; the **Walls-Template** material is assigned to *Walls*.

Creating and Applying Multi/Sub-Object Materials to the Roof

The materials applied to the roof should look like different from the interior of the room as compared to the exterior. You will create and apply multi/sub-object materials for the roof.

1. Select the next available sample slot in the **Material Editor** dialog box.

2. Change the **Arch & Design** material type to **Standard** type as discussed earlier. Select **Blinn** from the drop-down list in the **Shader Basic Parameters** rollout, if it is not already selected.

3. Expand the **Maps** rollout and then choose the **Diffuse Color** button which is currently labeled as **None**; the **Material Map/Browser** dialog box is displayed.

4. Select **Bitmap** from the **Maps > Standard** rollout and then choose the **OK** button; the **Select Bitmap Image File** dialog box is displayed. As the project folder is already set, the *images* folder of this project is displayed in the **Look in** drop-down list.

5. Select the file **RoofTiles.Jpg** and choose the **Open** button to load it into the **Material Editor** dialog box. Next, choose the **Show Shaded Material in Viewport** button to activate it.

6. Select the next available material sample slot in the **Material Editor** dialog box. Change the **Arch & Design** material type to **Standard** type as discussed earlier. Select **Blinn** from the drop-down list in the **Shader Basic Parameters** rollout, if it is not already selected.

7. Choose the **Diffuse** button in the **Blinn Basic Parameters** rollout; the **Material Map/ Browser** dialog box is displayed.

8. Select **Bitmap** from the **Maps > Standard** rollout and then choose the **OK** button; the **Select Bitmap Image File** dialog box is displayed. As the project folder is already set, the *images* folder of this project is displayed in the **Look in** drop-down list.

9. Select the file **Ceilings.Linear.Silver Grey.Jpg** and choose the **Open** button to load it into the **Material Editor** dialog box. Next, choose the **Show Shaded Material in Viewport** button to activate it.

10. Select the next empty sample slot in the **Material Editor** dialog box.

11. Choose the **Arch & Design** button in the **Material Editor** dialog box; the **Material/Map Browser** dialog box is displayed. Next, select the **Multi/Sub-Object** material type and choose the **OK** button; the **Replace Material** dialog box is displayed. Now, select the **Discard old material?** radio button and choose the **OK** button.

12. In the **Multi/Sub-Object Basic Parameters** rollout, choose the **Set Number** button; the **Set Number of Materials** dialog box is displayed. Set the value **2** in the **Number of Materials** spinner and then choose the **OK** button to exit the dialog box.

13. Drag and drop the file **RoofTiles.Jpg** onto the button for the first sub-material; the **Instance (Copy)** dialog box is displayed. Make sure the **Instance** radio button is selected in this dialog box. Choose the **OK** button to close this dialog box.

14. Similarly, drag and drop the file **Finishes.Ceilings.Linear.Silver Grey** onto the button for the second sub-material; the **Instance (Copy)** dialog box is displayed. Make sure the **Instance** radio button is selected in this dialog box. Choose the **OK** button to close this dialog box.

15. Rename the **Multi/Sub-Object** material as **Roof**.

16. Select *Roof* in any viewport and then choose the **Assign Material to Selection** button in the **Material Editor** dialog box to apply the material to *Roof*. Now, close this dialog box.

The material is applied to *Roof*. The top and two sides of *Roof* appear covered in tile. The bottom and other two sides of *Roof* appear to be covered in corrugated aluminum. Since the top and all four sides of *Roof* need to be covered in tile, you need to adjust the material IDs of some of the faces of *Roof*.

17. In the Front viewport, zoom in on *Roof*. Make sure *Roof* is selected and then choose the **Modify** tab in the **Command Panel**. Select **Mesh Select** from the **Selection Modifiers** section of the **Modifier List** drop-down list. Expand the **Mesh Select Parameters** rollout and choose the **Face** button, if it is not expanded.

18. Choose a spot in the Front viewport above and to the left of *Roof*. Drag the cursor to the right and about halfway down *Roof*. Release the mouse button; all the faces on the sides and top of *Roof* are selected, but none of the faces are selected on the bottom of *Roof*.

19. Choose the **Modify** tab in the **Command Panel**. Select **Material** from the **OBJECT-SPACE MODIFIERS** section in the **Modifier List**. In the **Parameters** rollout for the modifier, make sure the value **1** is set in the **Material ID** spinner.

    This leads to assigning the material ID 1 on the top and on all four sides of *Roof* and material ID 2 on the bottom faces of *Roof*. Note that *Roof* material now appears correct in the viewport.

Creating and Applying Multi/Sub-Object Materials to the Floor

In this section, you will create and apply multi/sub-object materials for the floor.

1. Select the next available material sample slot in the **Material Editor** dialog box. Change the **Autodesk Solid Glass** material type to **Standard** type as discussed earlier. Select **Blinn** from the drop-down list in the **Shader Basic Parameters** rollout, if it is not already selected.

2. Choose the **Diffuse** button in the **Blinn Basic Parameters** rollout; the **Material Map/ Browser** dialog box is displayed.

3. Select **Bitmap** from the **Maps > Standard** rollout. Next, choose the **OK** button; the **Select Bitmap Image File** dialog box is displayed. As the project folder is already set, the *images* folder of this project is displayed in the **Look in** drop-down list.

4. Select the file **Flooring.Tile.Square.Jpg** and then choose the **Open** button to load it into the **Material Editor** dialog box. Next, choose the **Show Shaded Material in Viewport** button to activate it.

5. Rename the material to **Carpet** and then select the next available material sample slot. Change the **Autodesk Ceramic** material to **Standard** as discussed earlier. Choose the **Diffuse Color** button currently labeled as **None**; the **Material Map/Browser** dialog box is displayed.

6. Select **Bitmap** from the **Maps > Standard** rollout. Next, choose the **OK** button; the **Select Bitmap Image File** dialog box is displayed. As the project folder is already set, the *images* folder of this project is displayed in the **Look in** drop-down list.

7. Select the file **ConcreteFlatGrey.Jpg** and then choose the **Open** button to load it into the **Material Editor** dialog box. Next, choose the **Show Shaded Material in Viewport** button to activate it. Name the material as **Concrete**.

8. Make sure the **Coordinates** rollout is expanded and then select the **Use Real-World Scale** check box, if it is not selected. Set the value **0'10 1/2″(0.914)** in the **Width: Size** and **Height: Size** spinners.

9. Select the next unused sample slot in the **Material Editor** dialog box. Choose the **Autodesk Wall Paint** button; the **Material/Map Browser** dialog box is displayed. Next, choose the **Multi/Sub-Object** material from **Materials > Standard** rollout. Now, choose the **OK** button; the **Replace Material** dialog box is displayed.

10. In the **Replace Material** dialog box, select the **Keep old material as sub-material?** radio button and choose the **OK** button; *Carpet* material is changed from the **Autodesk Wall Paint** material to the **Multi/Sub-Object** material. Note that the original material is loaded into the first sub-material slot.

11. In the **Multi/Sub-Object Basic Parameters** rollout, choose the **Set Number** button; the **Set Number of Materials** dialog box is displayed. Set the value **2** in the **Number of Materials** spinner and choose the **OK** button to exit the dialog box.

12. Drag and drop an instance of *Concrete* material onto the second sub-material sample slot.

13. In the Front viewport, select *Floor*. In the **Material Editor** dialog box, choose the **Assign Material to Selection** button to apply the material to *Floor*. Close the **Material Editor** dialog box.

14. Make sure *Floor* is selected and then choose the **Modify** tab in the **Command Panel**. Select the **Mesh Select** modifier from the **Selection Modifiers** section of the **Modifier List**.

15. In the **Mesh Select Parameters** rollout, choose the **Face** button. Next, invoke the **Select Object** tool from the **Main Toolbar**. In the Front viewport, pick a point below and to the right of *Floor*. Drag the cursor to a point to the left of and about halfway up *Floor*.

    The faces on the sides and bottom of *Floor* are selected, but none of the faces are selected on the top.

16. Select **Material** from the **OBJECT-SPACE MODIFIERS** area in the **Modifier List**. Expand the **Parameters** rollout and set the value in the **Material ID** spinner to **2**.

    Next, you will change the names of the material objects.

Creating and Applying Remaining Materials

In this section, you will create and apply the materials to the objects.

1. Select *Monitor Base01* and *Monitor CRT01* from the **Scene Explorer**.

2. Invoke the **Material Editor** dialog box by pressing the M key and select the next available sample slot. Change the **Autodesk Metal** material type to **Standard** type as discussed earlier. Select **Blinn** from the drop-down list in the **Shader Basic Parameters** rollout, if it is not already selected.

3. Choose the **Diffuse** color swatch in the **Blinn Basic Parameters** rollout; the **Color Selector:Diffuse Color** dialog box is displayed.

4. Set the color values in the spinners of this dialog box as given next:

    Red: **234**   Green: **226**   Blue: **211**

5. Close the **Color Selector:Diffuse Color** dialog box.

6. In the **Material Editor** dialog box, rename the material as **Computer_Case** and choose the **Assign Material to Selection** button to activate it.

7. In any viewport, select *CRT Tube01* and invoke the **Material Editor** dialog box, if it is not already invoked.

8. Select the next available material sample slot. Change the **Arch & Design** material type to **Standard** type as discussed earlier. Select **Blinn** from the drop-down list in the **Shader Basic Parameters** rollout, if it is not already selected.

9. Make sure the **Blinn Basic Parameters** rollout is expanded and set the value **75** in the **Opacity** spinner and then choose the **Diffuse** color swatch; the **Color Selector:Diffuse Color** dialog box is displayed.

10. Set the color values in the spinners as given next:

    Red: **0**   Green: **0**   Blue: **0**

11. Close the **Color Selector Diffuse Color** dialog box.

12. In the **Specular Highlights** area of the **Blinn Basic Parameters** rollout, set the value **95** in the **Specular Level** spinner and **45** in the **Glossiness** spinner.

13. Rename the material as **Computer_Screen** and then choose the **Assign Material to Selection** button to assign the material to the object. Make sure the **Show Shaded Material in Viewport** button is chosen.

14. Load and assign materials to the remaining objects in the scene as directed in the following table:

Object(s)	Maps
Ground	Sitework.Planting.Grass.jpg
Flower Bed	Sitework.Planting.Soil.jpg
Path	Sitework.Paving & Surfacing.Pavers
Table and Side01	Woods & Plastics.Finish Carpentry.Wood.WhiteAsh.jpg
Seat01and Back01	Furnishings.Fabrics.Plaid.jpg
Chair Frame	Metals.Ornamental Metals.Chrome.Satin.jpg
PivotDoor001	Door_Template (Multi/Sub-Object)
FixedWindow001	Window_Template (Multi/Sub-Object)

Mapping Coordinates

Now, all the materials are assigned. The objects, however, need their mapping coordinates adjusted to make the materials look right.

1. Select *Ground* in the Top viewport and then choose the **Modify** tab in the **Command Panel**. In the **Modifier List** drop-down list, select **UVW Map** in the **OBJECT-SPACE MODIFIERS** section.

2. Make sure the **Planar** radio button is selected. If needed, set the mapping coordinates in the **U Tile** and **V Tile** spinners as per your requirements.

3. Select *Path* and apply the **UVW Map** modifier, refer to step1.

4. Similarly, set the mapping coordinates for all other materials as required to get the desired output.

Copying the Furniture

Now, one computer station is complete. You will copy this station to create the remaining stations in the computer center. The **Array** command is used to complete this method.

1. Make sure the Top viewport is active and select *Back01, Chair Frame, CRT Tube01, Monitor Base01, Monitor CRT01, Seat01, Side01,* and *Table01* from the **Scene Explorer**.

2. Choose **Group > Group** from the menu bar; the **Group** dialog box is displayed. Enter **CompAssy01** in the **Group name** text box.

3. Choose **Tools > Array** from the menu bar; the **Array** dialog box is displayed, as shown in Figure P5-18.

Figure P5-18 *The* ***Array*** *dialog box*

4. Set the value **4'7"(1.397m)** in the **Incremental Y** spinner in the **Move** row. In the **Type of Object** area, select the **Copy** radio button. In the **Array Dimensions** area, make sure the **1D** radio button is selected and then set the value **4** in the **Count** spinner. Choose the **OK** button; the array is created.

There are now four computer stations inside the computer center on the left wall, as shown in Figure P5-19.

Figure P5-19 *The first row of computer stations created*

5. Hide *Chair Rail Shape* and *Chair Base Shape*.

6. Select all the four computer stations in the Top viewport. Invoke the **Use Selection Center** tool from the **Main Toolbar**. Next, invoke the **Mirror** tool; the **Mirror: Screen Coordinates** dialog box is displayed.

7. In the **Mirror Axis** area, select the **X** radio button. Also, set the value **7'4 1/2"(2.26m)** in the **Offset** spinner. Select the **Copy** radio button in the **Clone Selection** area, if it is not selected.

8. Choose the **OK** button; the objects are mirrored and you will notice that four more computer stations are created on the right wall.

9. With the four mirrored computer stations selected in the Top viewport, move them up **4'5"(1.378m)** on the local Y axis.

    The mirrored computer stations are aligned with the wall opposite the window, as shown in Figure P5-20. The inside of the computer center is completed.

Figure P5-20 *The second row of computer stations created and aligned*

Make a note of the door's location. If needed, move the door down in the Top viewport so that it does not overlap the first computer station.

Setting a Background

Now, you will set a background scene. You will begin by loading the map into the **Material Editor** dialog box. Then, you will adjust its position so that the desired portion of the map will be visible above the horizon. Finally, you will load the map as a background.

1. Invoke the **Material Editor** dialog box and select the next available material sample slot. Choose the **Arch & Design** button to change the material type to **Standard** as discussed earlier.

2. Select **Blinn** from the drop-down list in the **Shader Basic Parameters** rollout, if it is not already selected.

3. Expand the **Maps** rollout and then choose the **Diffuse Color** map button, currently labeled as **None**; the **Material/Map Browser** dialog box is displayed.

4. Select **Bitmap** from the **Maps > Standard** rollout and then choose the **OK** button; the **Select Bitmap Image File** dialog box is displayed. As the project folder is already set, the *images* folder of this project is displayed in the **Look in** drop-down list.

5. Select **DUSKCLD.JPG** and then choose the **Open** button to load it into the **Material Editor** dialog box. Next, choose the **Show Shaded Material in Viewport** button to activate it.

6. In the **Coordinates** rollout, select the **Environ** radio button and set the value **0.35** in the **V: Offset** spinner. Also, set the value **1.0** in the **U: Tiling** and **V: Tiling** spinners and close the **Material Editor** dialog box.

   This moves the map up so that the horizon in the map will roughly correspond with the horizon in the scene. You may need to fine tune the **V: Offset** spinner setting after the camera is added.

7. Choose **Rendering > Environment** from the menu bar; the **Environment and Effects** dialog box is displayed.

8. Expand the **Common Parameters** rollout, if it is not already expanded and choose the **Environment Map** button currently labeled as **None**; the **Material/Map Browser** dialog box is displayed.

   In the **Sample Slots** rollout of the **Material/Map Browser** dialog box, all the maps currently loaded into the **Material Editor** dialog box are displayed in the **Sample Slots** area.

9. Locate and select the **Diffuse Color: Map #XX (DUSKCLD.JPG)** entry and choose the **OK** button; the **Instance or Copy?** dialog box is displayed. Next, select the **Instance** radio button, if it is not selected and choose **OK** to exit the dialog box.

10. Close the **Environment and Effects** dialog box.

Adding Lights

You will now add lights to the scene that will complement the background, thereby creating a lighting effect simulating the dusk on a cloudy day. The long, late afternoon shadows will be cast by a single omni light. This light will be placed such that the shadows it casts are consistent with the sun's position in the background image. Two additional omni lights are added inside the building to create the appearance of fluorescent lighting.

1. Activate the Top viewport and choose **Create > Lights** in the **Command Panel**. Select the **Standard** option in the drop-down list. Invoke the **Omni** tool from the **Object Type** rollout; various rollouts are displayed.

2. Expand the **General Parameters** rollout and make sure the **On** check box in the **Shadows** area is selected. Next, select **Ray Traced Shadows** in the drop-down list under the **Shadows** area, if it is not selected.

    Ray-traced shadows are required to cast illumination through transparent materials, such as the window glass.

3. Expand the **Intensity/Color/Attenuation** rollout and make sure the value **1** is set in the **Multiplier** spinner. Select the color swatch next to the **Multiplier** spinner; the **Color Selector:Light Color** dialog box is displayed.

4. Set the color values in the spinners given next:

    Red: **161**   Green: **152**   Blue: **139**

5. Choose the **OK** button in the **Color Selector:Light Color** dialog box; the color of the omni light is adjusted to simulate the color of light produced by the setting sun.

6. In the Top viewport, select a point just to the right of the building and just above *Ground*. In the Front viewport, move the omni light so that it is at the top of the canopy of the tree.

7. In the **Name and Color** rollout, rename the light as **Sun**.

    This location approximates the location of the *Sun* in the background map. From this location, the omni light will cast shadows and create highlights that are consistent with the background.

8. Expand the **Shadow Parameters** rollout and set the value **0.7** in **Dens** spinner under the **Object Shadows** area. Also, use the **Color** swatch to set the color gray.

9. Choose **Create > Lights** in the **Command Panel** and then invoke the **Omni** tool from the **Object Type** rollout.

10. Expand the **Intensity/Color/Attenuation** rollout and choose the color swatch next to the **Multiplier** spinner; the **Color Selector:Light Color** dialog box is displayed.

11. Set the color values in the spinners as given next:

    Red: **226**   Green: **237**   Blue: **250**

12. Close the **Color Selector:Light Color** dialog box.

13. In the Top viewport, select a point centered left and right and about a third of the way up from the bottom of the computer center and then move the light in the Left viewport so that it is near the ceiling. In the **Name and Color** rollout, enter the name of the omni light as **Fluorescent01**.

14. In the Top viewport, select the omni light you just created. Next, hold the SHIFT key and drag the omni light about a third of the way down from the top of the computer center; a copy of light is created, as shown in Figure P5-21.

Figure P5-21 *The omni lights created and aligned in the viewports*

15. Choose **Rendering > Environment** from the menu bar or press 8; the **Environment and Effects** dialog box is displayed. In the **Common Parameters** rollout, choose the **Ambient** color swatch; the **Color Selector:Ambient Color** dialog box is displayed.

16. Set the ambient light values in the spinners as given next:

    Red: **35**   Green: **35**   Blue: **35**

17. Close the **Color Selector:Ambient Color** and **Environment and Effects** dialog boxes.

A small amount of ambient light is added to the scene to simulate the ambient light of an overcast late afternoon/early evening. The ambient light brings out a little bit of color and detail in areas that are not directly illuminated by the lights in the scene.

18. Activate the Perspective viewport and then invoke the **Render Production** tool from the **Main Toolbar** to see the effects of the lights. Make adjustments to the view and lights as needed.

Setting the Animation Length

In this section, you will create a path for a walkthrough animation. You will also animate the entrance door. First, set the total number of frames in the animation.

1. Choose the **Time Configuration** button; the **Time Configuration** dialog box is displayed.

2. In the **Animation** area, set the value **1000** in the **Length** spinner and then choose the **OK** button.

The number of frames is set to 1000, which is about 33 seconds of playback.

Animating the Camera along the Path

1. Activate the Top viewport and choose **Create > Shapes** in the **Command Panel**. Next, invoke the **Line** tool from the **Object Type** rollout.

2. Choose a series of points in the Top viewport to create a line that roughly follows the path, as shown in Figure P5-22.

Figure P5-22 Line created as Camera Path

The line should also pass through the door and enter the computer center. In the **Name and Color** rollout, enter **Camera Path**.

Use a path of your own design.

3. In the Left viewport, move the *Camera Path* up by 5'6"(1.676m).

4. With *Camera Path* selected, choose the **Modify** tab in the **Command Panel**. Choose the **Vertex** button in the **Selection** rollout to enter the vertex sub-object mode. Modify the path as needed to create a smooth curvature. Then, choose the **Vertex** button again to exit the sub-object mode.

5. Choose **Create > Cameras** in the **Command Panel** and then invoke the **Free** tool from the **Object Type** rollout. In the **Parameters** rollout, choose the **35mm** button in the **Stock Lenses** area.

6. Place the camera anywhere in the Front viewport.

7. Choose **Animation > Constraints > Path Constraint** from the menu bar.

8. In the Top viewport, select *Camera Path* created for the camera; the camera is placed at the start point of *Camera Path*, as shown in Figure P5-23.

Figure P5-23 The camera placed at the start point of Camera Path

9. Choose the **Parameters** button in the **Selection Level** area, if it is not chosen. In the **Path Parameters** rollout, select the **Follow** check box in **Path Options** area and the **Y** radio button in the **Axis:** area.

10. Activate the Perspective viewport and press the C key to switch to the Camera01 viewport.

11. Choose the **Play Animation** button to view the animation.

    Notice that the camera turns to follow the path. The result is not entirely realistic. A real person walking along the path would tend to look toward the door rather than perfectly straight ahead. If time permits, you can add keys by toggling animation mode and rotating the camera so that its line of sight seems more natural. You can animate the **Lens** of the camera in the **Parameters** rollout to get a better view.

12. Move the **Time Slider** right and left to preview the animation. Determine the frame on which the camera is ready to enter the door.

Animating the Door

When you preview the animation, you may notice that the camera is passing through the door. Therefore, the door needs to be animated so that the camera can enter the computer center without passing through the door.

1. Move to the frame at which the camera is about to enter the computer center.

2. Choose the **Toggle Auto Key Mode** button to enter the animation mode.

3. Activate the Top viewport and select the door. Next, choose the **Modify** tab in the **Command Panel**.

4. In the **Parameters** rollout, set the value **90** in the **Open:** spinner.

5. Choose the **Toggle Auto Key Mode** button to exit the animation mode.

    The door now begins to open at frame 0. The animation needs to be adjusted so that the door remains closed until the camera approaches it.

6. With the door selected, highlight the key at frame 0 in the track bar below the time slider. Move the key to about 100 frames before the keyframe where the door is fully open.

Rendering the Final Animation

In this section, you will render the final animation.

1. Make sure the Camera viewport is activated and then invoke the **Render Setup** tool from the **Main Toolbar**; the **Render Setup: NVIDIA mental ray** dialog box is displayed.

2. In the **Time Output** area, select the **Active Time Segment** radio button. In the **Output Size** area, choose the **320×240** button.

3. In the **Render Output** area, choose the **Files** button; the **Render Output File** dialog box is displayed. As the project folder is already set, the *renderoutput* folder of this project is displayed in the **Save in** drop-down list.

4. Select **AVI File (*.avi)** from the **Save as type** drop-down list. In the **File name:** text box, enter **Project05** and then choose the **Save** button.

    If the **AVI File Compression Setup** dialog box appears, choose the **OK** button to accept the default settings.

5. In the **Render Setup** dialog box, choose the **Render** button.

    It will take some time to render the animation. After the rendering is complete, close the **Rendered Frame** window and the **Render Setup** dialog box.

6. Choose **Rendering > View Image File** from the menu bar; the **View File** dialog box is displayed. Select the **Project05.avi** and choose the **Open** button; the rendered view of the final animation at frame 0 is displayed, as shown in Figure P5-24.

Figure P5-24 *The rendered view of the final animation at frame 0*

Student Project

PROJECT DESCRIPTION

Create a walkthrough animation in a house that consists of a drawing room, bedroom, kitchen, dining room, drawing room, bathroom, and lawn; refer to Figures SP-3 to SP-19.

You need to download the AutoCAD drawing file *Student_Proj_MaxDesign_2015.zip* from the CADCIM website, refer to Figure SP-1. This figure will give you an idea about the dimensions of the objects in the project. The path of the file is as follows: *Textbooks > Animation and Visual Effects > 3ds Max Design > Autodesk 3ds Max Design 2015: A Tutorial Approach*

Hint:

To measure the dimensions of the rooms in the house, you need to import the AutoCAD drawing file in 3ds Max Design 2015, refer to Figure SP-2. To do so, follow the steps given next.

1. Choose **Application menu > Import** from the menu bar; the **Select File to Import** dialog box is displayed. In the **Files of type** drop-down list of this dialog box, select the **AutoCAD Drawing (*.DWG,*.DXF)** option. Browse to the *student_project_drawing.dwg* file that you have downloaded from the CADCIM website. Pick the **Open** button; the **AutoCAD DWG/DXF Import Options** dialog box is displayed. Use the default settings and pick the **OK** button; the AutoCAD drawing file, *student_project_drawing.dwg,* is displayed in all viewports.

2. Click anywhere in the viewport and press CTRL+A keys; all parts of the AutoCAD drawing file are selected. Now, group them as *reference drawing*.

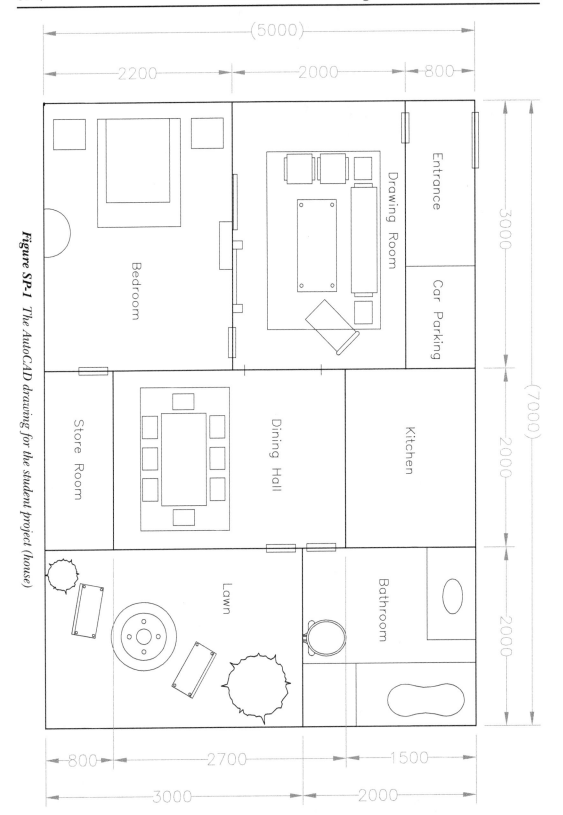

Figure SP-1 *The AutoCAD drawing for the student project (house)*

3. Select the *reference drawing* in the Left viewport and right-click on the **Select and Rotate** tool in the **Main Toolbar**; the **Rotate Transform Type-In** dialog box is displayed. In the **Offset: Screen** area, set the value **90** in the X spinner; the *reference drawing* gets rotated.

4. Now, create the scene in the Top viewport using the dimensions given in the *reference drawing* file.

You can view the rendered images of the scene by downloading them from *www.cadcim.com*. The path of the files is as follows: *Textbooks > Animation and Visual Effects > 3ds Max Design > Autodesk 3ds Max Design 2015: A Tutorial Approach*

Figure SP-2 *The drawing file imported in Autodesk 3ds Max Design 2015*

Figure SP-3 *Bedroom (View 1)*

Figure SP-4 *Bedroom (View 2)*

Figure SP-5 *Bedroom (View 3)*

Figure SP-6 *Kitchen*

Figure SP-7 *Dining room (View 1)*

Figure SP-8 *Dining room (View 2)*

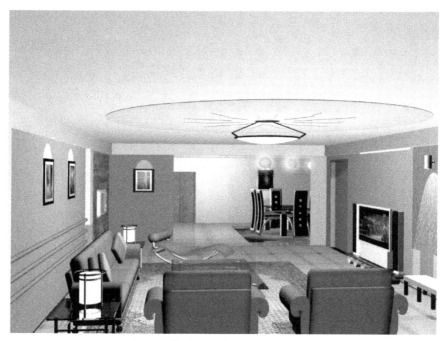

Figure SP-9 Dining room (View 3)

Figure SP-10 Drawing room (View 1)

Figure SP-11 *Drawing room (View 2)*

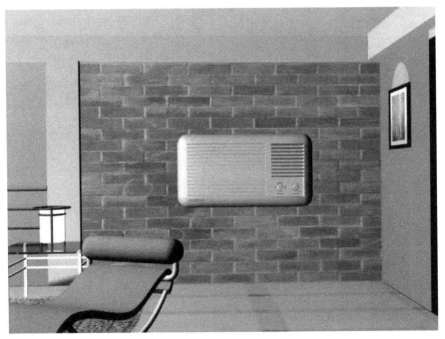

Figure SP-12 *Drawing room (View 3)*

Figure SP-13 Bathroom (View 1)

Figure SP-14 Bathroom (View 2)

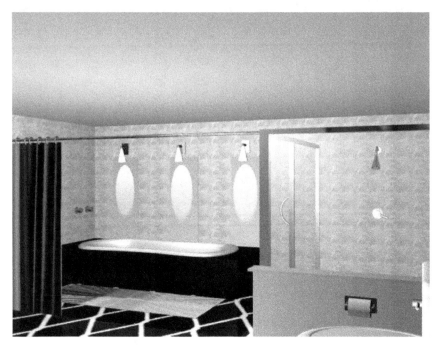

Figure SP-15 *Bathroom (View 3)*

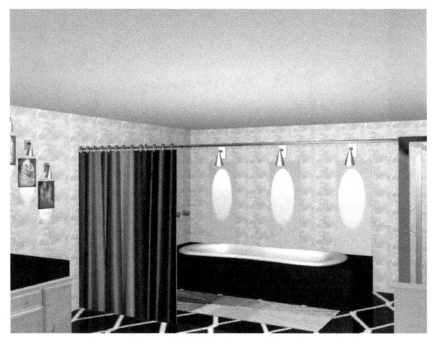

Figure SP-16 *Bathroom (View 4)*

Figure SP-17 Bathroom (View 5)

Figure SP-18 Bathroom (View 6)

Figure SP-19 *The lawn*

Index

Other Publications by CADCIM Technologies

The following is the list of some of the publications by CADCIM Technologies. Please visit www.cadcim.com for the complete listing.

Autodesk 3ds Max Design Textbooks
- Autodesk 3ds Max Design 2014: A Tutorial Approach
- Autodesk 3ds Max Design 2013: A Tutorial Approach
- Autodesk 3ds Max Design 2012: A Tutorial Approach
- Autodesk 3ds Max Design 2011: A Tutorial Approach
- Autodesk 3ds Max Design 2010: A Tutorial Approach

Autodesk 3ds Max Textbooks
- Autodesk 3ds Max 2015: A Comprehensive Guide
- Autodesk 3ds Max 2014: A Comprehensive Guide
- Autodesk 3ds Max 2013: A Comprehensive Guide
- Autodesk 3ds Max 2012: A Comprehensive Guide
- Autodesk 3ds Max 2011: A Comprehensive Guide
- Autodesk 3ds Max 2010: A Comprehensive Guide

Autodesk Maya Textbooks
- Autodesk Maya 2015: A Comprehensive Guide
- Autodesk Maya 2014: A Comprehensive Guide
- Autodesk Maya 2013: A Comprehensive Guide
- Autodesk Maya 2012 A Comprehensive Guide
- Autodesk Maya 2011 A Comprehensive Guide
- Character Animation: A Tutorial Approach

CINEMA 4D Textbooks
- MAXON CINEMA 4D Studio R15: A Tutorial Approach
- MAXON CINEMA 4D Studio R14: A Tutorial Approach

Fusion Textbook
- The eyeon Fusion 6.3: A Tutorial Approach

Flash Textbooks
- Adobe Flash Professional CC: A Tutorial Approach
- Adobe Flash Professional CS6: A Tutorial Approach

ZBrush Textbook
- Pixologic ZBrush 4R6: A Comprehensive Guide

Premiere Textbooks
- Adobe Premiere Pro CC: A Tutorial Approach
- Adobe Premiere Pro CS6: A Tutorial Approach
- Adobe Premiere Pro CS5.5: A Tutorial Approach

Nuke Textbook
- The Foundry NukeX 7 for Compositors

Autodesk Softimage Textbooks
- Autodesk Softimage 2014: A Tutorial Approach
- Autodesk Softimage 2013: A Tutorial Approach

AutoCAD Textbook
- AutoCAD 2014: A Problem Solving Approach

SolidWorks Textbooks
- SolidWorks 2014 for Designers
- SolidWorks 2013 for Designers
- SolidWorks 2012 for Designers
- SolidWorks 2014: A Tutorial Approach
- Learning SolidWorks 2011: A Project Based Approach
- SolidWorks 2011 for Designers
- SolidWorks 2010 for Designers

Autodesk Inventor Textbooks
- Autodesk Inventor 2015 for Designers
- Autodesk Inventor 2014 for Designers
- Autodesk Inventor 2013 for Designers
- Autodesk Inventor 2012 for Designers
- Autodesk Inventor 2011 for Designers
- Autodesk Inventor 2010 for Designers

Solid Edge Textbooks
- Solid Edge ST6 for Designers
- Solid Edge ST5 for Designers
- Solid Edge ST4 for Designers
- Solid Edge ST3 for Designers
- Solid Edge ST2 for Designers

NX Textbooks
- NX 8.5 for Designers
- NX 8 for Designers
- NX 7 for Designers
- NX 6 for Designers

EdgeCAM Textbooks
- EdgeCAM 11.0 for Manufacturers
- EdgeCAM 10.0 for Manufacturers

CATIA Textbooks
- CATIA V5-6R2013 for Designers
- CATIA V5-6R2012 for Designers
- CATIA V5R21 for Designers
- CATIA V5R20 for Designers

Pro/ENGINEER / Creo Parametric Textbooks
- Creo Parametric 2.0 for Designers
- Creo Parametric 1.0 for Designers
- Pro/ENGINEER Wildfire 5.0 for Designers
- Pro/ENGINEER Wildfire 4.0 for Designers

Creo Direct Textbook
- Creo Direct 2.0 and Beyond for Designers

Autodesk Alias Textbooks
- Learning Autodesk Alias Design 2012
- Learning Autodesk Alias Design 2010
- AliasStudio 2009 for Designers

ANSYS Textbooks
- ANSYS Workbench 14.0: A Tutorial Approach
- ANSYS 11.0 for Designers

Customizing AutoCAD Textbook
- Customizing AutoCAD 2013

AutoCAD LT Textbooks
- AutoCAD LT 2014 for Designers
- AutoCAD LT 2013 for Designers
- AutoCAD LT 2012 for Designers

AutoCAD Plant 3D Textbook
- AutoCAD Plant 3D 2014 for Designers

AutoCAD Electrical Textbooks
- AutoCAD Electrical 2014 for Electrical Control Designers
- AutoCAD Electrical 2013 for Electrical Control Designers
- AutoCAD Electrical 2012 for Electrical Control Designers
- AutoCAD Electrical 2011 for Electrical Control Designers
- AutoCAD Electrical 2010 for Electrical Control Designers

Autodesk Revit Architecture Textbooks
- Autodesk Revit Architecture 2015 for Architects and Designers
- Autodesk Revit Architecture 2014 for Architects and Designers
- Autodesk Revit Architecture 2013 for Architects and Designers
- Autodesk Revit Architecture 2012 for Architects and Designers
- Autodesk Revit Architecture 2011 for Architects & Designers

Autodesk Revit Structure Textbooks
- Exploring Autodesk Revit Structure 2015
- Exploring Autodesk Revit Structure 2014
- Exploring Autodesk Revit Structure 2013
- Exploring Autodesk Revit Structure 2012
- Exploring Autodesk Revit Structure 2011

AutoCAD Civil 3D Textbooks
- Exploring AutoCAD Civil 3D 2014
- Exploring AutoCAD Civil 3D 2013
- Exploring AutoCAD Civil 3D 2012
- AutoCAD Civil 3D 2009 for Engineers

AutoCAD Map 3D Textbooks
- Exploring AutoCAD Map 3D 2014
- Exploring AutoCAD Map 3D 2013
- Exploring AutoCAD Map 3D 2012
- Exploring AutoCAD Map 3D 2011

Autodesk Navisworks Textbooks
- Exploring Autodesk Navisworks 2015
- Exploring Autodesk Navisworks 2014

Paper Craft Book
- Constructing 3-Dimensional Models: A Paper-Craft Workbook

Computer Programming Textbooks
- Learning Oracle 11g
- Learning ASP.NET AJAX
- Learning Java Programming
- Learning Visual Basic.NET 2008
- Learning C++ Programming Concepts
- Learning VB.NET Programming Concepts

AutoCAD Textbooks Authored by Prof. Sham Tickoo and Published by Autodesk Press
- AutoCAD: A Problem-Solving Approach: 2013 and Beyond
- AutoCAD 2012: A Problem-Solving Approach
- AutoCAD 2011: A Problem-Solving Approach
- AutoCAD 2010: A Problem-Solving Approach
- Customizing AutoCAD 2010

Textbooks Authored by CADCIM Technologies and Published by Other Publishers

3D Studio MAX and VIZ Textbooks
- Learning 3DS Max: A Tutorial Approach, Release 4
  Goodheart-Wilcox Publishers (USA)
- Learning 3D Studio VIZ: A Tutorial Approach
  Goodheart-Wilcox Publishers (USA)

CADCIM Technologies Textbooks Translated in Other Languages

SolidWorks Textbooks
- SolidWorks 2008 for Designers (Serbian Edition)
  Mikro Knjiga Publishing Company, Serbia
- SolidWorks 2006 for Designers (Russian Edition)
  Piter Publishing Press, Russia
- SolidWorks 2006 for Designers (Serbian Edition)
  Mikro Knjiga Publishing Company, Serbia

NX Textbooks
- NX 6 for Designers (Korean Edition)
  Onsolutions, South Korea
- NX 5 for Designers (Korean Edition)
  Onsolutions, South Korea

Pro/ENGINEER Textbooks
- Pro/ENGINEER Wildfire 4.0 for Designers (Korean Edition)
  HongReung Science Publishing Company, South Korea
- Pro/ENGINEER Wildfire 3.0 for Designers (Korean Edition)
  HongReung Science Publishing Company, South Korea

Autodesk 3ds Max Textbook
- 3ds Max 2008: A Comprehensive Guide (Serbian Edition)
  Mikro Knjiga Publishing Company, Serbia

AutoCAD Textbooks
- AutoCAD 2006 (Russian Edition)
  Piter Publishing Press, Russia
- AutoCAD 2005 (Russian Edition)
  Piter Publishing Press, Russia

Coming Soon from CADCIM Technologies
- The Foundry NukeX 8 for Compositors
- NX 9.0 for Designers
- NX Nastran 9.0 for Designers
- Exploring AutoCAD Civil 3D 2015
- Autodesk Raster Design
- Primavera P6
- Bentley's Staad Pro.
- Energy Analysis Using Vasari and Green Building Studio

Online Training Program Offered by CADCIM Technologies

CADCIM Technologies provides effective and affordable virtual online training on various software packages including computer programming languages, Computer Aided Design and Manufacturing (CAD/CAM), animation, architecture, and GIS. The training will be delivered 'live' via Internet at any time, any place, and at any pace to individuals as well as the students of colleges, universities, and CAD/CAM training centers. For more information, please visit the following link: *www.cadcim.com*
